THE GREEK WAY OF LIFE

The Greek Way of Life

FROM CONCEPTION TO OLD AGE

Robert Garland

CORNELL UNIVERSITY PRESS
Ithaca, New York

First published 1990 Cornell University Press
Second printing 1990

Library of Congress Cataloging-in-Publication Data

Garland, Robert.
The Greek way of life : from conception to old age / Robert Garland.
p. cm.
Includes bibliographical references.
ISBN 0-8014-2335-X (alk. paper)
1. Greece—Social life and customs. 2. Life cycle, Human.
I. Title.
DF78.G28 1989
306′.09495—dc20 89-42955

The author and publisher are grateful to the following for supplying and giving permission to reproduce illustrations: Antikenmuseum Berlin, Staatliche Museen Preussischer Kulturbesitz: 13, 15; Ashmolean Museum, Oxford: 29, 35; Brauron Museum, Attica: 24; British Museum, London: 2, 6, 7, 9 (below), 10, 11, 17, 19, 21, 25, 32, 33, 36, 45; Eleusis Museum: 40; Alison Frantz: 22, 23; German Archaeological Institute, Athens: 30, 37; Herakleion Archaeological Museum: 31; Hirmer Fotoarchiv: 41; Michael Holford: 9 (above), 12; Metropolitan Museum of Art, New York (Purchase, Bequest of Joseph F. Durkee, Gift of Darius Ogden Mills and of C. Ruxton Love, 1972): 38; Musée du Louvre: 39; Museo Archeologico Regionale 'P. Orsi' di Siracusa: 5; National Archaeological Museum, Athens: 3, 14, 18, 28, 34; Ronald Sheridan: 4; Staatliche Antikensammlungen und Glyptothek München: 26; Staatliches Museum Schwerin: 27; Susan Woodford: 42.

Contents

For my son Richard, the father of this book

Preface

This book is intended to be a companion to my *The Greek Way of Death*, published in 1985. The idea for it grew out of an article which I wrote for *History Today* entitled 'Mother and child', and, like its predecessor and forebear, it has been written partly, though not exclusively, with the non-specialist reader in mind. Let me say at once that it is not intended to be exhaustive. Though certain phases of Greek life, most notably adolescence and coming of age, have been much discussed in recent years, conception, pregnancy, birth and old age have received only scant attention from scholars. As far as has been practically possible, therefore, I have focussed my attention primarily upon those aspects of the life-cycle where I believe I have some contribution to make, though not, I hope, to the detriment of the book's overall structure and unity. Athletic training, the sophistic movement, educational theory, girls' choirs, homosexuality and marriage are therefore treated only cursorily as they have already been the subject of detailed investigation. The emphasis tends to be on Athens in the Classical period, for that is the source of most of the evidence. However, it would have been quite impossible to write a *continuous* account of the Greek life-cycle by confining myself to one period or to one community. Little can be said about birth, still less about conception and gestation, for instance, without drawing upon non-Athenian, largely post-Classical sources.

I would like to express my sincere gratitude to Mary Lefkowitz who read the first two chapters of this book in draft form and commented expertly upon them; and to Susan Cole and Lauren Taaffe, the readers of Cornell University Press who read the whole ms. with great patience and sensitivity. My thanks are also due to Alan Booth, Helen King and Christopher Pelling for allowing me to cite from their (as yet) unpublished work. Two generous research grants from Colgate University made the undertaking possible.

While I was working on 'Mother and child' my wife was

pregnant. The same week that *The Greek Way of Death* was published, she had a miscarriage. She became pregnant again a little more than a year later and at the same time the present project was conceived and began its life in my mind. If I had not experienced all this, in particular if I had not witnessed my son's birth, I could not have written this book. These are the facts of my life. That is why it is dedicated to him.

Easy does it, old son.

R.G.

Illustrations

Abbreviations

Ancient authors and their works

Aes(chylus) *Agam(emnon), Ch(oêphoroi), Eum(enides) Supp(liants)*
Ail(ian) *V(aria) H(istoria)*
Aischin(es)
A(nthologia) P(alatina)
Apul(eius) *Apol(ogia), Met(amorphoses)*
Ar(istophanes) *Ach(arnians), Ekkles(iazousai), Lys(istratê), Pl(outos), Thesm(ophoriazousai)*
Arist(otle) *G(eneration of) A(nimals), H(istory of) A(nimals), P(arts of) A(nimals), Pol(itics), Phys(ics), Rhet(oric)*
Artem(idorus) *Onirok(ritikon)*
Athen(aios) *Deipn(osophistai)*
Censor(inos) *(De) D(ie) N(atali)*
D(iodorus) S(iculus)
D(iogenes) L(aertios)
Eur(ipides) *Alk(êstis), And(romache), Ba(cchai), El(ektra), Hek(abê), H(ercules) F(urens), Hipp(olytos), I(phigeneia at) A(ulis), I(phigeneia at) T(auris), Med(ea), Or(estes), Phoin(issai), Supp(liants), Tr(ojan Women)*
Gellius *A(tticae) N(octes)*
Harp(okration)
Herod(as)
H(ero)d(o)t(os)
Hes(iod) *Th(eogony)*
H(e)s(y)ch(ios)
Hipp(okrates)*
Hom(er) *Il(iad), Od(yssey)*
Hom(eric) h(ymn to) A(phrodite)
Hom(eric) h(ymn to) Del(ian) Ap(ollo)
Hom(eric) h(ymn to) Dem(eter)
Hyper(ides) *Epitaph(ios)*
Isai(os)

* denotes works attributed to Hippokrates

Isok(rates)
Josephus *A(ntiquities of) J(udea)*
Kall(imachos) *Ait(ia)*, *Epigr(ammata)*, *h(ymn)*
Lucr(etius)
Luk(ian) *Makrob(ioi)*
Lys(ias)
Men(ander)
P(apyrus) Oxy(rhynchos)
Paus(anias)
Phil(ostratos) *Ap(ollonius of) T(yana)*, *Gym(nastikos)*, *V(itae) S(ophistarum)*
Pi(ndar) *O(lympian)*, *N(emean)*, *P(ythian)*
Pl(ato) *Euthyd(emos)*, *Menex(enos)*, *Parm(enides)*, *Phaidr(os)*, *P(o)l(i)t(ikos)*, *Prot(agoras)*, *Rep(ublic)*, *Symp(osion)*, *Tim(aios)*, *Theait(êtos)*
Pl(i)n(y) *N(atural) H(istory)*
Plu(tarch) *Alk(ibiades)*, *Arist(ides)*, *Comp(arison between) Lyk(ourgos and) Num(a)*, *Kleom(enês)*, *Kim(ôn)*, *Lyk(ourgos)*, *Lys(ander)*, *Mor(alia)*, *Sol(on)*, *Them(istokles)*, *Thes(eus)*
Poll(ux) *Onomast(ikon)*
Pol(ybios)
Porph(yry) *(On) Abst(inence)*
Ps(eudo)-Ar(istotle) *A(thenaiôn) P(oliteia)*
Ps(eudo)-Dem(osthenes)
Ps(eudo)-Luk(ian) *Am(ores)*
Ps(eudo)-Pl(ato) *Ax(iochos)*
S(ophokles) *Ant(igone)*, *Oedipus at Kolonos*, *O(edipus) T(yrannos)*, *Trach(iniai)*
Sor(anos) *Gyn(aecology)*
Str(abo) *Geog(raphy)*
Th(eo)gn(is)
Th(eo)phr(astos) *Char(acters)*, *H(istory of) P(lants)*
Thuk(ydides)
Vitruvius *Praef(atio)*
Xen(ophon) *Ages(ilaus)*, *Anab(asis)*, *Hell(ênika)*, *Kyr(opaedia)*, *L(akedaimoniôn) P(oliteia)*, *Mem(orabilia)*, *Oikon(omikos)*, *Por(oi)*, *Symp(osion)*

Periodicals

ABSA = *Annual of the British School at Athens*
AC = *L'Antiquité classique*

AJPh = *American Journal of Philology*
AM = *Mitteilungen des deutschen archäologischen Instituts*
Annales (ESC) = *Annales: Économies, Sociétés et Civilisations*
ASAA = *Annuario della Scuola Archeologica di Atene*
BICS = *Bulletin of the Institute of Classical Studies*
CP = *Classical Philology*
CQ = *Classical Quarterly*
CR = *Classical Review*
CRAI = *Comptes rendus de l'Académie des Inscriptions et Belles-Lettres*
CSCA = *California Studies in Classical Antiquity*
CW = *Classical World*
EMC = *Échos du Monde classique*
G&R = *Greece & Rome*
HSCP = *Harvard Studies in Classical Philology*
HT = *History Today*
JbAC = *Jahrbuch für Antike und Christentum*
JdAI = *Jahrbuch des deutschen Archäologischen Instituts*
JHS = *Journal of Hellenic Studies*
JPh = *Journal of Philosophy*
JRS = *Journal of Roman Studies*
LEC = *Les études classiques*
PCA = *Proceedings of the Classical Association*
PCPhS = *Proceedings of the Cambridge Philological Association*
QUCC = *Quaderni Urbinati di Cultura Classica*
REA = *Revue des Études anciennes*
REG = *Revue des Études grecques*
RH = *Revue historique*
RHR = *Revue de l'Histoire des Religions*
RhM = *Rheinisches Museum*
STHist = *Sources travaux historiques*
TAPhA = *Transactions of the American Philological Association*
TLS = *Times Literary Supplement*
YCS = *Yale Classical Studies*
ZPE = *Zeitschrift für Papyrologie und Epigraphik*

Other abbreviations can be found in the Bibliography.

Γηράσκω δ'αἰεὶ πολλὰ διδασκόμενος
(Solon fr. 18 *IEG*)

Introduction

> Life is like a daylong period on guard and the length of life is like one day, as it were, and when we have looked upon its light we hand over our guardianship to the next generation.
>
> (Antiphon the Sophist, *DK* 87 B 50)

The structure of human life

Human life is finite, structured and divisible. Only death is not. In Hades the great sinners such as Ixion, Oknos, Sisyphos, Tantalos and the Daneids are literally deadlocked – condemned to futile, endless and repetitive labours. Each is confined within his own time-warp, unable to complete and unable to progress. The fact that this is their torture reveals a great deal about the Greek way of life and the Greek way of death. In life, as in passing from life, the ripeness or *hôraiotês* is all. This explains the fear of being stranded on the hither side of the River Styx when seeking to gain entry to Hades, and hence, too, the need for burial. 'Bury me as quickly as possible so that I can enter the gates of Hades', pleads the shade of the dead Patroklos to Achilles in a dream (*Il.* 23.71). It explains, too, the anxiety which the Greeks focussed on moments of transition, principally birth, coming of age and marriage, all regarded as fraught with lethal danger for the individual concerned.

The gods, as the poets never tire of telling us, are 'forever deathless and ageless'. All had their birth, most attain adulthood (Eros is an exception), many reach middle life (Zeus, Hera and Poseidon are but three examples), but none progresses to old age. The Graiai, who are virtually unique among the gods in being elderly, are so because they were grey-haired at birth (Hes. *Th.* 271). Ageing, like dying, is therefore part of what makes us human. Only at the moment of decease does the entity which survives death, the *psuchê* or *eidôlon* as it is referred to by medical writers and poets alike, finally become immune to the passage of time, destined to remain for all eternity what it was when death struck. The epigram on a fifth-century BC Attic grave-marker commemorating a woman called Ampharete (Fig. 30) puts this clearly: 'I am holding the dear child of my daughter, which I did when we looked upon the rays of the sun, and now that we have both passed away I hold her still upon my knees.' So does another commemorating a maiden called Phrasikleia (*Epigr. gr.* 6; *NM* 4889): 'I shall for ever bear the name of unmarried girl or *parthenos** because the gods assigned me this name in place of marriage.' Age at death materially affected the treatment which the dead received, though archaeological reports rarely shed light on this subject.

The belief that human life comprises a series of periodisations is prominent in western culture. Shakespeare's lines from *As You Like It* (act 2, scene 7)

> All the world's a stage,
> And all the men and women merely players.
> They have their exits and their entrances,
> And one man in his time plays many parts,
> His acts being seven ages ....

dominate our thinking even today. The editors of a modern investigation into developmental biology and psychology entitled *The Seven Ages of Man* state candidly (p. vi) that the structure of their work 'obviously was suggested by the famous lines from William Shakespeare's comedy' (Sears and Feldman 1973). Since they further acknowledge that 'the division of the book into ages ... is for expository convenience only', it is clear that they regard neither this nor presumably any other system of dividing life into ages as possessing any genuine claim to be an objective representation of human life. My division of the Greek way of life into six chapters is not intended to be prescriptive either, though I like to think that expository convenience is not its only guiding principle. In undertaking a broad-based survey of Greek age-classes it simply becomes impractical to separate early from late childhood or even middle from old age, chiefly because the Greek language itself does not always observe and reinforce distinctions of this kind.

The concept of the seven ages of man is of very great antiquity. The Hippokratic school of medicine, which was established in the late fifth century BC, also analysed human

* A glossary of age-terminology is given on pp. 291-3.

life into seven *hêlikiai* or age-groups, each of which was seven years in length. Quoting Hippokrates as his authority, Pollux (*Onomast.* 2.4) states:

> The first from birth to 6; the second from 6 to 13; the third from 13 to 20; the fourth from 20 to 27; the fifth from 27 to 34; the sixth from 34 to 41; the seventh from 41 to 48. The first, *paidion*; the second, *pais*; the third, *meirakion*; the fourth, *neaniskos*; the fifth, *anêr*; the sixth, *gerôn*; the seventh, *presbutês*.

Shakespeare's seven ages may well derive ultimately from Hippokrates, since the concept is also propounded in the sixth book of a French encyclopaedia entitled *Le grand propriétaire de toutes choses*, which was published in 1556 and contains a compilation of data culled from Byzantine writers. The underlying thesis of this work, which itself derives from antiquity, is the unity of all natural phenomena, one of its assumptions being that the seven ages of man correspond to the seven then-known planets (cf. Ariès 1960, 19f.).

The shaping of human life into *hêlikiai* was profoundly influenced by a conviction in the magical power inherent in certain numbers, notably seven and three. Periods of seven years known as *hebdomades* (singular: *hebdomas*) were thought to be highly significant, particularly when they occurred in multiples of three. The earliest allusion to the system of dividing human life into *hebdomades* occurs in a poem by Solon (fr. 27 IEG), who lived in the late seventh and early sixth centuries BC:

> A prepubescent child (*pais anêbos*) who is still a young child (*nêpios*) grows teeth and loses them for the first time in his seventh year. When god accomplishes his fourteenth year, he shows(?) indications of the beginnings of puberty (*hêbê*). In his third (sc. *hebdomas*) his limbs wax strong, his chin becomes bearded and he acquires a bloom (*anthos*) upon his skin. In the fourth *hebdomas* all men are at their peak of strength, which in an adult male (*anêr*) is the limit of physical excellence. In the fifth it is the right time (*hôrion*) for an *anêr* to think of marriage and offspring to come after him. In the sixth the mind of an *anêr* is disciplined in all things and he does not want to do what is unlawful (or 'what is impossible'). In the seventh and eighth *hebdomades*, which comprise fourteen years, intellect and power of speech are at their peak. In the ninth he is still capable, but his speech and discrimination are feebler than they were. If a man finally reaches the full measure (*metron*) in the tenth, let

him receive the apportionment of death (*moira thanatou*), not dying prematurely (*aôros*).

Aristotle, too, lent his authority to this theory by stating (*Pol.* 7.1336b40-2): 'Those who divide *hêlikiai* into *hebdomades* are more or less correct, and we ought to observe the division which nature (*phusis*) makes.' In *De die natali* or *Birthdays*, a valuable compilation of Greek and Roman sources on human life and time, the third-century AD Roman grammarian Censorinus reports (*DN* 14.9):

> The writings of philosophers and doctors contain plentiful comment on the subject of *hebdomades*, from which it can be seen that in illness periods of seven days should be treated with caution and are called critical (*krisimoi*); in the same way during one's lifetime a *hebdomas* is dangerous and, so to speak, critical, for which reason they are called climacterics (*klimaktêrikoi*).

Censorinus further observes (*DN* 14.10) that astrologers believe that 'one should pay particular attention to years which fall at the end of every series of three *hebdomades*, that is 20, 41, 62 and lastly 80'. Elsewhere he observes (*DN* 7.3-4) that while some youths experience puberty within their second *hebdomas*, all do so by their sixteenth year (i.e. 13 + 3). The hebdomadal theory enjoyed wide currency throughout antiquity at all levels of society. On the occasion of his sixty-fourth birthday, the Emperor Augustus is said to have written a letter to his grandson Gaius in which he expresses considerable satisfaction and relief at having 'survived my climacteric, the sixty-third year, common to all men' (Gell. *AN* 15.7.3).

In the Greek world a threefold division of life probably served most practical purposes. A few examples will prove the general point. An epigrammatic fragment of Hesiod (fr. 321 Merkelbach and West) reads: 'The deeds of the young (*neoi*), the counsels of the middle-aged (*mesoi*), the prayers of the elderly.' At the beginning of Sophokles' *Oedipus Tyrannos*, when a priest is supplicating Oedipus on behalf of the entire citizen body to secure Thebes' release from the grip of the plague, he alludes comprehensively to the population as follows (ll. 15-19):

> You see of what various ages (*hêlikoi*) are we who cling to your altars: those who do not yet have the strength to fly far from the nest, those who are heavy with age, priests, I of Zeus ... and the picked ones among the men who are unmarried or *êitheoi*.

Although there is no explicit allusion in the play to the riddle which the sphinx had put to Oedipus and whose solution earned him the kingship – 'What animal goes on four legs in the morning, two at mid-day and three in the evening?' – the priest's words here are surely intended to be reminiscent of it. In Euripides' *Bacchai* (l. 694) the herdsman informs Pentheus that the followers of Dionysos comprise 'young and old women, and unyoked girls (*neai, palaiai, parthenoi t'et'azuges*)'. The exhortation which closes the Classical Athenian funeral oration conventionally identifies three generations: first the dead and their contemporaries, next their fathers, and lastly their sons (cf. Loraux 1975, 2). With reference to the biological differences between the three age-groups Aristotle (*Rhet.* 1.1361b7-14) states:

> There are different forms of beauty according to each age-group (*hêlikia*). In a youth (*neos*) beauty consists in possessing a body that can withstand exertion, either in athletics or in trials of strength, and it is a pleasure to look upon .... In a young man at the peak of his physical condition (*akmazôn*) beauty consists in being adapted to the labours of war and it is pleasurable and frightening to look upon. In an old man (*gerôn*) it consists in being capable of enduring necessary labours and in not causing annoyance (or 'not suffering from pain') because one does not have the defects of age.

In the Nemean, Isthmian and Panathenaic games contestants were grouped into three age-classes, *paides, ageneioi* or beardless youths and *andres*. The 'boys' were aged eleven to fifteen, the 'beardless' fifteen to nineteen and the 'men' nineteen and upwards (cf. Pl. *Laws* 8.833cd). Plutarch (*Lyk.* 21.2) tells us that at Spartan festivals there were three choirs 'corresponding to the three *hêlikiai*'. The choir of old men (*gerontes*) would chant first: 'We were once bold youths (*neaniai*).' Then young men at their physical peak (*akmazontes*) would respond: 'We are so now, if you wish look and see.' Finally the third choir, that composed of boys (*paides*), sang: 'We will be mightier men (*andres*) by far.' The author of the Hippokratic work *Peri trophês* or *Nutriment* (41) recommends three different ways of preparing food for three different age-groups: *akmazontes*, *neoi* and *gerontes*. Often when a twofold division is indicated, a threefold division can be inferred. Aristotle in the *Politics* (7.1329a30-2) subdivides the adult citizen body into those of military age (*to hoplitikon*) and those of councillor age (*to bouleutikon*); the third group comprised those below military age. So, too, in the Homeric poems those of military age are designated youths (*kouroi*), those above *gerontes* (see below, p. 164).

The Pythagoreans identified four ages of man, namely *pais, neos, anêr* and *gerôn*, in line with the four seasons, assigning spring to the *pais*, summer to the *neos*, autumn to the *anêr* and winter to the *gerôn* (D.S. 10.9.5 = Thesleff 1965, 233). Plato (*Laws* 2.658cd) likewise distinguished four ages and attributed to each a different level of spiritual and intellectual enlightenment. Very tiny children (*panu smikra paidia*), he claimed, are most diverted by puppet shows, older children (*meizous paides*) by comic plays, educated women, youths (*nea meirakia*) and the general public by a performance of tragedy, and *gerontes* by recitations of the poems of Homer and Hesiod. A fourfold division of human life is also prominent in Hippokratic writings, allied to the celebrated doctrine of the four cardinal humours of the body as well as to the belief in a natural correspondence between the ages of human life and the four seasons. The author of *Peri diaitês* or *Regimen* (1.33) argues that a *pais* is moist and warm, a young man (*neêniskos*) dry and warm, an *anêr* dry and cold, and a *presbutês* moist and cold. Similarly in *Nature of Man* illness and ageing are explained as being due to changes in body fluid and body temperature. In the first phase of life blood predominates, in the second yellow bile, in the third black bile and in the fourth phlegm. The physician Galen (19.373f. *K*), who lived in the second century AD, also identified four *hêlikiai*, affirming that *neoi* are hot and moist like spring, *akmazontes* hot and dry like summer, those in middle life (*mesoi*) cold and dry like autumn, and *gerontes* cold and moist like winter.

Analogies between the human life-cycle on the one hand, and the seasons, times of day, plant growth and the life of the cosmos on the other abound in Greek as they do in English. In a speech perhaps delivered on behalf of those who died fighting on Samos in 439 BC Perikles made the unforgettable observation that the removal of youth (*neotês*) from the *polis* as a result of the heavy casualties which Athens had sustained was 'like the spring being taken out of the year' (Arist. *Rhet.* 1.1365a31-3). Mimnermos (fr. 2 *IEG*), an elegiac poet who lived in the seventh century BC, likened the bloom of youth (*anthea hêbês*) to 'the swift blossoming and withering of leaves', and the harvest of youth (*hêbês karpos*) to 'the brief moment when the sun spreads its dawn rays over the earth'. The fifth-century BC philosopher Philolaus of Kroton used a newborn baby's first intake of breath as an analogy for explaining how the cosmos, enveloped by fire, manages to avoid becoming overheated, in accordance with his belief that a baby cools itself down by inhaling and expelling air (*DK* 44 A 27; cf. Burkert 1972, 271).

Many words which primarily describe the natural world and its cycles are used metaphorically of man's physiological and biological condition. *Karpos*, for instance, whose primary meaning is 'fruit', also denotes an embryo or foetus. *Hersê*, which means 'dew', is applied by Homer to 'a young and tender animal'. *Theros*, 'summer' or 'harvest', vividly connotes the ripeness of pubescence, as in Kallimachos' bold phrase 'the first harvest of downy growth (*theros to prôton ioulôn*)', which evidently alludes to the first signs of hair on a young man's upper lip and chin (*h. Del.* 298). *Anthos*, whose literal meaning is 'bloom' or 'flower', is used with *hêbê* in poetic contexts from Homer onwards to refer to 'the bloom of youth' (see above). *Hôra* or *hôrê* can mean either 'the springtime of the year' or 'the springtime of life'. *Akmê*, 'highest or culminating point', describes either corn that has ripened to perfection, high summer, or the condition of being at one's physical peak, and there is no indication that one usage is semantically prior to any other. The metaphor of the child as a plant is elaborated in the *Odyssey* (6.163) into an arresting simile when Odysseus compares the beautiful Nausikaa to a young palm tree. In a familiar cliché Empedokles of Akragas describes old age as 'the evening of life, just as evening is the old age of the day' (*DK* 31 B 152). These equivalences were not merely worn-out analogies, as they have become in our language, but reflect a view of the universe as an integrated and interlocking whole. It is appropriate to point out that Milesian cosmogony, being hylozoistic (i.e. holding the doctrine that inert matter is invested with the power of generation and growth), derived the cosmos from a seed. Speculations of this kind were not exclusive to Greek philosophy. In mythical thinking, too, birth rather than an abstract notion of 'creation' was the main explanatory model (cf. Furley 1987, 18).

Not all Greek states possessed equally complex and ramified age-classification systems. In Classical Athens boys were not formally organised into a year-class until they reached their eighteenth year, whereas their Spartan counterparts had already been placed in a year-class at about the age of six. We may speculate that in earlier times Athens, too, had an equally extended system of age-classes which became attenuated around the end of the sixth century in line with the constitutional and political changes introduced by Kleisthenes (see Pélékidis 1962, 51-70; Rhodes 1981, 503). Changes in systems of age-classification inevitably reflect changes in society as a whole, while their preservation, as in the case of Sparta, signifies a deliberate and conscious attempt to resist change. The importance which a society attaches to its age-classification system is, moreover, closely related to the emphasis which it places upon peer-group bonding. In Homeric society, for instance, *homêlikiê* or sameness of age carried with it a sense of strong and even binding moral obligation, as can be seen from the following examples. When Sthenelos captures the much-prized horses of Aeneas, he entrusts them to his beloved companion Deïpylos 'whom he honoured above all men in his *homêlikiê*' (*Il.* 5.325f.). The crew who accompany Telemachos on his voyage from Ithaca to the mainland are 'companions in the same *homêlikiê* who went along with him out of love' (*Od.* 3.363f.). In formal supplications *homêlikiê* is cited as constituting compelling grounds for rendering assistance to one in need. Being eager to depart from Pylos without being waylaid by his host Nestor, Telemachos appeals for help to the old man's son Peisistratos in his capacity of guest-friend and co-eval (*Od.* 15.196f.); and when Odysseus supplicates Mentor – actually the goddess Athena in disguise – for assistance in his battle against the suitors, he likewise reminds his old friend of his past services and their *homêlikiê* (*Od.* 22.208f.). Peer-group bonding seems to have existed no less strongly among women, though there is inevitably less reference to it. When Helen confesses to Priam her longing for home, she alludes nostalgically to the *homêlikiê erateinê* or 'lovely girls in my age-group' whom she left behind in Sparta in order to accompany Paris to Troy (*Il.* 3.174f.). *Homêlikiê* was requisite among members of girls' choirs partly for harmonic purposes and partly for the sense of shared identity which found expression in the subject-matter of the songs which they sung.

Age-distinctiveness can be reinforced by spatial separation. In his discussion of the physical layout of the ideal state Aristotle (*Pol.* 7.1331a37-8) proposes that its gymnasium should be divided up according to *hêlikiai*: he may have wished to discourage homosexual liaisons between older and younger men of the kind which a gymnasium is likely to foster. A chaste separation of the population into well-defined age-classes was perhaps viewed as consistent with propriety and moral wholesomeness. It is surely for this reason that Xenophon (*Kyr.* 1.2.3-4) opens his discussion of the measures adopted by the Persians to ensure that their citizens 'shall not be of such a kind as to desire anything shameful or immoral' by a description of the spatial layout of the 'free agora' in the Persian capital. Four sectors are identified, one reserved exclusively for *paides*, another for those occupying the status between child and adult (*ephêboi*), a third for 'full' adults (*teleioi andres*), and a fourth for those over-age for military service (*geraiteroi*). The *paides* and *teleioi andres* were required to be in their respective sectors at daybreak, whereas the *geraiteroi* were free to come or go at whatever time they wished except on certain specified days when their attendance was compulsory. Finally, unmarried *ephêboi* had to spend the night in the agora dressed in light armour. Though the institution which Xenophon is describing is entirely non-Greek, his evident approval of it argues the existence of a mentality which accepted the premiss that spatial and temporal distinctions complement and reinforce those that are age-related.

The Greeks believed that character, temperament and life-goals are influenced and modified by a person's age. Hesiod gives the following advice to the peasant farmer (*Works and Days* 441-7):

> Let an active fellow in his fortieth year follow (sc. the plough and oxen) ... who will attend to his work and plough a straight furrow, one who is no longer of an age to stare after girls of his own age (*homêlikai*) – a man who will keep his mind on the business in hand. No younger man (*neôteros*) will be better at scattering the seed than he is, nor at avoiding having to sow it twice. For a man who is a mere stripling (*kouroteros*) will get excited by his *homêlikai*.

The further notion that there exists a close correspondence between physical development on the one hand and cognitive and emotional development on the other underlines the widely-held ancient theory of the impressionability (*euplasteia*) of the newborn infant, i.e. that an infant's body is susceptible to moulding in the literal sense of the word just as its mind is susceptible to it in the figurative sense (see below, p. 82).

Both the age-related visual imagery of Greek art and the terminology for the different ages of life functioned as an integral part of the value-system to which the individual members of a community were expected to subscribe, a point which has been recently demonstrated with reference to the representation of age among the figures on the Parthenon frieze (Osborne 1987, 103). In this celebrated image of the polity at worship the men, both human and divine, are all depicted either in the bloom of youth or in the ripeness of older age. This binary system of classification duplicates and reinforces that which we encounter in the Classical Athenian funeral oration, where *neotês* is used to describe and define the totality of Athens' fighting stock, just as *kouros* defines the totality of fighting stock in Homer (cf. Loraux 1975, 9-18). In contrast the single iconographic category in which women, both mortal and divine, are placed (youthful and unmarked by age) underscores the fact that a woman remained a woman (*gunê*) whatever her years (see below, p. 243).

The assimilation of Athenian youth to the Athenian hoplite force in its totality may have been prompted in part by the fact that the military call-up probably fell most heavily upon those in their twenties. The temperamental opposition between youth and age is, however, a commonplace in Greek literature. Thus, in the words of a Greek proverb, 'Action is for *neoi*, counsel for *geraiteroi*' (*CPG* I, p. 436.6). Again, as Pausanias (7.19.2) observed: 'It is somehow characteristic for old age to be generally hostile to *neoi*, and to be particularly unsympathetic in matters that have to do with love.' The young are habitually characterised as rash, headstrong, impetuous and desirous of honour, and the elderly as cautious, endowed with a superior capacity for engaging in rational discourse (commonly referred to as *logismos* or *to eu phronein*), disengaged from public life and over-preoccupied with money. From the fifth century onwards, however, philosophers and orators challenged these stereotypical portraits by claiming for the elderly the positive qualities conventionally associated with youth. In the celebrated Funeral Oration for the Athenian dead delivered in the winter of 431/0 Perikles asserts that love of honour is the only attribute that is ageless (*agêrôn*), i.e. the only life-goal not influenced by the ageing process, adding that 'in the useless time of (sc. old) age or *hêlikia* the greatest pleasure is not, as some say, in making money but in being honoured' (Thuk. 2.44.4). Even so, the antithesis between youth and age constituted a highly significant feature of the collective consciousness of the Greeks and remained the most commonly remarked upon age-distinction in Greek oratory.

According to the Judaeo-Christian world-view death and physical decline constitute features of the postlapsarian universe that we currently inhabit. The same belief is detectable in Greek thought, notably in Hesiod's *Works and Days* whose celebrated Myth of the Ages (ll. 106-201) draws upon deviant human development models as a means of characterising the five races that have lived on earth. The Golden race, who lived in the time of Kronos, died as though overcome by sleep without experiencing the hardship of old age. The Silver race, who followed after, took one hundred years to reach puberty (*hêbê*), while the remainder of their life was brief. The third race, that of Bronze, was the first to experience the phenomenon of death. The myth culminates in an apocalyptic vision of cultural and biological degeneration in its description of the fifth race, that of Iron, which in Hesiod's evolutionary schema represents his own contemporary world, destined to so degenerate that 'a time will come when children will be born with grey hair on their temples'.

Finally, the Greeks, like the Elizabethans, were strongly impressed by the circularity of human life. 'Never do good to a *gerôn* nor to a *pais*' was a Greek proverb (cf. Strömberg 1954, 80), its point presumably being the eminently practical one that neither a child nor an old man is in a position to return the favour. The child grows to manhood but the man in old age reverts to second childishness, as the chorus of old men in Aeschylus' *Agamemnon* (ll. 73-82) peevishly remark when they characterise their own strength as 'childlike (*isopais*)' and that of a child's as 'old-manlike (*isopresbus*)':

> Dishonoured because of our aged flesh, left behind by the expedition of yore we support a child's strength on our staves. For the youthful marrow <leaps up (*anaissôn*)> within the breasts (sc. of the very young), but warlike valour has no place within it, since it is like that of old age; while extreme old age, its leafage once shed, goes on three legs, in no way stronger than a *pais*, and fades like a dream as dawn breaks.

What follows, as Shakespeare observed, is mere oblivion.

Problems in methodology

At first sight a cross-cultural investigation of age-classes appears to be entirely non-problematic. What could be more 'universal' than the fact that people are born, grow up, grow old and die? The researcher has merely to identify the basic age-classification system of the culture he is investigating and then interrogate his data accordingly. If that seems simple it is not, for we at once encounter a fundamental difficulty which has to do with the signification of age and the division of human life into age-classes.

Let me spell out the problems in detail. The dividing up of human life into stages or ages, even when those divisions have some basis in observed physiological and psycho-social changes, none the less remains to a large extent culture-specific. To take a simple example, modern medicine divides pregnancy into three distinct phases, by identifying the fourth to eighth weeks of human development as the embryonic period, in distinction to the foetal period which follows and the zygotic period which precedes. It does so on the grounds that dramatic changes take place in the fourth week of pregnancy in connection with nervous system, blood supply and cellular structure. Even so, the fourth week remains a somewhat arbitrary moment to select, since it privileges these three developments over other, arguably no less dramatic developments which occur both earlier and later during pregnancy. In other words, the terminological distinction is essentially ideological, being based more on convention than on fact.

The Greeks did not divide up pregnancy in this way. Their word *embruon*, which is derived from the verb *bruo* meaning 'swell' or 'expand' and the preposition *en* meaning 'inside, within', and which of course gives us our word 'embryo', does not, unlike its English descendant, denote merely the first months of pregnancy. Instead it not only covers the entire period of gestation, there being no Greek word exactly equivalent to our word 'foetus', but it is also used post partum of a child or an animal which is suckling. The same is true of *brephos*, which likewise denotes both an unborn and newborn child. The implication of these usages would seem to be clear: the Greeks were disposed to regard the entire period of development during which young are dependent on their mother for food whether inside or outside the womb as one continuous and uninterrupted whole. That this view conforms to reality as much as does our modern distinction between 'embryo' and 'foetus' requires no laboured proof. The different perspectives on pregnancy and birth suggested by the different meanings of *embruon* and 'embryo' indicate, moreover, that an increase in linguistic precision often, perhaps invariably, contains within itself the seeds of semantic loss.

Terminology conditions social thinking. To take an extreme example, the verb *paidoktoneô*, which means 'commit infanticide', is never used in extant Greek literature of the practice of exposing an unwanted infant except where there is 'clear polemical and dramatic intent' (Patterson 1985, 105). The preference for neutral verbs such as *apotithêmi* or *ekballô*, which literally mean to 'expose', should not be interpreted as moral evasiveness. On the contrary, it highlights and exemplifies an essential fact of Greek life: that the newborn had yet to acquire a social entity and could not therefore be a victim of murder.

Many age-related terms in Greek pose similar problems since they cannot be translated accurately into English. Take *numphê*, whose meaning in the Greek lexicon (*LSJ*[9]) is given as (1) 'young wife, bride' and (2) 'marriageable maiden', but which seems to refer more particularly to a young woman's imminent or first experience of sexual intercourse. Like *embruon* and *brephos*, *numphê* indicates that the Greeks identified as a single, indivisible and uninterrupted whole a period of life which we tend to think of as consisting of two opposed social statuses, namely marriageable but unmarried on the one hand and recently married on the other. In cases of this kind it is not wholly satisfactory to adopt the view that 'following the context, this term signifies either the young girl as *parthenos* or as newlywed' (Calame 1977, I, p. 63), since what *numphê* really signifies is a continuous state of being, part biological and part social, which is neither limited nor modified by its context, and which occupies the interval between *parthenos* and *gunê* ('woman' or 'wife').

A further difficulty is that the terminology used to denote and define age-classes tends to carry overtones of an educational, legal, physiological, political, religious or social nature. Certain expressions cannot therefore be properly understood, and may have no real meaning, outside their specific context. Consider, for instance, in English the extensive range of ideas and images associated with such words as 'minor', 'teenager', 'adolescent', 'juvenile', 'stripling', 'lad', 'youth', 'youngster' and 'young person'. Although these terms overlap in regard to the period of life which they denote, they do not necessarily cover the exact same span of years. And the same appears to be true of age-terminology in languages the world over.

The Greek language contains a remarkably rich variety of expressions to denote ages and times of life. Pollux, a grammarian who lived in the second century AD, lists (*Onomast.* 2.8) no fewer than twenty words for a newborn child or infant. Yet the problem for this study is that age-related terms are not always used in precisely the same way from one community to the next or even, to cite an extreme case, by the same author within the space of two sentences (cf. Lys. 3.10; Hdt. 3.53; Antiphon 3.4.6 and 8). A source of particular confusion surrounds the vocabulary for denoting young persons, which includes *pais, meirakion, ephêbos, kouros, neanias, neos, neôteros* and *neaniskos*. All these terms could be used either in a technical sense to denote persons within a very narrow age band or in a non-technical, broadly descriptive sense to denote the entire period of life between childhood and adulthood. *Neôteros*, for instance, is used variously by different communities as an equivalent to *ephêbos* (approximately seventeen to nineteen years old), as a synonym for *neos* (approximately nineteen to twenty-nine years old), as a comprehensive term for both *ephêbos* and *neos*, and as a description of those who are pre-ephebic (cf. Forbes 1933, 60-1). In Athens *hêbê* denoted either the precise moment at which an adolescent youth was presented to his phratry or else puberty in general. In Sparta *pais*, in addition to its general meaning 'child', was used in a specific sense to describe the members of a single year-group, the seventeen-year-olds.

Scholars remain undecided as to how the Greeks actually reckoned a person's age in years. The age at which Spartans were recruited into the educational system known as the *agôgê* is especially problematic, depending as it does on the meaning of the phrase *heptaeteis genomenous* in Plutarch's *Lykourgos* (16.4), which has been variously translated as 'on their seventh birthday', 'at the age of seven' or 'in their seventh year'. Since the Greeks, like the Romans, counted inclusively, it seems preferable to translate 'in the seventh year'. I have adopted this interpretation consistently when translating, though I acknowledge that the same method of age-reckoning is unlikely to have been employed in the same way by all our sources. In view of the fact that the Spartans, to keep with the example, were hardly in a position to be meticulous about a person's exact age, having no birth-certificates and a most complicated calendar, however, the problem is essentially academic (cf. MacDowell 1986, 160). And what was true of a relatively illiterate society such as Sparta was hardly less true of a highly bureaucratised and literate one such as Athens where difficulties could arise in deciding which of two friends – or even which of two half-brothers – was the elder (Pl. *Lysis* 207bc; Dem. 39.27-9). For determining a person's exact age the state was ultimately dependent upon the sworn testimony of the individual or, in the case of a minor, that of his father. Thus the oath taken by jurors at the beginning of their year of office, for instance, required each candidate to swear that he was 'not less than in his thirtieth year' (Dem. 24.151). Birth certificates or *hupomnêmata epigennêseôs* such as were issued under Roman rule in Hellenised Egypt were reserved exclusively for the upper classes, who thereby sought to ensure that the privileges which they enjoyed would be handed down to their children (cf. Wallace 1938, 105).

The material upon which this survey is based varies greatly in representativeness. Most of the evidence regarding conception and gestation is provided by scientific and medical writers, whereas for the study of old age we are to a large extent dependent on stereotypical literary portraits of the elderly provided by philosophy and drama. For no aspect of this investigation does there exist 'hard' data of the kind which can be subjected to quantitative and qualitative statistical analysis. So we can do little more than speculate, for instance, about questions such as how frequently the typical Greek mother went into labour or what percentage of her confinements resulted in a successful delivery. But this should not deter us from at least *asking* these kind of questions.

Moreover, the fact that our main source of evidence is casual remarks scattered about in literary sources is not grounds for complete despondency. It is at least as important to be able to establish the significance, say, of the practice of exposure or the high rate of infant mortality, as it is to establish their precise rate of occurrence (cf. Patterson 1985, 123). There is after all 'a limit to what we can do with numbers, as there is to what we can do without them' (Nicholas Georgescu-Roegen, quoted by Paul Cartledge in *TLS*, 12 September 1986).

The investigation of the Greek life-cycle from conception to old age is admittedly an impressionistic and somewhat artificial exercise in view of the fact that we cannot examine in detail the life of even one historical individual from beginning to end. Biography as a literary genre did not emerge until the Hellenistic era and even then its concern was never with the entirety of a person's life (see below, p. 141). So the best we can do is to examine the collective representation of the human life-cycle as it is delineated in an arbitrary assortment of texts.

Among the questions which seem to me to lie at the heart of this inquiry are the following:

(1) To what extent do the age-classes identified by the Greeks conform to systemic changes in the physical, mental and emotional qualities that occur in a person's lifetime?

(2) To what extent is it possible to identify different systems of age-structuring in different Greek states and what conclusions can be drawn about those societies as a result?

(3) What social and other functions are chiefly served by the identification and categorisation of the population into age-classes?

(4) To what extent do male and female age-classes and their corresponding rites of passage balance and complement each other, and to what extent do they reveal a disjunction between the perception and treatment of the two sexes?

(5) In what ways (if any) is age-classification a function of a particular social class? Is it, for instance, more marked among the aristocracy than among lower social groups?

(6) What evidence is there for diachronic change in the emphasis placed upon age-categorisation as a means of organising society?

1

Conception and Pregnancy

How can hair come from non-hair and flesh from non-flesh?
(Anaxagoras *DK* 59 B 10)

Inasmuch as the primary function of marriage in Greek society was procreation, the primary value of a married woman was as a reproductive machine. This culturally determined role was reinforced by medical lore which taught that a woman who did not engage in sexual intercourse could seriously endanger her health. The Hippokratic work entitled *Peri gonês* or *Seed* (4), for instance, states:

> Women who have intercourse with men are healthier than women who abstain. For the womb is moistened by intercourse and ceases to be dry, whereas when it is drier than it should be it contracts violently and this contraction causes pain to the body.

The inescapable conclusion to be drawn from passages such as these is that women's psychological health was believed to be determined by their biological function as childbearers, a fact which gave the male an essential curative as well as therapeutic role as the bringer of both health and sanity to the pathological and imperfect female organism. It will be obvious from the start, therefore, that the study of conception and gestation is inseparable from the study of social values.

None of the testimonies that we shall be examining in this chapter is supplied by a woman, first because there was no prominent female biologist or gynaecologist in the ancient world whose work has survived and secondly because we do not have any commentary furnished by the patients themselves during their period of pregnancy and delivery. Although Pliny alludes to several female authorities when he discusses gynaecological issues, he does not tell us when any of them lived and we cannot assume that they wrote anything down. To aggravate matters medical writers appear to have attended to what women had to say about matters obstetrical only when it confirmed their own presuppositions. True, an 'experienced woman' was credited with the ability to determine whether she had conceived immediately after intercourse had taken place (Hanson 1987, 598f.). But that was about as far as her knowledge was believed to extend. The author of the Hippokratic *Peri heptamênou* or *Seventh-Month Foetus* (4) seems to be arguing for a reversal of normal medical practice when he urges:

> We must not disbelieve women with regard to childbirth. For they constantly and repeatedly make assertions about everything, and nothing can persuade them, neither argument nor evidence, that they are ignorant of what is happening in their bodies.

Even here, however, it is impossible not to detect a note of professional male vexation at the mere fact that women presume to express an opinion about their bodies at all.

But bias in the evidence is one thing. Bias in scholarship is quite another. Only recently has Greek gynaecology begun to attract the attention which both the subject and the sources deserve. So the picture of conception and gestation which has come down to us both at the level of transmission and at that of interpretation reflects an almost exclusively male viewpoint, even though, as we shall see, the reproductive theories that were generated in the Greek world do not uniformly proclaim a belief in the inherent superiority of the male (cf. Lloyd 1983, 60; below, p. 34).

Apart from Greek myth, Attic tragedy and a handful of fragmentary sacral laws, we have very little evidence that is not scientific in orientation, even though it may be folkloristic in origin. Interest in reproductive theory is evident among medical writers and Milesian philosophers from around the middle of the fifth century BC onwards. The questions which chiefly concerned both these and later researchers are the following:

(1) How is semen formed and what is its nature?
(2) What is the respective contribution made by the male and the female in reproduction?
(3) What determines the sex of the offspring?
(4) How are hereditary characteristics transmitted?

(5) How many months does gestation last?

No fewer than ten of the treatises in the Hippokratic corpus deal either largely or exclusively with embryological and gynaecological issues. A further major source is the fourth book of Aristotle's *Peri zôiôn genêseôs* or *Generation of Animals*, which is largely devoted to an investigation into the claims of the two main rival reproductive theories known as pangenesis and epigenesis (see below, p. 30ff.). Finally Soranos, a Greek doctor from Alexandria who practised medicine in Rome during the reigns of the emperors Hadrian and Trajan and wrote an immensely influential treatise entitled the *Gunaikeia* or *Gynaecology*, provides us with the earliest extended discussion of obstetrics in the history of medicine. Plato, incidentally, shows remarkably little interest in reproductive theory and, so far as we can tell, seems not to have read any of the embryological works included in the Hippokratic corpus. The few scattered allusions to reproduction which we find in his dialogues are invariably located in a mythological or poeticised context.

Although a certain advance in the understanding of conception and gestation is detectable over the period covered by this survey (roughly sixth century BC to second AD), progress was slow and old ideas died hard. Galen indicates that the discovery of the ovaries was made by the physician and anatomist Herophilos of Chalkedon who practised medicine at Alexandria in the first half of the third century BC. But Herophilos' discovery by no means won general acceptance and the debate concerning the respective roles of male and female in the reproductive process was subsequently waged in apparent ignorance of his pioneering researches. The heavy weight of past tradition, especially that associated with the Hippokratic school, is indicated by the fact that Soranos still felt the necessity to refute theories which had been propounded by 'the ancients (*hoi palaioi*)' over half a millennium previously.

Judged by modern standards, no ancient treatise on reproductive theory written before the Hellenistic age can properly claim to be scientific since, so far as we can tell, no ancient medical practitioner before that era had any eye-witness knowledge of the human womb. Empiricism thus played a relatively minor part in the formulation of embryological theories. The chief explanation for this seems to be that the dissection of the human body, though not of course that of

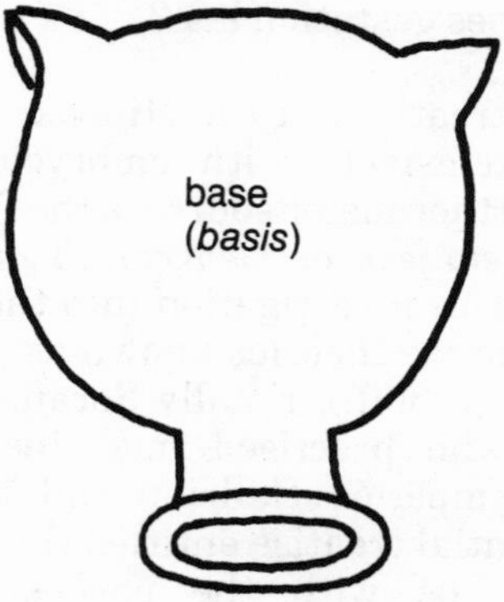

Fig. 1. Diagram of the human uterus as envisaged by Soranos in his *Gynaecology*, c. AD 900.

animals, was prohibited on religious grounds. The limitations upon the accuracy of deductions which hence proceeded in utter ignorance of even a rudimentary appreciation of the construction of the human womb is nowhere better demonstrated than by the fact that doctors, having only seen the bicornuate or double uterus of animals, blithely assumed that the human womb, too, was dual-chambered (cf. Lefkowitz 1981, 13). In the absence of any first-hand knowledge of either ovulation or the structure of the uterus, medical theories of reproduction tended to draw upon a hotchpotch of ideas which included the following:

(1) inferences drawn from observable physiological changes in the female body that take place during pregnancy, such as cessation of menstrual flow;

(2) analogies from the plant and animal kingdoms and from the physical world generally;

(3) cultural presuppositions based largely on a view of women's mental and physical inferiority;

(4) abstract logic and 'common sense';

(5) elementary deductions based on the dissection of brute animals including horses and cows.

The origins of sexual dimorphism

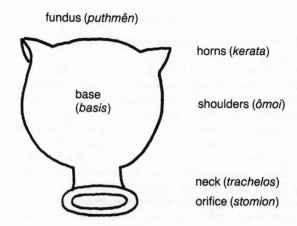

To understand the development of Greek embryology it may prove useful to begin by examining mythological beliefs about the origins of sexual dimorphism, that is, the origins of the sexual differences between male and female. Let us take as our starting-point the book of Genesis which addresses the problem by evoking the image of a benign and compassionate deity who, taking pity on man's solitary state in the Garden of Eden, decided to provide this genderless or unisex human entity with a companion and helpmeet. The poet Hesiod offers a strikingly different explanation which is commonly interpreted as evidence of a passionately hostile attitude to women on the part of all Greeks. He reports in the *Theogony* (ll. 570-602) that Zeus ordered Hephaistos to fashion out of earth 'the likeness of a bashful *parthenos*' as a 'beautiful evil (*kalon kakon*)' in order to punish the human race for Prometheus' theft of fire. In other words, the reason for devising the *parthenos* was to torment man, rather than to console him. The Hesiodic account further differs from Genesis in that this creature was not, like Eve, the mother of the entire human race but merely the mother of the female sex or *genos gunaikôn thêluteraôn* (l. 590; cf. Loraux 1978, 44f.). This myth therefore offers no solution to the problem as to how coitus became established as the necessary means by which the human race is propagated, but instead seems to imply that man was once somehow capable of reproducing himself without woman. Zeus' designation in Hesiodic and other epic poetry as 'the father of gods and men or *andres*', if taken literally, further suggests that every male offspring, though not every female, contains within himself a spark of the divine. Hesiod therefore differs from Genesis in his account of the origins of sexual dimorphism in the following particulars:

(1) he assigns evolutionary precedence to the male;
(2) he explains the creation of woman as a malicious and punitive measure on the part of an outraged and vindictive deity as opposed to a sympathetic action on the part of a concerned and fatherly one;
(3) he derives the entire female sex from a single female being who was herself unrelated to the race of men;
(4) he privileges man to a divine ancestry and woman to what is virtually a diabolical one.

In sum, sexual dimorphism is seen here as the consequence of two biologically separate and unrelated acts of creation.

Hesiod's view of women as a necessary evil was not short of

advocates in fifth-century Athens. Male characters in Euripidean drama, when exasperated either by women's lasciviousness or by their irrationality, rail constantly against the father of gods and men for having made women vital to human propagation. The outraged Hippolytos, for instance, when he learns of his stepmother's illicit infatuation for himself, bawls out in anguished perplexity (*Hipp.* 616-24):

> Oh Zeus, why did you bring women into this world, a false evil for mankind? If you wanted to propagate the human race (*broteion ... speirai genos*) you ought not to have done it by using women. Men might have dedicated bronze or iron or weighty gold in your temples, each man according to his capacity, in order to purchase the seed of offspring, and then we could have lived in our houses free of women's presence.

The underlying assumption is that women's main function is a biological one but that their warped natures render them unserviceable for even this humdrum, routine activity. The male members of Euripides' audience were evidently expected to recognise, even if they did not fully endorse, the cause of Hippolytos' frustration and the type of sentiments to which it gave rise.

Hippolytos' outburst may not have struck Euripides' audience as being quite so cranky and outrageous as it does us. Coitus after all was not the only reproductive mode envisaged by the Greeks. Testaceans, fish and insects were thought to reproduce themselves by spontaneous generation (cf. Balme 1962). In addition, there are numerous instances in Greek mythology of autochthonous generation, or birth from the soil. This latter reproductive mode served to explain both the birth of an individual, as in the case of Erechtheus/Erichthonios, a mythical Attic king, and the birth of a new race, as in the case of the Spartoi who sprang from the Theban soil after Kadmos had sown it with the dragon's teeth. A fragment of Empedokles (*DK* 31 B 62) even deploys it as an explanation for the origins of the entire human race. He claims that before sexual dimorphism occurred

> Whole-natured forms (*oulophueis tupoi*) first rose from the earth, possessing a measure of both water and heat, whom fire sent forth wishing to find their like, creatures which did not yet display a lovely form of limbs nor voice nor member specific to man.

In other words, at an earlier evolutionary stage than the present the earth spawned creatures who superficially resembled human beings although they lacked physical grace, the power of speech and the ability to reproduce.

This theory is famously parodied by Aristophanes in his speech in praise of Love in Plato's *Symposion* (189c-193b) where the comic poet fantasises that there was once a time when the earth was peopled by whole-natured forms which were globular in shape and had four arms, four legs, two heads and two private parts. There were also three sexes – male, female and an androgynoid combination of both. Because of their arrogance, however, Zeus bisected them, thereby creating the human race as we know it today. Out of pity for our ancestors who were threatened with extinction, he turned their private parts around to the front so that they would be able to mate and reproduce; previously these parts had been attached to the outside, which now became the rear. Though Aristophanes' parody is on one level pure fun, it touches upon many of the issues which preoccupied Greek embryologists. Empedokles assigned to Love a paramount role in the ordering of his cosmos, thus paralleling the vital role which this account assigns to love in human mating (cf. Furley 1987, 98), for, as Aristophanes points out in conclusion, each one of us is yearning after – quite literally – his or her other half, that missing portion of ourselves from which we have been severed and by union with which we will become whole-natured once again. The fantasy also explains why some people are homosexual and others heterosexual, since in our original, whole-natured form we were each conjoined with either a same- or other-sex half. Finally, it serves to remind us of the unique nature of human loving: we are the only species in the world that mates face-to-face, and we do so whatever our culture, whereas in animals who experiment with sexual positions face-to-face sex is an abnormal mode.

Conception

The Greeks held the view that the successful implantation of seed in the womb is a delicate and difficult operation, on the grounds that the mouth of the womb must close immediately after ejaculation has occurred in order for the seed to be retained. This is indicated by the fact that the verb *sullambanô*, which is regularly used in the sense 'conceive' (e.g.

Arist. *HA* 7.582a20-1 *T*; *GA* 1.727b8; Sor. *Gyn*. 1.28), means literally 'lay hold of' or 'seize'. For this reason Aristotle (*HA* 7.583a15-25 *T*) claimed that conception takes place more readily if the lips of the orifice (*ta cheilê tou stomatos*) are 'rough, adherent and thin', adding that if they lacked those properties then 'the part of the uterus on which the seed falls should be anointed with cedar oil, ointment of lead, or frankincense mingled with olive oil.' Hence, too, Soranos defined conception as 'a prolonged detention (*kratêsis*) of the sperm or embryo (or embryos) in the uterus due to natural causes' (*Gyn*. 1.43.1). In Graeco-Roman Egypt amulets have come to light which depict the uterus provided with a lock and key (cf. Bonner 1950, 84-5, 275-7). Though the symbolism is ambivalent, it is possible that some were intended to promote conception since they are inscribed with the exhortation 'Close, womb' (cf. Hanson 1987, 598).

Since conception was regarded as anything but an automatic consequence of intercourse it is not surprising that medical writers paid considerable attention to factors which were believed to be determinant in ensuring a healthy or unhealthy implantation of seed. Most of the concoctions for insertion into the vagina which are described in gynaecological works were in fact intended either to encourage conception or to prevent miscarriage, rather than to serve as a contraceptive (cf. Preus 1975, 247f.). Anxiety about conception is detectable already around the beginning of the eighth century BC and persisted into the Christian era. The earliest advice comes from Hesiod (*Works and Days* 735f.) who urged the peasant farmer 'not to sow his seed (*spermainein geneên*) after returning from an ill-omened funeral but from a banquet held in honour of the immortal gods'. His remark may have been inspired by a whole complex of feelings which included the belief that contact with the dead temporarily reduces fertility, whereas the consumption of food has a vitalising effect upon the system; that grief reduces one's appetite and aptitude for love-making, whereas a sense of well-being enhances it; that days which are sacred to the gods facilitate the implantation of seed, whereas those devoted to the dead impede it; and finally, perhaps most fundamentally, that death and sex make uneasy bed-partners. There is inconclusive evidence to indicate that women of childbearing years may have been banned from entering a house of mourning or attending the graveside lest their wombs be rendered infertile (cf. Parker 1983, 70 n. 123 with Dem.

43.62 and Pl. *Laws* 12.947d).

Medical writers cite the physical condition of the parents-to-be, climate, locality, time of year, and time of month as contributing materially to a successful implantation of seed. While not lending it his support, Soranos (*Gyn.* 1.41.1) reports the belief, no doubt of immemorial antiquity, that a waxing moon is propitious for conception on the grounds that:

> Things on earth are alleged to be in sympathy with things up above ... and the generative faculties (*hai spermatikai dunameis*) in us and in all living creatures increase when the moon is waxing and decrease when it is waning ...

The Hippokratic author of *Peri epikuêsios* or *Superfetation* (30) recommended that the man should have imbibed at most only a moderate quantity of strong, pure wine and have partaken of food that is nutritious, not have had a hot bath prior to intercourse, and be healthy and strong. Citing what was probably a widely held opinion, Plutarch (*Mor.* 1d = *Education of Children* 2) claimed that men should procreate when sober on the grounds that 'the offspring of fathers who conceive when drunk are themselves liable to grow up to be drunkards'. Soranos (*Gyn.* 1.38 and 40) suggested that the woman should take some nourishment and be given a massage shortly before intercourse. The former, he argued, promotes the desire for intercourse, while the latter, by encouraging bowel-movement and the evacuation of waste-matter, tones up the body so that it is more ready to receive and retain the sperm. In justifying these recommendations, Soranos used the much-worn analogy of the male as farmer and the female as cultivable soil, the latter needing to be purged of extraneous matter before productive sowing can begin.

Only in Sparta, so far as we know, did the state require mothers-to-be to participate in an arduous training programme which included running, wrestling, and discus- and javelin-throwing, with the aim that (Plu. *Lyk.* 14.2):

> the root of what they have conceived [i.e. the embryo] should have a strong beginning in strong bodies and that they themselves by enduring labour with fortitude should struggle effectively and easily with labour pangs.

Recommended ages for procreation

The concern to identify the optimum conditions for a successful implantation of seed generated argument about the ideal time of life for men and women to conceive. Plato, for instance, declared (*Rep.* 5.460e) that a man reaches the height or *akmê* of his physical powers in his thirtieth year and a woman in her twentieth. Aristotle, who regarded thirty-six and seventeen as the ideal ages at which to marry and start a family for the man and woman respectively, was of the opinion that men could no longer produce children after seventy nor women after fifty (*Pol.* 7.1335a7-10). However, the desirable upper age limit for procreation should not be much above fifty in the case of the man, since 'the offspring of too elderly parents (*presbuteroi*), like those of too young ones (*neôteroi*), are defective in both body and mind, while the children of geriatrics (*gegêrakotoi*) are weaklings' (1335b29-31). The strikingly late age for marriage suggested here and elsewhere for men may to some extent have been conditioned by the belief that 'the initial seminal emissions are infertile, until the twenty-first year' (Arist. *HA* 7.582a17f. *T*).

No Greek community is known to have adhered to these recommendations, which appear to have been based loosely on Spartan practice. In Classical Athens, which is the only Greek community whose marriage-patterns we can attempt to analyse in any detail, the majority of well-to-do girls seem to have been married around the age of thirteen or fourteen to men who were about thirty (see below, p. 210ff.). Thirteen, too, is likely to have been the age when most girls experienced menarche (below, p. 167f.). A large proportion of them probably became pregnant in their mid-teens, though there is no actual evidence about age-specific patterns of fertility. While the effect which either pre-menarcheal or early post-menarcheal sexual relations may have had on fertility cannot be gauged, there is little doubt that the early age at which many girls first gave birth greatly increased the risk of infant mortality, since those who become pregnant within two years of menarche put both themselves and their child at high risk. The following statement by Aristotle (*Pol.* 7.1335a12-17) seems to indicate some awareness of this fact, though it is unlikely to have had any impact upon sexual mores:

> The mating of the young (*neoi*) is bad for reproduction. In all species the offspring of the young are deformed and more likely

to be female and underdeveloped, and it is necessarily the case that the same occurs with regard to the human race. The proof is that in all communities where it is the custom for young men and young women (*neoi* and *neai*) to copulate, the bodies (i.e. of their children) are small and deformed.

Intercourse as a possible source of pollution

Intercourse does not appear to have been regarded by the Greeks as ordinarily polluting or dangerous for the participants. Even intercourse with a menstruating woman was not generally discouraged, as it is in many non-industrial societies (cf. Nag 1962, 143). In fact both Aristotle (*GA* 1.727b12-14) and Soranos (*Gyn.* 1.36.2) were of the opinion that a woman is most likely to conceive when her period is drawing to a close. Nor is there anything to indicate that the Greeks thought it necessary to purify themselves after having intercourse; if they did the procedure was probably perfunctory. The post-coital fumigation and ablution rites practised by the Babylonians, which required both the man and the woman to squat over burning incense and to take a bath the morning after love-making, were clearly considered by Herodotos (1.198) to be an anthropological oddity for which there was no Greek equivalent. In rustic communities, however, sexual purity or even sexual abstinence may have been insisted upon for the performing of important agricultural tasks such as sowing, planting and harvesting (cf. Parker 1983, 77f.). Pseudo-Lukian's observation (*Am.* 42) that 'women are so filthy that you need a bath after sleeping with them' does not of course imply the need for ritual purification and is unlikely to be representative of the majority view.

Like all bodily functions, intercourse was strictly forbidden within sanctuaries. According to Herodotos (2.64.1) what distinguished the Greeks and the Egyptians from almost every other race on earth was the fact that 'they do not have intercourse (*misgesthai*) inside sanctuaries nor do they enter a sanctuary without washing after having been with a woman (*apo gunaikôn*)'. Though the prohibition is likely to have arisen primarily from the desire to avoid imperilling the sanctity of the gods and hence arousing their anger, it may also reflect the fear that a god, like a corpse, is potentially noxious to an embryo.

Procreative predominance of sperm over womb

In Aeschylus' *Eumenides* (ll. 658-60) Apollo makes the notorious observation that 'the mother is not the begetter (*tokeus*) of that which is called the child, but only nurse (*trophos*) of the newly-implanted seed. It is the one who mounts who is the true begetter.' Further traces of the same belief are evident in the practice adopted by the Athenian democracy at the end of the sixth century BC of identifying citizens merely by their patronymic and demotic (i.e. X, son of father Y, of the deme Z). For administrative purposes the mother simply did not count. Milesian philosophers, who applied the notion of growth from seed as the chief explanatory model for their cosmogonical theories (above, p. 7), likewise attributed the capacity to promote growth to the semen alone, either because of the moisture which it contains, or because its foamy property indicates the presence of air, since water and air were regarded as essential for life by Thales and Anaximenes respectively (cf. Furley 1987, 21f.).

The theory of male reproductive predominance finds an echo in myths where Zeus takes upon himself the role of surrogate mother. When Zeus' first wife Metis became pregnant, Ouranos and Gaia advised the god to swallow her whole, since, if she bore him a son, it was destined to be mightier than its father. Zeus took their advice, but when he quarrelled with Hephaistos, the latter cracked him on the skull with an axe, whereupon his daughter Athena, adult and fully dressed in the panoply of war, sprang out of the cleft with a mighty shout (cf. Hes. *Th.* 886-900). The myth of the double birth of Dionysos goes even further in devaluing the role of the woman by attributing to Zeus the capability of taking over the female function once conception has taken place. Dionysos was conceived by his mother Semele whom Zeus incinerated with his lightning at the moment of impregnation. The embryo was subsequently sewn into the thigh of Zeus and delivered in perfect health at full term. In the myth of the birth of Erectheus/Erichthonios the role of the female is equally attenuated and nebulous. When Hephaistos tried unsuccessfully to rape Athena, he ejaculated over her leg. In revulsion she wiped the seed away with a piece of wool which she then threw upon the ground. The seed was engendered in the earth and the infant king was thus born (Apollod. 3.14.6). Instances in Greek myth of the appropriation of the female principle by the male are, however, matched by others which illustrate examples of parthenogenesis. Her lack of a bed-partner did not prevent Night from giving birth to a large and gruesome litter which included Doom, Fate, Death, Blame, Woe and other monstrosities (Hes. *Th.* 211-25).

Belief in the primary procreating function of the male sperm did not go entirely unchallenged in the Greek world, however, and in a number of Hippokratic works, notably *Regimen* 1, *Seed, Nature of the Child* and *Diseases* 4, the woman is portrayed as playing an equivalent role in determining the sex of the embryo (cf. Lloyd 1983, 66). In this particular area of embryological debate Aristotle's contribution to the discussion was wholly negative. For though he acknowledged that women contribute not only the place but also the matter necessary for the formation of an embryo, he asserted a belief in the inherent superiority of the male, whereas his opponents, the pangenesists, in their supposition that both the male and the female produce seed, attributed approximately equal significance to both partners. It must, however, be borne in mind that the speculations of philosophers are unlikely to have impinged much, if at all, upon the popular imagination.

What did impinge was Perikles' citizenship law, passed in 451/0 BC, which required both partners to be of pure Athenian descent in order for their (male) offspring to claim Athenian citizenship. Although the primary intention of the law was probably to limit the franchise rather than to preserve the purity of Athenian blood, such a regulation implies the belief that a woman's contribution to the production of an offspring is (or at least could be represented as being) active and vital, perhaps even equivalent to a man's.

Reproductive theories

The reproductive theory which enjoyed greatest support in medical circles down until the time of Aristotle was that known today as pangenesis or preformation, which taught that the seed is extracted or 'drawn off' – the technical verb used for this process is *aperchomai* – from the whole body. It was a perfectly 'natural' theory to hold, given the Greeks' ignorance as to the reproductive purpose of the testicles and ovaries (cf. Phillips 1987, 62). The earliest surviving reference to pangenesis is in an obscure fragment of Demokritos of Abdera (*fl.* 420 BC), which states (*DK* 68 B 32):

> Sexual intercourse (*sunousia*) is a minor apoplexy. For man (*anthrôpos*) burst forth from man, and is separated by being severed by a kind of blow (*plêgê*).

Pangenesis is the reproductive theory uniformly advanced in the embryological treatises of the Hippokratic corpus. The writers of these works analyse sperm into a compound substance whose elements are blood, bile, water and phlegm. These elements constitute bodies (*sômata*) of varying strength or weakness. Sperm is produced by both male and female partners and is diffused throughout the whole body. Fertilisation is therefore the product of a fusion between male and female *sômata* which combine in several different ways to produce various kinds of male and female embryos (see below, p. 30f.). The author of *Seed* (1), for instance, describes a man's orgasm as a warming of bodily fluid which leads to the secretion (*apokrisis*) of foam. He continues:

> This fluid is diffused from the brain into the loins and the whole body, but in particular into the spinal marrow: for passages extend into this from the whole body, which enable the fluid to pass to and from the spinal marrow. Once the sperm has entered the spinal marrow, it passes in its course through the veins along the kidneys. ... From the kidneys it passes via the testicles into the penis – not however by the urinary tract since it has a passage of its own which is next to the urinary tract. (tr. G.E.R. Lloyd)

Later in the same work it is stated that the pleasure and heat experienced by the woman during intercourse 'reach their peak simultaneously with the arrival of the sperm in the womb, and then they cease' (*Seed* 4), for it is an assumption of pangenesis that both partners must achieve a simultaneous orgasm in order for conception to take place. The discharge of sperm into the vagina is compared to the effect of pouring wine onto a fire. Initially the flame (i.e. the woman's orgasm) flares up and becomes more intense, but soon after it dies away and is extinguished.

The wide acceptance of pangenesis in medical circles in the fourth century BC is indicated by the fact that it is this theory which Aristotle sets out to demolish in Book IV of his polemical and pioneering embryological treatise entitled *Generation of Animals*. Aristotle's own theory of reproduction is the one which today goes under the name of epigenesis. It is based on the essentially correct belief that the parts of the body do not all develop simultaneously at the moment of conception but are brought into being by successive accretions. Defining semen as 'a residue (*perittôma*) from useful nourishment and in its final form' and menstrual fluid as 'impure sperm needing treatment (*ergasia*)', he evaluates the differing reproductive roles of the two sexes as follows (*GA* 1.728a17-21):

> A boy actually resembles a woman anatomically speaking (*kata morphên*) and a woman is, so to speak, an infertile male. She is female because of a kind of inadequacy (*adunamia*), being unable to concoct semen from nourishment in its final form [i.e. blood or its equivalent in bloodless animals] owing to the coldness of her nature (*phusis*).

Like his predecessors, Aristotle completely failed to comprehend the significance of the testicles, about which he wrote (717a34-6):

> The testicles (*orcheis*) do not form an integral part of the sperm ducts (*poroi*) but are attached to them just like stone weights that women attach to their looms when they are weaving.

Thus the male semen and the female menses are allied and analogous to one another. The menstrual discharge which women produce is merely an inferior type of sperm, a more plentiful but less pure and less concentrated kind of 'residue' which has to be activated by the male (cf. 726b30ff.). The respective functions of male and female at time of conception are defined as follows (729a9-11): the male supplies the form (*eidos*) and the principle of movement (*hê archê tês kinêseôs*), whereas the female supplies the body (*sôma*) and the substance (*hulê*). This substance, which Aristotle subsequently describes as prime matter (*hê prôtê hulê*), is contained within (or else is consubstantial with) whatever portion of the menses is not discharged externally (729a32). The male sperm is thus identified as the creative partner in the fusion, its function being analogous to that of a carpenter who fashions wood into a bed, the wood being the raw material provided by the female (729b16-17). It is by virtue of its potency (*dunamis*) that the sperm gives a particular stamp to the form (*hulê*) and nourishment (*trophê*) produced by the female. In sum Aristotle propounded that the efficient cause, the agent which sets the generative process underway, is the male sperm, while the material cause, the matter out of which the embryo is formed, is menstrual fluid coupled with the nourishment which the female supplies, both before and after birth.

Sex differentiation

There existed a multiplicity of theories purporting to explain what differentiates the sex of the embryo. Alkmaion of Kroton (*DK* 24 A 14) apparently asserted that it was dependent upon the parent who produced the most seed. Hippon of Rhegion (*DK* 38 A 14) alleged that females come from more watery sperm and males from thicker sperm, a theory that was also advanced by Aristotle (*HA* 7.582a30-2 *T*). Both Demokritos (*DK* 68 A 143) and Parmenides (*DK* 28 A 54) held the view that a war took place between the male and female seeds. Empedokles of Akragas stated (*DK* 31 A 81): 'Males come from sperm produced by parts on the right, females from parts on the left'; and elsewhere (*DK* 31 B 67; cf. B 65): 'The warmer part of the uterus (*gastêr*) receives seed which conceives the male.' Likewise Parmenides claimed (*DK* 28 B 17): 'Males (*kouroi*) come from the right, females (*kourai*) from the left.' A similar view was propounded by Anaxagoras (cf. Arist. *GA* 4.763b30-764a1; discussed by Kember 1973, 1-14). The association of males with the right side of the body and females with the left is attributable to the belief in the inherent superiority of the right and thus, by implication, of the inherent superiority of males: it is not known what evidence, if any, was cited in its support (cf. Lloyd 1962, 60-1).

The Hippokratic school claimed that the sex of the embryo was determined by the potency and quantity of the seed emitted from each partner and that this in turn was determined by the part of the body from which the seed was mainly drawn, since 'weak sperm comes from the weak parts and strong sperm from the strong parts' (*Seed* 8; cf. *Airs, Waters and Places* 14). The treatise *Superfetation* (31), however, in line with the beliefs of Empedokles and Parmenides, advised a man who wished to beget a male offspring to have intercourse either after the woman's period has ceased or when it is drawing to a close and to 'thrust as much as he can until ejaculation takes place', after previously tying a knot around his left testicle in order to render it inoperative. Diet, too, was believed to be capable of influencing the sex of the child: *Regimen* (1.27) states that in order to produce a male offspring both partners should submit themselves to a regimen based on fire and in order to produce a female to one based on water, significantly adding: 'And not only the man, but also the woman. For it is not only what is secreted (*apokrithen*) by the man that contributes to growth, but also what is secreted by the woman.' In order to increase their chances of giving birth to a male offspring women were further advised to eat roast veal together with the herb birthwort or 'Aristolochia' (literally 'of best birth') round about the time of conception.

Genetic transmission

It is self-evident that belief in the doctrine of pangenesis goes hand in hand with the theory that characteristics which have been acquired during a person's lifetime (*ta epiktêta*), such as diseases and deformities, are transmitted along with those which are genetically ingrained (*ta sumphuta*). The author of the Hippokratic *Peri hierês nousou* or *Sacred Disease* (5), for instance, commenting that 'seed comes from every part of the body, healthy seed from healthy parts, unhealthy seed from unhealthy parts', was of the opinion that epilepsy is a hereditary disorder. Even the epigenesists seem to have conceded this point: Aristotle reported as fact the case of a Chalkedonian who was branded on his arm with a letter and whose offspring bore the same mark 'though somewhat faint and hard to make out' (*GA* 1.721b34). Observing that this particular kind of occurrence was rare, Aristotle none the less asserted (*HA* 7.585b30-3 *T*) that:

> Deformed children come from deformed parents, lame from lame and blind from blind, and in general they often resemble their parents in regard to unnatural features such as pimples and scars.

The Hippokratic *Airs, Waters and Places* (14) put forward the view that acquired characteristics could ultimately become inherited if they were transmitted through a sufficient number of generations. As an example the author instances long-headedness, a characteristic which he claims is initially produced by the practice of applying force to the skull but which ultimately becomes 'a natural endowment (*en phusei*) no longer requiring practice to enforce it'.

Despite the broad acceptance of a belief in the superior reproductive capacity of the male, some embryological writers none the less maintained that the contribution of each partner is equally determinative in the transmission of physical characteristics. One of the earliest surviving statements to this effect is by Empedokles, who observed (*DK* 31 B 63): 'The nature (*phusis*) of the limbs is divided. One part comes from the man's <sc. body and another part from the woman's>.' Manifesting the same awareness that transmission through the female line is no less decisive than that which passes through the male, Plutarch (*Mor.* 1d = *Education of Children* 2) praised the Spartans for fining their king Archidamos for having married a diminutive wife since they rightly (in his view) feared that such a union would produce 'kinglets instead of kings'. To Plutarch, too, we are indebted for one of the most moving definitions of conception in all Greek literature (*Mor.* 140ef = *Advice on Marriage* 20):

> Nature joins us through our bodies, so that, taking a portion from each partner and mixing it together, she produces the offspring that is common to both, so that neither party can distinguish what is his or what is hers.

The mental condition of the mother-to-be at the moment of conception was also thought to play a significant part in the transmission of physical characteristics. Empedokles (*DK* 31 A 81) claimed that the mother's sensory impressions (*phantasiai*) decisively influence the physical appearance of the child, stating that 'Women who have fallen in love with statues and pictures frequently give birth to children who resemble them.' The truth of the claim was still being hotly debated in the Roman era. Soranos (*Gyn.* 1.39), for instance, alleged that women who see monkeys during intercourse give birth to monkeys. He also told the story of a misshapen Cypriot tyrant who practised amateur eugenics by compelling his wife to gaze upon beautiful statues while having intercourse and who begat beautiful children as a consequence. That is why, he concluded, a woman should be sober during intercourse since when she is inebriated 'her soul (*psuchê*) becomes prey to wild imaginings'.

Finally, the reason why Indians and Ethiopians are dark-skinned according to Herodotos (3.101) is because the sperm which they emit is black. We may look with a more charitable eye upon the lunacies of the Greeks if we note that as late as 1894 in England it was claimed that if a mother held a piglet by its tail during pregnancy, her baby would be born with a caudal appendage.

Twins

Greek medical writers believed that there were two factors which could influence the production of twins: first the shape of the mother's womb and secondly the quantity of seminal emission. The mistaken belief that the human womb is bicornuate committed the Hippokratic school to the view that the production of twins is natural and inevitable when conception takes place under optimum conditions. Conversely, the fact that women are seen to be capable of producing twins served this school as evidence of the womb's bicornuate structure. *Regimen* (1.30) asserts that if a womb has developed 'equally on both sides of its mouth', then it has every chance of producing twins, provided that the seed produced by the man is of sufficient quantity to divide upon contact with it. By contrast Aristotle maintained that twins are frequently formed in the same part of the womb and that it is simply the quantity of residue (*perittôma*) that determines how many fetations occur at any one time (*GA* 4.764a33-4; 772a4-8). Identical twins have a better chance of survival than fraternal twins, he argued, because male and female foetuses do not develop at the same rate (*GA* 4.775a22-4; cf. *HA* 7.585a2-3 *T*). Finally, Plutarch (*Mor.* 3d = *Education of Children* 5) ingeniously proposed that the reason why women have two breasts is precisely so that 'if they produce twins, they will then have a double source of nourishment to give them'.

Superfetation

Superfetation or *epikuêsis*, which is the fertilisation of a second ovum after a previous conception has taken place but before the first delivery, was thought to be a morbid condition due first to the overheated condition of the man and the woman at the time of intercourse, and secondly to the failure of the uterus to close up after the first implantation of seed. *Regimen* (1.31) states that the phenomenon tends to occur 'when the womb is naturally hot and dry, and the woman is hot and dry, and the sperm is likewise'. The treatise named *Superfetation* (1) maintained, however, that a secondary conception takes place 'when the neck of the uterus (*stomachos*) has not closed up completely after the first conception or, if it has done, when the signs [of pregnancy?] have yet to appear'. If the first embryo has established itself in the centre of the womb it will be expelled by the second implantation, whereas if it has settled in one of its horns (*kerata*), the woman will first successfully deliver a healthy offspring and then subsequently eject the superfetation in the form of a stillborn foetus. In the majority of cases, the author continues, the second fertilisation exists for only for a short period of time, destroying along with it the embryo already growing in the womb.

As an explanatory ploy which was incapable of being tested, superfetation could usefully explain why many pregnancies did not reach full term.

Fertility and sterility

The desire to become pregnant must have been very keenly felt on the part of all Greek wives since those who failed in this essential wifely duty might well have felt an object of suspicion in the eyes of their husbands and in-laws. In communities such as Athens and Sparta the failure to produce an offspring and heir almost certainly constituted one of the principal grounds for divorce. A preoccupation with childlessness is reflected in Attic myths which deal with the problem and its cure in the royal house of Athens, especially in connection with the aged king Aigeus and his wife Kreousa. It is hardly surprising, therefore, that anxiety on the part of women regarding pregnancy and uterine disorders features prominently among the miraculous cures recorded on the inscribed stones which have been discovered at the sanctuary of Epidauros in the Peloponnese. Epidauros, sacred to the healing god Asklepios, was arguably the foremost healing shrine in the ancient Greek world and may be compared with present-day Lourdes. Sick pilgrims who visited it were treated to a potent and in modern eyes mystifying mixture of magic and medicine in varying proportions, the treatment being revealed to the patient by incubation within the sanctuary.

One inscribed stone dated to the fourth century BC tells of a certain Ithmonike of Pellene who came to the sanctuary and dreamt that she asked the god to make her pregnant with a girl. Asklepios said that he would grant her request and that if she had any other favour to beg he would grant that too. Ithmonike blithely replied that she wanted nothing further

Fig. 2. Thank-offering for a successful pregnancy? Terracotta model of a womb from a Roman Asklepieion, third to first century BC

and in time duly became pregnant. Having remained in this condition for three years, she returned to Epidauros in order to ask the god why she had not yet delivered. Asklepios appeared to her a second time in her sleep and mischievously informed the woman that she should have been more specific in her request. What she had asked was to become pregnant; what she wanted was to give birth. Because she had come as a suppliant, however, he agreed to accede to this additional request. No sooner had Ithmonike left the sanctuary, the inscription alleges, than she gave birth to a daughter. The case of Ithmonike is by no means unique; the same stone records a five-year pregnancy in the case of a woman called Kleo. After sleeping in the shrine Kleo left the temple precinct and gave birth to a son who immediately washed himself in a fountain and walked about with his mother. A three- or five-year pregnancy is, of course, a medical nonsense. Though the true source of these women's complaints and their cures eludes us, it is just possible that what we are dealing with is an extreme case of amenorrhea, that is to say, the cessation of menstrual flow in a woman of childbearing years, a condition which in the ancient world might possibly have been diagnosed as an extended pregnancy. Dedications made of terracotta in the form of a pair of female breasts, the uterus or an ovary, which have been found at various Asklepieia, may, in some cases at least, be a thank-offering for a successful pregnancy, while that in the form of the male genitals perhaps celebrates the re-acquisition of potency (Fig. 2; cf. Lang 1977, 22-3 with figs 22 and 23).

What percentage of those who came to Epidauros went away cured is impossible to estimate. But in the final analysis this sanctuary and the two hundred-odd others dedicated to Asklepios scattered throughout the Greek world were important not primarily because the people who visited them were occasionally healed in a 'miraculous' way but because they enabled the sick to go on *hoping*. And in the case of childless couples, visiting such a sanctuary would have furnished the further comfort that they had done everything possible to alleviate their condition.

In Greek religious belief sterility was commonly explained as divine retribution for an offence against the gods. In Hesiod's *Works and Days* (ll. 240-5), for instance, famine, plague and infertility – or possibly the propensity to miscarry – are seen as punishments which Zeus inflicts upon a whole community for the insolence and immorality of just one of its members. This explanation persisted into the historical period. Herodotos (6.139.1) describes how the wives of the Pelasgians became infertile in consequence of their husbands' wholesale slaughter of Athenian women and children. The plot of Sophokles' *Oedipus Tyrannos* rests upon the assumption that an undetected murderer, or rather a combined parricide and regicide, was capable by contagion alone of blighting the human womb.

Rivers and streams were believed to have fertilising powers. Strabo (*Geog.* 15.1.22; cf. Arist. fr. 284 *T*) asserts that it was due to the generative properties of the Nile that 'Egyptian women sometimes produce quadruplets'. Sanctuaries connected with fertility tended therefore to be established in close proximity to water. In Attica a shrine sacred to Aphrodite situated on Mount Hymettos was celebrated for the fact that water from its fountain was believed to promote easy delivery and make sterile women fertile (cf. Paus. 1.14.7). Though goddesses and female spirits were most closely associated with fertility, the god Dionysos was also thought capable of promoting human fecundity. An Attic black-figure vase-painting which depicts Dionysos holding a cornucopia and facing a mother who is holding twins is probably intended to be an allusion to the god's fertilising power in view of the fact that multiple births were commonly regarded as evidence of superabundant fecundity.

By the beginning of the fifth century BC scientific explanations of sterility begin to appear. Alkmaion of Kroton, who advanced the influential theory that health consists of an equal balance (*isonomia*) of what he called 'powers (*dunameis*)', wrote (*DK* 24 B 3): 'In mules the males are sterile because of the fineness and coldness of the seed, and the females because their wombs do not open up.' His observation is important not only because it offers a challenge to the view of sterility as a form of divine punishment, but also because it apportions equal responsibility to both male and female. Alkmaion's theory of *isonomia* anticipates the celebrated Hippokratic doctrine of the four humours (heat, cold, moistness and dryness) of which all life was thought to be composed and in accordance with which barrenness is essentially the product of a physiological imbalance in the humours. As *Aphorisms* (5.62) explains:

> Women who have wombs that are dense and cold do not conceive; women who have wombs that are watery do not conceive because the seed is quenched. Women who have parched and over-heated wombs do not conceive because the seed perishes through lack of nutrition. Those who have a proper blend of both can conceive.

The fact that sterility is one of the most extensively discussed subjects in the gynaecological treatises of the Hippokratic corpus constitutes further evidence that childlessness was a major problem for many couples. In *Peri aphorôn* or *Sterile Women* about a dozen different causes of sterility are analysed, based on the theory that the sperm is either unable to enter the uterus, or alternatively that having entered the uterus it is unable to implant itself successfully owing to the unhealthy condition of the womb. It follows that a woman is incapable of conceiving if the mouth of her uterus is at an oblique angle to her vagina; if its mouth is partly or completely closed; if the uterus is ulcerated; or if it is unable to discharge all or part of the menses. The treatise naturally makes no mention of the possibility of an infection in the ovaries as a cause of sterility owing to its author's ignorance of the workings of this gland. There is little discussion of male infertility in the Hippokratic writings, though the explanation for this omission should not necessarily be ascribed to the fact that infertility was regarded as an exclusively or even predominantly female complaint. It may be due in part to the fact that the same condition in a man is less traceable and so less easy to treat.

The Hippokratic corpus recommends a number of tests designed to discover whether a woman who failed to conceive was infertile. These were based on the notion that the passage between a woman's mouth and her uterus resembles a kind of funnel which must remain clear and unconstricted. *Aphorisms*, for instance, proposes (5.59) that the woman should be covered with cloaks and incense burned beneath her. Then if the smell of the incense appears to pass right through her body and into her mouth and nostrils, she is capable of conceiving; otherwise she is not. *Sterile Women* (3.214) recommends giving the woman a pat of butter together with the milk of a mother who is weaning. Then 'if she vomits, she will conceive; if she doesn't, she won't'. Treatments for infertility included the insertion into the neck of a womb of a woollen suppository (*prostheton*) which had been dipped into a medicament composed of rose oil, marrow of ox, myrrh, cassia and cinnamon; or the burning of incense concocted out of a variety of substances including brimstone, garlic and beavers' testicles (*Superfetation* 32-5, 37 and 39). Another method was to flush out the womb by pouring milk into a tube which had been inserted into the vagina (*Gyn*. 3.222).

Factors which were reckoned to influence fertility included climate, occupation, body-weight and length of penis. North winds were widely reported to be more favourable for conception than those which blow from the south (Arist. *Pol*. 7.1335b1-5). *Airs, Waters and Places* (3-4) claims that cities exposed to hot winds induce barrenness and abortions and that those exposed to cold winds are equally injurious to health on the grounds that their drinking-water is 'hard, indigestible and cold'. The same work states that the nomadic Skythians suffered from occupational sterility because they spent too much time jolting up and down on their horses, thereby rendering themselves unfit for sexual intercourse (21). According to *Aphorisms* (5.44 and 46) excessively thin women have a tendency to miscarry, while excessively fat ones are unable to conceive owing to the fact that the mouth of their womb cannot open. Aristotle likewise believed (*GA* 1.726a3-6; cf. *PA* 2.651b13-17) that 'fat people are less fertile (*agonôteroi*) than those who are slim because when the body is overfed, the residue (*perittôma*) that is discharged is converted into fat'. He also maintained that men with large penises are less fertile than those with moderate-sized penises on the interesting grounds that 'the sperm cools down by being transported too far [along the reproductive tract] and sperm that has cooled down is not generative' (*GA* 1.718a22-5).

Pregnancy

Modern medicine divides pregnancy into three separate phases which it identifies as zygotal (weeks 1-2), embryonic (weeks 2-8) and foetal (weeks 8-40). A somewhat comparable method of systematising gestation is evident in Aristotle's statement: 'Deaths that occur up to seven days (sc. after conception) are termed *ekrusis*, those up to forty days *ektrôsmos* ... and most pregnancies fail within this term of days' (*HA* 7.583b12-15 *T*). As noted in the Introduction (p. 12), however, the Greeks used *embruon* to denote the unborn child throughout the entire period of gestation. Other expressions include *heptamênon* and *oktamênon*, which describe a foetus at seven and eight months respectively. Ideologically neutral, so to speak, these terms indicate that the entity within the womb was not invested with an enlarged biological persona as it developed and grew. Instead it remained as anonymous, so to speak, at the moment of parturition as it was at the moment of conception.

Although the Greek language failed to enforce any distinction comparable to that implied by our terms 'embryo' and 'foetus', some medical writers did clearly wrestle with the notion that the entity inside the womb was gradually assuming an identity of its own. This is well-illustrated in the Hippokratic *Nature of the Child* (12-29) which provides the following detailed account of foetal development. First, the author states, the seed (*gonê*) that is produced by both partners 'mixes' in the womb. Then it acquires breath (*pneuma*). As the mother inhales, the *gonê* grows warmer and becomes filled with *pneuma* until a fissure is created through which the breath escapes. Cold *pneuma* then enters and the cycle is repeated. The process is likened to the heating of green wood, which causes hot air to escape into the atmosphere and be replaced by cold air. In time a red, circular membrane (*humên*) forms around the surface of the seed composed of thick, white fibres (*ines*). In the middle of the *humên* is what appears to be the navel, though at this stage (six days) it is difficult to make out (13). The *gonê* in the *humên* 'has breath both inside and outside' and feeds on menstrual blood which causes 'the living creature-to-be (*to mellon zôön*)' to enlarge (14). Flesh begins to form and the *gonê* draws in more blood (15). 'As the entity in the womb increases (*auxomenou tou en têsi mêtrêisin eneontos*)', further membranes form, especially on the outside (16). Respiration causes the various types of flesh to join up together (heavy-textured with heavy, light with light, moist with moist, etc.) and articulation commences. The bones harden under the impact of heat while the eye-sockets become filled with pure moisture (17). The formation of a *paidion*, so-named and identified for the first time, takes forty-two days in the case of a female and thirty in the case of a male (18). Eventually the extremities are formed, just as the outermost branches of a tree finally put forth leaves (19). After the fingers and toes have been formed, nails and cephalic hair 'take root (*rhizountai*)' (20). Movement or quickening occurs at three months in the case of a male, four in the case of a female, this distinction being due to the fact that the male is stronger than the female and comes from stronger, thicker seed (21). As soon as the *embruon* (sic) moves, milk indicates its presence in the mother. This final change of terminology is apparently intended to signal the concluding stage of development, marked by dependency on the mother's milk rather than on her menses.

Medical writers were much exercised as to whether the constituent parts of the embryo develop simultaneously or successively, and if successively then in what sequence. Aristotle (*GA* 2.734a18-20; cf. *DK* 1 B 10a) ascribes to what he calls 'the so-called Orphic poems' the view that the parts of the body are formed successively 'in the way that a net is plaited'. A similar view is found in Demokritos who wrote (*DK* 68 B 148): 'The navel is implanted (*emphuetai*) first in the womb, as an anchor against tossing and wandering, as a cable and as a branch for the fruit (*karpos*) that is engendered and yet to come.' According to *Nature of the Child* (12) the respiratory system is the first organ to enter actively into its functions. By experimentation with hen's eggs, however, Aristotle correctly observed that within three days of fertilisation the heart is detectable in the albumen as a blood spot which 'throbs and moves as if endowed with life (*empsuchos*)' (*HA* 6.561a12-13 *T*). From this he concluded that the heart is the principle or *archê* of life (cf. *GA* 2.740a17-19), even though it is not present from the beginning in a perfected form (*GA* 2.734b17-19). Pangenesists were committed to the belief that the gestation period was devoted merely to the enlargement of what was already present in a perfected form from within a few days of conception having taken place. The Hippokratic author of *Flesh* (19) writes:

> When the seed (*gonos*) enters the womb (*mêtrai*) within seven days it has all the parts of the body articulated ... Public prostitutes, if they have a large number of clients, when they go with a man know whether they conceive. Then they destroy what is inside them, and when it is destroyed, it drops out like flesh. If you place this flesh in water and examine it in the water, you will find that it has all its limbs, and eye sockets, ears, members, the fingers of the hands, the legs, the feet, the toes, the genitals and all the rest of the body are evident.

In the absence of any secure method of determining precisely when a conception had taken place, and in consequence, too, of the inclusive method of counting by which part months counted as whole, the period of gestation was judged to be capable of varying from seven to eleven months (e.g. Hipp. *Seventh-Month Foetus* 4; Gell. *AN* 3.16).*

In both medical and non-medical circles it was universally agreed that the most dangerous period of late pregnancy for both the mother and the foetus was the eighth month. The author of the *Seventh-Month Foetus* asserts (3-4) that women themselves rightly claim that the eighth month is the 'most difficult', but, as if to display his erudition, adds that one should include a few days at the end of the seventh and a few at the beginning of the ninth, so that the period of danger is actually some forty days in length. When it is over, the author

* The uncertainty about length of gestation merely foreshadows a continuing ambivalence in modern medical circles about expected date of confinement (EDC) where the issue depends on whether one calculates from the moment of fertilisation, in which case gestation is 38 weeks in length, or from the beginning of the last menstrual cycle (known as Naegele's Rule), in which case it is 40 weeks.

continues, 'The inflammations (*phlegmonai*) in both the foetus and the mother subside, the belly is relieved, and the burden descends from the abdomen and from the flanks towards the lower parts in a manner that is favourable for delivery.' The following obscure passage in the Hippokratic treatise entitled *Peri trophês* or *Nutriment* (42) is probably intended to provide the reader with a description of seventh- and eight-month pregnancies:

> For formation 35 days, for movement 70 days, for completion 210 days; others, for shape 45 days, for movement 90 days, for completion 210 days; others, for shape 50 days, for the first kick 100 days, for completion 300 days. For distinction of limbs, 40 days; for *metabasis* [quickening?] 80 days, for detachment [i.e. delivery], 240 days. It is not and it is.

Certainly Aulus Gellius understood the passage to be referring to non-viable pregnancies, for he quotes the statement 'It is and it is not' with *ta oktamêna* (eighth-month foetuses) as subject, and then goes on to quote the Hippokratic commentator Sabinus as follows (*AN* 3.16.7-8): 'They exist because they appear to exist as living creatures (*zôia*) after the miscarriage (*ektrôsis*). But they do not exist because they die thereafter.'

Why the eighth month? The reason is to be found in the Hippokratic *Seventh-Month Foetus* (9) whose author dogmatically asserts that eighth-month foetuses are incapable of surviving 'owing to the imperfection inherent in an even number', thereby affording us a classic instance of the overlap between popular belief and scientific tradition. While it is impossible for the modern mind to comprehend fully in what precisely that imperfection consists, it evidently resided in the belief that oddness and evenness exert a 'characteristic influence (*idiê dunamis*)' upon the human body. Like superfetation, therefore, belief in the non-viability of an eighth-month child served a useful psychological function in the case of a stillborn delivery, first by relieving the parents of guilt feelings and secondly by exonerating the midwife and birthing attendants of negligence (Hanson 1987, 601-2). If, conversely, a foetus believed to be eight months old survived delivery, the midwife could always claim that the woman had conceived without realising it.

Foetal superiority of the male

The view prevailed in antiquity that the male foetus develops earlier, is physically more resilient, and imposes less of a burden upon its mother than the female. In *Aphorisms* (5.42) it is alleged that if a woman is pregnant with a boy she has a healthy complexion, and if with a girl a pale complexion (cf. *Sterile Women* 3.216 and *Superfetation* 19). *Nature of the Child* (18) claims that a male foetus takes a maximum of 30 days to become fully articulated, whereas a female takes 42; correspondingly, the lochia is discharged after 30 days in the case of a boy but 42 in the case of a girl. The author of *Seventh-Month Foetus*, who proposes a somewhat longer period of development for the articulation of the foetus, has the following explanation for the more rapid growth of the male. At the end of forty days, he writes:

> The foetus is stronger and the parts of its body become distinct. In boys everything becomes very distinct, though in girls the flesh at this time shows only excrescences (*apophusiai*). Like remains like in the like for a longer time and is distinguished later because of habit and affinity.

The last sentence seems to mean that it takes longer for a female foetus to establish its separate identity since it is consubstantial with the flesh of the woman who bears it. As we have seen, males were thought to be carried on the right of the womb and females on the left, a theory determined by the assumption that right was naturally superior to left (see above, p. 32; cf. Hipp. *Aph.* 5.48; Pln. *NH* 7.4.37). Aristotle was essentially of the same opinion, though he pointed out (*HA* 7.583b2-10 *T*) that instances were reported of a female manifesting movement on the right and a male on the left.

The belief in the inherent superiority of the male over the female foetus indisputably reflects the fact that the birth of a boy was often attended with greater joy and less ambivalence than that of a girl (see below, p. 86f.). It is not without its echo in today's world. A modern medical handbook on pregnancy states: 'More boys tend to be born in the first few years after marriage; immediately following a reunion after a long parting; and in younger parents' (Rose-Neil 1984, 25). The Greeks do not, however, seem to have subscribed to the widely-held belief that the begetting of boys is a sign of manliness on the part of the father. Herodotos (1.136.1) observes it to be an oddity of the Persians to regard a man's ability in this area as the next most important indication of character after his prowess in battle.

The pregnant woman

In the Hippokratic *Illnesses of Women* (1.25) it is stated: 'One needs much precaution and knowledge to bring a foetus to term and nourish it in the womb (*dienenkein kai ekthrepsai to paidion en têisi mêtrêisi*)'. The delicate condition of the pregnant woman, often referred to merely as *gunê en gastri echousê* or 'a woman who is carrying in her belly', is a subject of particular attention in *Aphorisms* which asserts that if a pregnant woman is attacked by an acute disease, the disease proves fatal (5.30); if she is bled, she miscarries (5.31); if she has frequent diarrhoea, she is in danger of miscarrying (5.34); if her breasts suddenly become thin, she miscarries (5.37); if her womb is attacked by erysipelas – a febrile disease sometimes called St Anthony's fire – it proves fatal (5.43); if she is unnaturally thin, she will miscarry unless she puts on weight (5.44); if she produces an abundance of milk, then the foetus cannot be healthy (5.52); if she succumbs to fever, she will either have a difficult and dangerous labour or else miscarry (5.55); and if she bleeds, the foetus cannot be healthy (5.60). The desire to eat non-food substances such as earth and coal, a harmless craving known today as pica and in antiquity as 'ivy sickness (*kissa*)', is noted in *Superfetation* (18), where the author darkly warns that if the craving is gratified, 'when the *paidion* is born a sign of such things appears on its head' (cf. Arist. *HA* 7.584a18-20 *T*; Sor. *Gyn*. 1.53). The view that the pregnant woman is highly susceptible to illness just as she is highly susceptible to pollution (see below) is clearly an expression of the fear that the pregnancy will not reach full term.

A woman was believed to be most likely to miscarry during the first forty days of her pregnancy. The author of *Seventh-Month Foetus* (9) writes:

> The first forty days are critical for the *embruon*. Women who get through the first forty days generally avoid miscarriages or *trôsmoi*. More miscarriages occur in the first forty-day period than in the remaining period of pregnancy.

The fear and incomprehension occasioned by the sudden

ejection from the uterus of a successfully implanted seed is graphically illustrated by Pliny's assertion (*NH* 30.44.130) that 'if a pregnant woman steps over a raven's egg, she will miscarry through the mouth'.

In order to safeguard the unborn child in the womb Plato (*Laws* 7.789b-d) advocates prenatal gymnastics on the grounds that 'all bodies are beneficially braced by every sort of shaking and stirring'. More moderately, and with the interest of the mother uppermost, Aristotle (*Pol.* 7.1335b12-14) urged pregnant women to take exercise and eat well. A daily constitutional to the shrine of the deities who protected women in labour would in his view satisfy this requirement, while also, it may be suspected, fulfilling the deep psychological need for regular communion with the divine. He also warned against excessive eating of salt and maintained that alcohol taken during pregnancy induced stupor and debilitation (*HA* 7.585a33-4 *T*).

There were conflicting opinions as to whether a pregnant woman should engage in sexual intercourse. *Aphorisms* (4.1) declared that a woman should be purged 'if she experienced excitement (*ên orgai*)' – a form of words presumably intended to include sexual stimulation – at any time during the fourth to eighth months of pregnancy. Aristotle, who claimed that intercourse during pregnancy was beneficial, none the less pointed out that if it occurred after the eighth month the child would emerge covered in a slimy mucus (*HA* 7.585a24-6 *T*). Soranos believed it to be harmful on the grounds that 'the womb is forced to endure a movement that is contrary to the essence of conception' (*Gyn.* 1.56.3).

There is little evidence that pregnant women were deemed capable of polluting, partly perhaps because there was no definite way of knowing whether a woman was pregnant until after a month had elapsed after conception. Censorinus writes (*DN* 11.7): 'In Greece they treat fortieth days as important. For pregnant women do not visit a shrine before the fortieth day.' What precisely 'fortieth days' means is not clear, but the period is probably to be calculated from the moment when a woman first becomes aware that she is pregnant (cf. Parker 1983, 48). The ruling is not referred to anywhere else and we cannot know whether it was enforced in earlier times. It may have had something to do with the alleged high incidence of miscarriages in the first forty days after conception. In later pregnancy, however, women were not generally debarred from visiting shrines; on the contrary they made regular visits to the sanctuaries of the birth goddesses in order to elicit their goodwill and support (see below, p. 66).

Although pregnant women were a source of only very weak pollution themselves, they were extremely vulnerable to pollution from others. Iphigeneia in Euripides' *Iphigeneia in Tauris* (ll. 1126-9), for instance, warns those devoting themselves to temple service, those who are about to get married, and those who are close to giving birth, to stay well clear when she leads the polluted matricide Orestes through the streets. No doubt proclamations of this kind were uttered in real life.

While none of the information we have been discussing tells us much about the care and attention that were bestowed upon pregnant women, the perception of them as extremely vulnerable both to illness and pollution strongly suggests that they were treated with considerable care and respect.

Contraception

Greek literature in general and the Hippokratic corpus in particular shed little light upon methods of contraception, arguably because the practice of exposure served instead as an *ex post facto* regulator of family size (cf. Phillips 1987, 112). What is abundantly clear, however, is that in antiquity, just as today, the responsibility for preventing a conception rested mainly with the woman. Such a bias is to some extent inevitable, for 'common sense' suggests that it is easier to block the entry to the womb than it is to control seminal emission. There seems to have been hardly any objection to contraception on religious grounds in ancient Greece and such objections as are found relate mainly to fringe sects. True to the standards of extreme ascetic rigour that permeated all aspects of their existence, the Pythagoreans, for instance, held that intercourse should take place exclusively between husband and wife and was justifiable only between partners 'who intended to create life (*zôiopoiein*) and to bring a being to birth (*genesis*) and existence (*ousia*)' (*DK* 58 B 8, p. 476.14-15).

In modern non-industrial societies the most popular and effective method of birth-control is coitus interruptus. A possible description of its application during a premarital sexual encounter occurs in a fragmentary poem by Archilochos, a native of Paros who lived in the seventh century BC. Having described how he gave a young girl his assurance that he would withdraw before ejaculation, the poet continues:

> I took the *parthenos* and laid her down among the flowers. I covered her with my soft cloak and held my arm around her neck. She stopped trembling like a fawn; I touched her breasts gently with my hand; she revealed her new young skin. I touched her fair body everywhere and sent my white force aside, touching her blonde hair. (tr. M.R. Lefkowitz)

Strictly speaking, it is uncertain whether the procedure described here is intended to prevent conception or merely serves to avoid rupturing the hymen. Coitus interruptus is not referred to in any of the gynaecological treatises and there is no other evidence to suggest that it was practised by the Greeks. In fact the earliest incontrovertible allusion to its use as a method of birth control dates to the first century BC (cf. Lucr. 4.1269-73). It goes without saying that this method necessitates considerable self-control on the part of the man, a self-control, we may note, which many men may be either unable or unwilling to exercise. It is not surprising, therefore, given the presumptions of ancient society, that the medical profession should have sought to suggest that it was not essential for the man to withdraw at the moment of orgasm. As the following passage from Soranos indicates, a little vigilance and dexterity on the part of an understanding woman at the moment of ejaculation will ensure that the sperm does not actually attach itself to the womb (*Gyn*. 1.61.1):

> During intercourse, at the moment of orgasm, when the man is on the point of orgasm, the woman should hold her breath and shift her position slightly beneath him so that the seed does not spurt too far into the recess of the uterus. Getting up immediately and adopting a squatting position, she should make herself sneeze and wipe the vagina all around and even drink something cold.

Thus the onus and responsibility for the use of a method of contraception that depends for its effectiveness almost wholly upon the man is transferred to the woman, thereby leaving the man free to enjoy his orgasm unimpeded.

The assumption behind the procedure recommended by Soranos is that conception only occurs if most of the sperm remains inside the womb (see above, p. 23) and that post-coital loss of semen serves as a preventative. A remarkable testimony to the belief that sperm could be expelled from the uterus by violent movement even six days after intercourse is contained in the following description of the ejection from the uterus of what the Hippokratic author identifies as a healthy six-day ovum or *gonê* – in reality probably a blood mole or blighted ovum partly surrounded by blood clots (*Nature of the Child* 13):

> A kinswoman of mine owned a very valuable danseuse, whom she employed as a prostitute. It was important that this girl should not become pregnant (*labein en gastri*) and thereby lose her value. Now this girl had heard the sort of thing women say to each other – that when a woman is going to conceive, the seed (*gonê*) remains inside her and does not fall out. She digested this information, and kept a watch. One day she noticed that the *gonê* had not come out again. She told her mistress, and the story came to me. When I heard it, I told her to jump up and down, touching her buttocks with her heels at each leap. After she had done this no more than seven times, there was a noise, the *gonê* fell out on the ground, and the girl looked at it in great surprise. (tr. G.E.R. Lloyd)

The Greeks put great faith in an assortment of concoctions which they applied to the vaginal area to prevent the sperm from passing into the fundus. Soranos, who is our most important source for the contraceptive techniques employed in antiquity, recommends (*Gyn.* 1.61.2-3) old olive oil, honey, cedar resin, juice of balsam, and a paste made out of myrtle oil and white lead. These devices are categorised as either styptic (i.e. having the power to contract the entry to the uterus), clogging (i.e. forming a barrier) or cooling (i.e. spermicidal). Other concoctions were taken internally. Under the influence of the Pythagorean doctrine that souls reside in beans, the author of *Nature of Women* (98) recommended that if a woman drank a mixture of beans and water she would be rendered proof against pregnancy for a year, on the grounds that beans would cause a blighted pregnancy to develop (cf. Lefkowitz and Fant 1982, 98 n. 6).

Male absenteeism occasioned by warfare and military training may well have had a significant effect on fertility, particularly in Sparta where males under the age of 30 were permitted to visit their wives only under cover of darkness (see below, p. 224). On Crete association (*homilia*) between males, which does not necessarily imply homosexual intercourse, was recommended as a means of regulating population size (Arist. *Pol.* 2.1272a23-5).

Vase-paintings depicting intercourse between prostitutes (*hetairai*) and their clients indicate that the Greeks practised oral, manual and intercrural sex, all of which undoubtedly served as methods of birth control. Anal intercourse between husband and wife, however, was regarded with utter repugnance, at least among members of the Athenian aristocracy. The disgust it aroused is well demonstrated by Herodotos' anecdote (1.61.1-2) about the tyrant Peisistratos who allegedly owed his first exile to the fact that he refused natural intercourse with his wife and lay with her 'in violation of customary practice (*ou kata nomon*)'. The wife confided in her mother, who in turn protested to her husband Megakles, a member of the powerful Alkmaionid *genos*. Megakles felt that his own honour had been impugned by Peisistratos ('*ton de deinon ti esche ... atimazesthai*') and was so outraged by the discovery that he patched up his differences with his political opponents and succeeded in driving Peisistratos into exile. Herodotos does not bother to tell us whether Megakles expressed any sympathy towards his daughter – perhaps he felt disgusted by her as well – nor indeed whether she herself felt equally aggrieved. Since a predilection for unnatural sexual practices constitutes one of the hallmarks of the Greek stereotype of a tyrant – Periander of Corinth, for instance, was said to have practised necrophilia on his wife's corpse (Hdt. 5.92) – the incident, whether factual or not, would seem to provide us with good evidence for the supposition that this taboo was not confined to Athenian aristocrats.

Finally, the 'rhythm method' was almost certainly practised, though probably without much success since it was believed that women were most likely to conceive when they were menstruating. There is no evidence for any device resembling a condom.

In summary, it is extremely doubtful whether any of the contraceptive devices employed by the Greeks was particularly effective in limiting family size. The fact that there is so little discussion of the subject in the Hippokratic corpus may be taken not only as evidence that it lay outside the concern of the medical profession, but also that limiting a woman's reproductive capacity was not regarded as a high priority or even a useful objective in a society which was primarily concerned with achieving the opposite result and where abortion and exposure could be practised as an effective last resort.

Abortion

Discussion of abortion is complicated by the fact that the Greek language did not fully distinguish between a procured abortion and a miscarriage. Words like *amblôsis, ektrôsmos, ektrôsis, phthora* and *diaphthora* refer merely to the fact of the foetus' expulsion and fail to indicate whether it was induced or spontaneous (cf. Parker 1983, 355).

It is well-known that Greek medicine, officially at least, did not condone abortion. The celebrated Hippocratic oath, which probably dates to the fourth century BC, required those who took it to declare unequivocally: 'I will not give a pessary to cause abortion (*pesson phthorion*).' It has been suggested that the oath furnishes evidence of Pythagorean influence, on the grounds that the Pythagoreans, who maintained that the embryo was animate from the moment of conception, would have been the sect most likely to raise objections to abortion (Edelstein 1967, 18f.). Although Pythagorean influence cannot be ruled out, the aversion may primarily derive from the fact that there was no known method of inducing an abortion which was not likely to result in permanent, perhaps even fatal injury to the mother, as is expressly stated in the following extract from *Illnesses of Women* (1.72):

> Women who have abortions (*hai phtheirousai*) are more at risk (i.e. than those who give birth). For abortions (*phthorai*) are more painful than births (*tokoi*). It is not possible to abort the embryo or foetus (*embruon*) except violently, that is, with drugs, potions, food, suppositories or something else. But violence is bad, because it involves the risk of ulcerating or inflaming the womb.

How widely observed was the Hippokratic oath? The mere inclusion of the ban on abortifacients is regarded by many scholars as unequivocal proof that many doctors did indeed prescribe and recommend abortifacients, not only for therapeutic purposes but also as a way of disposing of unwanted foetuses. Yet no abortifacients are recommended by any of the treatises in the Hippokratic corpus and the only instance of an abortion being performed by a member of the Hippokratic school for non-therapeutic purposes is the alleged case of a pregnant dancing girl whose owner, a woman, arranged for her to have the operation in order to preserve her market value (Galen 4.525f. *K*).

Certainly by the beginning of the Christian era and possibly earlier, the ethics of abortion had become a subject of lively controversy. Soranos (*Gyn.* 1.60.2-3) alludes to the existence of rival factions, one banning abortion altogether, the other condoning it when a woman's health was put at risk but forbidding it 'when a woman wishes to destroy the embryo because of adultery or in order to preserve her youthful beauty (*hôraiotês*)'. He himself, however, had no objection to the performing of an abortion for thearapeutic reasons. His contemporary Plutarch spoke scathingly (*Mor.* 134f = *Advice on Health* 22) of licentious women who 'employ drugs and instruments to perform an abortion (*ekbolia* and *phthoria*) for the pleasure of being stuffed and enjoying themselves again', and further urged a young married couple not to initiate a pregnancy unless both parties were willing that an issue should result (*Mor.* 144b = *Advice on Marriage* 42).

Soranos (*Gyn.* 1.64-5) is in fact the first medical writer to discuss abortifacients, recommending that a woman who wished to abort her child should walk about energetically, be shaken by draught animals, leap up and down, and carry objects that were too heavy for her. In addition, she should take protracted baths, eat little food, abstain from wine, use a diuretic which has the power not only to empty her bladder but also to cause her to bleed, insert suppositories into her vagina so as to dilate her uterus, and be bled profusely.

Although we do not know whether the opinions of women were ever canvassed in the debate, it seems that a number of them actually tried to perform abortions on themselves and were subsequently forced to seek medical assistance to correct their errors. The author of *Illnesses of Women* (1.67) writes:

> When a woman suffers from a deep wound as a result of an abortion (*trôsmos*) or the uterus (*mêtrai*) has been damaged by powerful suppositories, as a lot of women are constantly doing, 'curing' themselves ... if she is treated promptly she will regain health but remain sterile.

The fact that many women would resort to such desperate measures cannot, of course, be taken as evidence of any reluctance on the part of the medical profession to perform abortions, since the majority of individuals would probably have been unable to afford the high fees charged by doctors.

Greek law in distinction to Greek medicine freely permitted abortion, merely seeking to ensure that the father's rights were upheld. It was accordingly illegal for an expectant mother to undergo an abortion without first securing her husband's consent. A reference in Lysias (fr. 8 *T*) to the existence in Athens of a *graphê amblôseôs* or 'criminal charge for abortion' is tantalisingly obscure and of dubious authenticity. A suggestion has been made that the *graphê* was invoked in cases where 'the father is dead and where it might be very much in the interest of the embryo's next-of-kin to procure an abortion' (Harrison 1968, I, p. 72f.). More probably, such an action might have been brought by a husband against a wife who underwent an abortion without first securing his consent. In Cicero's speech *For Cluentius* (11.32), for instance, the story is told of a Milesian woman who was executed for having been bribed by the non-immediate heirs (*heredes secundi*) to undergo an abortion.

Some branches of Greek philosophy actively promoted abortion. Plato prescribed it along with exposure in the case of offspring born to parents who have passed the legal age of childbearing in order to prevent the procreation of defective stock (*Rep*. 5.461bc). Aristotle, who laid down maximum and minimum ages for procreation as well as an upper limit for the number of offspring permitted to each couple, recommended that if these regulations were exceeded and if social ethics forbade the exposure of infants, then (*Pol*. 7.1335b24-6):

> Abortion should be practised before the embryo has developed sensory perception (*aisthêsis*) and life. For the boundary between what is consistent with divine law (*to hosion*) and what is not will be marked by its having *aisthêsis* and life.

It is by no means clear what lower time limit Aristotle is proposing, though the reference to *aisthêsis* suggests that it was probably a fairly advanced state. As the context of the remark makes plain, however, Aristotle's primary concern is fear of the increased pollution which a later abortion would cause, rather than any 'embryonic' regard for the rights of the unborn child. The Stoics had no objection to abortion since they regarded the embryo as a functioning part of the mother whose ensoulment only took place at birth. Conversely the Pythagoreans believed that the embryo was imbued with life at the moment of conception and thus vehemently opposed abortion.

It is in our understanding of sacred law that the failure of the Greek language to distinguish between a miscarriage and an abortion is most problematic. The earliest surviving reference to the subject is in the cathartic law from the sanctuary of Artemis in Cyrene, Libya, dated to the fourth century BC. Like Aristotle, this law too makes a distinction between a formed and unformed foetus:

> If a woman throws out (*egbalêi*, i.e. has a miscarriage or abortion) when the foetus is fully formed (*diadêlos*), members of the *oikia* are polluted as they would be if someone had died, whereas if it is not fully formed, the *oikia* is polluted as if by childbirth (*apo lechos*).

Similar provisions are contained in inscriptions found at Delos, Philadelphia, Ptolemais, Lindos and Smyrna (see Parker 1983, 355).

Religious, legal, medical and moral considerations thus intersect and overlap, complicating and obscuring any straightforward assessment of a Greek 'attitude' to abortion.

We know little about the reasons that would induce a woman to undergo an abortion in antiquity. *Prima facie*, however, *hetairai* are likely to have constituted the largest group, since their livelihood must in many cases have depended on their ability, or at least their willingness, to dispose of an unwanted foetus from time to time. It was perhaps members of this profession who most commonly attempted to perform abortions on themselves, with varying degrees of success. Except when the risk to her life was unacceptably high, we should expect a typical Greek housewife to endure the trauma of birth and exposure in preference to abortion, but in making this assumption we may be underestimating her confidence in the powers of her midwife, who was actually believed capable of inducing a miscarriage (see below, p. 63).

A fascinating anecdote in Plutarch supplies us with rare data concerning the circumstances surrounding an abortion, albeit from the world of legend. The Spartan lawgiver Lykourgos is said to have opposed and thwarted an attempt to perform such an operation by his brother's wife who 'had been willing to destroy the embryo (*brephos*) on condition that he married her when he became king of Sparta' (*Lyk*. 3). What is significant is that the initiative is taken by the woman, the motive is selfish and personal, the procedure is deemed to be hazardous, and the operation is shown to be furtive and conspiratorial (see further Nardi 1971, 41).

Conclusions

From a twentieth-century standpoint it is difficult to comprehend how any Greek woman could have engaged in sexual intercourse without experiencing certain qualms, the fear of not being able to conceive if she wanted to become pregnant being matched by the fear engendered by the consequences of becoming pregnant against her will.

The gynaecological evidence upon which medical writers chiefly rely appears to have been provided by prostitutes. The reasons for this are twofold: first, prostitutes were credited with a more intimate knowledge of the workings of the female body than married women due to their sexual 'experience'; and secondly, they were much less inhibited than married women in talking openly about matters relating to sex.

It is abundantly clear that the reproductive theories which have here occupied the central position in the discussion of gestation and pregnancy would for the most part have been of very marginal concern to prospective parents. It is difficult, for instance, to see how the rival claims of pangenesis and epigenesis could have aroused much interest outside medical circles since they lacked any practical application whatsoever. The debate is perhaps chiefly of interest today for the fact that it was based on a fundamental misapprehension about the structure of the womb and proceeded in complete ignorance of ovulation. In this case as in others, much of what paraded itself as science was no better than dogmatism and pure bluff. A number of assumptions that appear in medical writings, such as the belief in the inherent superiority of the right side of the body, had their origins in what today would be termed superstition. The fact that they pervaded all levels of thought merely demonstrates the impossibility of drawing a firm distinction between scientifically based ideas and those rooted in popular folklore.

It is highly questionable whether medical science significantly affected attitudes towards pregnancy and gestation other than in the one area of sterility and its attempted cure. Though here at least we might expect there to have been a heated and acrimonious debate between medical practitioners on the one hand who ascribed it to a physiological defect and sought to treat it as such, and defenders of the religious world-view on the other for whom it manifested a type of divine displeasure, there is little to indicate whether this was so in practice. We lack information about the differing circumstances in which a woman suffering from sterility would, for instance, choose to go either to Epidauros or to the nearest physician. Which would have been the first and which the last resort, so to speak – if indeed that is the appropriate language in which to evaluate religious and medical procedures?

Religion played little part in regulating when and in what manner a couple should have intercourse. The banning of sexual intercourse within the sanctuary precinct appears to have been the only universally upheld taboo. A few cults insisted on sexual abstinence in their priests, priestesses and celebrants, but they were the exception rather than the rule and even for priests and priestesses the requirement seems generally to have been for a limited period only. The conclusion is irresistible that Greek religion did not invest the sexual act with anything like the same degree of anguish, guilt and shame as Christianity has done from the time of St Paul onwards. Nor in general did it seek to pronounce upon the ethics of birth control and abortion, other than in order to ensure that pollution be kept to a minimum.* There is no discussion of the right to life of the unborn in any Classical source, evidently for the simple reason that the unborn was not considered to be a person. *A fortiori* if the Greeks were prepared to tolerate the exposure of a newborn child (see next chapter), they were hardly in a strong position to question the ethics of abortion.

We do not know whether a pregnant woman was subject to any restrictions additional to those that were imposed on any freeborn woman attached to an *oikos*. From the fact that she was expected to make frequent visits to the shrines of birthing deities, however, it may have been the case that she was temporarily granted greater freedom of movement.

*The only evidence to the contrary known to me is an inscription dated to the late second or early first century BC relating to the management of a private cult at Philadelphia (Alasehir) in Lydia which contains a clause (ll. 17-18) banning from its precincts 'those who use ... an abortifacient (*phthoreion*), a contraceptive ([*at*]*okeion*) or any other device for killing children ([*allo ti paido*]*phonon*) or who encourage others to do so or who act as an accomplice in their use'. For text and translation, see Barton and Horsley (1981, 7-41). See also O. Weinreich ('Stiftung und Kultsatzungen eines Privatheiligtums in Philadelphia in Lydien' [*Sb. Akad. Heidelberg* Abh. 8], 1919); *SIG*[3] 985; *LSAM* 20. For its date, see Nardi (1963, 65 n. 45).

Pregnancy and giving birth, like growing old and dying, are mainly mortal experiences. While it is true that the twelve Olympians constituted a family in both the biological and social sense of the word, once their number became canonically fixed at twelve they were doomed for all eternity to practise safe sex without issue.

Medical writers tended to perceive the female body as a biologically defective and subservient organism whose proper functioning requires the action of the male. If anything can be said in defence of such a bias it is that the physical and emotional frailty ascribed to women may in part have been inspired by compassion for the greater biological constraints to which they are inherently subject. Less generously we may observe that it reinforced and gave credibility to the dominant cultural perception of women as inferior beings. Indeed it may be considered a supreme irony that whereas women were evaluated primarily in terms of their reproductive capacity, the dominant role in the reproductive process tended to be assigned to the man. No embryological treatise summarised matters more succinctly nor more smugly than this Greek proverb: 'No woman has ever produced a *paidion* except by having intercourse with a man' (Plu. *Mor.* 145d = *Advice on Marriage* 48).

2

Childbirth

> You surely don't suppose that people make babies (*paido-poieisthai*) because of sexual desire, when the streets and the brothels are full of those who will satisfy this need?
>
> (Xen. *Mem*. 2.2.4)

Giving birth, like dying, is a phenomenon which combines the universal with the particular, the biological with the culture-specific. In all human societies the treatment of birth is subjected to a strictly defined set of social regulations which provide little scope for personal initiative. Innovative practices and experimentation tend to be regarded with fear and suspicion even when the current birthing system is – when judged by modern standards – woefully inadequate. Conversely, as the previous chapter has demonstrated, the biological understanding of pregnancy and, we will now add, that of parturition, is likely to reflect that society's social organisation. This chapter accordingly proceeds from the assumption that childbirth is not only a physiological function but also a cultural production whose management is rooted in social as well as physiological-medical factors.

The limitations upon an investigation of the birthing system (or rather systems) that prevailed in Greek culture are severe. In the first instance there is no agreement among anthropologists as to what data should be collected and what criteria used in order to evaluate birth-practices cross-culturally and thus determine what significantly differentiates one birthing system from another. Secondly, childbirth is an intimate experience from which outsiders are normally and naturally debarred. Informed first-hand commentary is thus intrinsically hard to obtain. In ancient Greece birth was handled almost exclusively by women, yet no woman, midwife, birthing assistant or mother, has left us a detailed account of 'what it was like' to give birth. In other words, we lack the experiential register. There is thus a very real danger that our narrative will do no more than take us to the fringes of the study of childbirth as an experience in the lives of women and men. Although the gynaecological works in the Hippokratic corpus contain a number of observations on childbirth, there is no treatise devoted to obstetrics, which at first sight appears somewhat surprising in view of the fact that these writings constituted the medical Bible of the ancient world. The explanation for the omission is that physicians did not attend routine deliveries; they encountered childbirth only in its pathological aspect, as a situation fraught with crisis, and hence largely restricted their writings to the procedures to be adopted in the case of severely complicated deliveries. Indeed the fact that their presence was not normally considered necessary or even appropriate constitutes one of the most significant and telling features of the way in which birth was handled in ancient Greece. The earliest treatise to discuss routine birthing procedure was probably a lost work of Herophilos of Chalkedon, written in the first half of the third century BC. The earliest surviving account, however, is contained in the *Gynaecology* of Soranos, without which it would scarcely be possible to investigate this subject at all. The final limitation is that we know very little about birth as an occasion for ritual because no one wrote about it in that way, though there is sufficient to indicate that it did unquestionably have a highly ritualised structure.

Despite these drawbacks, we can none the less explore a range of options in order to arrive at a very broad definition of how the Greeks handled birth and the mood in which they typically confronted it. Possible models include:

(1) a dramatic yet normal part of family life;
(2) an unnatural and fearful event which can be attended with success only if divine agency is invoked;
(3) a physiological crisis, the handling of which is exclusively given over to a highly trained body of professionals.

In order to determine which model best suits the evidence this chapter will examine such issues as the birth-setting, the role and identity of the practitioners and their assistants, the incidence of perinatal deaths, the scope and effectiveness of emergency procedures, the strength and nature of pollution beliefs, and finally the social identity of both the mother and her newborn infant. Consideration will also be given to the question whether there is evidence of conflict between such interest groups as the immediate family, midwives, physicians and exponents of Greek religion. I shall also include investigation of the immediate postpartum period in order to demonstrate that the Greeks regarded birth, like death, not so much as an event as a process, one which took days rather than hours to complete. I would emphasise at the outset that, given the diversity of Greek culture, it is probably safe to assume that there existed a greater degree of flexibility in the negotiation of birth than is currently available in most modern birthing systems.*

The birth setting

As there were no hospitals in ancient Greece birth usually took place in the home. To my knowledge there is no source which tells us which area of the living quarters was allocated for birth, though the most likely setting is the *gunaikeion* which was reserved exclusively for women. That is because the *gunaikeion* was the most sheltered part of the house, a fact which was important not only for the preservation of privacy, but also for the containment of birth's pollution. Towards this end some purificatory ritual was probably performed in advance of delivery, but we know nothing of it.

Midwives and assistants

In all known societies access to birth is strictly limited. Those who are most commonly prohibited include children, men – sometimes with the exception of a male obstetrician and the husband – and women who have not given birth themselves. In Greece delivery took place exclusively in the presence of women. In Aristophanes' *Ekkleziasousai* or *Women in Assembly* (ll. 526-34) the heroine Praxagora justifies her early-morning absence to her husband by claiming that she had been assisting one of her friends to give birth; she would hardly have used this excuse if it had been customary for men

*In England and Wales flexibility in this area has sharply decreased over the past twenty years or so. In 1964, 70.1 per cent of all confinements took place in hospital and 28.4 per cent in the home, whereas in 1984 the figures were 98.9 and 1.0 respectively (G. Chamberlain in *The Practitioner*, July 1988, p. 771, table 1).

to be present at a delivery. Similarly in *Thesmophoriazousai* (ll. 507-9) the mother-to-be dispatches her husband from the birthing room as soon as her contractions begin. Sculptural representations of women in labour invariably depict their attendants as female (see Fig. 3) and likewise in the case of divine births it is the goddesses, not the gods, who assist at the birth of a deity (e.g. *Hom. h. Ap.* 119-22).

The most important assistant was the midwife or *maia*. Though a fairly humble profession, midwifery was none the less widely regarded as serving an essential function. That is the reason why Sokrates in the *Theaitêtos* (149b-151d) describes himself as a midwife in relation to the birth of ideas among his philosophical interlocutors. The only qualification, or perhaps more accurately the only stipulation that we hear about is that midwives were required to be above childbearing years. The popular explanation for this, Sokrates tells us, is that the goddess Artemis, being herself childless, 'assigned the privilege to women who were past childbearing years out of respect to their likeness to herself' (149c). A further possible explanation is that constant exposure to the pollution of childbirth was believed capable of rendering the womb sterile, though I know of no actual evidence to support this. It is unclear whether midwives were required to have given birth themselves. Perhaps, then, no other qualification than seniority of years was necessary in order to set up practice. Their success-rate as practitioners may well have been qualification enough.

Guidelines for distinguishing between competence and excellence in midwifery are set out by Soranos (*Gyn.* 1.3-4). A competent practitioner, he asserted, 'should be literate in order to comprehend her art through theory'. What he evidently means by this is that she should be able to read handbooks on 'How to be a good midwife', such as the one he wrote. In earlier times, before such handbooks were available, literacy is unlikely to have been an issue. A midwife should be reasonably intelligent, respectable and robust, Soranos continued. In addition, 'she must have long slim fingers with short nails, so as not to irritate any inflammation that may lie deep inside [the vagina]'. The very best midwives are those who are qualified dieticians, surgeons and pharmacists. They should not be members of ecstatic or orgiastic cults but be 'free from superstition so as not to overlook what is expedient on account of a dream or omen or customary ritual or popular superstition'. This is precisely the kind of observation lodged in a medical text that is most valuable for this study because it suggests that even in Soranos' day midwives did commonly resort to dreams and omens, presumably in order to determine when a woman would begin to go into labour, and that rituals and superstitious practices constituted an intrinsic part of their art. It may also hint darkly at the existence of an obstetrical controversy between midwives and the medical profession which may have originated with the birth of Greek medicine.

Whether the midwife made prenatal visits to the home of the pregnant woman is not known. It must, however, rate as a high probability on *a priori* grounds since it is of crucial importance that a woman giving birth should have full confidence in her chief helper. The powers of a Greek midwife were extensive. Probably her first duty was to supervise the purification of the *oikos* in general and the *gunaikeion* in particular, preparatory to the imminent birth. By administering drugs and intoning incantations or *epôidai* she was believed to be capable, with assistance from the deity with whom she and the mother had to be in good faith, of accelerating or allaying labour pains, easing a difficult labour, and even of causing a miscarriage if that were deemed desirable (Pl. *Theait.* 149d). To what extent her sphere of competence (or *technê*) was based on a sound medical appreciation of the contingencies and hazards of childbearing and to what extent she functioned as a mediator between the mother and the deities in charge of childbirth is impossible to determine. I assume that her skill was of a 'mixed' variety. In view of the fact that the medical profession regarded breech and transverse presentations as life-threatening to both mother and child, it is very likely that the midwife attempted to alter the position of the baby *in utero* into the head-down position by *psêlaphêsis*, that is, by massaging or palpating the mother's belly (cf. *Nature of the Child* 30; *Sterile Women* 1; *Superfetation* 4). Probably it was her unpleasant task to remove the foetus in the case of a stillbirth (cf. the reference to the *iêtreuousa* or female physician in Hipp. *Gyn.* 1.68). It was also her duty to cut the umbilical cord, judged to be an extremely delicate and highly skilled operation and one no doubt surrounded by a certain aura of mystery (Arist. *HA* 7.587a9f. *T*). Just how vital a part of her profession this action constituted is indicated by the fact that *omphalêtomos* or 'navel-cutter' occasionally serves as a synonym for *maia* (e.g. Hipp. *Gyn*. 1.46). Finally, midwives were uniquely well-placed to act as go-between on behalf of a woman who failed to conceive or produced a stillborn child and one whose infant was unwanted. In the *Thesmophoriazousai* (ll. 340, 407 and 502-18) Aristophanes suggests that some women even went so far as to feign pregnancy and delivery, presumably with the connivance of a midwife, so as to smuggle a bought baby into the house under the noses of their unsuspecting husbands!

It was in the immediate postpartum period that prompt action on the part of a midwife was reckoned to be particularly efficacious. Aristotle (*HA* 7.587a22-5 *T*) refers to experienced practitioners who are capable of saving the life of a newborn child if it happens to be bleeding from the umbilical cord by squeezing the blood back along the cord. After safely delivering the baby, the midwife perhaps carried out a series of tests to determine whether the infant should be reared or exposed (cf. Sor. *Gyn*. 2.79), bathed it and then, where it was the practice so to do, wrapped it in swaddling bands. If, however, it was decided on her recommendation or for any other reason not to rear it, then it was her task to remove the infant and dispose of it, as Sokrates threatens to do in his capacity as intellectual midwife if his interlocutor delivers a defective idea (cf. Pl. *Theait*. 151c). Her ministrations probably extended at least until the celebration of the Amphidromia when the pollution caused by birth began to diminish, though she may have continued to perform rituals on behalf of the newborn until the fortieth-day celebration (see below, pp. 93 and 97). In view of the fact that the midwife would herself have become contaminated by birth, she was perhaps initially debarred from offering her services elsewhere.

Female relatives, friends and neighbours also were present at the birth. The Hippokratic school took it for granted that there would be at least four women available in case it became necessary to induce labour (*Cutting Up of the Embryo* 4). Likewise Soranos (*Gyn*. 2.5) recommended that there should be at least three women present in addition to the midwife so that they can 'gently calm the fears of the woman giving birth, even if they do not happen to have experience in childbirth'. No doubt it was their duty to furnish the pregnant woman with the mental and physical support necessary for a successful delivery, and also to summon the birth goddesses by intoning and incanting under instruction from the midwife.

Deaths of women in labour

Childbirth was risky in ancient Greece, partly because standards of hygiene were completely inadequate and partly because the majority of mothers were barely past puberty when they first gave birth. The incidence of maternal mortality in prehistoric societies has been variously put at between 10 and 20 per cent (cf. Morris 1987, 63). Whatever the precise level, the phenomenon was sufficiently common to require effective action of a propitiatory nature on the part of all mothers-to-be (see below). In religious terms women who died in childbirth were probably regarded as victims of Artemis' continuing and unappeased wrath at the fact of their having yielded up their maidenhood, though this generic explanation may have been supplemented by allusion to particular offences thought to have been committed against the deity by an individual who met her death in this way. The perils and pains of childbirth are eloquently summed up by Medea in Euripides' play of that name (l. 250f.): 'I would rather stand in a battle-line three times than give birth once.' Whether Medea is conveying by this remark that childbirth was three times as dangerous as fighting or merely three times as laborious is unclear. On a somewhat more frivolous note Plutarch (*Mor.* 143e = *Advice on Marriage* 39) tells an anecdote about a woman in labour who, when urged to lie down on the bed, replied: 'How can a bed cure what I've got? It was by going to bed that I ended up like this.'

Medea's analogy between childbirth and warfare was neither eccentric nor perverse (cf. Loraux 1981, 37-67). Plutarch (*Lyk.* 27.2) reports that in Sparta the laws of Lykourgos permitted the names of the deceased to be inscribed on tombstones only in the case of men who were killed in war and, according to a textual emendation which has some epigraphical support, of women who died in childbirth. The explanation for the equivalent social rating of a dead mother-to-be and a dead warrior is patently obvious: both heroically lay down their lives while seeking to perpetuate the identity of the state. Probably few Spartans, however, were capable of appreciating the irony in the fact that members of the former group die while seeking to create life, members of the latter while attempting to destroy it. By awarding high honours to the victims of both childbirth and war Lykourgos no doubt intended to render the mortality rate associated with these 'high-risk occupations' acceptable to society at large. It may also have been to encourage women to hazard their lives in travail that in imperial Rome, as Pliny (*NH* 7.9.47) reports, 'the birth of a child was regarded as more auspicious if the mother died in labour'. In Athens women who died in childbirth seem also to have constituted a privileged group, their graves being marked by funerary reliefs depicting them being assisted on to a birthing stool immediately before delivery (see Fig. 3).

Finally, hazardous though it undoubtedly was to give birth in ancient Greece, the fact that instruments were rarely used in the delivery room meant that women are not likely to have suffered much from puerperal fever, an illness which is transmitted manually by doctors carrying bacteria from one patient to another. In the absence of hospitals women would also have been spared exposure to the germs that were rife in these institutions until the late nineteenth century.

Deities of childbirth

Even allowing for the considerable anxiety which still surrounds childbirth in modern society, it is scarcely possible to comprehend the terror that is aroused by such apparently inexplicable events as stillbirths, perinatal deaths, deaths of the mother in labour, abnormal births and even births of twins, either in cultures which lack any scientific tradition altogether or in those where the scientific tradition enjoys currency only among an educated minority. Given, moreover, the immense physical effort required to drive the baby through the birth canal, it is not surprising that the belief is widely reported by anthropologists that a successful delivery can only be achieved through the gracious intervention of a deity.

In ancient Greece the deities of childbirth, who are themselves invariably female, were conceptualised as the personified essence of accomplished midwifery whose presence was deemed to be essential both in order to sanction and to induce the delivery. They do on the divine plane, in other words, what midwives do on the human plane. The foremost deity who presided over women during this critical period seems to have been Eileithyia, whose worship in Greece dates as far back as the Bronze Age and may even be older. It is generally agreed that the name Eileithyia is most likely a corrupt form of 'Eleuthyia' meaning 'She who comes' (cf.

Pingiatoglou 1981, 11). The goddess should thus be understood as the ideal personification of a safe and quick delivery who is invoked by a woman in labour and her assistants. Hardly anything could more forcibly indicate that the delivery of an offspring as well as a woman's release from labour-pangs were perceived as events over which the birthing-deity had effective and ultimate control. The verbs *exagô* and *ekphainô* ('bring forth' or 'deliver'), which are used in Homer with Eileithyia as subject and the child as object, support the view that this deity was believed to assume the leading role at birth (cf. *Od.* 16.188 and 19.104). This finds confirmation in the fact that it is Eileithyia's arrival on Delos which instantly triggers Leto's delivery of baby Apollo (*Hom. h. Del. Ap.* 115f.). The most celebrated mythological instance of the exercise of her powers depicts the goddess in a more mischievous light, however, for it was by retarding the birth of Herakles that Eileithyia succeeded in rendering him subject to the domination of Eurystheus whose birth was at the same time accelerated to make him senior.

The goddess Artemis is also prominently associated with childbirth, though the reason why her goodwill was judged to be efficacious is not altogether clear in view of the fact that she was a chaste virgin who rigorously shunned sexual congress. Scholars usually argue that women invoked Artemis at the moment of delivery in order to appease her retrospectively for the loss of their virginity. We should not rule out the possibility, however, that more specific and personal reasons might also have been put forward in order to explain and justify a woman's death in labour. In Attica the goddess was closely associated with Iphigeneia, who was founding priestess of her cult at Brauron and buried inside her sanctuary precinct. It has been plausibly suggested that Iphigeneia's name means literally 'Strong in Birth' and that this was the cult epithet by which Artemis was invoked in her capacity as a deity presiding over the pubertal rites preceding marriage (see below, p. 187). Other childbirth goddesses include Hekate, Hera, the Erinyes (Furies), the Nymphs, the Moirai (Fates), as well as more localised deities such as the Boiotian Pharmakides (witches).

The Athenians are known to have worshipped a very large number of such deities, though our evidence does not permit us to determine whether they invested childbirth with an inordinately high level of anxiety compared with other Greeks.

A fourth-century votive plaque from Phaleron lists the following catalogue of divinities, all of whom in some capacity or other were evidently believed to have contributed to a successful delivery (*IG* II^2 4547) :

> Hestia, Kephisos, Pythian Apollo, Leto, Artemis Lochia, Ileithyia [sic], Acheloös, Kallirhoe, the honoured Nymphs of birth (*geraistai numphai genethliai*) and Rapso.

As was the case throughout the ancient world, rivers and streams were believed to be able to cure infertility and also to accelerate or ease delivery. The river Kephisos, which flows into Phaleron Bay in southern Attica, is described by Sophokles (*OK* 685-9) as birth-hastening or *ôkutokos*, and the stream Kyllypera, which rises in the foothills of Mount Hymettos, was credited with the power to promote an easy delivery (above, p. 38). There was also a cult of Aphrodite Kolias in association with a group of minor deities of childbirth known as the Genetyllides (birth-hour goddesses) situated near Cape Kolias on the east of Phaleron Bay (Paus. 1.1.5).

An easy birth is not the only blessing for which a pregnant woman might pray; it is at least equally important that her offspring should be healthy and well-formed. An Athenian divinity who went under the title Kalligeneia, the personification of the 'bearer of a beautiful or healthy offspring', was summoned on the final day of the Thesmophoria, the principal festival held in honour of Demeter. Kalligeneia was presumably invoked by her celebrants collectively on behalf of all Athenian women who would give birth in the coming year. Since there does not appear to have been any sanctuary devoted to Kalligeneia in Attica, it is possible that this is merely a cult epithet of Demeter in her specialised capacity as the bearer of beautiful offspring.

The very large number of deities protecting childbirth, both chthonic and Olympian, who received cult in ancient Greece is a sure reflection of the extremely high level of anxiety generated by the activity of giving birth, as too is the fact that no single deity ever succeeded in establishing outright control of this branch of human activity.

Labour and delivery

We pass now to a discussion of birth itself. As indicated at the beginning of this chapter, our evidence for the procedure is mainly scientific. The earliest surviving description of a normal, vertex presentation occurs in the Hippokratic *Nature of the Child* (30):

> When it is time for the mother to give birth, what happens is that the *paidion* by the spasmodic movements of its hands and feet breaks one of the internal membranes. Once one is broken, then the others of course are weaker, and these break too in order of their proximity to the first, right up to the last one. When the membranes are broken, the *embruon* is released from its bonds and emerges from the womb all bunched together. ... Once the *paidion* is on its way, it forces a wide passage for itself through the womb, since the womb is resilient. It advances head first – that is the natural position, since its weight measured from above the navel is greater than it is below. (tr. G.E.R. Lloyd)

Most notable here is the observation that it is the child and not any external agency that by its own efforts initiates the birthing process.

In line with the 'common sense' observation that water causes any surface to become slippery and helps to reduce the friction which an object passing along it will encounter, medical texts recommend the application of a variety of emollients in order to moisten the womb and birth canal immediately before delivery (*Superfetation* 4; Sor. *Gyn*. 1.56.7). Thus the nearer to the time of delivery a woman's waters break, the less painful are her contractions (*Cutting Up of the Embryo* 3). Possibly with the same theory in mind Aristotle maintained (*HA* 7.584a31-2 *T*) that the man should assume an active and instrumental role at the end of parturition just as he does at the beginning, on the grounds that 'women who have intercourse with their husbands before giving birth do so more quickly'. Belief in the natural superiority of the male over the female, a feature, as we have seen, of attitudes surrounding conception and gestation, is possibly detectable in Aristotle's claim that when a woman is giving birth to a girl her labour tends to be 'sluggish and protracted', whereas in the case of a boy it is 'painful and far more difficult'. The author of *Nature of the Child* (30) correctly observes that women experience more pain during their first delivery, but he does so on the erroneous grounds that they are unaccustomed to travail. A variety of sources refer to a drug called *ôkutokion* (sc. *pharmakon*) which, as its name signifies, was believed to accelerate the delivery.

Fig. 3. Attic grave-relief commemorating a woman who died in childbirth, fourth century BC. She is being assisted onto a birthing stool by two female assistants. On the left is a grieving relative, probably her husband. From Oropos, Attica.

Soranos (*Gyn.* 2.2-2.3.1) lists the equipment which a well-prepared midwife was expected to have at her disposal as follows:

> oil for injections and cleansing, hot water in order to wash the affected area, hot compresses to relieve the labour pains, sponges for sponging off, wool for covering the woman's body, and bandages to swaddle the baby in, a pillow so that the infant may be placed on it below the mother until the afterbirth has been taken away; scents, such as pennyroyal, sparganium, barley groats and quince, and if in season citron, or melon and anything similar to these, for the recovery of the mother's strength; a birthing stool or *diphron maiôtikon* [literally 'chair belonging to the midwife'] so that the mother may be arranged on it ... a wide space in a crescent shape must be cut out in it .... (tr. O. Temkin)

What percentage of deliveries took place in these optimum conditions – even in the second century AD – is impossible to determine. Moreover, it is important to emphasise that although this passage seems to indicate that in Soranos' day there existed a general appreciation of the need for cleanliness, it is extremely unlikely that the precise causal connection between dirt and disease was fully understood.

In the event of a delayed or difficult delivery the author of the Hippokratic *Cutting Up of the Embryo* (4) recommended the following procedure for inducing labour:

> Re: shaking [a pregnant woman] up and down. Wrap a blanket around the woman, make her lie down, place another around her genital area so that it is hidden and pass the blanket around both her legs and both her arms. Two women should take hold of each leg and two others should take hold of each arm. Then, grabbing her tightly, shake her up and down at least ten times. Next place the pregnant woman on a couch with her head down. Raise her legs and make all the women grab hold of her legs, after releasing her arms. Then make the women shake her shoulders several times and throw her onto the couch so that the baby, as it is shaken up and down, turns into a more favourable position and can come out naturally. If you have any Cretan dittany (*origanum dictamnus*), give her some to drink. Otherwise, boil castor oil in Chian wine.

Alongside the scientifically-based procedures described by writers such as Hippokrates and Soranos, there were others whose roots lay in folklore. We gain some impression of the latter from the writings of Pliny. Though there is no earlier testimony for most of the practices he records, there can be little doubt that they were widely accepted throughout the Graeco-Roman world, not least because Pliny himself, affluent and educated though he was, seemingly had confidence in their efficacy (cf. French 1988, 1357). For reducing labour pains he recommended the following (*NH* 28.6.33-4):

> Hurl a projectile over the house where the woman in labour is lying – a stone or some other object which has killed three living creatures with a single blow apiece, a human being, a boar and a bear. The ideal implement is a cavalry spear which has been extracted from a man's body without touching the ground.

To hasten childbirth Pliny advised tying above the pubic area of the mother (*NH* 28.9.42):

> a stone which has been ejected by a person suffering from bladder trouble .... Granius [not otherwise known] adds that the stone has greater potency if it has been excised by an iron knife. The man by whom the woman has conceived hastens the delivery if he unties his belt and ties it around her waist and then unties it, delivering the prayer: 'I bound you and I will untie you', before he departs.

Fig. 4. Terracotta figurine of a woman in the act of giving birth in an upright position, sixth century BC. A birthing assistant supports the mother from behind.

The position in which women give birth is to a large extent culturally determined. Though the seated position seems to have been preferred, it was not the only method of giving birth in ancient Greece. Leto, for instance, the mother of Apollo and Artemis, is said to have given birth to Apollo in a squatting position with her arms clasped around a palm tree (*Hom. h. Del. Ap*. 117f.). As the passage from Plutarch quoted above (p. 65) indicates, some women gave birth lying on a *klinê* or couch. Soranos in fact asserted that the seated position should only be used if the mother was calm and strong and that otherwise she should deliver lying down, on the grounds that 'this method is less disturbing and less frightening' (*Gyn*. 2.4.3). Noting that a birthing stool might not always be available, he recommended that in its absence the mother should sit on a woman-helper's lap (2.5.2). His injunction to the midwife 'to refrain from staring directly at the parturient's genitals in case she feels ashamed and her body becomes contracted' (2.6.2) is of particular importance in helping us to arrive at an appreciation of the male attitude towards the body of a woman in labour, and echoes the instruction to place a blanket around the genital area of the woman in labour that we encountered previously in a Hippokratic work (above, p. 71).

The importance of correct breathing during labour and delivery is frequently stressed in obstetrical and folkloristic writings. Conflicting views were held on the subject. According to Hippokrates a sneeze is beneficial in the case of a difficult delivery (*Aph.* 5.35). On the other hand, both Aristotle (*HA* 7.587a 4-6 *T*) and Pliny (*NH* 7.6.42) urge women to hold their breath during delivery in order to ease the contractions, the latter adding menacingly that if a woman should happen to gape during childbirth 'it may prove fatal'. Soranos was of the opinion that everything should be done to ensure that the woman's breathing is unconstricted, though not, it is important to note, to the extent of recommending that she be naked during labour. He writes (*Gyn.* 2.6.1):

> One must advise the parturient to drive her breath down into her thighs not with screaming, but rather with groaning and retention of her breath .... To which end, namely for the unrestrained passage of her breath, it is necessary to untie the girdle (*zônê*) and to free the chest of any constraint, not on account of the popular belief according to which women are unwilling to endure any fetter and for this reason <also> loosen their hair, but rather for the previously-mentioned reason that even loosening the hair effects good tonus of the head.

It is precisely in this attitude, ungirdled and with hair flowing loose, that women are depicted giving birth on Athenian gravemarkers (Fig. 3).

Sympathetic magic played a major part in the handling of birth. Pliny suggested that women who were about to give birth should eat wolf 's meat, or, if they were already in labour, have someone sitting beside them who had recently partaken thereof, evidently in the conviction that this would give added strength. Midwives used the left hand to deliver the baby for no better reason, according to Soranos (*Gyn.* 4.12), than because 'serpents too are lifted with it'.

At the moment of delivery the women helpers uttered a ritual cry of joy known as the *ologugê*, as do Leto's divine helpmates at the birth of Apollo (*Hom. h. Del. Ap.* 119). After the midwife has determined the sex of the infant, Soranos (*Gyn.* 2.10.1) tells us, she should announce it 'as is the custom among women (*kathôs gunaixin êthos*)', presumably to the father and the other male members of the household. She must then place the infant on the ground and examine it carefully in order to discover whether it is worth rearing or not (2.10.2-5). Then she has to cut the umbilical cord, 'at a distance of four fingers' breadth from the stomach' (2.11.1). Soranos informs us that the majority of midwives used a piece of broken glass or a potsherd on the grounds that 'cutting is deemed of ill omen during the earliest period [of a child's life]', since it causes the baby to cry, which itself bodes ill for its future health. He himself none the less advocates the use of an iron blade. The severing of the umbilical cord was undoubtedly a solemn act attended with ritual but we lack any description of it.

The mother and her newborn baby then bathed together, most commonly in pure water which had been drawn from a sacred spring in order to purge away the defilement or *lumata* of birth (*Hom. h. Ap.* 120f.; Kall. *h. Zeus* 15-17). Soranos (*Gyn.* 2.12-13), however, refers scathingly to the custom of bathing the newborn 'in wine mixed with brine or in pure wine or in the urine of an undefiled *pais*'. The practice is reminiscent of the bathing of the infant Achilles in the River Styx, its waters having the property of rendering the human body inviolable to injury. In some communities the bath appears to have been not only purificatory but also probative. Plutarch (*Lyk.* 16.2) states that in Sparta, for instance:

> Newborn babies (*brephê*) were bathed not with water, but with wine in order to test their constitution (*krasis*). For it is said that epileptic and sickly children experience convulsions as a result of contact with unmixed wine, whereas healthy ones are tempered and strengthened by it.

The Hippokratic school recommended that the mother should be fed wormwood, dittany, white violet flowers and silphium in order to aid the separation of the afterbirth from the inner wall of the uterus (*Nature of Woman* 32). A more ingenious procedure was the following (*Superfetation* 8):

> Let the woman sit on a night-stool. Let something elevated be set up in order that the baby (*embruon*), being suspended, draws out the placenta (*chorion*) by its own weight. Do this gently, not violently, lest unnatural straining cause inflammation. It is necessary, therefore, to place a very large quantity of newly carded wool beneath the *embruon*, together with two animal-skins tied together and filled with water, so that they

> gradually deflate. The wool is above the skins and the *embruon* above the wool. Then pierce one of the skins with a needle so that the water flows out slowly. As the water flows out, so the skins deflate. As they deflate, the child draws out the umbilical cord and that in turn draws out the placenta.

Next, as we read in *Cutting Up of the Embryo* (5):

> When the placenta (*husterai*) is delivered, either as the result of pain [i.e. presumably as a result of failure] or as a consequence of delivery – if the patient you are dealing with has experienced this recently, then you should do the following. If not, then let it be. Proceed as follows: cut around the hymen of the womb following its natural shape and obliquely. Rub it with a piece of linen as if it were inflamed, then dab it with either fish-oil or pitch, make a poultice of pomegranate seeds, and then, when you have moistened some soft sponges with wine, apply them and bind them around the woman's shoulders. Then make her lie down with her legs raised as high as possible and let her have a little to eat.

As upon the occasion of the severing of the umbilical cord, the midwife probably now performed ritual acts.

To indicate that a delivery had been successful, it was customary in Athens to hang up a crown of olive on the front door of the house marking the arrival of a boy and a tuft of woollen material that of a girl. According to the sixth-century AD lexicographer Hesychios, who is our earliest authority for the practice, woollen material denoted a girl 'because of the spinning' (s.v. *stephanon ekpherein*). This cryptic observation should perhaps be interpreted as meaning that in the writer's view at least a woman's essential identity was conveniently and aptly symbolised by an allusion to her association with spinning. The crown of olive, by contrast, may have been intended to symbolise male athletic prowess, this being the prize that was awarded at the Olympic games. The original purpose behind the custom of publicising birth in this way can only be guessed at. Apart from serving to announce the fact of delivery to those outside the family circle, it presumably warned non-relatives of the risk of pollution. It may even have provided a kind of two-way protection both for and from mother and child. The sign remained on the front door at least until the celebration of the Amphidromia, after which it was probably removed (cf. Ephippos, *CAF* II, p. 251f.3; see below).

Stillbirths

Since it is extremely unlikely that many Greek (or indeed Roman) obstetricians ever attempted to perform a Caesarean section, a regular task facing medical practitioners would have been the extraction of a stillborn foetus. There were two alternatives available. He (or she) could either dismember the foetus while it was still *in utero* or remove it whole by means of forceps. The former procedure, known as an *embruotomê* or cutting up of the foetus, is the subject of the Hippocratic monograph that goes under that name. It does not make pleasant reading (1):

> Re: non-routine pregnancies where the foetus has to be cut up in the womb. First of all place a linen sheet around the woman, make a knot above her breasts, and cover her head so that she will not be frightened by witnessing what you are doing. If the foetus, lying in a transverse position (*plagion parapeson*), puts forth its arm [i.e. into the birth canal], grab hold of it and drag it out as best you can, excoriate the flesh from the arm and strip it down to the bone, then wrap some fish skin around two fingers of your hand so that the flesh does not elude your grasp. Next make an incision all around the shoulder and remove it up to the joint. Then push the head around into its normal position [i.e. for a vertex presentation] and draw it out. Move around the foetus inside with your finger. Otherwise puncture the ribs or the collar-bone with a knife so that the flatus is released, the foetus comes out, and the delivery is made more easy. As for the head, if you can extract it naturally, well and good. But if not, smash it and in that way remove the foetus. Next pour plenty of hot water around [the perineum], dab it with olive oil, order the woman to lie down with her legs crossed and to drink pure sweet white wine, and give her a potion of resin, wine and honey. In all other respects, treat her as you would an ordinary parturient woman or *lechô* ....

The treatise correctly notes (2) that a transverse presentation, i.e. one in which the baby's arm appears first, is usually to be interpreted as a sign that the infant is stillborn, on the grounds that 'the umbilical cord is twisted around the neck and is obstructing the delivery of the baby (*embruon*)'. An embryotomy was performed with an instrument known as an *embruothlastês, thlastês* or *piestron*, all of which words indicate that the medical practitioner first had to smash the foetus before removing it. It was the final medical option in cases where the foetus could not be removed in any other way.

The less radical procedure was to perform an *embruoulkia* or an extraction of the foetus by means of hooks. In view of the fact that these hooks, according to Soranos (*Gyn.* 4.10.1), were most effectively inserted into 'the eyes, the back of the head, the roof of the mouth, the collarbones and the region below the ribs', it is evident that the foetus, even if delivered alive, would have emerged in a horribly mutilated condition. There is very little to indicate that either the Greeks or the Romans possessed any surgical instruments for delivering a child alive. We may conclude, then, that if labour became prolonged or difficult a critical situation very soon developed which could only be resolved by recourse to highly lethal techniques, commonly resulting in permanent damage to the mother.

Following a stillborn delivery some couples may have requested the midwife to provide them with a substitute child. It is precisely this kind of situation that is envisaged in Herodotos' tale of the adoption of the infant Kyros, where the wife of the servant appointed to expose the child has recently given birth to a stillborn child (Hdt. 1.108ff.; below, p. 90).

Premature births

As noted in the previous chapter, the Greeks believed that children could be born in the seventh or ninth month of pregnancy but not in the eighth. A wide variety of medical and non-medical evidence upholds this claim. The comic writer Epicharmos of Syracuse, who was active during the first quarter of the fifth century BC, stated flatly, 'Birth in the eighth month is impossible' (*DK* 23 B 59), and the Hippokratic author of *Flesh* (19) alleged equally emphatically that 'an eighth-month child (*genomenon*) never ever lives'. Empedokles' description of women as 'double-bearing (*digonoi*)' may be a reference to the same belief (*DK* 31 B 69). The impossibility of a woman having a successful delivery in the eighth month is clearly the explanation for Herodotos' assertion (6.69.5): 'Not all women complete a tenth-month pregnancy. Some give birth in the ninth month, others in the seventh.' Though some Hippokratic writers were of the opinion that a baby born in the eighth month did have a slim chance of survival, they maintained that such children usually turned out to be handicapped (cf. *Seventh-Month Foetus* 5). Aristotle (*HA* 7.584b7-9 *T*) alleges that eighth-month babies generally only survived in Egypt. It was equally widely believed that

Fig. 5. Statue of a woman, possibly a fertility goddess, nursing twins, early sixth century BC. From Megara Hyblaia in Sicily.

seventh-month children could survive if given intensive care. Thus *Flesh* (19) states: 'A *paidion* of seven months is born by reason (*logos*) and lives. It has reason and a number that is in conformity with *hebdomades* [i.e. series of sevens, see above, p. 3]'.

Multiple births

It has only been in the last two decades that, thanks to the use of fertility drugs, the chances of a mother producing triplets, quadruplets or even sextuplets at a single delivery has come to be accepted as a fairly routine occurrence. It is not surprising, therefore, that in the ancient world multiple births, being extremely rare, were believed to portend disasters. Pliny (*NH* 7.3.33) records that on the day of the funeral of the Emperor Augustus a woman named Fausta produced two male and two female infants 'which certainly portended the famine shortly to follow'. He further notes that instances of more than three children being born at once were generally regarded as portentous throughout the ancient world – 'except in Egypt where the drinking of water from the Nile causes fertility'. Aristotle (*HA* 7.584b29-35 *T*) similarly alleged that while most women give birth to only one child at a time, twins are common everywhere, particularly in Egypt. He also stated that the largest number of offspring ever produced at a single delivery was five, a feat achieved by one woman on no fewer than four occasions! It is not, to my knowledge, indicated in any source whether a mother who had given birth to multiple offspring or the offspring itself would have been regarded with fear or suspicion, but given the essentially negative feelings aroused by the production of multiple births the possibility cannot be ruled out.

Monstrous births

If multiple births caused anxiety, monstrous births, defined by Aristotle (*GA* 7.767b6 *T*) as 'whatever does not resemble its parents in some way', must have aroused yet greater alarm, the popular belief being that monstrosity was a heaven-sent punishment for serious offences against the gods. Foremost among these offences was breaking an oath to which the gods had been summoned as witnesses. Thus the oath which was taken by the Athenians before the battle of Plataia in 479 BC and subsequently administered to ephebes in the fourth century contains the following dreadful proviso:

> If I remain faithful to the inscribed oath, may women give birth to children who resemble their parents. If not, may they give birth to monsters (Tod, *GHI* II 204.39-45)

Since the oath constitutes a decree passed by the Athenian assembly, it is safe to conclude that the sanction was treated with some seriousness.

Alongside this 'religious' explanation of monstrosity, however, there existed various scientific explanations, of which the following fragment by Parmenides is an early example (*DK* 28 B 18):

> The power which shapes <the embryo> in the veins from different blood only forms well-proportioned bodies if it preserves moderation [or moderate temperature?]. For if the powers war with one another when the seed is mixed and do not make one [kind of being?], they will grievously disturb the growing embryo owing to the twofold seed of the <different> sexes.

Parmenides' rationalistic explanation of monstrosity need not be viewed as an attack on Greek religion. Religious and scientific explanations do not cancel each other out, just as in the field of philosophical inquiry a teleological explanation is not necessarily incompatible with a mechanistic one. It is not inconsistent to hold a belief in divine intervention while maintaining as well that there exists a perfectly rational explanation for everything that happens on this earth; in other words, to perceive the gods as exercising their will in accordance with, not in defiance of, natural law and natural processes.

Monstrous births feature prominently in mythology, often as the product of a union betwen gods disguised as animals and mortal women. A celebrated example is the union between the bull of Poseidon and Pasiphae which produced the Minotaur. Such stories seem to be inspired not so much by fear of giving birth to a monster, which is a widespread and presumably natural parental anxiety, as by the question, 'What would happen if a beast were to mate with a human being?'

Day-superstition

According to Herodotos (2.82.1) it was the Egyptians who invented the practice of 'foretelling by the date of a man's birth his fortunes, the day of his death and his character'. The earliest reference to day-superstition is in Hesiod's *Works and Days* (ll. 780-813) where it is stated that the sixth, ninth, tenth and sixteenth days of the month were favourable for the birth of boys. Only two days of the month, namely the ninth and the fourteenth, were regarded as auspicious for the birth of girls, however, while the first and the sixth were judged positively unfavourable. No day is alleged to have been inauspicious for the birth of a boy. We may reasonably ask what action a Boiotian peasant would have been expected to take in the light of such information. Would he, for instance, have been more inclined to expose a girl if she was born on an 'unfavourable' day?

Hesiod also subscribed to the belief that a child's birthday determined, or at any rate influenced his character. Boys born on the sixth of the month, for instance, were thought to grow up to be 'sarcastic, untrustworthy, cunning and deceitful', while those born on the twentieth were thought to become wise men. There is little evidence for day-superstition in later Greek literature. Though this may simply reflect the bias of our sources, it is worth mentioning that the three Fates, Klotho, Lachesis and Atropos, were believed to apportion good and evil at a person's birth in a manner that is wholly inscrutable and does not depend upon the timing of that birth. There is no evidence that the Greeks believed that human life was in any way influenced or determined by planetary or sideral positions at time of birth.

Swaddling the newborn

In a number of Greek communities including Athens but excluding Sparta (below, p. 137) it was customary to envelop the newborn baby in swaddling bands known as *spargana*. Vase-paintings and sculptures often depict *sparganiôtai* or children in swaddling bands so wrapped from neck to toe and wearing a pointed cap which covers the ears and the back of their neck (Fig. 7). Soranos (*Gyn.* 2.13-14) recommended the use of 'soft woollen bandages which are clean and not too threadbare, some three or four fingers in breadth'. He states (2.42.1) that these bands were generally kept on until the sixtieth day after birth, though some people removed them on the fortieth day, others on or after sixty days had elapsed. It is evidently intended to be perceived as a mark of Apollo's divinity, as well as of the nutritional value of nectar and ambrosia, that as soon as the infant god tasted this heavenly food 'he could no longer be restrained by his golden cords nor did the fastenings confine him, but their ends were loosed' (*Hom. h. Del. Ap.* 127-9).

Fig. 6. Red-figure *hydria* by the Oinanthe Painter depicting Gaia (Earth) giving birth to Erechtheus/Erichthonios, 480-450 BC. Athene prepares to wrap the newborn in a blanket while a winged Victory holds out swaddling bands. From Vulci, Etruria.

The practice of swaddling seems to have owed its origins to the fear, by no means confined to the ancient world, that the limbs of the newborn, unless constricted, are likely to become misshapen through violent movement. Plato (*Laws* 7.789b) actually recommended that physical training ought to begin while the foetus is still being nursed in the mother's womb, in the belief that the impressionability or *euplasteia* of the infant is a physical as well as a mental characteristic. This theory of plasticity persisted into Roman times. Both Plutarch (*Mor*. 3e = *Education of Children* 5) and Soranos (*Gyn*. 2.14.2) similarly asserted that it was essential immediately after bathing the newborn to mould (*plattein* or *diaplassein*) its limbs according to their natural shape so that they become straight and not misshapen. According to Aristotle (*Pol.* 7.1336a10-12) certain tribes even employed what he darkly refers to as 'mechanical devices (*organa mêchanika*)' on newborn infants, perhaps as a safeguard against deformity. We also hear of a gruesome custom practised among a semi-barbarian people known as the Longheads or *Makrokephaloi* who, in the belief that the longest heads are the noblest (Hipp. *Airs, Waters, Places* 14),

> remould (*anaplassein*) the child's head with their hands as soon as it is born, that is, while it is still soft and the body is tender, and forcefully elongate it by applying bandages and other suitable appliances, thereby spoiling the roundness of the head and increasing its length.

Apart from its supposed physiological side-effects, swaddling also had the benefit of freeing the mother to attend to her household chores.

Thank-offering for delivery

Shortly after giving birth the mother would be expected to visit the sanctuary of the birth-goddess or goddesses with whom she had been in close communion throughout her long ordeal in order to render thanks for her delivery. It was also customary to make a votive offering to the Nymphs who had presided over the stream from which the pregnant woman had drunk as an aid to her fertility, particularly in view of the fact that these deities would continue, it was hoped, to watch over the newborn (see below, p. 112). When Orestes is told that his mother's paramour Aigisthos is praying to the Nymphs, he reflects upon his own neglect at her hands and sardonically inquires: 'For the sake of the nurturing of children or before some impending birth?' (Eur. *Or.* 624-6).

A common, perhaps even obligatory gift was that of the clothes which the woman had worn during pregnancy and childbirth. A moving epigram by Phaidimos, who lived in the third century BC, reads (*AP* 6.271):

> The son of Kichesias dedicated sandals to you, Artemis, and Themistodike simple folded woollen garments, lady, because you came gently to her when she was in labour, without your bow, and held your two hands above her. Artemis, grant that

> Leon should live to see his baby boy (*pais nêpiachos*) wax strong in limb as a young man (*kouros*).

In Attica records of dedications to Artemis Brauronia are preserved in a set of fourth-century inventories of the treasurers of Artemis which have come to light on the Acropolis (*IG* II^2 1514-31). Inscribed chronologically, they give the name of the dedicant together with a brief description of the garment (e.g. 'dotted, sleeved tunic', 'cloak with a broad purple border in a wavelike design', etc.). Though the dedicant is invariably a woman, it is certain that some were dedicated after the parturient's death in childbirth (cf. Eur. *IA* 1464-7), 'as if the miscarriage indicated a debt which must be settled posthumously' (Burkert 1985, 70). Other objects dedicated to Artemis Brauronia include bronze mirrors, gold jewellery and ornaments (cf. Hollinshead 1979, 46). Elsewhere votive offerings have come to light in the form of terracotta figures of pregnant women and women in the act of delivery, as well as replicas of the uterus (Fig. 2; cf. van Straten 1981, 99f.).

Exposure

It is something of an anomaly in our eyes that while the Greeks expressed certain reservations about terminating a pregnancy, they paid not the least regard to the rights of a newborn child, for the unpleasant truth of the matter seems to be that certain Greeks at least were prepared in certain circumstances to put down any child whom they did not wish to rear. In what appears to us to be a totally hypocritical way of salving a bad conscience at the cost of every shred of human decency, the Greeks did not, however, actually kill unwanted babies, apparently because had they done so they would have incurred blood-guilt. Instead they practised exposure, known as *ekthesis* or *apothesis*. That is to say, they entrusted the unwanted child either to the midwife or to a household slave who would carry it outside the residential area and abandon it in some deserted spot to the mercies of the elements. Alternatively, and perhaps more commonly, they might deposit it in some well-frequented place, such as a crossroads or a shrine, in the hope that a passer-by or the temple authorities would take pity on it and rear it. The motive for exposure in the individual instance presumably dictated the place of abandonment. In view of the high level of infant mortality, however, there may well have been a considerable demand for healthy offspring. At least some unwanted infants must have been reared as foundlings (*threptoi*).

The investigation of exposure in antiquity involves at least four main lines of inquiry:

(1) What were the chief motives for practising exposure?
(2) Which categories of infants were most at risk?
(3) What consequences did the practice have for the morale of a woman giving birth?
(4) What differences can be detected in regard to attitudes towards exposure at various levels of society in different communities and at different times?

Let it be said at the outset that the apparent acceptance by certain Greeks of this practice is arguably what separates us most radically from their mentality, and in order to comprehend it we need to appreciate just how tough the fight for survival was in the ancient world. It may help to point out that in England as recently as two and a half centuries ago children were being abandoned on the doorsteps of houses and in churchyards in such numbers that in 1741 it was decided to establish the London Foundling Hospital, which in the first four years of its existence admitted no fewer than 15,000 newborn children. The modern equivalent is the 'trashcan baby', frequently reported in the American press. With reference to pre-industrial societies Weiss (1972) has identified four conditions as particularly favouring the decision to practise infanticide. They are the following: when the child is weak and deformed, when its mother is too young to nurse it, when its environment cannot support it, and finally when it has siblings who are still dependent on nursing. In the eighteenth century abandonment was a desperate remedy resorted to by families whose living conditions were already so appalling that they were quite unable to contemplate an increase in the number of mouths to be fed, particularly if the mother herself was engaged in productive labour and could not be spared to nurse her child. A similar situation must have confronted a great many Greek households.

Ancient Greece in general and the Greek city-state in particular are, however, by no means typical of pre-industrial societies, and though the factors enumerated by Weiss probably accounted for a great many of the decisions to 'put out' an infant, they were certainly not the only ones. In Athens and elsewhere the laws governing inheritance also militated against the production of large families, since the testator was required to divide his property among all his male heirs. Any claim that it was *exclusively* poorer families who were constrained on economic grounds to limit the number of their offspring is therefore quite untenable. Impoverishment does not act as a regulator of family-size in Third World countries today, and even in the USA it is the prosperous Whites, rather than the economically depressed Blacks and Hispanics, who choose to limit their family-size by practising effective birth-control. Myths telling of the exposure of royal infants as well as the comedies of Menander suggest that the practice was in fact prevalent or at least tolerated at all levels of society. Oedipus, a royal infant who was abandoned in response to a prophecy which forecast that when he grew up he would kill his father and marry his mother, is the most celebrated example from mythology. Yet what the myth actually explores is the fear of producing a child who is destined to grow up to be what today would be termed a sociopath. Even so, economic constraints are likely to have served as the *primary* motive for exposing a newborn infant. According to Diodorus Siculus (1.80.6) the reason why Egypt was so populous was because 'the entire expense incurred by the parents of a child until it reaches *hêlikia* [i.e. coming of age] is not more than twenty drachmas'.

There are four categories of newborn babies which were at high risk in ancient Greece, namely girls, deformed or sickly infants, illegitimate offspring and the offspring of slaves. Girls are likely to have been abandoned more frequently than boys for the simple reason that they offer less of an economic return and are more expensive to bring up. Poseidippos, who lived in the third century BC, in fact stated (*CAF* III, p. 338.11) with comic exaggeration: 'If you have a son, you bring him up, even if you're poor, but if you have a daughter, you expose her, even if you're rich.' Not only is a girl's capacity for productive labour more limited than that of her brothers, but she also has to be provided with a dowry at marriage (cf. Dem. 27.5, 11-13; other references in Golden 1981a, 195f.). It follows that families with more than two daughters may have been rare except among the well-to-do. The lower social value placed on girls is strikingly illustrated by Herodotos' comment on the Spartan king Kleomenes who 'died childless (*apais*), leaving only one daughter, Gorgo' (5.48). The preference for boys over girls is poignantly revealed in a letter written on a papyrus dated 1 BC from a Greek soldier called Hilarion billeted in Alexandria in Egypt to his pregnant wife Alis in Oxyrhynchos, which contains the following instruction (*P. Oxy*. 4.744): 'If you happen to give birth, if it is a boy let it be, but if it is a girl cast it out (*ekbale*).' In Longus' novel *Daphnis and Chloe* (4.35) a father is forced to expose his baby girl because he does not wish to rear her in poverty. A set of inscriptions from the city of Miletos on the west coast of Turkey dated between 228 and 220 BC which records the names of all the mercenaries who had been enrolled as Milesian citizens during that period also suggests that the selective exposure of girls was practised in the Greek world, since out of a total child population of 215 only 46 of those registered are female. While it can be argued that females commonly go uncounted on census lists, mercenaries would surely have been vigilant in ensuring that the names of their daughters no less than those of their sons were inscribed on the list, since no other proof would have existed to justify the claims of their children to Milesian citizenship (cf. Pomeroy 1983, 209-18). Even if this evidence has been correctly interpreted, however, mercenaries are an unrepresentative sample of the population and we should be wary of drawing deductions from their behaviour about social practice in the Hellenistic world in general (cf. Patterson 1985, 111).

Whether female exposure was an accepted practice in Classical Athens is a matter of continuing controversy. Gomme (1933, 80) rejected the suggestion entirely on the basis that 'most of the evidence depends on the romantic plots of tragedies and comedies'. One recent estimate, however, puts the level of female exposure as high as 10 per cent of all female births (Golden 1981a, 321) on the grounds that there is likely to have been an oversupply of marriageable women which would have resulted in a 'marriage squeeze', whereas another argues that the percentage would have been negligible, given the demographic constraints facing any ancient or pre-industrial population (Engels 1980, 112). Neither examination of the subject is particularly compelling.

Secondly, physically handicapped and sickly children of either sex risked abandonment, a practice which in Sparta was demanded by law. Plutarch (*Lyk*. 16.1) informs us that the father of a newborn child, who unlike his counterpart in most other Greek states was not legally responsible or *kurios* for its upbringing, had to present his offspring to the elders of the tribes (*presbutatoi phuletôn*) in a place called the Lesche (or Gallery) for inspection. If the child was strong and lusty, the elders ordered the father to raise it; if it was not, he had to expose it at a chasm-like place called Apothetai (literally 'Place of Exposure') at the foot of Mount Taygetos, 'in the belief that the life which nature had not provided with health and strength was of no use either to itself or to the state'. What criteria were used to determine whether the child was healthy and strong are not stated, but they may have been similar to those laid down by Soranos (*Gyn.* 2.79) for the purpose of determining whether a newborn infant should be raised. These were: that the mother herself had been healthy throughout her pregnancy; that the child was born 'at the proper time' (not in the eighth month or not on an auspicious day?); that it cried lustily when it was first placed on the ground after birth; that it was physically perfect; and, finally, that it responded to stimuli. Presumably infants who manifested convulsions when first bathed would also have been reported to the elders of the tribe (see above, p. 74). What is particularly noticeable is that neither here nor anywhere else is it ever suggested that the motive for exposing a malformed infant might be dictated wholly or in part by the assumption that such a being was evil or malevolent. On the contrary the decision appears to have been based wholly on practical considerations (cf. Roussel 1943, 14-17).

It is doubtful whether all Greek communities acted equally brutally towards children who were not physically perfect, and I know of no evidence to indicate that elsewhere in the Greek world deformed children were invariably exposed. In Plato's *Theaitêtos* (161a) Sokrates advises Theaitetos to inspect his spiritual offspring from every angle in order to make sure that he is not deceived by 'a lifeless phantom (*eidôlon*) not worth the rearing'. Sokrates then adds: 'Or do you think your infant must be reared in any case and not exposed? Will you bear to see it examined and not be upset if it is taken away, even if it is your first-born?' Though Plato leaves the reader in no doubt that Sokrates regards the rearing of deformed children as an act of irresponsible folly, the remark none the less constitutes recognition of the fact that some Athenian mothers did feel genuine tenderness and compassion towards even deformed and sickly offspring. Aristotle's recommendation in the *Politics*

(7.1335b19-21) that there should be a law to prevent the rearing of deformed children (*mêden pepêrômenon trephein*) further seems to imply that some parents *were* disposed to rear such children. The crucial factor in any decision to expose or rear a delicate or deformed child must surely have been the intensity of the desire with which that child had been awaited.

Evidence for the fact that children born out of wedlock were occasionally exposed derives exclusively from Attic drama. It is therefore of limited trustworthiness but should certainly not be discounted. Aristophanes states that he 'exposed' his first play *Banqueters* when he was a *parthenos* (*Clouds* 530-32); Kreousa in Euripides' *Ion* exposed the child of that name who was born to her as a result of intercourse with Apollo; and in Menander's *Arbitrators* a child is exposed who is the product of rape. Then as now an unmarried mother had to face strong social disapproval, beginning with her immediate family (cf. *Ion* 898). The fact that in Classical Athens illegitimate children could not inherit their father's property may also have acted as an incentive to exposure, given the bleak social and economic future that inevitably awaited such offspring (cf. Patterson 1985, 115-16). Illegitimates were not invariably repudiated in early Greek society, however, as evidence from Homer indicates: in the *Odyssey* (4.1-14) Menelaos celebrates in a very public manner the marriage of his illegitimate son by a slave girl, and there is certainly no indication that his son's patrimony is in any way compromised by his illegitimacy. We are told that Menelaos took the slave girl to bed because his wife Helen could only have one child. It is not improbable that many childless couples similarly sought the services of a surrogate mother who was a slave.

Finally, though household slaves may have been permitted to have intercourse with their own kind, there was an extremely high degree of probability that their offspring would not have been reared. Ischomachos in Xenophon's *Oikonomikos* or *Art of Household Management* (9.5) states that he locked the door of the *gunaikeion* with the express object of preventing theft and deterring the slaves 'from making babies without my knowledge'. Though Ischomachos is portrayed as somewhat old-fashioned, he none the less epitomises decent, middle-class Athenian values.

As the papyrus from Egypt discussed earlier unambiguously indicates, the final decision to raise an infant usually rested with the father, who, in the eyes of the law – Spartan law excepted – was the true 'owner' of the child. His rights were upheld by both Greek and Roman law, which regulated that if the father died, a newborn child must be handed over to its father's family. Likewise in the case of a divorce it was the father who retained custody of the child. This raises the question as to how a marriage could have survived in cases where the decision to expose was taken unilaterally by the father. The broad cultural acceptance of exposure is one thing; the means by which that acceptance was translated into practical effect in individual instances is quite another. The case-histories of mothers like Iokaste and Kreousa as we encounter them in tragedy indicate that the exposing of a child bequeathed the mother a legacy of bitterness and self-recrimination which might endure throughout her life. If exposure was occasionally practised in Classical Athens, that fact, far from inuring the mother against the loss of her child, may actually have had precisely the opposite effect, since the decision *not* to expose would presumably often be reached only after hard, painful and acrimonious bargaining with the father, during which the mother's attachment to the newborn may in some cases have constituted the determining factor.

Anecdotes as well as myths indicate that the task of exposing a newborn baby was regarded with abhorrence, a traditional feature of such stories being the inability of the person who has been delegated to perform the melancholy task actually to carry it out. Instances include the servant of Laios who lacks the heart to expose the infant Oedipus, and Mitradates, a herdsman of the Persian king Astyages, who swaps the infant prince Kyros for the stillborn baby of his wife (Hdt. 1.108-14). Mitradates' wife was called Kyno or 'Bitch' (1.122.3) and the folktale motif of the exposed infant who is suckled by a bitch or a she-wolf, as in the story of Romulus and Remus, should perhaps be seen as a type of wish-fulfilment expressive of deep misgivings at the thought of a newborn infant being mauled and devoured by a wild beast.

The unnaturalness of infanticide is humorously portrayed in Herodotos' account of the failed attempt upon baby Kypselos' life by the Corinthian Bacchiadai (5.92). Hearing of a prophecy which foretold that Kypselos would overthrow their rule, the Bacchiadai instantly dispatched no fewer than ten assassins to the mother's house in order to kill the newborn child. In the course of their journey they agreed that whoever picked the baby up first should dash its brains out on the ground. When the first man picked it up, however, Kypselos smiled. Unable to kill him, the man passed the child to the next assassin in line who was similarly overcome with pity. In this way the baby was transferred from one hardened criminal to the next until each had been reduced to putty by his charms.

A variety of sources suggest that in late fifth- and early fourth-century Athens the ethics of exposure had become a subject of controversy. Encounters between children who had been repudiated by their parents and those parents in later life, currently a highly problematic and sensitive area of human interaction, are self-evidently potentially catastrophic in cases where a child who has been left to die none the less survives to encounter the parents who exposed him, a subject which Sophokles explores in the *Oedipus Tyrannos* and Euripides in the *Ion*. Both dramatists emphatically indicate, moreover, that they regarded the practice of exposure with repugnance and horror. In the *Ion* as nowhere else in surviving Greek literature Euripides repeatedly dins into his audience's heads the sheer inhuman brutality of exposure and forces them to think the practice through to its logical conclusion by insisting that a newborn baby so treated becomes 'a prey for birds', 'a meal for wild beasts', and the like (cf. ll. 348-52, 503-5, 903, 917, 933, 951). The point is further driven home in the following lines of dialogue between an old man and Kreousa, the child's mother (ll. 954-63). We might dismiss them as melodramatic, if we doubted the passionate sincerity of the poet's moral outrage:

– Who exposed the child? Obviously you couldn't have done.
– I did. I swaddled him in my woollen garment at night.
– Didn't anyone know of the exposure?
– Only misery and secrecy knew of it.
– How could you bring yourself to leave the child in the cave?
– How else but with a pitiable lament.
– You acted harshly. The god [Apollo, the child's father] more so.
– Oh, if you had only seen the child stretching forth its hands towards me!
– To suck your breast, to lie in your arms?
– For that which was rightfully his, had I been a decent mother.

Again in the *Oedipus Tyrannos*, at the devastating climax to the stichomythia between Oedipus and the old servant of Laios, when Oedipus asks why the old man handed the infant over to the Corinthian instead of exposing him as instructed, the servant replies, 'Out of pity, master ...' (l. 1178).

Yet it is difficult to know how much weight to attach to such evidence. Euripides' and Sophokles' hostility to exposure may or may not be representative of contemporary Athenian attitudes and certainly tells us absolutely nothing of the prevalence of the practice at the time when they are writing, anymore than does the motif of the exposed child in New Comedy a century later. In the end we can say nothing with certainty about exposure in Athens, other than that intellectuals were divided on the issue – Euripides and Sophokles disapproved, while Aristotle recommended it as part of his population policy (see below, p. 100). Isokrates (*Panath.* 121-2) by contrast proclaimed exposure to be a crime against the gods and patriotically alleged that it was only ever practised by non-Athenians and in early times. It must be reiterated that not a single real-life instance of exposure is documented for Classical Athens.

It would seem a sensible precaution to provide an abandoned child with absolutely nothing that could possibly connect it to its parents, should it happen to be retrieved. In mythology and drama, however, parents regularly furnish it with objects known as *sunektithemena*, such as a ring or an amulet or a distinctive item of covering, which subsequently serve as *gnôrismata* or tokens of recognition by which a grown-up child and its parent(s) come to identify one another in later life. The most famous use of this device is the pinning together of infant Oedipus' ankles, which functions as a grotesque kind of identity bracelet. The fact that *gnôrismata* were a necessary plot device for stories involving abandoned infants who survive to adulthood does not, of course, prove that they were used in real life, although it seems unlikely that the custom was a complete fabrication on the part of the mythopoeic mind. If the practice occurred in real life, it may have reflected a sentimental desire to provide the newborn either with protection against evil or with a limited kind of identity in order to facilitate its passing to the world beyond (cf. Cameron 1932, 107).

As the Greeks themselves would have hotly contended, the abandonment of a child is not tantamount to causing or even willing its death. Some parents may have sincerely believed that exposure placed their child in the care of the gods. The pinning of Oedipus' ankles together in order to deny him any chance of survival is unique even in Greek myth. Many infants were exposed in public places, evidently with the deliberate intention that they would be retrieved, perhaps by a childless couple or by a slave dealer (cf. Eyben 1980-1, 15 n. 39). Only in Sparta was it probably illegal to retrieve an abandoned infant, since the infant in question had in effect been officially condemned to death (cf. MacDowell 1986, 53). Perhaps as a deterrent to exposure, Athenian law granted the finder of an exposed child the right neither to adopt it nor to sell it. The child remained the property of its father or, in the case of a slave, of its master, either one of whom was permitted to repossess his 'property' by a procedure known as *aphaireisthai eis eleutherian* (to release into freedom) or *agein eis douleian* (to bring into slavery). Except in the realm of drama and romance, the right of the father or that of the slave owner to repossession would of course have been virtually impossible to prove.

At least two Greek states are known to have introduced legislation, possibly in the Hellenistic period, either regulating exposure or banning it altogether. In Thebes exposure was entirely prohibited, although a father who pleaded extreme poverty could entrust his child to the magistrates, who sold it for a nominal fee. Then, when the child grew up, 'The rearer takes its enslavement in return for the rearing' (Ail. *VH* 2.7). In Ephesos, too, exposure was banned except in cases where 'the ankles have become enlarged as a result of famine', in which case the infant was evidently deemed to be beyond all hope of survival (Plu. *Hes*. fr. 69 *T*).

The Amphidromia

In Athens any decision about whether to put out a newborn child had to be taken in the very first days of its life because, probably on the fifth day after birth, a ceremony called Amphidromia was held in the baby's home which marked its official entry into the family. From now on, being a recognised member of the family, the infant acquired the right of life, which previously it had been denied. Very likely this was the first occasion that the new arrival left the *gunaikeion*, in which till now it had been confined with its mother.

The ritual performed at the Amphidromia, which may have taken place in the *andrôn* or men's quarters, bears a superficial resemblance to a christening or baptism service, but with three important differences: first, like many Greek rituals, it took place in a home and not in a church or temple; secondly, again like many Greek rituals, no priest was required to be present; and thirdly, instead of being baptised in water the baby was carried – possibly at a run – around the domestic hearth, either by the women who had delivered it or else by its father. According to one source the carriers were naked when they performed the rite. The Amphidromia, whose name means literally 'a walking or running around', undoubtedly had a deeply religious meaning for those who performed it, since fire is a well-known purifier, the hearth was the centre of the home, and Hestia, the goddess of the hearth, was the protectress of both the home and family life. It evidently served first to place the child under the protection of Hestia, and secondly as a kind of initiation ceremony or rite of passage, the first of many within the individual's life and similar in meaning to the service which was performed on behalf of brides and slaves when they were introduced to the *oikos* (see below, p. 221). The Amphidromia probably ended with a sacrifice performed as a thank-offering to the gods and the whole occasion is likely to have been productive of much merriment and feasting. The comic playwright Ephippos (*CAF* II, p. 251.3) describes it as an occasion when it is appropriate to 'toast hunks of Chersonese cheese, boil cabbages gleaming in olive oil, bake fat breasts of lamb, pluck the feathers of doves and thrushes and finches all at the same time, nibble squid with cuttlefish, tenderise the tentacles of many octopuses, and drink many goblets of barely diluted wine'. Only among the excessively rational Trausioi, a Thracian tribe, did relatives of the newborn 'sit around and lament at the thought of all the sufferings that the infant must endure' (Hdt. 5.4.2).

Either now, or at a later ceremony connected with birth, relatives and friends brought gifts called *optêria* which were presented on the occasion of seeing the child for the first time. The expression 'birthday gift (*dosis genethlios* or *genethlia*)' seems to have referred exclusively to a gift that was presented 'on behalf of the day of a person's birth' (cf. Hsch. s.v. *genethlia*) and may have been identical with the *optêria*. It may also have been now that magic charms known as *baskania* or *probaskania* were attached by a cord around the neck of the infant as a protection against bad luck, illness, or the evil eye (Fig. 8).

It was at a tenth-day ceremony known simply as *dekatê* or 'tenth' that the baby was given its name, which in the case of a first-born boy would commonly be that of his paternal grandfather. This may have been a more formal occasion than the Amphidromia, one to which relatives and others were invited with the express purpose of witnessing the father's acknowledgment that the newborn child was a legitimate offspring. Although in the majority of cases this was probably no more than a formality, there is a distinct possibility that some husbands may have used this occasion to denounce their wives publicly for having produced an offspring which bore no resemblance to its father, a circumstance which was judged to provide evidence of infidelity (cf. Pythagorean treatise on chastity in Thesleff 1965, 15ff.). In Athenian lawcourt speeches dealing with disputed inheritance, it is often one's naming at the *dekatê* that is cited as proof of legitimacy (e.g. Dem. 39.20 and 22). Besides the tenth-day ceremony, we also hear of a seventh-day one as well, though the explanation may be that the day fixed for the naming of the child varied from time to time and from place to place. Whatever the exact sequence of postnatal rituals, we can be certain that the various elements constituted an integrated series whose purpose was to introduce the newborn first to its immediate family and then to its more distant relatives through the vehicle of gifts and feasting (cf. Furley 1981, 70). It is to be noted that the birth of an Athenian baby was not registered officially outside the home, an indication that at this tender age it did not possess any political, legal or civic identity.

All the testimonia that we have been considering pertain exclusively to Athens. Although we do not know how extensively postpartum rites were practised outside Attica, it is very likely that they existed in some form throughout the Greek world for the purpose of marking the acceptance of the newborn within the circle of the home since, given the high incidence of perinatal deaths in ancient Greece, delayed inclusion might have been regarded in part as serving to limit the psychological involvement of the parents until the new family member had demonstrated its capability to survive the crisis of birth. Aristotle (*HA* 7.588a8-10 *T*) actually affirms that the reason for the delay in naming the newborn child is because most infant deaths occur in the first week after birth, particularly if this happens to coincide with a new moon.

The Greeks did not perform circumcision, though they acknowledged its hygienic value. Herodotos (2.36.3-37.2), who believed that the practice originated in Egypt, disdained it on aesthetic grounds. He writes:

> While men of other races leave their genitals as they were at birth, the Egyptians and those who have adopted the practice from them perform circumcision .... They circumcise their genitals for the sake of cleanliness, preferring to be clean rather than of comely appearance.

Evidence from vase-painting also indicates that the Greeks regarded an uncircumcised penis as elegant and dainty.

Pollution

Throughout her confinement a woman was regarded as ritually unclean. In sacral laws avoidance of contact with parturients was commonly enjoined upon priests, priestesses and temple servants. Though the lexicographer Photios (s.v. *miara hêmera*) alleges that the house in which a birth was taking place was smeared with pitch 'in order to drive away spirits (*daimones*)', more plausibly the purpose of the custom was to prevent the pollution inside the house from seeping into the community outside. The mother did not cease to be unclean once she had delivered, as is intimated by the fact that the word *lechô*, which is used of a woman in childbed, also denotes one who has just given birth (e.g. Eur. *El.* 652, 654, 1108). Being the term most commonly applied to a woman who is impure by reason of childbirth, it perhaps covered the whole birthing period from labour to postpartum.

Though details of pollution-belief during the postpartum period are unclear, it seems likely that one became contaminated simply by entering the house in which confinement took place, irrespective of whether one actually had any physical contact with the mother and child. The fourth-century cathartic law from Cyrene, for instance, states:

> The woman in childbed shall pollute the *oikos*. [...] she shall not pollute [the person who is outside the *oikos*?], unless he comes in. Any person who is inside shall be polluted for three days, but shall not pollute anyone else, not wherever this person goes. (tr. R. Parker)

Judging from the limited circle of persons affected by the pollution, it is abundantly clear that birth was not considered to be anywhere near as contaminating as death, even though Theophrastos seems to indicate that a superstitious man would have felt equally threatened by both crises (*Char.* 16.9).

Notable, too, is the fact that members of the *oikos* are placed in the safe category of 'polluted but incapable of polluting others'. It may have been in part to reduce the level of pollution to which a *lechô* was herself subject and in turn subjected others that it was customary to put women who had delivered on a diet of cabbage, loosely described as a kind of antidote or *antipharmakon* (Ath. *Deipn*. 9.370c).

In all probability the mother, the house of confinement, and those who had assisted in the delivery remained ritually unclean until the Amphidromia ceremony. No doubt the family was under some obligation throughout that period to take all proper precautions to ensure that the pollution of childbirth was adequately contained. The Amphidromia would have been an appropriate moment to mark the fact that miasma was now deemed to have run its course for all the participants, excepting only the mother herself. How those who had been polluted now purified themselves is not recorded, though the methods are likely to have resembled in attenuated form those which were adopted by persons who had been in contact with the dead (cf. Garland 1985, 41-7).

As the pollution gradually lifted from around the mother, she was able to return to her normal existence and re-integrate herself into the social life of the community. In addition to the fifth- and tenth-day rites already alluded to, there is a reference in Censorinus (*DN* 11.7) to a joyous celebration called *Tesserakostaion*, meaning 'Fortieth', which was held in the home, presumably on the fortieth day after delivery. Though the testimony is late, there are grounds for supposing that the rite was an ancient one. It may not be wholly accidental that its date is approximately coincident with the time around which the lochial discharge from the uterus generally tapers off. Very possibly, therefore, it was at this fortieth-day ceremony that the miasma surrounding the mother finally expired.

Ancient gynaecological treatises devote considerable attention to variations in the flow and colour of the lochia as an indicator of the mother's health. According to the author of *Seed* (18) the lochial discharge should cease within 30 days if the child is a boy and 42 if it is a girl. The supposition that women bleed for a longer period after delivering a girl finds an echo in Leviticus (12:1-6) where it is stated that postpartum purification requires 40 days in the case of a boy and 80 in the case of a girl. *Seed* (18) further alleges that purgation takes longer in an older woman than in a younger woman and that it is more painful for a woman who is delivering for the first time than for a multipara.

Numbers of offspring per family

In what appears to be the classic Greek formula by which a woman became betrothed to her future husband the bride's father publicly declared to the groom: 'I give you my daughter for the ploughing of legitimate children' (Men. in *CAF* III, p. 205.720). How many children did the average couple produce? Obviously the answer depends upon which period of history, which Greek community and which socio-economic group is under investigation. Factors to be taken into consideration include age at marriage, age at first birth, the interval between marriage and first birth, and the duration of the subsequent intervals between births. The problem, as usual, is that we have only literary evidence to go on. Hesiod states in the *Works and Days* (ll. 376-8):

> May there be only a single male child (*mounogenês pais*) to consume his father's *oikos* for in this way wealth will increase in the halls. But if you leave behind a second son, may you die an old man (*geraios*).

It has been inferred from this remark that Hesiod is writing 'in or of a period of rapid population growth' (Sussman 1984, 89). This claim lacks foundation, however, for as the context makes clear the poet is not actually concerned with economic survival as such but rather with the accumulation of wealth. The view expressed by Hesiod actually holds good for all periods of history and certainly does not exclusively reflect the demographic realities of Archaic Greece. It was the rule throughout the Greek world that inheritance must be divided equally among the sons, and so the head of household was under a strong compulsion to limit his family in order to avoid dissipating his estate and impoverishing his heirs. The desirability of having only a single male heir was, moreover, advocated by a variety of philosophers and legislators in all periods of Greek history, including Lykourgos, Xenokrates (fr. 97 Heinze) and Plato (*Laws* 5.740b).

It is probably safe to assume that the desire for children would have been closely linked to the recognition that if a couple reached old age and ultimately became incapable of productive labour, their only source of livelihood would be that provided by their offspring (cf. Isai. 2.10-12; Xen. *Oikon.* 12.19). It has been suggested that in societies where infant and child mortality rates are extremely high, five or six offspring are needed to guarantee that at least one infant survives to adulthood (cf. Stone 1977, 265). In Homer three sons appears to be typical (*Il.* 11.59, 14.115, 20.231), though both Nestor and Dolios had six (*Od.* 3.412, 24.497). Several of the Athenian families who employed the services of a professional orator in the fourth century BC did actually have as many as five children. Since the majority of them were involved in disputes over inheritance, however, they must all have been extremely wealthy and cannot be regarded as a representative sample of family-size. Multiple procreation is, after all, a long-term investment in which only the relatively well-off can afford to speculate. For those at the lower end of the economic scale it may spell short-term financial ruin.

In mainland Greece, according to a celebrated comment of Polybios (36.17.5-10), there was at the time of his writing (i.e. around the middle of the second century BC) 'universal childlessness (*apaidia*) and depopulation (*oliganthrôpia*)'. Polybios ascribes this phenomenon to moral degeneracy in general and to pretentiousness (*alazoneia*, aspiring to a more elevated life-style), plain greed and idleness in particular. The consequence, he states, is that 'People do not marry or if they do they do not rear the children born to them or at most generally only one or two, so that they can leave them in affluence and rear them in luxury.' The remedy, he concludes, lies not in praying to the gods for salvation, but in changing people's values, or, failing that, in passing laws making child-rearing compulsory. Whatever the accuracy of Polybios' diagnosis of the ultimate cause of childlessness in Hellenistic Greece, there are no good grounds for challenging his basic observation that the average couple produced two children at the most. It does not take a degree in statistics to identify widespread depopulation, and Polybios had no particular reason to lie. Moral degeneracy may of course have played some small part in all this; more significant were the troubled economic and political conditions that prevailed in Greece under Roman rule.

Population policy

How closely did a Greek state monitor its birth-rate and how preoccupied did it become in the event of either a shortfall or a steep increase? To what extent was child-rearing subject to centralised control? For both fiscal and military reasons it may at times be necessary to cast a supervisory eye over the size of the citizen body. Certainly this could have been done with comparative ease in a state such as Athens, either by adding together the totals of the 140-odd deme registers or else, more accurately, by comparing annually the size of the in-coming *hêlikia* at the age of seventeen with that of its immediate predecessors (see below, p. 180). That the Athenian Demos actually did this in practice, however, is less than likely.

Both Athens and Sparta did, however, operate population policies aimed at keeping their citizen body up to full strength. In Athens a childless man was excluded from high office. Spinsters, on the other hand, were not penalised, the assumption perhaps being that no woman would remain single unless she was incapable of attracting a husband owing to circumstances beyond her control (cf. Daube 1977, 14f.). We can only speculate about the date when the Athenian state became officially committed to the promotion of fertility. A likely possibility is in the second quarter of the fifth century BC when her population is known to have experienced a rapid increase, in part perhaps due to the threat posed by the numerically much superior Persian forces (cf. Labarbe 1957, 211; Daube 1977, 13f.).

Athens' problems were mild compared with those faced by Sparta whose *oliganthrôpia* became so acute as to threaten the state with virtual extinction. Just how acute we can discover by comparing a statement made by Herodotos (7.234.2) that in 480 she had a fighting force of 8,000 with another by Aristotle (*Pol.* 2.1270a29-32) that by the time of his writing in the 330s or possibly as early as 371 the number had fallen 'to below 1,000'. Though both figures have been challenged, there can be little doubt that they are substantially correct (cf. Cartledge 1987, 37f.). By the mid-third century Sparta's military manpower had dwindled even further, to a mere 700 (Plu. *Agis* 5.6). It is generally agreed that this decline was due primarily to economic constraints imposed on the citizen body by the Spartan landownership system which resulted in the concentration of landed property in an ever-diminishing propertied élite. The disenfranchisement of many Spartiates who defaulted on their mess-contributions was one consequence; the attempt to limit their offspring ideally to a single male heir another. With characteristic shortsightedness and hamfistedness the state responded to this crisis by addressing the first problem and ignoring the second, not realising that the two were interrelated.

Among the measures which were introduced was exemption from military service for the father of three sons, and exemption from all public duties for the father of four sons or more (Arist. *Pol.* 1270a40-b7; Ail. *VH* 6.6). Wife-sharing was also encouraged in order to maximise women's procreative capacity. Thus married men, in particular older men, who failed to produce offspring would have been under strong public pressure to invite other men to impregnate their wives (Plu. *Lyk.* 15.6-7; cf. Xen. *LP* 1.7-9). In the case of a marriage between a young girl and an old man (*geraios*), the latter was permitted to beget offspring 'by bringing in whoever he admired because of his physique and temperament' (Xen. *LP* 1.7; cf. Plu. *Lyk.* 15.7). Bachelors were penalised by being debarred from seeing young men and girls perform naked at the festival known as *Gymnopaidia*; in winter they were publicly humiliated by being required to march naked in a circle around the agora like naughty little boys, chanting that they were being justly punished for having disobeyed the laws; and when they grew old they were denied the honour and attention which youths customarily bestowed upon their elders (Plu. *Lyk.* 15.1-2). Imaginative though these measures undoubtedly were, they signally failed to produce the desired effect.*

Both Plato and Aristotle advocated population policies for their ideal states. In the *Republic* Plato places men and women under a duty to procreate for the sake of the state, though he is also anxious to prevent over-population. Parents should only have as many offspring as their means allow because too many children are a cause of poverty and war (2.372b). The best men should have intercourse with the best women as frequently as possible and only their offspring should be reared 'in order that

*The measures applied by Sparta to increase the birth-rate may be compared with those currently employed in the Soviet Union, also troubled by its birth-rate, where the Order of Maternal Glory and Hero Mother of the Soviet Union are awarded to women who give birth to between seven and nine and over ten children respectively.

the herd should be of the highest possible quality' (5.459de). As a prize for distinguished service in war young men will be permitted to have more frequent intercourse with women (5.460b). The children of inferior parents and any child of good parents who is born defective 'the officials will hide, as is fitting, in a secret and unknown location' – apparently a reference to exposure (5.460c). Men and women should beget children only while they are at their physical and mental peak, that is, between the ages of twenty and forty in the case of a woman, and thirty to fifty-five in the case of a man (5.460e-461a).

In the *Laws* Plato's population policy is aimed at ensuring that the optimum number of 5040 households is maintained but not exceeded. To this end he argues in favour of raising only a single male heir (5.740b-e). Other male offspring should be handed over to childless couples. If too many children are born, then the state should intervene by introducing 'measures to keep the birth-rate in check (*epischeseis geneseôs*)'. Regrettably, as Aristotle (*Pol.* 2.1265a38-42) comments, Plato does not tell us what specific measures he has in mind. Perhaps he felt inhibited in talking openly about such matters. If the population continues to increase the state should sponsor new colonies in order to rid itself of surplus citizens. Conversely, in order to promote the birth-rate, Plato laid down that a man who fails to marry by the age of thirty-five will be required to pay a fine to the goddess Hera (6.774ab). The minimum acceptable number of offspring per couple is to be fixed at one boy and one girl (11.930cd). Finally, newlyweds are to be supervised for ten years to ensure that the state has an abundance of citizens and if they fail to produce offspring within this period they will be required to separate (6.784ab).

Much of Book 7 of Aristotle's *Politics* is about determining and maintaining the optimum number of citizens, which the author defines (7.1326b22-4) as 'the greatest surveyable number for the attainment of a life of self-sufficiency', where 'surveyable' indicates the ability of all the citizens to know one another personally. Exposure is to be permitted only in the case of deformed children and the principal check on over-population is by recourse to abortion (7.1335b19-26). Men are to procreate only between the ages of thirty-seven and fifty, and women once they reach eighteen. Advocates of population policy are not found in Greek literature after Plato and Aristotle.

Conclusions

There is no means of telling how closely the Greek world as a whole conformed to the birthing system outlined in this chapter. Major regional and social variants undoubtedly existed. Whereas all classes of society relied on the services of midwives, however, we can be confident that only those births accompanied by severe complications would have taken place in the presence of a doctor. In the light of all the evidence gathered here it should anyway be abundantly clear that neither the baby's nor the mother's chances of survival would have been improved by the presence of a physician with the possible exception of a stillborn delivery, while in most situations they would have been seriously reduced.

As noted at the beginning of this chapter, it is intriguing to speculate whether in the period from the late fifth century BC to the second century AD midwifery and medicine were complementary or competitive areas of competence. In other words, did the Greek physician see himself as providing an *alternative* response to the traditional birthing technique of midwives or merely as capable of enhancing their recognised skills in an emergency? On the whole the evidence we have been considering suggests the latter. Certainly the Hippokratic school of medicine expected the midwife to be in charge even in the case of a difficult labour. It seems at least possible then that upon some occasions doctor and midwife might have been in the birthing-room together.

A second area of potential conflict involves the general relationship between medicine and religion. On *a priori* grounds we should expect them to be antagonistic to one another, but in practice there is little evidence to support this claim. As in the case of many Greek rituals, no priest was required to be present – indeed priests who were members of the family would also have been debarred from entering the house of confinement – but the midwife herself acted in a religious capacity, as a mediator between the human world and the divine.

Who actually controlled the birth? Though the midwife obviously orchestrated the drama, it is uncertain how much initiative she was able to exercise. Could she for instance override the wishes of the family in the event of a crisis? What exactly was the authority of the husband? Could a midwife be accused of negligence or malpractice in the case of a traumatic, perhaps even fatal delivery? If so, what charges could be brought against her? My own conviction is that it was not possible to sue midwives, simply by virtue of the fact that they acted as representatives of the gods and could always defend themselves against charges of negligence by alleging either that the mother had incurred divine disfavour or that the foetus had been born in the eighth month.

Though the study of parturition potentially offers to enrich and broaden our understanding of the organisation of female networks, interests and strategies, the results are in the end somewhat disappointing. We have to acknowledge that we possess less information about the role of women in childbirth than we do, for instance, about their role in handling death. This is in large measure due to the fact that whereas there exists copious iconographic material on vases about the handling of death, childbirth is very rarely represented. What is striking, however, is that whereas men were entirely excluded from the birth, their power immediately reasserted itself in the postpartum period by virtue of their exclusive right to determine whether the offspring was legitimate.

Belief in symbolic associations pervaded the handling of birth and the treatment of the newborn, as it did attitudes surrounding conception and gestation, insofar as we find evidence for belief in the superiority of odd over even, of right over left, and of male over female. There was thus no clear dividing line between the nostrums of Greek medicine and those of folklore, and the latter clearly influenced the former.

Birth was a ritual, although its structure can only be dimly perceived. Very possibly appropriate ritual action was taken by the mother-to-be and her household as soon as a pregnancy had been diagnosed or even suspected. Other rituals included the taking of omens in advance of delivery, the invoking of deities in order to induce and expedite labour, the uttering of the *ololugê* or ritual cry at the moment of delivery, the ritual bathing of the newborn and of its mother, and the various postpartum practices and rituals held on the fifth, seventh, tenth and fortieth days after delivery. The fact that birth – like death – was perceived to be an extended process rather than an instantaneous event is suggested first by the delay in naming the newborn and granting it formal admission into the family circle; secondly by the perception of the mother as a source of continuing pollution over a forty-day period; and thirdly by the time-span covered by such words as *lechô* and *embruon*.

I would propose that giving birth was regarded both as (1) a more or less normal part of family life and as (2) an event whose success depended upon supernatural agency. Only among the educated élite does it seem to have acquired the status of a physiological crisis.

Finally, in what mood did a pregnant woman approach the moment of delivery? Knowing what *we* know about birth, about the much greater likelihood of something going wrong, possibly horribly wrong, about the fact that in certain households a pregnant woman, like the woman from Oxyrhynchos, went into labour knowing that even if everything went right she would only have a fifty-fifty chance of keeping her baby, we would conclude: in a mood of profound anxiety, demoralisation, bitterness and frustration. But knowing what *they* knew, sustained by their belief in the gods, in the efficacy of prayer and of ritual, in the skill of the *maia*, and – let us not forget – in their own self-esteem as the means by which the family line is perpetuated, who knows but that their mood was not actually cheerful or at least resigned? Greek religion is not the spiritual vacuum that it is often claimed to be.

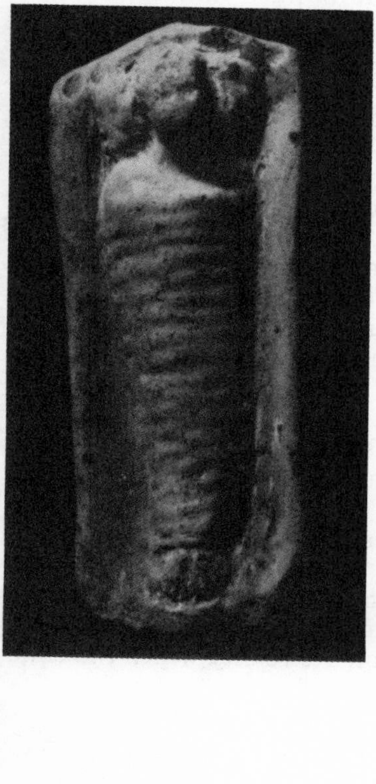

Fig. 7. Figurine of a swaddled baby lying in a cradle, *c.* 450 BC. From Taras, South Italy.

3

The Growing Child

> Child-rearing (*teknotrophiê*) is a perilous business. When it is successful it is attended by strife and care. When it fails there is no other pain to compare with it.
>
> (Demokritos *DK* 68 B 275)

This chapter covers the period from earliest infancy to pre-puberty. It was a period which the Greeks themselves seem generally to have regarded as a continuous whole since throughout its length the growing child was referred to as a *pais*, though an infant was more commonly described as a *paidion*. *Pais* has other meanings besides that of 'child' or 'young person'. It also denotes someone who is in a position of social or sexual subordination, such as either a male household slave irrespective of age or the junior (and passive) partner in a homosexual liaison, even when the latter is already sprouting a beard. The fact that boys, slaves and pathics were all addressed in this same way thus raises the interesting question as to how closely their social identities were conflated.

Let me emphasise at the start that we are dealing with a society where the average life expectancy at birth was probably no more than twenty-five (cf. Hopkins 1983, 225). Children would therefore have constituted a very much larger proportion of the population than they do in an increasingly 'grey' society such as present-day Europe or the United States where, if present trends continue, the over-sixty-year-olds may eventually become as numerous as the under-fifteen age group. In 1841 in England and Wales there were five children under fifteen for every one person over sixty. In ancient Greece the disproportion between the two categories was probably even greater.

The investigation of childhood may adopt two quite separate strategies. It may take the form of an attempt to enter the world of the child by focusing upon the reality which the child constructs around itself in response to the constraints, expectations, demands and so forth that are imposed upon it by parents, adults, teachers, peers and siblings. Alternatively it may take the form of an investigation into the ideological framework which is largely responsible for creating those constraints, expectations and demands in the first place. Most of the evidence for this chapter is provided by philosophers and therefore directs us towards the second type of investigation. The drawback is obvious since these writings merely provide us with testimony as to what a handful of highly unrepresentative, often eccentric, certainly unqualified and quite possibly childless adults happened to think was the right way to bring up children. Their interest in children is, moreover, not prompted by a humanitarian concern for their welfare. Nor, it may be noted, were their comments directed primarily to prospective parents. Plato, for instance, who of all ancient philosophers devotes perhaps the greatest attention to the upbringing and education of children, discusses the games children play merely as a way of illustrating important features of his philosophical system (see below, p. 127).

Modern investigative studies of the role of children in different societies often seek to determine 'how visible and how differentiated children are in the source evidence' (cf. Rawson 1986a, 170). The short answer to this investigative tactic with regard to ancient Greece is that children were practically invisible. Only when we reach the fourth century can we detect some increase in interest, as evidenced in particular by Greek art. The portrayal of children in fifth-century Greek tragedy contributes little to our investigation, since their appearances are generally confined to moments of crisis when their lives are endangered (cf. Sifakis 1979, 72f.). Their overriding dramatic function in other words is to extend the scope of the audience's sympathies outwards from the centre, by illustrating the devastating effect which tragedy has upon the lives of innocents and protagonists alike. What such evidence does not tell us, what no source tells us, is 'what it was like' to be a child in ancient Greece. So we find ourselves in much the same predicament as we were in the foregoing chapter, attempting to reconstruct a 'typical' pattern of behaviour in the absence of any testimony from the subjects themselves.

Infant mortality

Infant mortality, i.e. deaths occurring during the first year of life, was extremely high in ancient Greece even apart from the practice of exposure, so high in fact that the majority of couples could probably look forward to the death of at least one of their offspring shortly after birth. It has been estimated that in Rome 'more than a quarter (28 per cent) of all live-born Roman babies died within their first year of life' (Hopkins 1983, 225; cf. 1966, 263) and there is no reason to suppose that the incidence of mortality would have been any lower in a city such as Athens. Given the fact that girls were probably less well-treated and well-nourished than boys, infant mortality is likely to have been higher among females (cf. Plu. *Lyk.* 3; below, p. 120). As in the previous discussion about exposure, it is difficult to assess what impact the expectation and, in many cases, the experience of repeated bereavement occasioned by the loss of an infant may have had upon the parents (cf. Golden 1988a). Since the Greeks did not keep statistics they were at least spared the knowledge that an infant's chances of surviving to its first birthday were somewhat better than two in three. Infant mortality rate is unlikely to have been the same for all levels of society. It was undoubtedly highest among slaves and the urban poor; substantially lower among country-dwellers and the well-to-do.

Diarrhoeal diseases caused by the lack of clean drinking water and the absence of a satisfactory human waste disposal system probably constituted the foremost cause of infant mortality in the ancient world as they do in the under-developed world today. Although the plague described by Thukydides which afflicted Athens in the early 420s is often treated as a virtually unique occurrence in Greek history, it is extremely likely that outbreaks of cholera, typhoid, diphtheria and smallpox occurred throughout the Greek world with virtually annual regularity, if not quite on the same tragic scale, particularly in densely populated urban settlements. The fact that many women became pregnant again immediately after parturition owing to the absence of any completely effective method of contraception further aggravated the hazards facing the newborn, since a rapid succession of pregnancies greatly depletes a mother's nutritional reserves, thereby reducing the quantity and quality of her milk. Children born close together are therefore required to compete

Fig. 8. Limestone statue of a crouching child wearing a chain of amulets draped over his left shoulder and under his right arm, *c*. 300 BC. From the Sanctuary of Apollo Idalion on Cyprus.

with one another for limited physical resources, a situation which frequently results in the death of the weakest. Among the poorer sections of society, those that is who were unable to meet the expense of hiring a wet-nurse, the decision to expose a newborn infant may occasionally have been made on the basis of concern for the mother's health, rather than on the economic pros and cons of child-rearing as such. The fact that girls were typically married shortly after menarche substantially diminished their chances of delivering a healthy offspring. Wet-nursing is also likely to have contributed to the rate of infant mortality especially at the weaning stage, due to the fact that nurses premasticated food for their nurslings (cf. Stone 1977, 83). Finally, it is probable that swaddling created serious health problems for neonates since the bands would only have been changed infrequently.

Whereas there is little evidence to suggest that the medical profession had any real understanding of why so many infants died, far less about how to prevent them from dying, there was none the less an acute awareness of the extreme delicacy and susceptibility to disease of the newborn. The Hippokratic author of *Eighth-Month Foetus* writes here with some feeling of their plight (12):

> Instead of airs (*pneumata*) and humours (*chumoi*) whose nature is congenital to its own and whose familiarity and pleasantness are never denied him while inside his mother's womb, the newborn child is exposed to everything that is alien, everything that is more harsh, more dried up and less humanised (*exênthrôpismena*). The inevitable consequence is suffering and, in many cases, death.

It remains extremely doubtful, however, whether physicians were regularly requested to attend infants in the first months or even the first years of life.

Although a newborn infant was regarded as both fragile and vulnerable, parts of its body were thought to contain powerful healing qualities. Pliny (*NH* 28.9.41), who cites evidence that has its origins in a folkloristic tradition of immemorial antiquity, reports that 'the first crop of hair which is cut from a child's head is said to relieve gout, if tied around the affected area, as generally does the hair of all who have not yet arrived at puberty (*impubes*)'. He further ascribed magical properties to the first tooth which a child loses, claiming that 'so long as the tooth does not touch the ground, if set in a bracelet and worn constantly on the arm it will prevent a woman from suffering any discomfort in the pubic region'. Such beliefs no doubt enjoyed wide popularity throughout the ancient world.

Throughout the growing phase and not merely during infancy the life of the child was understood to be at grave physical risk. To be sure, mortality was higher in infancy than at puberty or adolescence, yet there was a high expectation that those who survived infancy would not reach adulthood. Only when the child actually stopped growing, it was believed, did its susceptibility to fatal diseases sharply decline. Although it acquired a name of its own within the first two weeks after birth, its identity probably remained low key. With few exceptions interest in the child's earliest development is singularly lacking in Greek culture, perhaps for the obvious reason that the existence of a creature whose chances of surviving its first year were less than bright scarcely merited serious attention. Just as a woman was for official purposes identified as someone's daughter or wife, so a child at this age was most probably identified as someone's child or *teknon* (cf. Montevecchi 1979, 113).

Divine protection of the growing child

In appreciation of the hazards which afflict the growing child Greek parents placed their offspring under the protection of *kourotrophoi* or 'fostering deities'. Hesiod (*Th*. 346-8) claims that the progeny of Tethys, wife of the earth-encircling stream Okeanos, included 'the sacred race of *Kourai* who, in conjunction with lord Apollo and the rivers, transform *kouroi* into men (*kourizousi*), this being the role they have had assigned to them by Zeus'. *Kourotrophoi* are closely identified with the Nymphs, spirits who haunt running water, and, like them, had the duty of nurturing children from birth to the end of adolescence. Their role as nurses commenced as soon as the child was born, as is indicated by the fact that the *Kourêtes*, the male equivalent of the *Kourai*, were present at the birth of Zeus (cf. Str. *Geog*. 10.3.11; 10.3.19). Among the very large number of deities and heroes who were accorded the title of *kourotrophos* we may note in particular Artemis, Demeter, Ge, Hekate, Hestia, Leto and Herakles. Having commended their child to the care of one or more fostering deities during its growing years, parents were obliged to render thanks later for the help they had provided. A votive relief from Phaleron dated *c*. 400 BC carries the following inscription (van Straten 1981, 90 with fig. 23; Athens *NM* 2756):

> Xenokrateia, daughter of Xeniades, from Cholleidai, has founded the sanctuary of Kephisos and has dedicated this gift for the rearing or *didaskalia* [of her son] Xeniades and to the gods who share his altar.

The prominence and prevalence of cults in honour of *kourotrophoi* throughout ancient Greece is no doubt due primarily to the high incidence of infant and child mortality which in turn prompted the belief that adulthood could only be attained if a child was spiritually adopted by a fostering deity. But there is another likely reason for their popularity. The term *kourotrophos*, which means 'nurse of the young', suggests that the deity or deities were expected to be intimately involved with the growing process, even perhaps to the extent of being instrumental in assuring physical development. That would explain why *kourotrophoi*, such as the three thousand Okeanidai in the Hesiodic passage referred to above, are frequently associated with running water, since rivers and streams were believed to promote fertility and growth. The association between water and the growing child, whether the *paidion* happens to be inside or outside the womb, may also have had something to do with the fact that the Greeks habitually thought of young people as plants. It is also likely to be part of the explanation for the custom of dedicating a lock of hair either to the local river god or to the nymphs as a thank-offering at the moment of transition to adulthood (see below, p. 187). It is worth adding that the attention which children received from the *kourotrophoi* was not invariably benign. Inscriptions on the gravestones of young children indicate that the Nymphs were held responsible for the disappearance or death of a child. This spiteful and sinister aspect of their nature was a mythological representation of the hazards and dangers that were believed to attend physical and psychological growth.

On one occasion at least, according to Herodotos (6.61.3-5), the deified Helen took a personal interest in the development of an ugly female infant. Every day her devoted nurse brought the infant to the goddess' shrine. Laying her down in front of the goddess' statue, she prayed to her to remove her ugliness. One day as the nurse was leaving the shrine she met a woman who asked to look at the baby. In spite of the fact that its parents had expressly forbidden her to allow anyone to gaze upon their offspring, presumably with the purpose of preventing themselves and it from becoming an object of ridicule, the nurse yielded to the woman's insistence. The stranger proceeded to stroke the baby's head and prophesied that it would grow up to be the most beautiful woman in all Sparta. Such *ex post facto* intervention was evidently remarkable and should perhaps be taken as a sign of Helen's exceptional ability to influence an offspring's appearance. Prudent mothers-to-be would surely have done all that they could in advance of their delivery to ensure that the goddess of good looks blessed the child in the womb.

There were more scientific explanations as to why children grow. An obscure and corrupt passage in Aeschylus' *Agamemnon* (l. 76f.) refers to 'the youthful marrow (*nearos muelos*) <leaping up (*anaissôn*)> within the breast (*sterna*)'. If the reading given here is correct, the presupposition would seem to be that growth occurs as a result of marrow being pumped through the bones rather like the sap rising in the spring. The Hippokratic school, which propounded that growth was associated with body heat and body moisture, claimed that the consumption of these elements during the growing period accounts for the fact that a youth is drier and cooler than a child (*Regimen* 1.33.1-2; cf. Gal. 1.583 *K*). Exercise was also thought to be capable of either accelerating or impeding growth. Thus Aristotle (*Pol.* 7.1336a25-6) advocated that the exercises required of children up to the age of five should not be too strenuous 'in order that there will be no impediment to their growth'. Finally, the Stoics attributed growth to the activity of vital breath or *pneuma*, which permeates and activates everything. They maintained that increase in height is facilitated by a modest intake of food on the grounds that over-eating impedes the upward progress of the *pneuma* by dispersing it over a greater physical area. Likewise Plutarch (*Lyk.* 17.4), himself a Stoic, stated that the reason why the Spartans are so tall is because they are undernourished during their growing years.

Nurses

Myths of divine infancies provide support for the belief that in early Greek society it was commonplace for members of the aristocracy to hire a wet-nurse or *titthê* to breastfeed an infant. The *Homeric Hymn to Delian Apollo*, for instance, states that Apollo was not breastfed by his mother Leto but handed over to Themis, who nourished him with nectar and ambrosia (ll. 123-5). That the Greeks perceived the humble and menial activity of nursing a child as not beneath the dignity of the goddess Demeter, the nurse of the infant Demophoön, may be further construed as evidence of the value and importance with which the work of this profession was generally regarded (cf. *Hom. h. Dem.* 219ff.). Spartan *titthai* enjoyed a particularly high reputation and were much sought after by other Greeks because of their training techniques, like Amykla the *titthê* of Alkibiades (Plu. *Lyk*. 16.3; *Alk*. 1.2).

The reasons behind the practice of hiring a wet-nurse are likely to have been similar to those which prevailed in modern Europe until the mid-eighteenth century when wet-nursing went out of fashion. These include: a lack of adequate milk supply in the mother as a result of sickness or exhaustion following childbirth; an intolerance of the discomfort and inconvenience caused by breastfeeding; a fear that breastfeeding might permanently impair the shape of the breasts and cause premature ageing; and finally, perhaps overridingly, a reluctance on the part of the husband to compete with the child for the mother's attention (cf. Stone 1977, 269f.). It goes without saying that the mother's death in labour would also have necessitated the hire of a wet-nurse. But there is yet another reason not included in this list. In view of the fact that women were charged with the management of the household, which included such chores as washing, cooking, gardening, weaving cloth, sewing clothes and supervising the slaves, how much time was actually available for childcare? In some cases at least the services of a wet-nurse and later a dry-nurse must have been engaged primarily because child-rearing took second place to domestic management. It would be interesting to know whether a nurse was hired at the insistence or recommendation of the husband or whether it was a decision usually reached jointly by both partners. The hypothesis that wet-nursing owed some of its popularity to the fact that it served to minimise the degree of parental involvement in the newborn until the latter had proved its capacity to survive and so provided 'a cushion against the foreseeable loss of children and the accompanying emotional trauma' (Bradley 1986, 220), cannot be disproved, though it is in the highest degree unlikely that the Greeks ever articulated the merits of the practice in this way.

The pros and cons of engaging a wet-nurse were hotly debated in philosophical circles. The hostility towards the practice which is expressed in several philosophical works is commensurate with the high value which their authors attached to the activity of child-rearing. In the *Republic* (2.373c), for instance, Plato places both wet- and dry-nurses in the same category as other frauds such as *paidagôgoi* (see below, p. 122), beauticians, barbers, cooks and chefs, who exist only in societies which are given over to profligacy and immorality. Even so Plato concedes that the mothers of the guardians, those who are destined to protect the constitution of the ideal state, should be assisted by nurses. The function of these nurses, however, will not be to lessen the mother's burden but rather to prevent her from recognising her own child, thereby ensuring her impartial devotion to the entire community (5.460c). Plutarch (*Mor.* 3c-e = *Education of Children* 5; cf. Sor. *Gyn.* 2.18.4) took a modern attitude to nursing, rightly observing that breastfeeding not only stimulates the degree of affection which a mother feels towards her child but also promotes bonding between the two:

> Mothers should nurture (*trephein*) their children themselves and supply them with their own breasts. For they will feed them with a greater degree of affection and more care since they love them from the inside and, as the saying goes, up to the ends of their fingers. But *titthai* and *trophoi* (wet and dry nurses) have spurious and insincere feelings because their love is bought .... Mothers who nurse become more sympathetic (*eunousterai*) and more affectionate towards their children. Inevitably so: for this shared nurture (*suntrophia*) is a strengthener of goodwill (*eunoia*).

Plutarch, however, concedes that a wet-nurse is necessary in cases where the mother is unable to produce milk either because of her physical weakness or because of her eagerness to have more children.

By the Hellenistic period at the latest considerable concern was being voiced about the quality and reliability of wet-nurses. A pseudepigraphical letter ascribed to the Pythagorean school dating to the third or second century BC and addressed to a woman called Phyllis who has recently given birth urges the latter to engage the services of a nurse who is 'not sulky nor a chatterbox nor a glutton, but self-disciplined, moderate, practical, and not foreign but Greek'. The implication would seem to be that wet-nurses were commonly perceived as dirty, drunken and disorderly; or in other words, that the profession tended to attract the absolute dregs of society. Despite all the objections raised by philosophers, however, wet-nursing remained standard practice throughout antiquity.

The advice offered to Phyllis is almost identical to that provided by Soranos, who observes that a wet-nurse should be 'self-controlled, sympathetic, well-tempered, Greek and tidy' (*Gyn*. 2.19.1). The concern for propriety which we encounter in both authors was reinforced by the conviction that a woman transmits her character along with her milk. A freeborn Greek woman therefore would have been much preferred over a slave or foreigner, despite the fact that slaves and foreigners were commonly employed as wet-nurses, particularly by the poor. Soranos further recommended that the wet-nurse should be aged between 20 and 40, healthy, of large build, be a mother of two or three children, and be abstemious in regard to both intercourse and alcohol. Finally, she should have been lactating for not more than two or three months prior to hire because otherwise her milk would be deficient.

The central importance of nurses within the Greek *oikos* is indicated by their prominence in Greek tragedy. Indeed the mere fact that nurses and *paidagôgoi* are among the very small group of non-royal persons to whom a speaking role is assigned indicates their proximity to the events which they are called upon to witness. The most sympathetically drawn is Kilissa, the *tropheus* of Orestes, who makes a brief but memorable appearance at a critical moment in Aeschylus' *Libation Bearers*. Kilissa fondly reminisces about the intimate chores that she performed long ago on behalf of her royal charge, much to the detriment of the audience's sympathy towards Orestes' own mother Klytaimnestra (ll. 749-60):

> How I devoted myself to that child from the moment that his mother gave him to me to nurse as a newborn babe! He kept me up every night, crying and screaming, he was a perfect nuisance and all for nothing. They're brainless things, you see, children. You have to nurse them as if they are animals and follow their moods. A babe in swaddling clothes can't tell you what the matter is – whether it's hungry or thirsty or wants to go to the potty – though of course babies can't control themselves, it just comes out and you can't do anything about it. You learn to tell the future in my profession, but, heavens above, I was wrong often enough and then I had to wash its clothing. I was a nurse and a washerwoman rolled into one!

Euripides' *Hippolytos* provides us with a very different image of the nurse. Theseus' wife Phaidra, demented with love for her stepson Hippolytos, can find no outlet for her guilty passion except by confiding in her old nurse on whom she wholly relies for the solution to her problem. When Phaidra finds out that the nurse has simply confronted Hippolytos with the information and that he is sickened by it, she sees no alternative but to kill herself, and in so doing brings about the ruination of the entire household. The outcome of the play seems to suggest that in the emotionally charged, all-female world of the *gunaikeion* the intimacy and trust which naturally existed between a nurse and her mistress could enable a well-intentioned but meddlesome slave to acquire a dangerous ascendancy over her mistress. In real life the dependency of a mistress on her nurse, often beneficial but occasionally fatal, must have been widespread in a society where men were absent or unavailable for long periods of time.

Nurses who were slaves remained with their owners' family until they died and several sepulchral inscriptions testify to the indebtedness that was felt towards them by their former charges. The following Homeric-style tribute composed by Kallimachos (*Epigr.* 50 Pfeiffer) on behalf of a foreign-born woman of low extraction is splendidly direct in its appeal:

> Mikkos provided for Phrygian Aischre, his good wet-nurse [literally 'his good milk'] as long as she lived and even in her old age. When she died he set up a dedication to her for future generations to see. So the old woman departs from this life, having received due recompense for her breasts.

Such testimonials can hardly be regarded as wholly representative, however, for the obvious reason that nurslings who felt no particular affection for their nurses have left no permanent record of their feelings. Since the relationship between the two parties was either mandated (in the case of a slave nurse) or mercenary (in the case of a freeborn one), we have to acknowledge that there may have been just as many negative or neutral relationships as there were positive ones (cf. Bradley 1986, 221).

In some households at least a nurse was expected to be skilled in magical practices in order to protect her ward against witchcraft and the evil eye. The divine nursemaid Demeter, when presenting her credentials to Metaneira, states (*Hom. h. Dem.* 226-30):

> I will nurse your child as you bid, and never, I confidently expect, by carelessness of his nurse (*titthênê*) will witchcraft do him injury nor the *hupotamnon* [see note on p. 317]. For I know

a very strong antidote to the *hulotamnon* [or *oulotamnon*: see note on p. 318] and I know an excellent safeguard against painful witchcraft.

Weaning and teething

A short and textually corrupt Hippokratic treatise entitled *Peri odontophuiês* or *Teething* contains a collection of aphorisms dealing with the prognosis of illnesses to which infants at the weaning and teething stages succumb. Among its claims are the following: babies who eat solids while being breastfed bear weaning more easily; those who drink a great deal of milk are generally drowsy; teething children are occasionally subject to an attack of convulsions which often proves fatal; such attacks are more likely to occur in the case of babies whose bowel-movement is irregular, those who do not experience any acute fever, and those who are comatose as a result of being well-nourished; and the best time of year for a child to be teething is during the winter. Virtually the sole piece of advice which the treatise offers regarding the care of babies in earliest infancy, however, is that if they are looked after properly they will more easily bear weaning (12). There is also a brief reference to the onset of dentition in *Aphorisms* (3.25), which states that this development is accompanied by 'inflammation of the gums, fevers, convulsions, diarrhoea, especially when cutting the canine teeth and in the case of very fat infants and in those whose bowels are hard'. Considering the highly generalised nature of these observations, and considering, too, the paucity of descriptions of infant diseases among case-histories in the Hippokratic corpus, it seems likely that the care of babies did not generally fall within the scope of the medical profession. Evidence for lack of medical interest in the physical growth and development of infants also resides in the fact that they are designated *paidia* whatever their exact age. There is no ancient equivalent for the modern practice of referring to children aged under two years by the number of months which they have attained.

For more helpful advice on how to look after a baby we must again turn to the pseudepigrahical letter addressed to Phyllis:

It is best, if the baby is put down to sleep when it is well filled with milk .... If other food is given, it should be as simple as possible. One should stay away from wine completely because it has such a powerful effect or else mix it sparingly with its

Fig. 9. Babies' feeding bottles of black-glazed ware. The one above carries the inscription 'Mamo', meaning 'Mummy', the one below says 'Drink, don't drop it'. Both are from southern Italy.

evening meal of milk. She [the wet-nurse] should not give him continual baths; it is better to have occasional temperate ones. Along the same lines the atmosphere around the baby should have an even balance of hot and cold, and his housing should be neither too airy nor too close. Moreover, his water should not be too hard nor too soft, nor his bed too rough – rather, it should fall comfortably on his skin. (tr. M.R. Lefkowitz).

As a supplement to human milk, infants were given a concoction of flour and water with a variety of additives such as hydromel, milk, sweet wine and honey wine (cf. Sor. *Gyn.* 2.46.3). It is extremely unlikely that animal milk would have been trusted for infants, given the belief that character could be transmitted through milk.

Soranos (*Gyn.* 2.46.3-4) recommended that the first solid food be given to a child in the sixth month, even though its weaning will not be completed until it is about eighteen months or two years old. He also suggested that when a child is very thirsty, water or watery wine be administered by means of what he calls 'artificial teats (*pephilotechnêmenai thêlai*)', probably made of leather or cloth, which were attached to terracotta feeding bottles (Fig. 9).

Soranos (*Gyn.* 2.49.2) further suggested that the discomfort caused by teething could be alleviated after the fifth month by softening a baby's gums during the bath with chicken fat applied to the end of a finger. Pliny's claim (*NH* 7.16.72) that it is 'a universal custom not to cremate a person before the teething stage' implies that an infant who had survived the difficult teething stage was credited with a new and enlarged physiological and social identity.

The lower social value placed on girls meant that in some households they received inferior attention and treatment to boys. Xenophon (*Lak. Pol.* 1.3) pays the Spartans the compliment of declaring that of all Greeks it is only they who devote as much attention to rearing girls as boys, stating:

> Others rear girls (*korai*) who are destined to become mothers and who are judged to be well brought up on the least amount of food possible and with the most meagre amount of cooked fare. Either they are not allowed any wine or if it is permitted it is diluted with water. Most Greeks expect *korai* to keep their mouths shut and attend to their wool in the manner of the majority of skilled sedentary workers.

Plato (*Rep.* 5.461d; cf. 7.541a) recommended removing infants from their parents shortly after birth and placing them in state nurseries, evidently in the belief that a child who is ignorant of its own parents will feel a stronger bond to the community as a whole. Such a violent rupture constituted merely the first step by which he sought to undermine the strength of the family unit, the chief obstacle, in his mind, to the establishment of a perfect world.

Registration of an Athenian infant in a phratry

In Athens and other Ionian communities an infant's first introduction to the world outside the family took place at the festival known as the Apatouria which was held annually in the month of Pyanopsion (roughly October-November). This was an occasion when all male citizens assembled in hereditary associations known as *phratriai*, sometimes loosely translated 'brotherhoods'. Well-born Athenians who belonged to the smaller hereditary associations known as *genê* probably registered their sons in these groups, too, soon after birth. The fact that the infant was now introduced not to the community as a whole but only to a subdivision thereof is a reflection of the bounds which were set upon its social persona.

On the third day of the festival called *Koureôtis* male offspring who had been born to members of the phratry since the previous celebration of the Apatouria were officially registered in that phratry in the presence of its *phratores* or phratry-members. The ceremony perhaps began with a sacrifice known as the *meion* or 'lesser', the victim being provided by the child's father. The infant was introduced – the Greek verb is *eisagein* – by either its father or legal guardian who was required to swear on oath before the altar of the phratry with his hand on the sacrificial offerings that it was 'in very truth the legitimate offspring of an Athenian woman who had been formally betrothed (*ê mên ex astês kai enguêtês*)' (cf. Isai. 8.19; Dem. 57.54; Ps.-Dem. 59.60). However, there is some evidence to suggest that the wording of the oath varied a little from phratry to phratry, and further that not all phratries were equally rigorous in the manner in which they administered the rules of procedure (cf. Isai. 7.16, with Sealey 1984, 121). If the claim was uncontested, the infant was duly admitted to the phratry, though by what rite of initiation is unclear. Though most infants were introduced to their phratry before they were one year old, there does not seem to have been any upper age limit for registration. Even so, delayed registration probably only occurred in cases where either the child's legitimacy or its entitlement to citizenship was for some reason contested, since it seems to have been regarded with some suspicion. It is not known whether girls as well as boys were registered in a phratry.

The *Choës*

A later, more public initiation ceremony for Athenian children took place at a ceremony known as the *Choës* or Pitchers which was held on the second day of the Anthesteria, a spring festival celebrated in the month of Anthesterion. At dawn on this day, which fell on the twelth of the month, the doors of the small temple of Dionysos in the Marshes (*en Limnais*), situated on the south slope of the Acropolis, were opened. They remained open until sunset, being closed for the rest of the year. All boys aged between three and four were deemed *choïkoi*, that is, eligible for participation in the *Choës* ceremony, which may have marked the end of infancy. As with the Apatouria, it is uncertain whether girls were also included. Each child who was *choïkos* was presented with a small pitcher *or chous* (see Fig. 13), from which the ceremony takes its name, and tasted therein his first drops of wine.

The importance of this ceremony perhaps lay primarily in the fact that wine was the gift of Dionysos. A child's first sip might therefore have established a covenant between the child and the god. Part of the reason for delaying a child's enrolment into the cult of a major state deity until his fourth year may have had to do with the fact that this period coincides with a decreased susceptibility to fatal diseases. To have introduced an infant to Dionysos any earlier might therefore have been considered an affront.

The *Choës* ceremony was almost certainly confined to Attica. Since it marked a child's first encounter with one of the state's major tutelary deities as well as the first encounter with its entire year-group or *hêlikia*, it laid the foundation stone for the development of a civic as opposed to merely intrafamilial persona. In a broadly social sense it thus marked the first stage in the child's passage towards incorporation within the full community.

Paidagôgoi

Both Xenophon (*Lak. Pol.* 2.1) and Plutarch (*Mor.* 439f = *Can Virtue be Taught?* 1) recommended that the services of a *paidagôgos* or child-attendant should be engaged as soon as the weaning period was over and the infant was able to comprehend speech. In words that closely echo the Pythagorean description of the ideal wet-nurse (see above, p. 115),

Fig. 10. Attic red-figure *pelikê* depicting a child receiving first lessons in walking, *c.* 440-420 BC. The scene is probably set in the *gunaikeion*. The elderly man leaning on a stick is either the child's father or its *paidagôgos*.

Plutarch (*Mor.* 3f-4b) states that the ideal *paidagôgos* should be of serious disposition, trustworthy, reliable, Greek and articulate, on the grounds that 'if you live with a lame man, you learn to limp'. Plutarch is highly critical of the current calibre of *paidagôgoi*, complaining that it is common practice to assign the delicate task of looking after the young to slaves who are drunk, greedy and idle. As their name suggests, one of the primary functions of *paidagôgoi* was to accompany their young masters outside the home. But they were also expected in some cases to have a formative influence upon their future career. The tomb of Konnidas, the *paidagôgos* of Theseus, was honoured by the Athenians as late as the second century AD with the sacrifice of a ram on the day before the *Theseia* or festival in honour of Theseus (Plu. *Thes.* 4). The personal trust invested in a *paidagôgos* could even determine the outcome of a war. Herodotos relates (8.75; cf. Plu. *Them.* 12.4) how Sikinnos, the *paidagôgos* of Themistokles' children, acting under instructions from his master, bore a message to the Persians before the battle of Salamis which was largely responsible for the subsequent Greek victory. Though mainly associated with boys, *paidagôgoi* were occasionally assigned to girls (cf. Euripides' *Iôn* and *Phoin.*).

Toys, games and pets

From finds in graves and representations on vases we know that favourite children's toys included rocking horses, hoops,

Fig. 11. Terracotta rattle in the shape of a pig, third or second century BC. From Cyprus.

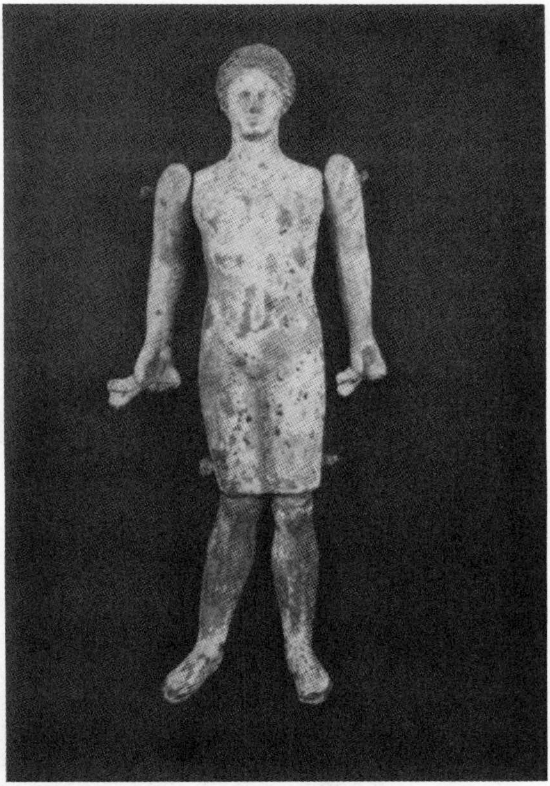

Fig. 12. Terracotta *neurospaston* or doll with movable limbs.

miniature carts, spinning tops, rattles, models of horses on wheels and boats, and dolls with jointed, movable limbs known as *neurospasta* (cf. Xen. *Symp*. 4.55; Fig. 12). Though there might have been one or two stalls in a Greek agora which specialised in models made out of terrracotta or wood, the majority of toys were probably made in the home, as is indicated by the following passage from Aristophanes' *Clouds* (ll. 877-81) in which a father boasts of his son's inventiveness:

> Oh, he's clever all right. When he was a little boy (*paidarion*) just so high, he made houses out of clay, and wooden boats, and chariots from bits of leather, and he carved pomegranates into the shape of little frogs – you just can't imagine how bright he was!

Evidence about children's games derives almost entirely from late lexicographical sources, notably Eustathios, Hesychios, Pollux and the Souda. There can be little doubt,

Fig. 13. Attic red-figure *chous* by the Shuvalov Painter depicting children playing the game of *ephedrismos*, a variant on 'piggy-back', *c*. 425 BC.

however, that the games which they describe are of very great antiquity. The conservatism of children's games throughout history is proved by a version of 'heads or tails' called *ostrakinda* or potsherd which is still played in parts of Europe today (Poll. *Onomast*. 9.111; cf. Sprague 1984, 283; Opie 1969, 101). The potsherd is smeared on one side with pitch and then tossed in the air by two teams of children, one called Night, the other Day. If it lands on the black side the Nights chase the Days, whereas if it lands on the white side the Days chase the Nights. Knucklebones or *astralagoi* were also extremely popular, both among adults and children. A game known as the bronze fly (*chalkê muia*) seems to have resembled blindman's buff. A blindfolded child tries to catch one of his playmates, saying as he does so: 'I am going to hunt a bronze fly.' His playmates circle around him, strike him with their hands or with bits of papyrus, and chant: 'You'll hunt but you won't catch anything' (Poll. *Onomast.* 9.123). A game called cooking pot (*chutrinda*) requires the child who has been designated the pot to sit in the middle while his playmates circle around him, taunting him and hitting him. When the *chutrinda* succeeds in touching one of his fellows with his foot, the boy who is caught has to take his place. Finally, in *ephedrismos*, a variant upon piggy-back (see Fig. 13), players aim an object at a stone target called a *dioros*. The child whose shot lands furthest from the mark is made to grope towards the *dioros* with his eyes blindfolded carrying one of the players on his back (Poll. *Onomast.* 9.119).

Popular pets for smaller children included birds, dogs, geese, cocks, hares, goats and monkeys (cf. Beck 1975, ch. 8 for illustrations). Among well-to-do youths tame panthers or cheetahs were *à la mode* (cf. Ashmead 1978, 38-47).

Children's play receives prominent attention in Plato who saw it as fulfilling a major role in the moulding of human personality and the developing of individual talent. He recommended that a child who is to become a farmer or a builder should play at farming or building and be given miniature tools by his *paidagôgos* so that he can gain an early apprenticeship in his profession (*Laws* 1.643bc). Plato further maintained that children who 'play the same games with the same rules and under the same conditions and take pleasure in the same toys' grow up to be tractable and quiescent (*Laws* 7.797ab). He was evidently unaware of their inherent conservatism.

Modes of child-rearing

The kind of treatment which parents mete out to their children inevitably reflects the kind of view which society as a whole takes of the child's innate, basic nature (cf. Stone 1977, 254f.). Adherents to the theory that man is born with the condition of Original Sin, for instance, maintain that the only way to discipline a child is by subjugating it and breaking its will. The dominant perception in the Greek world seems to have been that children and young people are innately deficient in intelligence and commonsense. The specific corollary to this theory was that the brain grows (or at least should grow) with

Fig. 14. Statue of a toddler holding a small dog. Roman copy of a hellenistic Greek original found in Turkey.

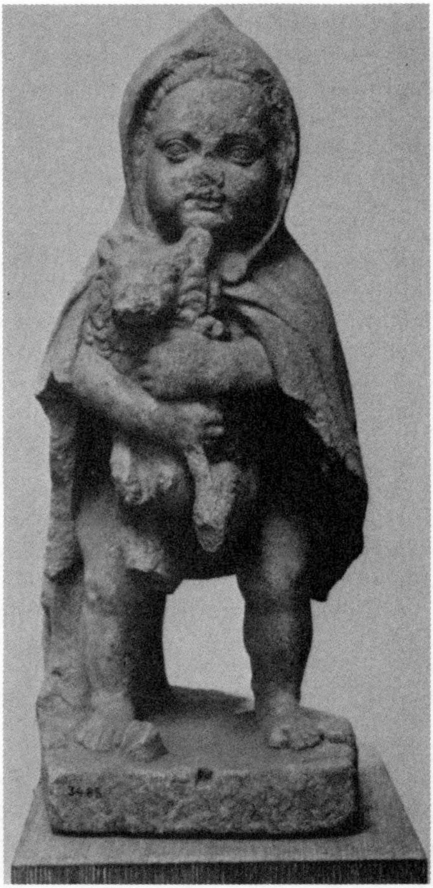

the body. In Homer *nêpios*, which means 'infant' or 'child', is regularly applied to adults who act without proper forethought, are careless, or simply plain ignorant of the facts of life (e.g. *Il.* 16.46, 22.445; *Od.* 9.44, 13.237). 'They're such utter *nêpioi*,' runs a Greek proverb, 'that they don't know that a half is better than a whole. For when someone wants more, he loses what he has' (*CPG* I, p. 437.7). In Plutarch's *Theseus* (8.2) Perigoune, the daughter of the bandit Sinis, is mocked for her childish stupidity which prompts her to supplicate wild asparagus and other plants in order to escape the clutches of her father's murderer Theseus. Young people who do not expect to grow old and die are ridiculed by Simonides (fr. 8.8-12 *IEG*) for being *nêpioi* or infantile. Disrespect for the intellectual capacity of the child is persistent and widespread in Greek literature, linked closely to the belief that intelligence is a function of age.

Other theories also prevailed in ancient Greece. Herodotos' account of the upbringing of the Persian prince Kyros affords a classic demonstration of the belief that a child's personality is wholly determined by heredity. Kyros was allegedly brought up in a simple peasant's cottage in complete ignorance of his royal parentage (see above, p. 90). This fact notwithstanding, he exhibited a proud and masterful disposition, as was revealed at the age of ten when he was chosen by his companions to act the part of king in a game of make-believe (Hdt. 1.114-15). When the son of a distinguished Mede refused to carry out his orders Kyros had him savagely beaten with a whip, thereby revealing his kingly origins along with his authoritarian nature. (What this implausible anecdote fails to reveal is how the son of an aristocrat happened to be playing with a mere peasant boy in the first place.)

There is evidence that in late fifth-century Athens parental discipline was perceived as being extremely lax. In Aristophanes' *Clouds* (ll. 39-80) the audience is clearly intended to sympathise with the elderly Strepsiades when he complains that his wife is ruining him by indulging his son's taste for expensive horses. Though part of the humour lies in the fact that Strepsiades, a thrifty peasant, is married to a gadabout from the big city, he none the less stands for decency, common sense and traditional values. The interest and involvement which he displays in the ethical content of his son's upbringing and education also represents a kind of ideal, one which, as the action of the play seems intended to imply, has lamentably passed out of fashion in Classical Athens.

The evil consequences of failing to instil a proper sense of discipline in one's child are forcibly underlined in Plato's cautionary observations about the treatment which Kyros' sons received from the women of the royal household in the absence of their father who entirely neglected their upbringing (*Laws* 3.694cd). These women 'would allow no one to cross such vastly superior beings in anything' but instead 'required everyone to commend all their sayings and doings' – with the inevitable result that the little princes grew up to be spoilt brats. Plato adds that the Spartan system of child-rearing was, by contrast with the Persian system, commendably egalitarian, for it meted out exactly the same treatment to royals as to commoners.

Plato was of the opinion that a child is born with a propensity towards neither good nor evil but is moulded wholly by experience. For that reason firm discipline is of the essence. In the *Laws* (7.808de) he writes:

> Of all wild creatures a *pais* is the most difficult to keep in check. Because he more than any other has a well of wisdom inside him which is still uncurbed, he is a crafty, mischievous, and most insolent beast. So he must be held in check, so to speak, by several bridles – first, when he is out of his mother's and nurse's charge, by *paidagôgoi* to care for his childish helplessness (*paidias kai nêpiotêtos charin*), and then secondly by all the masters who teach him all kinds of subjects, as befits a freeborn man. But further chastisement, as befits a slave, shall be inflicted both on the boy and on his *paidagôgos* and teacher as well, by any free person in whose presence he commits any fault.

Plato further maintained that the tenor and quality of a political system decisively influences children's attitude towards their parents. He observes in the *Republic* (8.562d-563c), for instance, that when anarchy replaces obedience to the law in a democracy, before long it begins to infiltrate private households as well with the result that sons no longer feel a sense of shame or fear towards their parents; to make matter worse, *gerontes* start to imitate *neoi* for fear of being thought loathsome and despotic – all of which is as deplorable in his view as slaves having as much liberty as their masters and women enjoying equal rights with men.

The vital importance of upbringing is nowhere more passionately defended than in the *Laws* (6.766a) where Plato states:

> Now man, we may say, is a gentle creature, but though he is likely to turn out most godlike and gentle if he has the right nature and gets the right education, if he is badly or inadequately trained, he is the most savage beast on earth.

Plato was what we would term today an environmentalist. He subscribed to the theory that a child is essentially a *tabula rasa*, neither good nor bad by nature and dependent for development solely upon upbringing. So, too, it seems, did Sokrates, who is credited with the statement that the most gifted individuals are capable of becoming excellent and useful if properly disciplined, but evil and depraved if left to their own devices (Xen. *Mem.* 4.1.4). Anticipating the modern theory which maintains that the earliest years of a child's life are decisive for character development, Plato argued that every effort should be made to keep infants from experiencing either distress, anxiety or pain until they are three years old (*Laws*

7.791b-792b). He also judged it to be important to monitor the kind of stories which nurses and mothers tell their children (*Rep.* 2.376e-378e). The ones which describe acts of violence perpetrated either by children against their parents or by parents against their children are the most likely to inculcate the wrong values. Eminently unsuitable, therefore, is the story of the castration of Ouranos by his son Kronos, and of the maiming of Hephaistos by his father Zeus.

Plato's strictures notwithstanding, it seems to have been common practice to instil discipline into temperamental or disobedient infants by terrorising them with tales of fiendish monsters or *mormolukeia* such as Mormo, Lamia, Gorgo and Empousa. In Theokritos' *Idyll* 15, Praxinoa, who is clearly intended to represent a very average Alexandrian housewife and mother, threatens her child with the bogey Mormo – described by the poetess Erinna (*Select Papyri* 3.120 in *LCL*) as a creature with large ears that walks on all fours and changes face – in order to quell its temper tantrums at being left at home with its nurse. Corporal punishment, too, was accepted as a proper way of instilling discipline in the growing child, though it was undoubtedly applied more savagely in Sparta than in Athens. We hear of no objections to the practice anywhere in the ancient world before Quintilian who wrote in the first century AD.

Environmentalism was undoubtedly the educational philosophy which prevailed in Sparta. Plutarch reports that in order to prove to his people the overriding importance of education in promoting excellence, the lawgiver Lykourgos separated two puppies which had been born in the same litter and reared them in totally different ways (*Mor.* 3ab = *Education of Children* 4; cf. 225f-226a). One puppy was trained to be greedy and ill-disciplined, the other to hunt. One day Lykourgos placed a bowl of food and a hare in front of both animals. The greedy puppy rushed to the bowl, whereas the well-trained one ran after the hare. Though this demonstration of the powers of environmentalism was lost on the dull-witted Spartans, it underlined and justified the whole tendency of the Lykourgan education system by proving, as Plutarch commented, that 'Training is more effective than nature for the good'.

The purpose, value and effectiveness of education were keenly debated in Athens from the second half of the fifth century onwards, due in no small measure to the activities of the sophists who purported to be able to teach *aretê*, a term which came to comprise the qualities that enabled a young man to succeed in Athenian society. Faith in the teachability of *aretê* was in fact the hallmark of the sophists' profession since their justification for charging fees for their services rested precisely on this claim. As Antiphon the Sophist confidently asserted (*DK* 87 B 60):

> In my opinion, education is of the highest priority among human activities. For if anyone starts any kind of project correctly, it is likely that he will end it correctly too. However one sows the seed in the ground, so one can expect to reap. And whenever one sows a noble education in a young body, this education lives and flourishes through the whole of his life, and neither rain nor drought carries it off.

The teachability of virtue is addressed on a number of occasions in the dialogues of Plato, notably in *Meno* and *Protagoras*. In *Protagoras* it takes the form of the question: 'Why do many sons of good fathers turn out to be of poor quality?' (326e). In conformity with the doctrine which he maintained elsewhere, Protagoras replies that everything is relative. Let us suppose, he says, that we lived in a community whose existence depended on everyone having to learn how to play a flute. Is it not the case that all the members of that society would be reasonably proficient in the art compared with children who grow up in societies where this skill is not deemed essential? So it is in Athens with regard to virtue. Everyone, and not merely the child's father, is actually teaching virtue constantly, with the result that everybody possesses it in some degree. Thus, even if the worst Athenian criminals were to be set beside the products of those communities where virtue was not of the utmost importance, they would appear to be paragons of excellence. It is hardly surprising, Protagoras concludes, in view of the numbers of instructors available in Athens, if the sons of good parents often turn out to be mediocre, while those born of mediocre parents turn out to be good.

This kind of reasoning easily leads to the conclusion that bringing up a child is anything but an exact science, and that even if the soundest educational principles are inculcated, there is no guarantee that one's offspring will grow up disciplined, virtuous and law-abiding. One of the most cynical observers of the pitfalls of parenthood was Protagoras' contemporary Demokritos of Abdera, who wrote (*DK* 68 B 276):

> I do not think one should have children. I perceive that in the possession of chidren there are many great dangers and many griefs, whereas there is only a weak and sickly crop of those that are well-suckled.

Acknowledging the deep psychological need for children, however, Demokritos conceded that anyone who wants a child should adopt one from a friend, rather than beget it himself, since then 'he will be able to select the kind of *pais* that he wants' (B 277). It is not known whether Demokritos sought to apply his philosophical principles to his own life.

Athenian education

There were two schools of thought in the Greek world as to whether the education of children should be left to the initiative of parents or provided by the state. In Athens, where the former doctrine prevailed, parents were expected to take full responsibility for the upbringing of their children until they reached their eighteenth year. Just how much education the average Athenian child received as a result of this *laissez-faire* policy is difficult to assess since we know very little about Athenian schools other than the kind of courses which they taught. Complaints by philosophers about the indifference of Athenian parents to their children's education need not be taken very seriously, however, since the complexity of Athenian society from the mid-fifth century BC onwards makes it certain that the majority of adult males were expected and required to be literate in order to discharge their state duties. As Aristophanes makes clear, even such a humble person as a sausage-seller knew how to read and write, though he would not have been educated in music (*Knights* 188-9). Though privately run, schools were subject to a strict code of practice. Schools, gymnasia and *palaistrai* were not permitted to open before dawn, and had to close by sunset. Children's age of admission and size of classes were also prescribed by law (Aischin. 1.10). It was also the case that an Athenian was exposed to a programme of indoctrination 'from the *ephêbeia* to the meetings of the assembly in which the citizen underwent his political apprenticeship, and in the ceremonies [Panathenaia, Dionysia or public funerals], intended to instil official values' (Loraux 1986, 145); and, we might add, from much earlier in his life, too, in ways that we can hardly detect.

Our first evidence for schools in the Greek world does not antedate the opening decades of the fifth century. Prior to that education would almost exclusively have been in the hands of private tutors. But even in the Classical era many Athenians were probably taught on a one-to-one basis, since little schooling can have been available in the country demes of Attica. The speaker in Lysias (20.11) states proudly that his own father received his education in Athens itself, in contrast to the oligarchic Phrynichos who, being a poor man, grew up looking after sheep in the countryside.

Until the age of six boys as well as girls probably spent most of their time confined to the *gunaikeion* where they would have been almost exclusively in the company of women. Aristotle (*Pol.* 7.1336a 23-34), who certainly had Athenian children partly in mind, recommended that they should not take any course of study nor be subjected to physical exertion. Instead they should receive plenty of exercise and be encouraged to play games, particularly those which are 'imitations of the serious pursuits of later life'. Contrary to Plato (*Laws* 7.792a), he was firmly of the opinion that little children should be allowed to cry if they wanted to, on the grounds that 'crying contributes to growth, since it serves in a way as exercise for the body' (*Pol.* 7.1336a34-9). Aristotle also urged that children should have as little as possible to do with slaves lest by consorting with baseborn persons they acquire a 'slavish' disposition.

Both Aristotle (*Pol.* 7.1336a41-1336b1) and the author of a spurious Platonic work entitled *Axiochos* (361d) recommended that formal education should begin around the age of six. Their views were probably based partly on Spartan educational practice (see below) and it may well have been the case that the majority of Athenian parents sent their boys to school when they were somewhat older. Primary education in the Classical period was essentially threefold. Its most important element was the teaching of letters or *grammata* by a *grammatistês* or 'letter-teacher'. This entailed learning how to read and write, and in addition committing to heart the works of Homer and other edifying poets (cf. Xen. *Symp.* 3.5). The second part of the curriculum was music, in particular learning to play the lyre or *kithara* while singing in accompaniment, a skill which was taught by a *kitharistês*. The lyre was judged to be such an essential part of a well-rounded Athenian education that in Aristophanes' *Wasps* the hero Bdelykleon says (l. 959) of the

Fig. 15. The music lesson. Attic red-figure *kylix*, first quarter of the fifth century BC. The bearded man in the centre is coaching a young boy in the recitation of epic verse from a tablet or scroll. To his right a seated *paidagôgos* watches. On the left another bearded teacher gives lessons in the *kithara* or lyre.

dog Labes: 'If he has filched anything, forgive him. He never learned how to play the lyre.' The remark, which presupposes a direct link between music and 'breeding', is evidently intended to imply that the canine is completely uncultivated. Athletic training, which was supervised by a *paidotribês* or boy-trainer, constituted the third part of the curriculum.

Boys probably left school around the age of fourteen, though as Protagoras asserts in Plato's dialogue of that name (326c) it was certainly the case then as now that: 'The sons of the richest men go to school earliest and leave latest.' While the sons of poor parents would have been put to work at fourteen, if not earlier, those from a well-to-do background seem to have enjoyed considerable freedom until they reached seventeen or so when they became liable for ephebic service. In Plato's *Laches* (179a) Lysimachos states that most Athenian parents 'allow their sons to do exactly what they like once they become lads (*meirakia*)'.

Sokrates in Xenophon's *Memorabilia* (1.5.2) implies that the three chief preoccupations facing a head of household are his son's education, his daughter's virginity and his *oikos*'s prosperity. This telling equation reveals that Athenian girls received nothing in the way of formal education. What they learned came to them impromptu. The heroine Lysistrate in Aristophanes' play of that name states candidly (ll. 1124-7): 'I'm a woman but I've got some intelligence .... Since I've often heard what my father and elderly persons (*geraiteroi*) say, I'm not completely uncultured (*ou memousômai kakôs*).' In a discursus on Athenian prehistory Herodotos (6.137.3) asserts that 'in olden days', i.e. in an age of ideal self-sufficiency, when neither the Athenians nor anyone else had slaves, menial tasks, such as fetching water from the communal well, were performed by the daughters of the household. It is questionable whether girls were better treated in historical times. Many must have been illiterate when they married and some husbands at least believed that it was safer that they should remain so all their lives. A fragment from a comedy by Menander reads: 'He who teaches letters to his wife does no good. He's giving additional poison to a horrible snake' (*CAF* III, p. 201.702). In light of this discussion, it may be no accident that the only female intellectual known to have lived in Athens during the Classical era was the foreigner Aspasia, the mistress of Perikles.

While Solon prescribed that an Athenian father must teach his son a skill in order to entitle himself to support from him in old age (Plu. *Sol*. 22), he did not require the father to provide him with a general education. The fact that Plato (*Laws* 7.804d) envisaged a system whereby all *paides* 'must, as far as possible, be compelled to receive education, inasmuch as they are *paides* of the state more than *paides* of their parents' further suggests that the Athenian state did not in practice regard it as its right or obligation to intervene in this matter. Aristotle (*Pol*. 8.1337a14ff.), again in opposition to contemporary Athenian practice, also argued that education should be one and the same for all and that the supervision of it should be public and not private. We must understand, however, that such lofty sentiments do not amount to a plea for equal educational opportunities for all, since both these philosophers excluded not only women but also the working classes from citizenship in their ideal states – traders and craftsmen in the case of Plato (*Laws* 5.741e; 8.846d-847a) and mechanics in the case of Aristotle (*Pol*. 3.1278a8).

Spartan education

Virtually from the moment they emerged from the womb Spartan infants of both sexes were treated in a way that was intended to ensure that they did not become cry-babies, as Plutarch approvingly tells us (*Lyk*. 16.3):

> In regard to child-rearing the Spartans combined care with skill. They did not place their children in swaddling bands, but let their limbs and bodies develop freely. They taught them to be peaceful, to avoid faddiness in their diet, to be fearless of the dark or of being left alone, not to sulk – a sign of low-breeding – and not to throw temper-tantrums.

At the age of about six Spartan boys left the home and entered the public educational system called the *agôgê* or 'guidance' whose purpose was to produce a well-drilled military machine composed of soldiers who were 'obedient to the word of command, capable of enduring hardship and victorious in battle' (Plu. *Lyk*. 16.6). Each boy was assigned to a herd or *agela* where he lived communally with other boys. Under this system literacy was not a high priority, boys being taught only 'what was enough to get by with (*heneka tês chreias*)'. *Paides* were also divided into age-classes known as *bouai*, each age-class having its own *bouagos* or 'oxen-leader'. The Spartan system thus sought to reinforce both tribal affiliation and peer-group bonding, at the expense, as has frequently been observed, of the development of close family ties. Yet despite the limited role which Spartan parents took in the upbringing of their sons, they were none the less responsible for instilling discipline in them, as is indicated by a brief anecdote told by Plutarch (*Mor*. 233f) of a father who was punished for allowing his two sons to quarrel together.

Entry to the *agôgê* was not restricted to the sons of Spartiates. A group called the *mothakes* or *mothônes* also entered the military training programme, even though they were not necessarily of Spartan descent. Phylarchos (*FGrH* 81 F 43 ap. Ath. *Deipn*. 6.271ef), an Athenian historian who lived in the third century BC, writes:

> The *mothakes* are *suntrophoi* or foster-brothers of the Spartans. Each of the citizen *paides* ... makes one, two or more his *suntrophos*. The *mothakes* are free but not Spartiates and they share in all their *paideia* or education.

Those eligible for inclusion under this heading were the sons of foreigners, the sons of Spartiate fathers and non-Spartiate mothers, and the sons of Spartiates who had lost their citizen status.

The next milestone in a Spartan boy's life occurred when he reached eleven. This was marked by an increase in the austerity of the training programme. Plutarch (*Lyk.* 16.6) writes:

> They no longer had a tunic, received one cloak a year, had hardened skin, and took very few baths and used practically no ointments, except on a few prescribed days of the year. They slept together according to platoon and herd (*kat' ilên kai agelên*) on pallet beds made of rushes which they plucked with their bare hands from the River Eurotas – no knives were allowed. In winter they added so-called lycophon or thistle-down to their beds, since this was thought to provide warmth.

Paides now 'lived with' or else 'were closely associated with' a lover or *erastês*; the verb *sunanestrephonto* which Plutarch uses here is perhaps intentionally ambiguous. The duty of the *erastês*, we are told, was 'to admonish and punish him [i.e. the *pais*]'. Xenophon (*Lak. Pol.* 2.13), who like Plutarch greatly admired the Spartan system and alludes to the same custom, is careful to point out that it was Lykourgos' intention and expectation that the *erastês* in question should be 'enamoured of the boy's soul (*agastheis psuchên paidos*)' and not 'desirous of the boy's body (*paidos sômatos oregomenos*)', and that if improper feelings were suspected they were condemned. Xenophon concludes by stating: 'The behaviour of *erastai* towards their *paidika* is as wholesome with respect to sexual feeling as is that of parents towards *paides* or brothers towards brothers.' On the basis of these two accounts it is entirely uncertain whether pederasty was actually 'institutionalised' in Sparta as is often claimed or whether there merely existed public acknowledgment and acceptance of the fact that the practice was extremely widespread.

Spartan girls also received formal education. Although it remains uncertain whether they underwent a course of training comparable to the *agôgê*, the evidence is sufficient to indicate that an attempt was made 'to maintain some form or degree of parity between the sexes' (Cartledge 1981, 93; cf. Nilsson 1908, 308-40). In addition, there were a number of

Spartan women who claimed to be learned and cultivated (cf. Pl. *Prot*. 342d).

Sparta was not the only Dorian community to favour state-sponsored education. A system similar to the *agôgê* operated on Crete where, according to the fourth-century BC historian Ephoros, boys when very young were taken to the public messes (*sussitia* or *andreia*) where they 'sit on the ground and eat together wearing shabby clothes, the same in winter as in summer, and wait on one another as well as on the men'. At a later age they were required 'to learn their letters and also the songs prescribed by the laws and certain types of music' (*FGrH* 70 F 149 ap. Str. 10.4.19).

Apprenticeship and child employment

We might suppose that Solon's stipulation that an Athenian father should teach his son a trade would have encouraged the use of child labour in Athens. There is, however, very little evidence to prove that this was actually the case. In fact virtually nothing is known about apprenticeship at all. In Sparta, however, as Herodotos (6.60) informs us, a number of professions were reserved in certain families. These included that of herald, flute-player and cook, whose expertise was passed down from father to son through successive generations.

Pederasty

The cultural acceptance of pederasty in Archaic Greece is demonstrated by the fact that Zeus himself was a pederast. The myth of his abduction of the beautiful youth called Ganymede was frequently depicted in art (see Fig. 16) and is alluded to by Pindar in *Olympian* 1 (ll. 44ff.), where it is given the status of a sodomites' foundation charter. So, too, Athenaios (*Deipn*. 10.424e) reports that 'in the old days' *paides* from the best families served as wine-pourers, by which he evidently means in the days before pederasty fell into disrepute. Although an increasingly hostile attitude towards this practice did evolve in Greece over the course of time, notably in Athens, the precise nature of the change is difficult to track down, owing to the flexible usage of the word *pais*, which could denote a passive homosexual of any age. In Classical Athens pederasty was an extremely serious crime,

Fig. 16. Divine pederasty. Terracotta statue from Olympia depicting Zeus abducting Ganymede, ostensibly to be his cup-bearer on Olympos, *c*. 470 BC. Ganymede holds a cock, a common love-gift among the Greeks. The statue originally crowned the pediment of a small temple or shrine, indicating broad acceptance, even approval, of Zeus' act.

punishable in certain circumstances by death. Thus to enter a classroom while pupils were present, except in the presence of a close relative, was a capital offence (Aischin. 1.12). Indecent assault against either a freeborn *pais* or a minor would also result in execution (1.16).

Representations of childhood in biography

Our modern belief that childhood experiences are formative in the development of the adult personality had no ancient equivalent, as is indicated by the relative unimportance attached to the pre-adult phase of life in ancient biographies. The majority of Plutarch's *Lives*, for instance, which include biographies of both historical and legendary figures, confine themselves to a description of their subject's life from the moment when he – it is invariably he – first appears on the public stage. While it can be objected that information about a person's childhood is intrinsically more difficult to obtain than that which relates to his adult life, this by itself hardly serves as an adequate explanation. The truth is that the Greeks did not perceive childhood as being coloured with highly individualised and individuating experiences in the way that we do today. Only in those cases where a man's personality or career was judged to be abnormal or bizarre to an extreme degree does there seem to have been any inclination to seek out some sort of explanation in his early years. Even then, however, the explanation is never provided in terms of unusual upbringing, eccentric parents or traumatic childhood experiences but simply in terms of the child's extraordinary precocity. What the biographical genre would therefore have us understand is that the truly unique and exceptional individual is such by virtue of the fact that he was a truly unique and exceptional child – and this of course explains nothing.

Let us take Plutarch's *Life of Themistokles*, a document which happens to be unusually detailed about its subject's early years. We are informed (2.1) that Themistokles 'did not play or idle away his time like the other *paides*', but instead composed speeches and practised delivering them to himself. Plutarch then goes on to say (2.2):

> In his education he applied himself diffidently and reluctantly to subjects which were intended to be character-forming, recreational or diverting, but paid close attention to those which were said to promote intelligence or those which related to

practical affairs, having confidence in his own innate ability (*phusis*).

In other words what Plutarch is telling us is that at a very early age Themistokles already had his sights set wholly upon the adult world and had no time for child-oriented pursuits. Further evidence of Themistokles' precocity is indicated by his boasting that although he never learned how to tune a lyre or play a harp, he knew how to take control of a *polis* that was small and insignificant and convert it into one that was great and famous. As is frequently the case in ancient biographical writings, the identity of his teachers was a matter of scholarly debate: Stesimbrotos of Thasos maintained that Themistokles was a pupil of Anaxagoras and Melissos the physicist, whereas Plutarch himself asserts that he studied under Mnesiphilos of Phrearrys. Commenting further upon his early behaviour, Plutarch alleges (2.5) that 'Under the impress of early youth (*en ... tais prôtais tês neotêtos hormais*) he was erratic and unbalanced', and adds that Themistokles 'admitted as much himself in later life by saying that the wildest colts, provided that they get proper instruction (*paideia*) and training (*katartusis*), make the best horses'. Plutarch dismisses (2.6-7) as fabrications the claims made by certain unnamed writers that Themistokles' father disinherited him by the procedure known as *apokêruxis* (see p. 182) and that his mother committed suicide because of her son's disgrace. Yet he repeats uncritically an apocryphal conversation which Themistokles had with his father in which the latter endeavoured to deter his son from going into politics by comparing some triremes that lay rotting on the seashore with the thankless way Athenians cast aside politicians once they have outlived their usefulness.

The same emphasis upon precocity is evident in Plutarch's *Life of Alkibiades* where it is stated (2.1) that Alkibiades' contentiousness and desire to be first are revealed in anecdotes relating to his childhood (*ta paidika apomnêmoneumata*). Once during a wrestling match Alkibiades is said to have bitten his opponent's arm in order to prevent himself from suffering a fall. When the other accused him of biting like a child, Alkibiades replied, 'No, like a lion' (2.2). On another occasion he risked his life by throwing himself in front of a loaded waggon merely to prevent it from rolling over his dice (2.2-3). Like Themistokles, Alkibiades had no interest in learning a

Fig. 17. Attic grave-relief commemorating Xanthippos, *c.* 430 BC. The deceased, who is holding a model of a foot, was probably a shoemaker by trade. He is attended by his two daughters, who are portrayed as miniature adults instead of with the proper proportions of childhood.

musical instrument. We are told that his contempt for those who practised the flute was so vehement that the instrument fell into utter disfavour and dropped out of the syllabus of a liberal arts education (2.4-6).

Representations of children in Greek art

Until the late fifth century artists invariably depicted children as miniature adults with heads disproportionately small for their bodies (see Fig. 17). From this period onwards, however, an attempt is made to represent them with the characteristics of their age, notably on red-figured *choës* and white-ground *lêkythoi* or oil-flasks designed exclusively for funerary use, and on grave monuments which commemorate the deaths of young children. Notable examples in this last category include the grave monument of Ampharete and her grandchild dated *c.* 410, one of the earliest successful renderings of a baby in Greek art (Fig. 30); and that of Mnesagora and her little brother Nikochares dated *c.* 430, which depicts a delightfully podgy infant straining upwards to reach a bird. Children now become a focus of artistic interest in their own right, whereas previously they had merely functioned as an appendage (cf. Zahn 1970, 23-5). An interest in child portraiture is also evident from the fourth century onwards, notably in the series of girls' heads from Brauron (see Fig. 24). It is difficult to determine, however, whether these developments argue an increased interest in children for their own sake or whether they merely reflect increased technical mastery in the pictorial and sculptural arts.

The role of children in religion

Children played a variety of significant roles in Greek religion. At the most mundane level they worked as temple servants, probably under the direction of a sacristan or *zakoros* who was responsible for the orderliness and upkeep of the sanctuary. Choirs of children were prominent in religious celebrations and devotions. Ten choruses of fifty boys apiece representing each of the ten Attic tribes competed in the performing of dithyrambic choruses at the City Dionysia and five choruses competed at the Thargelia (Ps.-Arist. *AP* 56.3). On the day of the *Koureôtis* children divided into their respective tribes and chanted poetry, including the works of the lawgiver Solon (Pl.

Tim. 21b; see below, p. 179). In certain cults children served as priests. At both Patrai and Aigeira the priestess of Artemis had to be a *parthenos* below marriageable years (Paus. 7.19.1 and 7.26.5). At Aigion the priest of Zeus was originally chosen from 'among the boys who won the beauty contest'; as soon as the incumbent began to sprout a beard the honour was conferred on another boy (Paus. 7.24.4). A boy or girl known as a *pais aph' hestias* or hearth-child, who functioned as an intermediary between those undergoing initiation and the divine (*to theion*), was elected annually by allotment to be initiated at public expense into the Eleusinian Mysteries (Porph. *Abst.* 4.5). Finally, children were included whenever the family held religious ceremonies inside the home, as is demonstrated by their frequent portrayal in vase scenes of the *prothesis* or laying out of the dead (cf. Zahn 1970, 22).

Why were children prominent in Greek religion? The most obvious explanation is that they symbolise purity. Ritual purity or *hosiotês* certainly seems to have been a requirement of temple service. In Euripides' *Ion* (l. 150) the youthful Ion, while performing his daily tasks in the sanctuary of Apollo at Delphi, boasts that he is 'unsullied by sexual intercourse (*hosios ap' eunas ôn*)'. Sexual abstinence does not seem to have played a particularly vital part in Greek religion, however, and it can be argued that Ion's pride in his own virginity was somewhat unusual or that he was interpreting *hosiotês* somewhat eccentrically. Another possible reason for their prominence is that children have been minimally polluted through contact with the dead. They therefore constitute less of a threat to the sanctity of the Olympian deities, who are required to shield themselves completely from all taint of physical corruption (e.g. Eur. *Hipp.* 1437f.; cf. Garland 1985, 18 and 44). Absence of close contact with the dead would explain the religious significance that attached to *paides amphithaleis* – children whose parents were still alive (cf. Poll. *Onomast.* 3.25). It was *amphithaleis*, for instance, who cut branches from the sacred olive trees out of which wreaths were fashioned for athletic victors at Olympia; who at the festival known as Pyanepsia carried the *eiresionê*, a bough wreathed with wool and laden with objects that symbolised fruitfulness; and who at weddings wore crowns made of thistles and oak leaves and carried a winnowing basket full of bread. The literal meaning of *amphithalês* is 'blooming on both sides', and we may speculate that such children were selected for such

Fig. 18. Hellenistic bronze statue of a jockey boy, third or second century BC.

sensitive functions not only because they were as yet touched by the taint of pollution, but also because they embodied the fruitfulness, increase and promise of renewal, which the duties they performed were intended to secure. In addition, a child who had both parents still alive was probably regarded as being specially marked out and endowed with divine favour, thereby making him the natural choice as a vehicle of communication between man and the gods (cf. Stengel s.v. *amphithaleis* in *RE* I.2 [1894] col. 1958).

Child heroes were venerated throughout Greece and often credited with awesome powers, possibly in the belief that those who died *aôroi*, i.e. before their allotted span of years had been fulfilled, constituted a category of the unhappy and vengeful dead and were thus appropriate deliverers of curse-tablets to the chthonic gods (cf. Garland 1985, 6 and 86). Pausanias (6.20.3-5) tells the peculiar story of the Elean Sosipolis (Polis-saviour), a baby-hero who was awarded this title because he helped the Eleans when they came under attack from the Arkadians. In response to a dream, his mother brought her infant to the Elean high command with the suggestion that it should fight on their behalf. The generals placed Sosipolis naked at the head of their army. When the Arkadians advanced he turned into a snake and routed the enemy. Since Sosipolis was worshipped as a baby he may have died in infancy. Other child-heroes include the offspring of Kondylea, who were stoned to death for pretending to strangle an image of Artemis and subsequently venerated by order of Delphi (Paus. 8.23.6-7); and the offspring of Medea, who were also stoned to death because of the deadly bridal gifts which they brought to their father's second wife, but later awarded yearly sacrifices, again by command of an oracle, in order to deter them from committing infanticide (2.3.6-7).

Mothers and fathers

In societies which experience a high level of infant or child mortality it is generally assumed that the degree of affect between parents and children is appreciably lower than in those where deaths of young persons are comparatively rare. Pomeroy (1975, 101), for instance, claims: 'The natural mortality of young children would seem to discourage the formation of strong mother-child bonds.' In support of her statement Pomeroy quotes a celebrated remark by Antigone to the effect that while she is willing to lay down her life for her brother Polyneikes, she would not be prepared to make the same sacrifice on behalf of a parent or offspring (S. *Ant.* 905-12). It is possible, however, that Antigone's sentiments – if indeed these lines are genuine – were intended to be regarded as an example of level-headed pragmatism pushed to an unnatural and somewhat forbidding extreme. They may well have been calculated, therefore, to cause an uneasy stir in an Athenian audience, rather than to stand as an expression of social norms likely to earn for the heroine the audience's uncritical and unquestioning approbation. Nor does Pomeroy's further observation that 'Patriarchal authority asserted that the child belonged to the father, not to the mother' add much weight to her claim that the mother-child relationship counted for little, since patriarchal authority, even if absolute, cannot prescribe emotional affect. What does seem clear is that the degree of affection which parents demonstrated towards their children depended partly on the sex of the child and partly on the size of the family. Particularly highly prized were only children, children who were last-born, or ones who were born to elderly parents, all of which meanings are contained in the epithets *têlugetos* and *opsigonos*. Special affection was also felt towards first-born children, partly perhaps because of a belief in their innate moral superiority.

Mythological accounts of infanticide, incest, the eating of children's flesh, matricide and patricide provide an inexhaustibly rich storehouse for Freudians in hot pursuit of evidence for psychosexual conflict between Greek parents and their children. What fantasies and phobias really lie at the heart of such grisly stories is not, however, a subject of inquiry that is susceptible to systematic analysis. As an example of the kind of difficulty that arises in attempting to use data of this sort in order to shed light on intrafamilial relationships, let us consider the story of Medea, which is most familiar from Euripides' play of that name. Medea is depicted as a barbarian who murders her children in order to have revenge on her husband Jason for his callous rejection of her for another woman. The myth as it has come down to us in its Euripidean version seems to question the very nature and validity of the maternal instinct, for it suggests that in a moment of extreme provocation that instinct may become overwhelmed by the need for revenge. Since the infanticide almost certainly did not constitute a feature of the myth's original structure but was invented by Euripides for his own dramatic purposes, however, any attempt to read into it evidence of unconscious tensions in the Greek mother-son relationship in society at large must first be subordinated to an appreciation and assessment of the aims of Euripidean dramaturgy (cf. Foley 1981, 138f.).

All the same, it is undeniable that Greek mythology contains what by any reckoning must be judged to be a disproportionate number of stories at the core of which is often a violent and destructive relationship between parent and child. Tantalos serving up his son Pelops at a banquet held in honour of the gods, Kronos castrating his father Ouranos and then devouring his own babies one by one for fear they would displace him, Agamemnon sacrificing his daughter Iphigeneia, Herakles slaughtering his children in a fit of madness, Agave killing and dismembering her son Pentheus under Dionysiac inspiration, Zeus ejecting his son Hephaistos from Olympos, Laios nailing his son Oedipus' ankles together before exposing him, Oedipus' subsequent killing of his father, Orestes murdering his mother Klytaimnestra in vengeance for her killing of his father – the list is seemingly endless and amounts to mythopoeic paranoia on a truly cosmic scale. The Greeks themselves were surely aware that there was something odd in all this. Herodotos at any rate was, for he found it appropriate to observe (1.137.2) that the Persians, unlike the Greeks, were incapable of contemplating patricide or matricide. Detailed investigation of the circumstances surrounding alleged instances of these crimes, the Persians maintained, invariably revealed that the child accused of the murder was the offspring of an adulterous affair. In the same vein Isokrates (*Panath.* 121-2) maintains that patricide and matricide were committed only by non-Athenians and in the dim and distant past. The fact that the Greeks as a whole acknowledged that such crimes do indeed take place does not, however, furnish evidence for the claim that parent-child relations in Greece were commonly attended by a disproportionate amount of violence and negativity. What it does indisputably indicate, however, is that the Greeks fully appreciated the extent to which a propensity towards violence is engendered in the home and has its roots in one's relationship with one's parents.

From an analysis of 65 representations of parent-child interactions in tragedy, Slater (1971) concluded that same-sex relationships (father/son and mother/daughter) were solidary, whereas cross-sex relationships were problematic or hostile. Identifying what he described as the 'repressed mother syndrome' among Athenian wives who were separated from their husbands for frequent and prolonged periods owing to the latter's absence on military campaigns, he argued that the sense of isolation which these wives experienced would have given rise to feelings of repressed aggression which they then directed outwards towards their male offspring. Sons were thus bombarded by alternating currents of stifling possessiveness and venomous hatred as their mothers vainly sought a substitute marital partner. In support of his theory Slater adduced the fact that heroines in Greek tragedy are sometimes extremely masculine and overbearing, and he concluded that this constituted evidence for the dramatist's own preoccupation with the ambiguous undercurrents in the mother/son relationship. Tendentious though such reasoning is, it may not be wholly wide of the mark, though the evidence which Slater cites does little to advance his argument. While it is true that Klytaimnestra and Antigone, for instance, both reject the role of mother, their behaviour can hardly be regarded as normative, far less as paradeigmatic. After all each has suffered a devastating loss. It is also worth noting that

Penelope in Homer's *Odyssey* in no way manifests the 'repressed mother syndrome', even though her condition – that of separation from her husband for some twenty years – conforms exactly to the pattern outlined by Slater.

Support for the thesis that sons were the focus of excessive attention from their mothers when the latter found themselves in an adversarial relationship with their husbands does, however, exist. One of the best examples is Plato's description of the timocratic man (*Rep*. 8.549c-550b) – possibly a self-portrait – who finds himself 'at the centre of a maelstrom ... subjected to a relentless pressure to succeed where his father is reputed to have failed by a mother who may realise her own thwarted ambitions only vicariously through her offspring' (Walcot 1987). Another is Aristophanes' portrait of Pheidippides (*Clouds* ll. 12ff.) who is indulged in his extravagant passion for chariot-racing by a mother who bitterly resents her marriage to a social inferior. In Sparta, where fathers spent most of their time living communally with their peers, the matricentral character of the home must have been particularly pronounced. Many Spartan mothers would therefore have identified with the grass widow Deianeira when she complains bitterly of her husband Herakles: 'Indeed we had children but he never saw them other than as a farmer sees an outlying field, at seed-time and when harvesting' (S. *Trach*. 31-3).

Spartan mothers had a reputation for putting extreme moral pressure on their sons, almost at the cost of their identity as mothers. A collection of their apocryphal utterances is preserved in Plutarch's *Sayings of Spartan Women* (*Mor*. 240c-242d), of which the most celebrated is the remark made by one mother to her son as she handed him his shield before he left for battle: 'Either with this or on this' (241f). The question is, however, whether this reputation was justified and whether it markedly distinguished Spartan mothers from other Greek mothers. For what the evidence is worth, Greek mythology also depicts mothers bullying their children into acts of heroism, as in Euripides' *Erechtheus*, where Praxithea agrees to allow her daughter to be sacrificed in Athens' defence; and in his *Suppliants*, where Aithra urges her son Theseus to assist the mothers whose sons died fighting at Thebes in order to recover their bodies for burial (cf. Lefkowitz 1988, 804). So maternal pressures of one kind or another may well have been pronounced throughout the Greek world.

One of the finest and most moving tributes to motherhood in Greek literature is Homer's portrayal of the sea-goddess Thetis, the mother of Achilles, who makes three brief appearances in the *Iliad*. Thetis exemplifies motherhood in its ill-fated and most tragic aspect. It is her unenviable fate to labour tirelessly on her son's behalf, serving as a humble go-between between him and Zeus, always haunted with the knowledge that her efforts are serving merely to increase his misery and hasten his doom. Immortal herself, Thetis is condemned not only to outlive her son – itself judged to be a terrible affliction for a mother – but also to be the unwitting means by which he accomplishes and expedites his own destruction. The goddess sums up her unenviable plight in the single word *dusaristokeia*, which awkwardly translates 'being the ill-fated mother of a splendid offspring' (*Il.* 18.54). It is one of the most beautiful *hapax legomena* in the Greek language and one of the most devastating oxymorons in any. Thetis is tragic in part because she cannot die. Mortal mothers, however, can, as in the case of Antikleia, the mother of Odysseus, who dies, possibly by her own hand, because she is unable to endure her son's long absence (*Od.* 11.202f.). A fourth-century Athenian epitaph commemorating a certain Xenokleia asserts that the woman died out of grief for the death of her eight-year-old son who met his death at sea (*IG* II^2 12335).

Poets and philosophers set an extremely high value upon the maternal instinct. 'Mighty for women are the offspring (*gonai*) of their travails', sings the chorus of Phoinician women in Euripides' play of that name (l. 255f.). When in Xenophon's *Memorabilia* (2.2.5) Lamprokles complains of harsh treatment at the hands of his mother, his father Sokrates roundly rebukes him and delivers the following eulogy upon the qualities demanded of motherhood in general:

> It is she who is impregnated, bears the load during pregnancy, risks her life for it, and supplies it with the food with which she herself is nourished; and then, having brought it into the world with much labour, she nourishes it and cares for it, although she has received no good and the infant (*brephos*) does not recognise its benefactress and has no means of signalling its desires. But a mother guesses what it needs and likes and tries to satisfy it, and rears it for a long time, toiling day after day, night after night, not knowing what gratitude she will receive in return.

Fig. 19. Terracotta figurine of a somewhat less than fully engaged mother nursing her child, mid-fifth century BC. The *polos*-style head-dress indicates that she is a goddess. From Taras, South Italy.

When Lamprokles later objects that his mother has a terrible temper, Sokrates, who does not actually attempt to refute the charge, forces him to admit, not without a pinch of irony, that it is not so harsh as that of a wild beast (*Mem*. 2.2.7). Again in the *Oikonomikos* or *Art of Household Management* (7.23-4) Xenophon argues that since women are biologically and psychologically conditioned by divine providence to lead an indoor life, they are innately more affectionate towards newborn babies (*neogna brephê*) than men are.

Pictorial representations of mother and child, one of the great and enduring iconographic images in Christian art from the tenth century onwards, do not occupy a position of comparable significance within the Greek artistic tradition, even though examples are plentiful (cf. Zahn 1970, 22). Just occasionally, however, the theme was treated with a degree of emotional involvement on the part of the artist which approaches, if it does not equal, such renderings in Christian art. Examples include a sixth-century BC sculpture from Megara Hyblaia depicting what is probably a fertility goddess suckling a pair of twins (see Fig. 5); and a fragmentary funerary relief from Anavysos in Attica dated *c*. 530 which shows a mother cupping the head of her infant in her hand in a gesture of exquisite tenderness that is virtually unique in Greek art (Fig. 20). The comparative dearth of such representations is perhaps best explained not so much by lack of interest in the subject as by the absence of an appropriate artistic genre through which to give it prominence.

Evidence about the strength and intensity of the father-son relationship is also conflicting. Herodotos (1.136.2) praises the Persians for their custom of not bringing boys into the presence of their fathers until their fifth year but instead confining them to the women's quarters with the humane intent of 'sparing their fathers the distress that would result if they died during the nursing period'. His account is significant first because it demonstrates an awareness of the very high level of infant and child mortality in the ancient world; secondly because it suggests that the distress of the mother occasioned by the death of one of her children was deemed unproblematic by both Herodotos and his Persian informants; and thirdly because it reveals that paternal involvement with a young child was, at least in Persia, ordinarily quite high. This last point is especially interesting precisely because it runs counter to what we might expect of a society in which fathers were customarily

Fig. 20. Fragmentary Attic grave-relief from Anavysos commemorating a mother(?) holding the head of a child, *c.* 530 BC.

absent from the home for long periods of time. And what was true of Persia may also have been true of Greece where the incidence of child mortality is likely to have been equally high and the absence of fathers no less frequent and prolonged. It is also interesting to note that although an adopted child was required by Athenian law to forego all kinship with his natural father, the requirement was often circumvented, evidently because it ran counter to natural feeling (Ps.-Dem. 44 and Isai. 10; cf. Humphreys 1983, 65).

There is, however, much to indicate that father-son conflict was widely recognised in Greek society. Pseudo-Demosthenes alleges (40.47) that the difference between natural sons and adopted ones is that whereas both habitually quarrel with their fathers while they are alive, only natural sons refrain from speaking ill of them when dead. A poignant anecdote in

Herodotos (3.50-3) concerns the problems which the ageing tyrant Periander of Corinth had with his younger son Lykophron who suspected him of killing his mother. At the end of his life Periander repeatedly made efforts to achieve reconciliation with his son but to no avail.

Homer's brief portrait of Achilles' old tutor Phoinix is one of the most compact and subtle illustrations of the father-son relationship ever drawn (*Il.* 9.444-95). As a young man Phoinix had, at his mother's bidding, slept with a slave woman in order to deter the latter from sleeping with his father Amyntor. Amyntor, infuriated by his son's meddlesomeness, cursed him with sterility. Phoinix was tempted to kill his father but instead left home and wandered through Greece till he came to the palace of Peleus in Phthia. There Peleus received and cherished him 'as a father cherishes his only beloved (*têlugetos*) who will inherit great wealth' (9.481-2). In return Phoinix acted as a male nurse to Peleus' son Achilles. The intimacy of their relationship is conveyed by the following reminiscence (9.485-91) which Phoinix shares with Achilles when he is urging his erstwhile ward not to desert the Greek army:

> I made you what you are today, godlike Achilles, loving you with all my heart, for you were unwilling to go with anyone to the feast or to eat in the hall before I had set you on my knees and given you the first cut of cooked meat and a sip of wine. Often you wetted my tunic, regurgitating your wine in your pathetic childishness (*en nêpieêi alegeinêi*).

What is significant in Phoinix's story is that, despite having been rejected and cursed with sterility by his father, he does not remain deadlocked in emotional and physical sterility as he might well have done. Instead he redirects his filial and paternal instincts towards Peleus and Achilles, who become his surrogate father and son respectively. Phoinix's own 'rebirth' in the home of Peleus is a wonderfully optimistic celebration of the father/son relationship, an admittedly ambivalent dynamic whose potential for good here succeeds in dispelling the negative impulses to which it had previously given rise. The intensity of the father/son relationship is again powerfully conveyed at the climax of the *Iliad* in Book 24. When Priam makes his way secretly through the Greek lines and arrives at the tent of Achilles to beg for the release of his son's body for burial, he appeals to his foe in the name of his father Peleus (l. 486f.).

Sepulchral inscriptions commemorating the deaths of young people seem at first sight to suggest that the father-son relationship greatly outweighed in importance that of father-daughter, mother-daughter or mother-son. A survey of fourth-century inscriptions from Attica produced some thirty examples which commemorate a father and son jointly, compared with only four which commemorate a father and daughter (Humphreys 1980). Mother and daughter appear together five times, mother and son just twice. Suggestive though this evidence is, it must be borne in mind that Athenian women were not permitted by law to possess money of their own, at least not enough to pay for the expense of a funerary monument. It remains questionable therefore whether Athenian mothers were economically empowered to publicise their grief for their children.

A change in burial practice that occurred in Athens in *c.* 760 BC has been taken as indicative of a re-evaluation of children's worth by parents around the time of Homer or somewhat earlier. Before this date young children were buried intramurally, often even under the floor of a house, while adults were buried outside the residential area. After that date, however, extramural burials for children become as numerous as intramural ones. Arguably the change in practice reflects the fact that parents were beginning to take a greater interest in children than they had done previously (cf. Sourvinou-Inwood 1981, 34), but the issue is unlikely to be that simple. The intramural burial of the infant dead probably derived from a complex and perhaps even conflicting network of feelings which comprised not only indifference and neglect but also tenderness and compassion. It may point to the fact that the dead child was intended to serve as a sacrificial offering to the spirits which guarded the home; that its corpse was not judged to be so polluting as that of an adult and so had no need to be banished beyond the residential area; that the child's existence had been confined wholly to the home and so its physical remains most appropriately belonged there too; or finally, that the emotions aroused by its death did not merit the effort and expense of more than a domestic funeral. It is noteworthy, too, that for the Early, Middle and Late Geometric I periods (*c.* 900-725 BC) only a very small number of child burials have come to light in Attica, prompting the speculation that most of the young were excluded from formal burial (Morris 1987, 61f.). But even if the archaeological record is accurate and even if this supposition is correct, any evaluation of this practice in terms of emotional ties can only be very cautiously advanced.

What, finally, of the sentiments felt and expressed by children towards their parents? The evidence seems to suggest that while filial devotion was commonly regarded as a fundamental attribute of any decent human being, in practice it was not invariably manifested, inasmuch as ill-treatment of parents came under the heading of impiety as a type of crime which the gods themselves would be minded to punish (cf. Mikalson 1983, 99f.). Thus the Athenian politician Lykourgos, who became prominent after 338 BC, maintained (*Against Leokrates* 94): 'It is the greatest impiety not to pass our lives benefiting those from whom we have received the beginning of life and those from whom we have received many benefits.' His view was not eccentric. An orator in a speech by Lysias (31.20-1) raises violent objections to the candidacy of a certain Philon to the office of councillor partly on the grounds that he mistreated his mother both during her lifetime and after her death. Significant, too, is the fact that the eponymous archon before assuming his office was required to state whether he treated his parents well (Ps.-Arist. *AP* 55.1-3).

Parental authority and the legal rights of children

Athenian children enjoyed little protection under the law, first because there was no public prosecutor in Athens, and secondly because as minors they had no access to the courts. In the eyes of the law an Athenian child was completely under the control of his father or legal guardian and, at least until the time of Solon at the beginning of the sixth century BC, could even be sold into slavery. Even after Solon a father or, if the father was dead, a brother, had the right to enslave a daughter (or sister) who had been caught in an act of illicit sexual intercourse (Plu. *Sol.* 13.3 and 23.2). Loss of legal protection was therefore the price which a *parthenos* had to pay for the loss of her virginity.

If a child happened to be the victim of physical assault or sexual abuse within its own family, there was no legal redress available. If, however, it was the victim of a civil injustice involving, say, an attempt by its guardian to deprive it of part or all of its inheritance, its interests could be represented procedurally in court by an adult male citizen. Only once, however, is there a reference to a guardian being charged with mismanagement of his wards' estate during their childhood and even then the suit was unsuccessful, since the guardian persuaded the jurors that he was fit to continue to administer the *oikos* himself (Dem. 38.23). Virtually the only course of action available was to wait until the attainment of legal majority in the eighteenth year. Even then, however, the proceedings are likely to have been protracted and the outcome uncertain. In the celebrated case of Demosthenes versus his guardians the plaintiff upon attaining legal majority discovered that only one tenth of the estate which his father had bequeathed to him was still intact, the remainder having been squandered by his three guardians (Dem. 27). The guardians spent three years attempting to reach a settlement, but when he was nineteen Demosthenes finally brought a successful action against them. Another two years were to elapse before he finally received full compensation.

Other than in the specialised area of property rights, where it was not so much the interests of the heirs as those of the *oikos* which they represented that Athenian law was minded to uphold, children were liable to find themselves at the complete mercy of vicious or neglectful parents on the one hand and unscrupulous guardians on the other.

Orphans

Since at least until the Hellenistic era the Greek world was in a state of almost perpetual warfare, a very great many children must have been fatherless. *Orphanos*, which gives us our word 'orphan', is in fact used primarily in the sense of 'a fatherless child'. While it might be argued that this usage merely provides further evidence of prejudice against the status and importance of the mother in Greek society and social thinking, it also constitutes acknowledgment of an unavoidable fact of Greek life – that a fatherless child was at grave risk whether or not its mother happened to be still alive. The following words uttered by the grieving Andromache upon learning of the death of her husband Hektor afford a terrifying glimpse into the plight of the fatherless child as a complete social reject (Hom. *Il.* 22.490-8):

> The day a child becomes an orphan he is separated from children of his own age. He goes always with his head bowed low and his cheeks wet with tears, and in his need he goes to his father's companions, grabbing one by the cloak another by the tunic. Anyone who feels pity for him briefly offers him his drinking cup and wets his lips but not his palate. But a child who has both parents still living (*amphithalês*) drives him from the feast, beating him and abusing him: 'Clear off! Your father does not dine among us.'

Girls were even more vulnerable than boys because, in Athens at least, they could not directly inherit even when they were heiresses. Much depended on the integrity of their guardians.

The most favoured orphans were those whose fathers died on the field of battle. Self-evidently the welfare of children in this category was of paramount concern to the state because the state needed to assure its citizens that if they laid down their lives in its service, their families would not be left destitute and bankrupt. Fear of destitution is a key concern in the *Odyssey*, where Odysseus' problematic status of 'missing presumed dead' enables the suitors to squander the assets of his household. To prevent just such a situation from arising in real life Greek states undertook to support orphans of the war dead at public expense until they came of age. In Athens, according to Diogenes Laertios (1.55), public support for war orphans was first introduced by Solon, though our earliest Athenian evidence for the practice does not predate *c*. 478-462 BC (Ps.-Arist. *AP* 24.3). The magistrate in charge of their welfare was the eponymous archon and the level of allowance, at least at the end of the fifth century, was probably one obol per child per day (cf. Stroud 1971, 199-200). We also hear of *orphanophulakes* or protectors of the orphans, who appear to have been specifically appointed to represent their interests (Xen. *Por*. 2.7); elsewhere these officials are referred to as *orphanistai*. Support lasted *mechri hêbês*, that is, until the orphan reached his eighteenth year (see below, p. 182).

Orphans who stood to inherit when they reached legal majority constituted a second group who were protected by Athenian law, their welfare also coming under the purview of the eponymous archon. In the words of Pseudo-Aristotle (*AP* 56.7):

> The eponymous archon supervises orphans and heiresses (*epiklêroi*) and women who profess to be pregnant in the event of their husbands' death, and has complete power either to fine

> those who commit crimes against them or to bring them into the court. He grants leases to the houses that belong to orphans and heiresses until the latter are in their fourteenth year (*tettarakaidekatis*) and he receives the rent, and, in cases where guardians fail to support their *paides*, he himself exacts the allowance.

The interpretation of this passage is problematical, but what it seems to indicate is that girls who have no legal guardian are to be treated as orphans until they reach thirteen. Thereafter those from propertied families are designated *epiklêroi* and would be expected and indeed required to marry. Boys, as we have just seen, were regarded as orphans until their eighteenth year, which was the age when they could claim, and if necessary contest, their inheritance. Though the situation must have been immeasurably bleaker for those who had little or no legacy left to them, the strength of the family unit probably ensured that in most cases orphans were rarely destitute.

Conclusions

The impression left by the evidence we have been considering in this chapter is that childhood was viewed by the Greeks as merely a preparatory stage of life. Apart from philosophy, which addresses the subject from a purely theoretical standpoint, other literature shows little interest in the subject.

By reason of the fact that children occupied a marginal status in Greek society with virtually no legal rights, they resembled both women and slaves. What basically differentiated boys from girls was that whereas boys ultimately achieved full integration within the community upon coming of age, girls achieved no comparable enlargement of their social identity.

How were Greek children treated in the home? Were they encouraged at an early age to behave like miniature adults or were they left more or less free to develop at their own pace? How much time did children of various economic and social groups spend typically in the company of their peers, their mothers and fathers (whether singly or jointly), their grandparents, their relatives and household slaves, and what impact did that have upon their upbringing? How did the frequent absence of a child's father affect his or her emotional and intellectual development? Our evidence sheds only a dim

Fig. 21. Attic red-figure *chous* depicting a child sitting on a potty and holding a rattle, *c*. 440-430 BC. The potty would have been in two sections so that the lower section could be removed while the child remained seated in the upper section.

light on these questions and much remains ambiguous. To re-state what was said at the beginning of this chapter, the world of the child eludes the investigator except insofar as that world is refracted through images provided by adults. We can with confidence state that a child of well-to-do parents would have spent a very considerable amount of time in the company of slaves and, moreover, that in the absence of infant schools the home would have been the centre of his early education. But the consequences that flowed from these 'facts' cannot be easily determined.

What is abundantly obvious is that Greek society was anything but child-oriented and that it made very little provision for the needs and wants of a child. Perceived as intellectually and morally inferior to an adult, the child was an incomplete and imperfect organism. Though there are some indications, notably from the presence of mass-produced toys in graves, from the production of specialised items manufactured exclusively for infant and child use, from iconography, and finally from developments in education, that from the fourth century onwards childhood began to arouse more interest than it had done earlier, it is probably safe to conclude that our modern sentimental view of childhood as a uniquely precious time of life to be indulged and prolonged as late as possible would have been regarded with derision by Greeks of all social strata.

The following saying, quoted by Artemidoros (*Onirok.* 1.15), is symptomatic of the very real fear engendered by child-rearing in Greece: 'Throughout human history a *pais* has meant one of two things for its father – either indigence or grief.' In other words, given the economic constraints of life in the ancient world and the high incidence of child mortality, the joy of parenthood was almost inevitably overshadowed by fear of impoverishment on the one hand and fear of bereavement on the other. Judged from a modern perspective, however, that fact merely constitutes a difference in degree rather than in kind, and at bottom serves to assimilate the Greeks to us rather than to set them apart.* After all, as Euripides (*HF* 636) incontrovertibly remarked, all humankind loves its own offspring.

*Infant mortality is mercifully much reduced in the modern western world, but impoverishment through child-rearing is very much alive. The *Daily Mail* of 30 March 1988 carried an article in which it estimated that the average cost of bringing up a child in the south-east of England is currently in the region of £115,000. Viewed as a *proportion* of family income, the cost of rearing a child in the ancient world would have been considerably less than it is today.

4

Coming of Age

> Was it not enough for you suitors to waste all my fine property when I was still a child (*nêpios*)? But now that I am fully grown (*megas*) and comprehend by listening to others, and the spirit (*thumos*) inside me is increasing, I will endeavour to hurl evil destruction upon you.
>
> (Hom. *Od.* 2.312-16)

Coming of age is both class-related and sex-specific. In the first instance the attainment of adulthood articulates, reinforces and 'justifies' sex distinctiveness by requiring boys and girls, young men and young women, to perform rituals which prepare them for sex-specific roles in adult life. The rituals which boys undergo at this period tend to be public and civic in orientation, while those undergone by girls are private and domestic. Again, those involving boys tend to focus upon the enhancement of their political status as citizens and their socio-economic status as heads of households, whereas those involving girls concentrate upon their biological status as child-bearers and their social status as wives. In the second instance, coming of age has meaning only in those communities and among those socio-economic groups where the attainment of adulthood is accompanied by increased legal, political and economic privileges (cf. Finley 1981, 160). For the poor, namely those who are unable to enjoy the luxury of extending their pre-adult years and who have to be put to work as soon as possible, childhood ends at between twelve and fourteen. An extended childhood is the mark of a society which is itself economically and socially advanced. That is because adolescence, like time itself, has no ontological reality but is merely an invention of the systematising mind. As Telemachos' threat to the suitors quoted at the head of this chapter reminds us, arrival at adulthood is measurable in terms of a threefold alteration in status which – to put it in our terms – comprises biological development, intellectual capacity and emotional stability. This chapter will attempt to explore all three.

Given the fact that between one half and one third of the population was probably below fifteen years of age (cf. Cipolla 1978, 90), it is hardly surprising that coming of age should have been seen as a major milestone for the rising generation and that a great deal of corporate energy should have been expended in ensuring that a young person, once having reached this milestone, should actually surpass it and attain adulthood.

Terminology

Some cultures do not have any word to describe the interval – as we identify it – between childhood and adulthood. Up until the eighteenth century in France, for instance, adolescence was 'confused' with childhood, so that *enfant* was virtually the only word used for the entire period from birth to late adolescence. Greek, too, has no word that is exactly synonymous with our concept of 'adolescent' and 'adolescence'. Take *parthenos*, for instance. Commonly translated 'virgin', it more precisely denotes the status of a young woman, less commonly that of a young man, who, having reached puberty, is not yet married. Its signification is therefore linked not only to age but also to status. Though the values of Greek society were such that *parthenoi* were certainly expected to be virgins when they got married, girls who engaged in premarital sex as well as those who were the victims of rape did not necessarily forfeit this title. Astyoche, who is alleged to have had intercourse with the war-god Ares, is described by Homer, somewhat ironically perhaps, as a 'bashful *parthenos*' (*Il.* 2.514), and there are many instances in later Greek literature to indicate that this usage was not confined to epic.

Another word which can serve to identify an adolescent is *koros* and its Ionic variant *kouros* (fem. *kourê*, *korê*). The age-span denoted by these terms was by no means limited to adolescence, however, for they could also be used of a foetus or a newborn child, as well as of a person of adult years. In Homer, for instance, *kouroi* designates those of military age, whereas *gerontes* denotes those above it. Like *parthenos*, *kouros* implies a kind of status, but in this case one that is social rather than biological, since the designation of a man as a *kouros* constitutes acknowledgment that he is of aristocratic

Fig. 22. On the verge of womanhood. The so-called Peplos *Korê*, *c.* 540-530 BC. From the Acropolis in Athens.

lineage. It has even been claimed that the term 'aims more at the quality and social situation of those whom it designates than their actual age' (Jeanmaire 1939, 36). An unequivocal instance of the use of *kouros* to denote people who belong to the aristocracy is provided by a sardonic question put by the suitor Antinoös upon learning of Telemachos' departure to the mainland: 'Who among the *kouroi* went with him? Were they the cream of Ithaca, or his own hired hands and domestics?' (*Od.* 4.642-64).

The word which actually comes closest to the notion of adolescence is *hêbê*, though 'puberty' is often a more satisfactory translation. For Homer *hêbê* is exclusively a physiological term of reference. Its lower age limit is identified in the case of a male by the first appearance of facial hair, as in the description of Hermes' epiphany before Odysseus 'in the likeness of a youth (*neêniês*), one who is just sprouting a beard on his upper lip, which is the most graceful time of *hêbê*' (*Od.* 10.279; cf. *Il.* 24.348). Its upper limit is only very hazily delineated. The description of Aeneas as being 'in the flower (*anthos*) of *hêbê* when physical strength (*kratos*) is greatest' unmistakably indicates that here the word is being used to denote early adulthood (*Il.* 13.484).

In later times the compounds *ephêboi*, *hoi hêbôntes* and *hoi eph'hêbês* were used to denote 'young persons at the period of *hêbê*', though in these instances *hêbê* denotes late adolescence rather than puberty. The appearance of a terminology to designate people in this age-group coincided with the establishment by many Greek states of a legal age of *hêbê* whose termination, generally in the twentieth or in some states in the eighteenth year, coincided with completion of military training. The duration of the ephebic period differed from state to state. In Athens it lasted for two years (i.e. about seventeen to nineteen), whereas in Sparta it lasted for six years (i.e. about thirteen to nineteen). To complicate matters further, *hêbôntes*, like *hê hêbêtikê hêlikia*, denoted Spartan youths aged about nineteen to twenty-nine, though this particular usage may have been colloquial rather than formal (cf. MacDowell 1986, 167).

Though the Greeks had no word which was exactly equivalent to our word 'adolescence', they none the less insisted upon a rigid distinction between childhood and adulthood. That distinction permeated virtually all aspects of Greek life. To take an example: at Eretria on Euboia excavations in a cemetery dated to the late eighth and early seventh centuries BC have brought to light contemporary inhumation and cremation burials whose distinctiveness is a reflection of the symbolic opposition between childhood and adulthood, since inhumation was reserved for boys and girls who had not yet reached adolescence, and cremation for 'marriageable girls and married women, and for youths and men able to use the lance and to take their place in battle' (Bérard 1970, 50, quoted by Vidal-Naquet 1974, 173). It would be fascinating to know just how rigorously the distinction between the age-groups was enforced and how broad was the period of overlap.

The vital importance of the rising generation both for the family and for the community at large, and the tragic sense of bereavement experienced by parents at premature loss, may be appreciated by the fact that in the Archaic period young adults constituted the largest single group of dead for whom Attic grave monuments were erected. Of the 20 inscriptions which record the relationship between the commemorator and the deceased that have survived from this period, no fewer than 13 refer to dedications erected by parents to their children (cf. Humphreys 1980, 104). Small though the sample is, it is none the less likely to be representative.

Age of puberty

Regarding age of puberty Aristotle (*HA* 7.581a11-581b7 *T*) states:

> Males generally begin to produce sperm for the first time when they have completed thirteen years. Simultaneously pubic hair begins to grow .... About the same time the voice starts to become harsher and less even, neither shrill as it was nor deep as it will be, nor all on one note, but like chords that are harsh and discordant. We say that the voice is breaking (*tragizein*) .... At around the same time a swelling of the breasts occurs in girls and what is referred to as menses (*ta katamênia*) begins to discharge. This resembles fresh blood .... Menses occurs in most cases when the breasts protrude by about two fingers' breadth.

Likewise Plato in the *Laws* (8.833d) implies that puberty occurs around thirteen.

There was a general appreciation that age of puberty is subject to environmental and other factors. The Hippokratic *Airs, Waters and Places* (4) states that puberty is delayed in the case of those who live in cities where cold winds blow throughout the winter, while Galen (17.ii.637 *K*) alleges that those who possess a warm constitution (*krasis*) attain maturity earlier than those whose constitution is cold.

Though ancient writers were in general agreement about the timing of the onset of puberty, they differed markedly in beliefs about its duration. Didymos, for instance, a grammarian who lived in the first century BC, is quoted (schol. on Aischin. 3.122) as saying that puberty began at thirteen and terminated at fifteen. Aristotle, who as we have just seen, maintained that males produce their first seed at the end of the thirteenth year, was of the belief that this seed did not become fertile (*gennêtikos*) until the twenty-first year (*HA* 5.544b27-8 *T*; cf. 7.582a17-8). Galen (17.ii.791-2 *K*), who also believed that puberty begins at thirteen, set its maximum upper limit at twenty-four. The worth of all these statements is questionable to say the least, in view of the fact that it is extremely doubtful whether any of these authorities had sufficient evidence to make a reliable pronouncement upon a statistical average. Nor can we be sure whether their reference group was the whole population or, as seems more likely, the upper classes to which they themselves belonged (cf. Hopkins 1965, 310-12).

Vulnerability at puberty

Medical writers were of the opinion that puberty is a time when the human body is particularly vulnerable to physical and mental illness. According to the author of the Hippokratic treatise entitled *Peri partheniôn* or *Illnesses affecting Virgins* (1) unmarried girls at menarche become delirious, fearful of the dark, and subject to visions which bid them either to throw themselves down wells and drown or else hang themselves, all because the menstrual blood cannot properly flow until the 'orifice of egress (*to stoma tês exodou*)' has been opened up through intercourse. Unable to find release the blood settles around the heart and becomes a burden to the body, thus producing heaviness, torpor and insanity. The cure was straightforward. 'My prescription', the no-nonsense doctor writes, 'is that *parthenoi* should marry as soon as possible when they experience these symptoms. If they become pregnant, they are cured. If not, then at *hêbê* or shortly afterwards she [sic] will succumb, unless some other ailment carries her off. Among married *gunaikes* the sterile ones are more prone to this condition.' Pliny (*NH* 28.10.44) shared the same belief, declaring that 'Many kinds of illnesses are cured by the first act of intercourse or by the first menstruation'. It was customary for *gunaikes* who had 'survived' menarche to dedicate their garments to Artemis, a practice alluded to by the author of *Illnesses affecting Virgins* and of which he is utterly scornful.

The emotional instability of *parthenoi* accounts also for the celebrated suicide epidemic at Miletos which Plutarch (*Mor.* 249b-d = *Bravery of Women* 11) reports. The epidemic was allegedly due to the peculiarity of the air in the town which caused the minds of young girls to become unhinged so that 'a sudden yearning for death, a manic desire to hang themselves affected them all'. Nothing could put a stop to the evil until eventually someone had the bright idea of suggesting that the bodies of the suicide victims be borne naked through the market place. The sense of shame at the prospect of being exposed in this manner paradoxically proved an effective deterrent for prospective suicides and the epidemic immediately subsided.

By the second century AD at the very latest less drastic remedies than defloration were being recommended to alleviate the condition of girls who were undergoing menarche. Soranos (*Gyn.* 1.25.2) suggested that they should take gentle walks, swing in a hammock for long periods of time, perform gymnastic exercises that are not too arduous, be massaged with plenty of fat, take a daily bath and have plenty of distractions to keep their minds occupied.

Quite aside from the particular problems associated with menarche, both men and women were believed at puberty to become susceptible for the first time to 'adult' diseases. The author of the Hippokratic *Koan Prognostications* (30.502) writes:

> These illnesses do not develop before *hêbê*: inflammation of the lungs, pleurisy, gout, nephritis, varicose veins in the legs, discharge of blood, non-congenital cancer, non-congenital elephantiasis, rheum of the spine, haemorrhoids and non-congenital disease of the liver. One need expect none of these illnesses before *hêbê*. From fourteen to forty-two the body becomes prone to every kind of illness.

The perils of self-abuse

In what appears to be a veiled homily upon the perils of self-abuse and premature sexual activity in general, Aristotle offers the following stern warning to parents (*HA* 7.581b12-21 *T*):

> They [i.e. adolescents] should be closely watched around this age [i.e. puberty]. For they exhibit a tendency to indulge the appetite for sexual gratification (*aphrodisia*) which is beginning

> to awaken inside them. As a consequence, unless they are guarded from arousal [?], apart from that which their bodies of themselves undergo [?], they are likely to acquire habits which will remain with them in later life (*eis tas husteron hêlikias*) even if they do not actively engage in sex. For girls (*neai*) who experience sexual gratification become more and more precocious, as do males, if they do not guard against either or both of these temptations. For the passages become enlarged and make the body open in this area.

Portraits of emergent adulthood

Homer's Telemachos is one of the most engaging portraits of a young man poised on the brink of adulthood in the whole of western literature. His personality and development dominate Books 1-4 of the *Odyssey*, which are appropriately designated the *Têlemacheia* in his honour, and feature prominently in Books 15-17 and 19-22. At the beginning of the poem Telemachos, who is about nineteen or twenty, is wholly lacking in motivation, moral fibre and self-confidence. By its end he is fully his father's equal in physical prowess, courage and social awareness. Telemachos' final attainment of manhood is symbolised by his ability to string his father's great bow, though he refrains from actually performing this feat in order to disguise his newly acquired strength from the suitors (*Od.* 21.128-9). Since the stages of his maturation are graded with considerable subtlety, it will be useful to examine the portrait in some detail.

Athena's arrival on Ithaca at the beginning of the poem is wholly motivated by her desire to foster Telemachos' emotional development. It is, she says, her intention to 'stir him up' and instil some moral fibre in him (*Od.* 1.88-9). Appearing in the guise of Mentes, an elderly family friend, she takes on the role of surrogate father by urging him to act like a grown-up (*Od.* 1.296-9):

> You should now refrain from childish behaviour (*nêpieê*), since you are no longer of an age (*têlikos*) where that is appropriate. Or haven't you heard what renown royal Orestes won throughout the world when he slew his father's murderer?

Her advice, as Telemachos himself says, is exactly what 'a father would give to his *pais*' (*Od.*1.307-8). What Telemachos has to do in fact is to take charge of the household as Odysseus' son and heir in order to prevent the total exhaustion of its resources by the suitors. Athena's presence at his side at this critical moment in his life is testimony to Homer's belief that the process of maturation is greatly facilitated by assistance from a father or father-image.

The start of Telemachos' journey to adulthood seems on one level to be marred by temper tantrums more characteristic of a pre-delinquent than of a young man poised to take charge of his own destiny. When his mother Penelope instructs the bard Phemios to refrain from singing of the Achaians' homecoming from Troy on the understandable grounds that the story is reawakening her grief for her long-lost husband, Telemachos sternly reprimands her and tells her to face up to the fact that Odysseus has undoubtedly perished. His concluding words are (*Od.* 1.356-9):

> Go back into the house, and attend to your own work, the loom and the distaff, and bid your handmaidens get on with their work also. Speech will be the concern of men, all men, but chiefly me. For mine is the power (*kratos*) in this household.

The key to the correct interpretation of this passage lies in understanding what is meant by 'power in this household'. It is the absence of any power in the household, the absence in other words of an adult male presence during the long years of Odysseus' absence, that has enabled the suitors to infiltrate that household, waste its wealth and importune its mistress with unwelcome offers of marriage. This parlous state of affairs could only be resolved in one of two ways: either Odysseus must return home and resume control, or, failing that, his heir must demonstrate his ability to take over the title to his estate. The climax and resolution of the poem in fact depend upon the exact coincidence of these two alternative solutions, for it is precisely at the moment when Odysseus reveals his true identity to the suitors that Telemachos finally attains adulthood, a transition that is symbolised, as previously noted, by his ability to match his father's strength in stringing the bow.

Immediately after rebuking his mother, Telemachos warns the suitors that he intends to call an assembly of the people of Ithaca in order to denounce them publicly for their outrageous behaviour in wasting his assets. The assembly duly takes place the following day and it is in tacit recognition of the fact that he is now of an age to assume the headship of his father's house and by extension overlordship of the entire island that the *gerontes* move aside when he sits down in his father's seat (*Od.* 2.14). The young man lacks sufficient self-mastery to handle the situation, however, becomes overwhelmed by his feelings, and finishes his speech in a flood of tears.

Telemachos' most enterprising act of self-assertion is his journey to the Greek mainland to discover news of his father's whereabouts. As it turns out his journey completely fails in its purpose. What it does do, however, is to provide him with the opportunity to win 'goodly fame among men', a necessary qualification for the attainment of adult status in the heroic world (*Od.* 1.95). The way in which that fame is achieved is measured wholly in terms of exacting social situations which take place at the courts of legendary kings. In other words, what Telemachos acquires is a set of social skills that enable him to move around with confidence at the highest level of society. A beautifully exact instance of 'ring composition' provides a clear indicator of the increase in self-confidence which Telemachos gains in the course of his journey. When the young man arrives at Pylos at the beginning of his travels, Athena urges him to question Nestor regarding news about his father. He is quite unable to do so, excusing himself by saying (*Od.* 3.23-4): 'I have absolutely no experience of discourse. A *neos* feels inhibition (*aidôs*) when addressing one who is *geraiteros*.' And the matter rests there, though later, thanks to the intervention of Athena, he does pluck up courage to question the old man. By the time he is ready to leave Menelaos' palace in Sparta at the end of his travels, however, he has not only acquired the strength of character to resist his host's well-meaning attempt to delay his departure but has also grown sufficiently assertive to reject his proferred gift of horses on the sensible grounds that he would have no use for them on a hilly island like Ithaca. He even has the temerity to ask instead for 'something that can be kept in store' (*Od.* 4.593-608).

What is the unifying link to this series of encounters which collectively are clearly intended to signify a young man's passage to adulthood? I believe they should be interpreted as not only progressive in the literal sense of movement outwards from the home but also cumulative, as Telemachos confronts in turn first his mother, secondly the *gerontes* and the people of Ithaca, and thirdly the *basilêes* Nestor and Menelaos. By moving from the *oikos* to the *polis* and then from the *polis* to the greater world that lies beyond the confines of Ithaca he is discovering and defining his identity in terms of an ever-widening and ever more challenging social milieu. But the most crucial encounter, the one which constitutes the first step towards an assertion of selfhood, is the one which he has with his mother. That is surely because a young man's journey to adulthood can only properly begin to gather momentum once he has distanced himself from his mother, a move which is almost inevitably accompanied by frustration and anger on one side, pain and confusion on the other. In other words, a young man must first die as a *nêpios* in order to be born as an *anêr*.

Telemachos' passage from childhood to adulthood is portrayed without allusion to any accompanying adolescent sexual awakening. By contrast the Phaiakian Nausikaa, who is depicted at the beginning of Book 6 as identically poised on the brink of adulthood, is described exclusively in terms of her budding womanhood. Nausikaa's sexual awakening is first hinted at in a dream where Athena appears to her in the guise of one of her companions who urges her to take thought of the fact that, being now of marriageable age, she should wash her clothes and smarten up (*Od.* 6.20-40). The full implications of her new status are brought home the very next day on the beach when she encounters Odysseus, a man old enough to be her father, emerging from the bushes with only a leafy branch to cover his nakedness. What makes the encounter even more dramatic is that just before it takes place Nausikaa is depicted in a state of archetypal innocence playing ball with her handmaidens. Homer compares the princess to Artemis, the chaste and maidenly goddess who delights in hunting and who ranges the mountain peaks in the company of the woodland nymphs. The simile concludes (*Od.* 6.108f.): 'Just as Artemis is easily distinguished from her companions, though all are lovely, so did Nausikaa, an untamed *parthenos*, stand out from her handmaidens.' The irony lies in the fact that the chaste and maidenly Nausikaa is about to experience a rude sexual awakening that will shatter the innocence of her childhood world once and for ever. Artemis is a goddess who presides over the transition from girlhood to womanhood, and that in essence is what this scene is all about. The characterisation of Nausikaa as an untamed *parthenos* thus constitutes a further element of irony, since *admês*, the word for 'untamed', is commonly used of a girl who has had no sexual experience, the belief being that girls who have arrived at puberty are extremely difficult to control until they have been 'tamed' by the loss of their virginity.

Only on Scheria could a meeting between a middle-aged naked man and a young girl take place, at least without unpleasant consequences, for Scheria is the Odyssean equivalent of Never-never-land. For the parents of a well-brought up girl an encounter of this kind represents the ultimate nightmare. For the well-brought up girl herself it may represent a type of wish-fulfilment, since unmarried girls had virtually no opportunity to associate with persons of the opposite sex. That Nausikaa's own emotions are somewhat stirred by the stranger but to no avail (*Od*. 6.244-5), that she is preoccupied with the danger to her reputation of being seen in the company of a stranger (6.273-88) – all this is entirely consistent with the real-life predicament of girls of her age and upbringing.

Homer's twin portraits of Telemachos and Nausikaa underline in their different ways the pain and isolation that mark the transition to adulthood. There can be little doubt that they are intended to be perceived as parallel and complementary portraits of emergent adulthood, not least because Athena serves in both cases as the catalyst by which each is propelled forward into a recognition of that new status. But there is a striking difference between the two portraits as well, and one which corresponds closely to the reality of their differing social statuses as man as woman. Telemachos achieves adulthood by moving outwards from the physical and emotional centre of his life into a world which constantly enlarges and redefines his social identity. Nausikaa, on the other hand, arrives at adulthood by a violent rupture from the world of childhood which simultaneously forces her to acknowledge her potential as marriage partner and childbearer.

Rites of passage

As is common the world over, Greek communities dramatised the transition from child to adult by rites of passage whose purpose was to safeguard the individual at what was judged to be a moment of extreme, even unparalleled danger in the young person's life. As identified by van Gennep (1909), rites of passage are tripartite in structure, consisting of rites of separation, rites of exclusion and rites of (re-)incorporation. Their structure symbolises and mirrors the threefold progress of the individual who must first dissociate himself or herself from the social group of which he or she is currently a member, then exist for a period of time as a member of no particular group, and finally become incorporated into a new, often enlarged social group with a correspondingly enlarged social persona.

With regard to Greece, however, there is a fundamental problem: how to identify and isolate what did or did not constitute a rite of passage in the exact sense of the term. It has been argued (cf. Brelich 1969) that in the historical period initiatory rites of the kind which we are considering were preserved only in conservative areas such as Sparta and Crete or backward areas such as Arkadia, whereas in more advanced societies such as Athens one of two developments occurred: either these rites became absorbed into the cult practices that were performed in connection with a leading divinity (as in the case of the *Arrhêphoria*, see below, p. 191), or else their identity as rites of passage remained intact but they were performed by only a token number of individuals (as in the case of the *Arkteia*, see below, p. 187). The objection to this hypothesis is that there is no shred of evidence to support it: we cannot know for certain whether the form in which these rites have come down to us was not actually the form in which they were originally conceived.

Our fullest account of what was undoubtedly a rite of passage concerns a bizarre Cretan initiatory ritual reported by Ephoros (*FGrH* 70 F 149 ap. Str. *Geog*. 10.4.21) who writes:

> The *erastês* or lover informs the friends of the *pais* three or four days beforehand that he intends to abduct him. It is most disgraceful for his friends to conceal the *pais* or to prevent him from journeying upon his appointed road, this course of action being regarded as a confession, so to speak, that the *pais* does not deserve the favours of such an *erastês*. When the encounter takes place, if the *erastês* is the boy's equal in social status (*timê*) as well as in other respects, the friends pursue the *pais* and gently lay hold of him, thereby satisfying the claims of custom (*to nomimon*). But in other respects they cheerfully consent to lead him away. If he is unworthy, however, they remove him. The abduction ends when the *pais* has been brought to the men's quarters (*andreion*) of his abductor. The Cretans think a *pais* worthy of love not for his looks, but for his manliness (*andreia*) and propriety of behaviour (*kosmiotês*).
>
> After giving the boy gifts, his abductor leads the boy off to any place in the countryside that he wishes. Those who were present when the abduction took place follow behind, and when they

> have feasted and hunted together for a period of two months (this being the maximum permissible period to detain the *pais*) they return to the polis. The boy is set free after receiving a military uniform, an ox and a goblet, which are the gifts required by law, as well as many other costly presents, to which his friends make a contribution because of the expense involved. He then sacrifices the ox to Zeus and gives portions to those who returned with him. Afterwards he discloses details about his affair with his *erastês*, whether he derived any satisfaction from it or not, the law granting him this privilege, so that if any force was applied to him at the time of the abduction, he would be able to avenge himself on his lover on the spot and so be rid of him.
>
> It is considered a mark of disgrace for those who are handsome and have illustrious forebears not to obtain a lover, the failure to do so being judged a mark of character (*tropos*). But the *parastathentes* [literally 'those who stand alongside or nearby', perhaps in the battle-line; see below, p. 184], which is the name given to those who are abducted, receive honours. In both the dances and the races they have the most honoured positions, they are allowed to dress differently from all the rest, that is, in the clothes they have been given by their lovers. And not only now [i.e. when they are still *paides*] but even when they are *teleioi* [i.e. fully adult] they wear a distinctive dress which indicates that each is regarded as 'celebrated (*kleinos*)'. They call the loved one '*kleinos*' or celebrated and the lover '*philêtor*' or paramour.

Ephoros' description is stiff with initiation motifs: the removal of the *pais* from society to an uninhabited region, expressly from the *polis* to the countryside, symbolises his liminality; the reference to hunting emphasises self-reliance and cultural regression, which are traditional elements in rites of passage; the suggestion of masquerade and play-acting, as indicated by the token resistance put up by the 'friends', is consistent with the basic ambivalence surrounding those who are interstitial; and the sacrifice of an ox as a thank-offering to Zeus signals the successful completion of the passage from one status to another. There are military overtones in the gift of an army uniform and corporate-convivial ones in that of a drinking-cup. The imagery seems to suggest that manhood was most importantly indicated by eligibility for military service and the right to attend the symposium or drinking-party. The reference to the 'illustrious forebears' of the *pais* strongly implies that initiation was confined to a social élite. Finally, the fact that *parastathentes* were accorded the title '*kleinoi*' and permitted to wear distinctive clothing indicates that the ritual conferred a permanent and visible alteration in social status.

To analyse and identify the structural elements contained in the ritual is, however, to fall far short of comprehending why the Cretans opted for a dramatisation of homosexual rape as a way of symbolising a young man's passage towards adulthood. Chronological uncertainties further compound the difficulty in arriving at a proper understanding of its meaning. We do not know when the ritual was first established nor how widely it was observed at the time when Ephoros wrote his description of it. Is what we have a description of an institution in decline preserved only in a small, backward community or that of one which commanded majority support in mainstream Cretan society? Ephoros' account indicates that the law insisted that the participants conduct themselves with a sense of propriety. We are told that the abductor, who is referred to as an *erastês* or lover, was required to obtain the favours of the *pais* 'by persuasion and not by force'. In other words, the author would have us understand that the drama which he is describing was not so much an abduction as a seduction. Whether the somewhat defensive strain that permeates the account is properly attributable to Ephoros himself, to an intermediary source, or to the actual practitioners of the ritual, cannot be determined. If we accept that propriety was indeed part of the ritual, it remains unclear whether this was a feature of the ritual when it was first established or whether, as would superficially appear to be more likely, it came about as a result of popular pressure in an age which looked somewhat askance at pederasty and was only prepared to tolerate it under the guise of pretended violence. The problem with this latter suggestion, however, is that masquerade and pretence are common elements within the traditional complex of initiation motifs and thus have a strong claim to being regarded as part of the ritual's deep structure. Finally we would wish to know the ages of the *pais* and his *erastês*. Interestingly it seems to be the *erastês* who determines the moment at which a *pais* is deemed ready for manhood, but what criterion did he use? Did the *erastês* have to be qualified to 'abduct' a *pais* or was it sufficient if he merely belonged to the same social status?

These problems aside, what can be said of the overall meaning of the ritual? In the first place, all our evidence about Greek initiatory rites indicates that they are sex-specific.

What the men do is one thing, what the women do quite another. And those who negotiate the transition are themselves invariably of the same sex as the initiates, no doubt because a role model is required to sponsor a young person's transition (see above, p. 171). Though no ritual comparable to the one we are discussing is known to have existed in Athens, a parallel situation did exist: an adolescent youth called an *erômenos*, meaning 'one who is the object of romantic attachment', was introduced into adult society by an older homosexual lover or *erastês*, most probably in his mid- to late twenties, who was expected to educate the *erômenos* and transfer him from subordinate to citizen status, in much the same way as Telemachos is transferred from the condition of *pais* to that of wielder of *kratos*. Was the Cretan ritual merely a primitive, barbaric and abbreviated variant? It is at least conceivable that the motif of abduction did not actually carry any sinister overtones at all. In the end the ritual may on one level have been intended to symbolise the initiate's natural reluctance to exchange the protected world of childhood for the exposed world of adulthood, while emphasising at the same time the inevitability and inescapability of physiological and psycho-social change.

The Spartan *ephêbeia*

In the fourteenth year a landmark was reached in the life of a Spartan *pais*, who now became an *ephêbos*. His new status probably marked the beginning of his military training in earnest. A gloss on Strabo (cf. Diller 1941, 500) states:

> A Spartan *pais* is an ephebe (*ephebeuei*) from thirteen to nineteen. In the first year he is called '*rhôbidas*', in the second '*prokomizomenos*', in the third '*mikizomenos*', in the fourth '*propais*', in the fifth '*pais*', in the sixth '*melleirên*', in the seventh '*eirên*'.

Though scholars have doubted whether the year-classes enumerated here denote the seven-year period leading up to the *ephêbeia* or the seven-year period of which the *ephêbeia* consists, the latter interpretation is certainly to be preferred since it seems to agree with Plutarch's somewhat obscure statement (*Lyk.* 17.2), 'They call *eirenes* those who for two years already have been out of the category of *paides* and the oldest of the *paides* are called *melleirenes*', which suggests that a Spartan became an *eirên* in his twentieth year (cf. MacDowell 1986, 162). Between the years seventeen and nineteen Spartan *ephêboi* served in an organisation known as the *krupteia* which resembled a kind of secret police (the literal meaning of the term) and whose purpose was to terrorise and demoralise the enslaved helot population. As *kruptoi* they lived outside society, probably secretly and in isolation. On completion of their period of service they were liable for regular military service, though they were not yet regarded as full citizens. The *krupteia* thus appears to have been equivalent to the *ephêbeia* within the life-cycle of an Athenian (see below, p. 183).

The *Koureôtis*

In Athens the period of transition from childhood to adulthood seems to have lasted from the sixteenth to twentieth year and was graded in such a way that youths became incorporated in an ever-widening social and civic milieu in line with their assumption of an ever-increasing variety of social and civic roles. Accordingly the groups to which they were successively admitted – first the phratry, second the deme, third the citizen body as a whole – themselves become progressively more representative of the body politic.

Upon attaining the age of sixteen or thereabouts an Athenian boy was probably introduced for the second time to his phratry on the day of *Koureôtis* during the *Apatouria* (see above, p. 121). As in the case of newborn infants, admission to the phratry was contingent upon a vote by all its members, the function of which was to establish and acknowledge publicly the applicant's legitimacy and entitlement to membership. From the time of Kleisthenes onwards (i.e. 508/7 BC) admission to a phratry does not seem to have carried with it any enhanced civic status and was only of significance within the phratries themselves. Before 508/7, however, it is likely that it guaranteed eventual access to political and legal rights. The *Koureôtis* takes its name from *koureion*, a word which referred both to the sacrifice which was now performed on the initiate's behalf – a more senior equivalent of the *meion*, so to speak – and to the ceremonial cutting of a young man's hair which almost certainly accompanied it. Conceivably this act may have symbolised the end of a young person's growing years, since it was widely believed that cutting the hair was liable to terminate growth. It may have been on this same occasion, but at any rate before the hair-cutting, that Athenian youths performed a ritual known as the *oinistêria*, in accordance with which 'they brought a measure of wine as an offering to Herakles, and, after pouring a libation to him, gave it to their companions' (Hsch. and Phot. s.v.; cf. Athen. *Deipn.* 11.494f.).

Enrolment on the deme Athenian register

An Athenian male attained civic majority in his eighteenth year. This status was publicly denoted by his enrolment on the register of demesmen or *lêxiarchikon grammateion* which was displayed in the agora of his deme. The Aristotelian *Athênaiôn Politeia* or *Constitution of Athens* (42.1) describes the enrolment procedure as follows:

> Those who are born from parents on both sides (i.e. of citizen descent on the mother's as well as father's side) are entitled to citizenship and they are registered among their demesmen in their eighteenth year. When they are being registered, their demesmen vote about the candidates on oath, first as to whether they appear (*dokein*) to have reached the legal age (*hê hêlikia hê ek tou nomou*) – if they are regarded as not having done so they return to the *paides* – and secondly on whether the candidate is free and was born in accordance with the law (*kata ton nomon*).

After a discussion of the appeal procedure adopted in cases where a candidacy is rejected, the author continues (*AP* 42.2):

> After this the Council scrutinises (*dokimazei*) those who have been enrolled, and if anyone is regarded as being younger than his eighteenth year it fines the demesmen who registered him.

Precisely what constituted evidence of a young person's age is not known. Though not too much credit should be attached to Aristophanes' suggestion (*Wasps* 578) that it was customary for the Council to scrutinise (*dokimazein*) the private parts of the *paides* in order to determine their ages, it seems inevitable that candidates must to some extent have been judged on their appearance of physical maturity (cf. the use of *dokein* in *AP* 42.1). As at previous registrations and inductions, a single annual ceremony was held in Athens, probably during the month of Boedromion (August-September), at which all citizens-elect in the year-group underwent *dokimasia* by the Council. Since Athenian parents did not officially register their

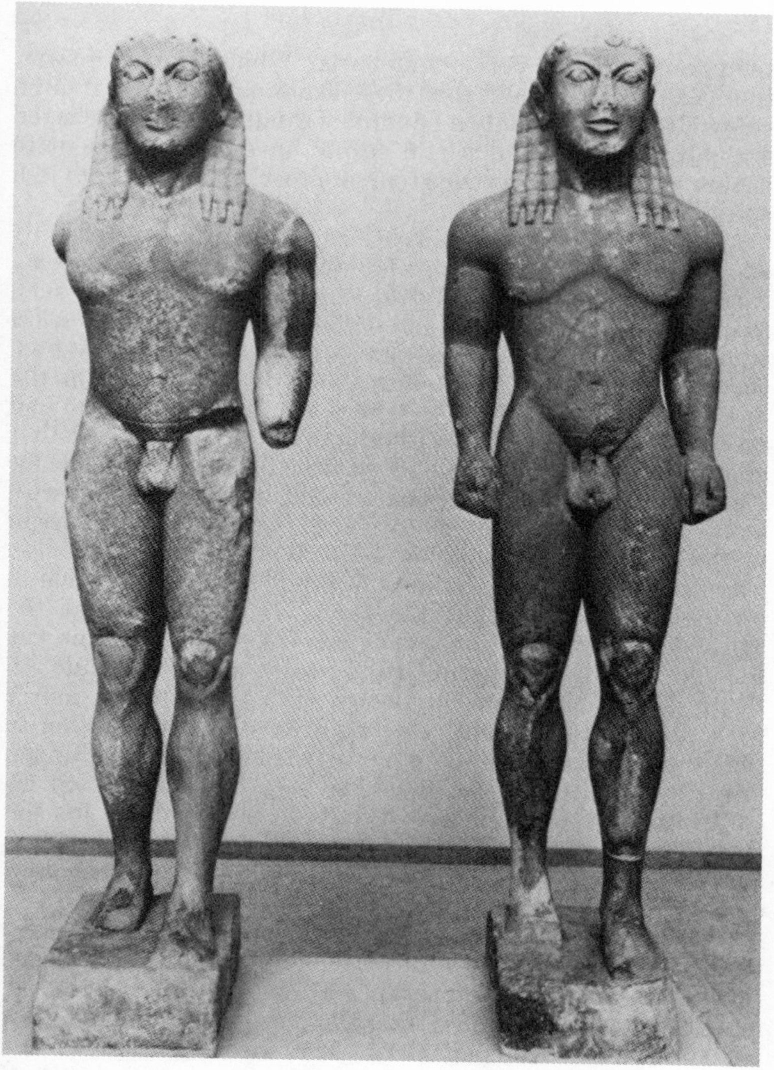

Fig. 23. On the verge of manhood. The twins Kleobis and Biton, *c.* 580 BC. Argive workmanship from the Sanctuary of Apollo at Delphi.

offspring at birth, this would have been the first occasion when the Athenian state formally acknowledged their existence. To what extent was the examination first by deme and then by Council essentially a formality and to what extent did candidates face a very real threat of rejection, whether on a temporary or on a permanent basis? Whatever the answer, there can be little doubt that these examinations were treated seriously, for even if only a handful of candidates were rejected annually, this in itself would surely have been sufficient to ensure that the entire year-group approached both events in a spirit of some trepidation.

A young Athenian who had cleared both hurdles successfully was judged to be an adult, as is indicated by the terminology used to describe his new status, which includes phrases such as *anêr gignesthai, andra einai dokimasthênai, dokimazesthai eis andras, exelthein ek paidôn* and *apallattesthai ek paidôn* (cf. Goldhill 1987, 67). Consequent upon his enrolment on the deme register, the citizen elect now acquired legal rights and ceased to be subject to the authority of his father, elder brother or guardian. Previously he had not been legally responsible for his actions and so could not be brought to court charged with any crime. Now, however, as Aischines reminds his audience in his speech *Against Timarchos* (1.18, 39 and 139), an Athenian was expected to know the laws of the *polis* and to be able to distinguish between right and wrong, having arrived at 'the age of discretion (*hê phronousa hêlikia*)'. Very possibly this was the age when he was permitted to recline at a symposium (cf. Booth 1988). Now, too, in theory at least he could marry without parental consent. The one area of absolute authority remaining to his father lay in the latter's ability to eject his son from the household by invoking a procedure known as *apokêruxis*, by which he may have been able to debar his son from his inheritance. No clear instance of the procedure has survived in our sources, however, and it is unclear how *apokêruxis* was implemented.

It was at this point, too, that orphans of the war dead ceased to be provided for by the state (see above, p. 159). To mark the conclusion of their period of maintained childhood, and, equally important, to underline the duties and obligations of citizenship by idealising those who died fighting for the community, an elaborate ceremony was staged on their behalf during the festival of the Great Dionysia. The ceremony is most fully described by Aischines, who makes it clear that it had been discontinued at some date before the time of his writing in 330 BC (3.154):

> Once upon a time on this day when as now tragedies were about to be performed, at a time when the *polis* had better customs

and better leaders, the herald came forward and introduced the orphans whose fathers had died in the war, *neaniskoi* accoutred in the panoply of war, and then he delivered the fairest of all proclamations and the one that serves most effectively as an inducement to valour: 'These *neaniskoi*, the sons of fathers who laid down their lives in the war and have become heroes (*agathoi*), have been supported by the demos until coming of age (*mechri hêbês*). Now, fully dressed in the panoply of war, the Demos dismisses them with prayers for their good fortune, each to his own home (*epi ta heautôn*), and it bids them to seats of honour in the theatre.' That used to be the proclamation, but not now ....

The Athenian *ephêbeia*

Immediately after passing the *dokimasia* Athenian youths began a two-year period of compulsory military training as *ephêboi* under the direction of a magistrate known as a *kosmêtês* or 'guardian of order', who was assisted by a board of ten (later twelve) *sôphronistai* or 'controllers of moderation'.

There is evidence for the existence of the Athenian ephebate from *c*. 370 BC onwards (cf. Aischin. 2.167), though its origins are undoubtedly much older. Our main source of information is provided by the Aristotelian *Athenaiôn Politeia* (42.3-5), which is dated *c*. 325. The chief problem is trying to determine which elements of the ephebate are 'traditional' and which form part of the innovations that came into effect in the fourth century, principally after the battle of Chaironeia in 338 as the result of a law introduced by Epikrates (cf. Harp. s.v. *Epikratês*). It is certainly possible that at the time of which Pseudo-Aristotle is writing all citizens irrespective of class were registered as *ephêboi*, even though the ephebic oath itself (see below) refers to the bearing of the heavy shield or *hoplon* from which hoplites take their name. Ephebes were maintained by the state and wore a broad-brimmed hat known as a *petasos* with a black travelling cloak known as a *chlamus*. Later, in the early second century AD, this was changed to white, thanks to the munificence of Herodes Atticus.

Ephêboi began their training by making an official round of the principal sanctuaries in the city (Ps.-Arist. *AP* 42). During their first year they resided in barracks on Akte peninsula and Mounychia Hill in the Piraeus and received instruction in both hoplite and light-armed warfare, including the use of the bow, the javelin and the catapult. At the end of the year they underwent a review in the deme theatre of the Piraeus at which each *ephêbos* was presented with a shield and a spear. Either now or possibly at the end of their second year they took an oath of loyalty to the state in the sanctuary of the goddess Agraulos situated on the north slope of the Acropolis. The words of the oath are preserved in a number of sources, including a fourth-century BC marble shaft or *stêlê* discovered in the deme of Acharnai which probably stood in the sanctuary of Ares in the Agora. The text reads as follows (Tod, *GHI* II 204):

> I shall not disgrace my sacred weapons (*hopla*) nor shall I desert my comrade at my side (*parastatês*), wherever I stand in the ranks. I shall fight in defence of both sacred and secular things and I shall not hand down a fatherland that is reduced in size, but one that is larger and stronger as far as in me lies and with the assistance of all. I shall be obedient to those who on any occasion are governing prudently and to the laws that are established and to any that in the future may be wisely established. If anyone tries to destroy them, I shall resist both as far as in me lies and with the assistance of all, and I shall honour the sacred rites that are ancestral. These gods are witnesses: Agraulos, Hestia, Enyo, Enyalios, Ares and Athena Areia, Zeus, Thallo, Auxo, Hegemone, Herakles, the boundary-markers of the fatherland, the wheat, barley, vines, olive trees and fig trees.

During their second year *ephêboi* served as patrolmen or *peripoloi* at various forts situated along the borders of Attica. Throughout their period of service they were not only exempt from taxes but also debarred from appearing in a law court either as prosecutor or defendant. In addition, they were required to take a leading role at festivals and on other state occasions. To give one example, it was *ephêboi* who at the celebration of the City Dionysia formed the procession which conveyed the cult statue of Dionysos from the Academy, which lies just outside the city wall, to the theatre of Dionysos on the south-east slope of the Acropolis.

At the end of their second year of service *ephêboi* were reincorporated into the citizen body as young adults or *neoi*. Most probably their names were now recorded on a register known as the *ekklêsiastikon pinax*, which indicated that they were entitled to attend the Ekklesia or Assembly, though a passage in Xenophon (*Mem.* 3.6.1) suggests that this right was conferred earlier. (A citizen's name was presumably struck off the *pinax* only if he became disqualified and when he died). They could now prosecute and be prosecuted. Militarily speaking, they constituted a *hêlikia* under the protection of an eponymous hero and until the age of fifty-nine were liable for annual military call-up, presumably on a rotating basis.

By the end of the fourth century ephebic service seems to have been no longer compulsory, and by 282 BC at the latest it had been reduced to one year. The institution had become militarily defunct by the end of the second century BC, even though numerous inscriptions record that *ephêboi* were still performing duties of a civic and religious nature. Foreigners, too, came to be admitted into its ranks. Philosophy and literature became part of the core curriculum, as is indicated by an inscription dated 123/2 BC which alludes to the attendance of *ephêboi* at lectures given at educational institutions including the Academy, Lykeion and Ptolemaion (*IG* II^2 1006). To this period, too, belong the earliest inscriptions referring to naval races between teams of *ephêboi* which were held in the Piraeus. These races constituted an important feature of the two most important festivals held in the port town, notably the Diisoteria, celebrated in honour of Zeus Soter and Athena Soteira, and the Mounychia, celebrated in honour of Artemis Mounychia. *Ephêboi* are last heard of in an inscription dating to the second half of the third century AD (cf. *IG* II^2 2245). The institution existed in numerous Hellenistic cities throughout the Greek world and constituted a powerful hellenising influence. When the high priest Jason decided to introduce Greek culture into Jerusalem he did so partly by organising the aristocratic youth into an ephebate and making them do exercises in the gymnasium (II Macc. 4:9, 12 and 14).

It has been observed: 'The *ephêbeia* is much more than a period of military service. It is the period of transition between childhood and complete participation in the life of the society' (Roussel 1921, 459). Like the Spartan *krupteia*, which the Athenian institution mirrors in a number of important particulars, young men were required to undergo a period of withdrawal from the community before full inclusion within the citizen body. This period of withdrawal served to underline the ambiguous relationship which young men aged about seventeen to nineteen enjoyed with the *polis* itself. Their liminal status as citizens-to-be was expressed in symbolic form by the aetiological myth explaining the origin of the Apatouria festival and in dramatic form by the military programme which as *ephêboi* they themselves fulfilled.

The myth of the Apatouria appears in a number of different versions which all derive the festival's name from the *apatê* or deceit practised by an Athenian called Melanthos (or Melanthios) over Xanthos, king of Boiotia, when the two were engaged in single combat to determine the sovereignty of disputed territory on the borders between Attica and Boiotia. According to one account the Athenian king Thymoites was himself unable to fight because he was too old, so he promised the throne to the youthful Melanthos if he won. As Xanthos and Melanthos took their stand opposite each other, the latter claimed to see a beardless man wearing a black goatskin standing behind Xanthos and cried out in protest. When Xanthos turned round to see who was there, he was struck by Melanthos and killed. The myth seems to provide a foundation charter for the ephebate itself in that (1) the action takes place at a frontier region, (2) the combat is based on a style and code (or anti-code) of military conduct that is completely counter to the hoplite ethic which *ephêboi* swear to uphold, and (3) the imagery of the narrative emphasises the ritual exclusion of the *ephêbos* from public life by repeated reference to the colour black, as in the name Melanthos which means 'the Black One', the black cloak of the mysterious helper, and, in some versions at least, in the name of the disputed territory Melainai (cf. Vidal-Naquet 1968).

According to this interpretation, the action of the hero thus provides a symbolic inversion of 'hoplitism', since it violates the honourable and corporate ethic upon which this style of fighting was based. One reservation needs to be expressed, however. We do not know for certain whether all citizens-elect qualified for the ephebate. The suggestion that ephebic training is likely to have excluded the *thêtes*, the lowest property-owning group, on the grounds that it was primarily in hoplite warfare is not wholly convincing (cf. Rhodes 1981, 503). The fact that at the time of the composition of the *Athenaiôn Politeia* ephebes were trained in the use of the bow, spear and catapult surely indicates that by the 320s at the latest it constituted all-round training appropriate for light as well as heavy infantry, though it must be conceded that *thêtes* would not have been included in the presentation ceremony at which ephebes received a hoplite shield and spear. Since, too, mercenaries occasionally served as *peripoloi* it is inherently unlikely that native-born citizens would have been excluded (cf. Aischin. 1.168). The interpretation of the Apatouria as an ephebic charter myth may therefore need modification if it turns out that there were those among the *ephêboi* who never actually graduated to hoplite status, since, if that is true, what the myth then provides (or at any rate came to provide) is not only an inverted model for hoplites but also an actual model for *thêtes*.

On completing his ephebic training a young man made a private dedication to the gods who had supervised his coming of age. The following epigram of uncertain date (*AP* 6.282) describes this solemn moment:

> To you, Hermes, did Kalliteles hang up [as a dedication in your temple] his felt hat made of well-carded sheep's wool, his two-pinned brooch, his strigil, his unstrung bow, his threadbare travelling cloak (*chlamus*) soaked in sweat, his javelins and his ever-spinning ball. Receive, I beseech you, friend of youth (*kôrophilos*), this gift of a well-ordered adolescence (*ephêbosuna*).

The homosexual phase

Typically around the age of eighteen an Athenian male entered a phase of life when his emotions and sentiments would be most powerfully directed towards a person of his own sex. This period may have lasted some ten years, in the course of which he would graduate from being the object of homosexual love as an *erômenos* to the victim of its assaults as an *erastês*, that is, from passive partner to active one, from pupil to teacher. Deviations undoubtedly occurred, however, and it would be foolish to pretend that every Athenian male passed through a homosexual 'phase' or, conversely, that homosexual activity was invariably confined to the period from twenty to thirty. The view none the less prevailed that homosexual activity was an 'episodic phenomenon', rather than one which reflected an individual's basic sexual orientation (cf. Dover 1978, 202f.).

The *Arkteia*

A highly problematic passage in Aristophanes' *Lysistratê* (ll. 641-7) has been interpreted by some scholars as indicating that Athenian girls underwent four stages in their transition to womanhood. The passage reads as follows:

> As soon as I was in my seventh year I became an *arrhêphoros*. Then in my tenth I was an *aletris* to the *Archêgetis*. Then, wearing a saffron robe (*krokôtos*), I was a bear (*arktos*) at the festival of Artemis Brauronia. Next, on becoming a beautiful *pais*, I performed the function of *kanêphoros*, wearing a string of figs.

Of the four rituals mentioned here, the one about which we are best informed is that of 'acting the bear', an allusion to a rite known as the *Arkteia* which was performed chiefly at the sanctuary of Artemis Brauronia at Brauron. The *Arkteia* took its name from the fact that during its celebration young girls called *arktoi* performed ritual acts in a bear-like manner (*arkteuein, mimêsasthai tên arkton*, etc.). According to an aetiological legend, the consecration of young girls to Artemis was a necessary act of atonement for the killing by some Athenian youths of a sacred animal which had broken into the goddess's sanctuary. Although Artemis initially demanded virgin sacrifice to avert a plague or drought (see below, p. 194), she was eventually deceived into accepting the sacrifice of a ram disguised as a she-bear. The *Arkteia* was hence explained as a re-enactment of the substitute-sacrifice performed in Artemis' honour. From the evidence supplied by figured decorations on special-shaped vases called *kratêriskoi* (miniature mixing bowls), which have been found at sites throughout Attica including Brauron, Halai, Mounychia, Eleusis and the Acropolis, it seems that *arktoi* either wore a short undergarment known as a *chitôn* or else went naked. The rituals which they were required to perform included dancing, running towards an altar, holding garlands and sacrificing a goat. Palm trees, which recall the circumstances of Artemis' own birth on Delos, are also occasionally depicted. The *kratêriskoi* were no doubt mostly used for libations, though some contain traces of ashes.

The suggestion has been made that the devotion of the *arktoi* to the goddess was originally seen as 'equivalent, within the life-cycle of females, to the period of withdrawal and seclusion that characterises the period of adolescence', as exemplified, for instance, by the Spartan *krupteia* and the Athenian *ephêbeia* (cf. Jeanmaire 1939, 260). How accurate is this claim? There are a number of problems. First, the girls' period of service was probably of very short duration, only a month or so at the most. Secondly, we do not know for certain at what age

Fig. 24. Head of a little girl, possibly a 'bear', late fourth or early third century BC. From the sanctuary of Artemis Brauronia in north-east Attica.

the girls became eligible for the *Arkteia*. The *Lysistratê* passage implies that *arktoi* had to be more than nine years old, whereas the scholiast (ad l. 646) states categorically that they were aged between four and nine. Another late source, Harpokration, informs us that the verb *arkteuein* is synonymous with *dekatuein* (s.v.), which should mean 'to be in one's tenth year'. The iconographical evidence is equally confusing. The girls depicted on the *kratêriskoi* appear to be aged between seven and eight (Karouzou, quoted in Kahil 1965, 25), whereas several statues dedicated in the sanctuary at Brauron appear to depict girls in their early teens, though it must be conceded that there is no proof that the latter are actually 'bears' (Lloyd-Jones 1983, 93). Indeed the fact that boys are more commonly represented than girls tends to suggest the contrary (cf. Hollinshead 1979, 42).

An attempt has been made to reconcile the conflicting testimonia by proposing that *arktoi* were originally selected from among girls who were experiencing the onset of puberty but that subequently their age was lowered 'proportionately as the original meaning of the rite was forgotten and service to Artemis took on a more restrained kind of character, preserved among a few traditionally-minded families which performed it out of a certain vanity' (Jeanmaire 1939, 259f.). The proposition is an attractive one, but it cannot be proved. Lowering the age-requirement of a rite of passage is widely attested by anthropologists, its occurrence perhaps being evidence of increasing urbanisation and social sophistication. In seventeenth-century England, for instance, aristocratic boys doffed long frocks to don breeches at the age of seven, whereas in the following century the switch to masculine attire took place as early as three or four (cf. Stone 1979, 258). That the *Arkteia* was in origin and essence a puberty ritual seems an obvious inference.

The scholiast to *Lysistratê* states that the ritual preceded marriage, that the girls had been 'chosen', and – contradictorily – that it was a compulsory undertaking for *all* girls before marriage. But although elements such as seclusion, cultic nakedness and the threat of maiden sacrifice constitute typical initiation motifs (cf. Burkert 1985, 263), we can hardly regard the *Arkteia* as an initiatory ceremony in the strict sense of the term in view of the fact that their service as *arktoi* did not, so far as we know, confer any new social status upon the girls. Despite the bold assertion made by the scholiast, only a small fraction of the female population of Attica are actually likely to have served the goddess in this capacity, as is indicated by the modest size of the Artemis sanctuaries and the relative paucity of finds which they have produced. It is probable therefore that the girls were either chosen randomly from the population at large or else belonged to an exclusive social élite, membership of which may have been confined to a limited number of Athenian *genê* or aristocratic kin-groups.

In view of the fact that the primary social function of Greek women was to marry and give birth to future citizens, the *Arkteia* probably negotiated a status-transition of an essentially physiological and private nature which had virtually nothing to do with the celebrants' public identity. It perhaps marked a young girl's graduation to the condition of 'marriageable but unmarried' as denoted by the term *parthenos*. Like other rituals and festivals, however, it was no doubt polyvalent and probably incorporated a whole complex of transitions at different levels of public and private consciousness, including the passage from girlhood to maidenhood, from guilt to expiation, from savagery to civilisation, from animality to domesticity, from anxiety to confidence, and finally from the threat of sterility to the promise of increase.

Since the aetiological myth of the *Arkteia* deals with the consequences of slaughtering what is wild, structuralists have interpreted it as a coded commentary upon man's guilt in the face of his own cultural evolution. Vidal-Naquet (1974, 179), for instance, writes: 'In exchange for the very advance in culture implied by the killing of wild animals, an advance for which men are responsible, the girls are obliged ... before puberty to undergo a period of ritual "wildness".' Analogously, but here with reference to the evolution of the individual rather than that of the whole group, Sourvinou-Inwood (1987, 144), has recently expressed the opinion that 'an important part of the initiatory function [of the ritual] pertains to the "domestication" of the partly wild girl, purging her of animality and thus taming her for marriage'. Plausible though these explanations are, they still leave unanswered the question why girls should be called upon to atone for the crime of young men. Even more problematically, they ignore the fact that the myth explains the ritual as a response to a *real* natural disaster. In view of the fact that the service of *arktoi* was deemed efficacious to prevent a recurrence of drought or plague, it seems appropriate to emphasise that the young girls' own socialisation may have been only a part of the ritual's total meaning.

The role of *parthenoi* in religion

Of the four duties mentioned in the *Lysistratê* only that of being a bear has any possible claim to function as a rite of passage. The previously-mentioned status, that of being an *arrhêphoros* at the age of seven, was reserved for two (or possibly four) young girls of noble birth who resided 'for a certain time' on the Acropolis (Paus. 1.27.3). Their duties included weaving Athena's *peplos*, tending her sacred olive tree, and carrying certain unspecified objects in a basket which was balanced on their heads to the shrine of Aphrodite in the Gardens on the north slope of the Acropolis, whence they returned similarly laden. Though initiation symbolism has been detected in the fact that the maidens 'encounter the domain of Aphrodite' (Burkert 1985, 264), it is unclear how a ritual requiring the services of a maximum of four ministrants can properly be understood as a rite of passage unless our evidence is describing a very attenuated manifestation of what had once involved a much larger number of girls. There is, however, absolutely no shred of evidence to suggest that being either an *aletris* ('baker' or 'grinder') of the *Archêgetis* (possibly a cult epithet of Athena) or a *kanêphoros* ('basket-carrier'), the other two sacred duties mentioned by Aristophanes, marked regular stages in a *parthenos*' preparation for adult life. It is best, therefore, to conclude that what the poet provides us with are the steps of a 'pseudo-cycle' (cf. Vidal-Naquet 1974, 179), though this is not to deny that one or two very privileged Athenian girls may occasionally have served in all four capacities. Athenian *parthenoi* performed many other religious duties. Two girls of noble birth, for instance, annually served as *loutrides* or *pluntrides*, their duty being to wash the robes that adorned the ancient olive-wood image of Athena Polias (Hsch. and Phot. s.v. *loutrides*; see Parker 1983, 26f.).

Parthenoi serving as priestesses or temple servants in expiation for crimes performed by men are attested in several cults outside Attica. As a punishment for the rape of Kassandra by Ajax son of Oileus, a crime perpetrated in the temple of Athena during the sack of Troy, the townspeople of western Lokri were required to send two *parthenoi* of aristocratic birth to the temple of Athena Naryka in the Troad. There they led a wretched existence performing menial tasks such as sweeping and washing the temple, going about barefoot, shaven-headed and wearing only a single undergarment. According to one tradition they remained in temple service for life, though another states that they were replaced annually. The latter is more probable in view of the fact that the evidence for perpetual chastity as a requirement of Greek religion is very slight.

Also widely-attested are premarital rituals involving *parthenoi*. On Keos, for instance, *parthenoi* were required to remain all day long in sanctuaries, engaged in play and dance under the scrutiny of their suitors, while by night they went from house to house on a rotating basis, waiting upon each other's parents and brothers 'even to the extent of washing their feet' (Plu. *Mor.* 249de = *Bravery of Women* 12). The ritual seems to have been intended to dramatise the complementary roles of both sex-partner and housekeeper which a Kean wife, like all wives, was required to fulfil.

Choirs of *parthenoi*

Choirs of *parthenoi* linked by *homêlikia* appear to have existed in very large numbers in both the Archaic and Classical periods. How closely 'sameness of age' was defined for choral purposes no doubt varied from choir to choir, though in some instances it undoubtedly denoted exact age-correspondence. Xenophon of Ephesos, author of a romance known as *Ephesiaka*, alludes (1.2.2 *T*) to a choir whose members were all aged sixteen, and Kallimachos (*h. Artemis* 13f.) in a mythological context to a choir of 60 Okeanidai all aged nine. What chiefly distinguished groups of female age-mates from their male counterparts was the fact that the bonds which linked the girls to one another and to their leader inevitably dissolved upon the occasion of their marriage. Post-marital female *homêlikia* was virtually non-existent.

For a brief period, however, as girls experienced the first onset of womanhood, they would have had an opportunity to 'compare notes'. The relations engendered within groups of this kind, temporary though they may have been, thus afforded a valuable breathing-space during which the girls' own feelings and identities could be the subject of legitimate interest and concern, prior to assimilation into their respective *oikoi* as wives and mothers. The female circle about which we are best informed is that for which Sappho composed poetry. Born in Mytilene on Lesbos in the early sixth century BC, Sappho wrote poems which were largely inspired by homosexual love. Her circle comprised young girls of marriageable age who, through the vehicle of dance and song, exchanged feelings of an intensely private nature. How long the girls remained in the circle is not known, though Sappho mentions knowing one pupil called Atthis when she was 'small and graceless' (fr. 49 *LP*).

On the fringes of the Greek world the natural competitiveness of *parthenoi* took a more barbaric turn. Herodotos (4.180) tells of a Libyan tribe who celebrated annually a festival in honour of Athena at which

> *Parthenoi* are divided into two groups and fight each other with sticks and stones, claiming that they are fulfilling their ancestral obligations to their native goddess whom we call Athena. *Parthenoi* who die of the wounds they receive are called *pseudo-parthenoi*. Before they join battle they do this in common. They attire the most beautiful *parthenos* in a

Corinthian helmet and Greek panoply, set her on a chariot and lead her in a circle around the lake.

Sacrifice of *parthenoi*

In Greek mythology the sacrifice of a *parthenos* is commonly performed as a prelude to war. It was in expiation for the killing of a pregnant hare before the despatch of the Greek fleet to Troy that the sacrifice of Iphigeneia, the daughter of Agamemnon, was demanded by Artemis. Belief in the supreme efficacy of virgin sacrifice certainly persisted into historical times. Just before the battle of Leuktra, which was fought in 371 BC, the Theban commander Epaminondas is said to have performed a substitute-virgin sacrifice at the tomb of two Boiotian *parthenoi*, daughters of a certain Skedasos, who had been raped by the Spartans and subsequently committed suicide out of shame. Skedasos had appeared to Epaminondas in a dream demanding the sacrifice of a Boiotian *parthenos* as the price for his support but was prevailed upon instead to accept that of a young filly which opportunely came forward to the altar at the moment the *parthenos* was due to be slaughtered.

Why sacrifice a virgin before going to war? I think there are several explanations. As a symbol of purity and innocence, a *parthenos* is antithetically related to the activity of war. She is by definition ripe for marriage, and marriage, since it implies love and fecundity, is the absolute negation of war. Virgin sacrifice before combat is thus a way of establishing one's priorities. A further reason is that only the life of a pure and unsullied human being can possibly be judged to be commensurate with the help that is sought from the gods at time of war. Lastly, virgin sacrifice may have been intended to heighten psychological motivation among the soldiery, by transforming what might otherwise have been regarded as an unwarranted act of aggression into a 'just' war of revenge. By a particularly twisted form of logic the sacrifice of an innocent may have been viewed as a pre-emptive act of atonement for the anticipated slaughter that will follow (cf. Burkert 1972, 65).

Inasmuch as it constituted the most potent form of offering, virgin sacrifice was also performed as a way of averting natural disasters such as famine or disease. Pausanias (7.19) reports that a *parthenos* called Komaitho who lived in Triklaria had

Fig. 25. Detail of a Tyrrhenian amphora attributed to the Timiades Painter depicting Neoptolemos sacrificing the virgin Polyxene upon the grave of his father Achilles, *c.* 570-560 BC.

a boyfriend called Melanippos. The parents of both parties objected to their relationship and in order to evade discovery the two made love in the temple of Artemis. In consequence of this flagrant act of impiety, infertility and plague spread throughout the land. To atone for the crime the inhabitants of Triklaria were required by the Delphic Oracle to make an annual sacrifice of the most beautiful *parthenos* and the most handsome *pais* to the goddess Artemis. In Athens virgin sacrifice was commemorated at a shrine called the Leokorion which marked the spot where the hero Leos sacrificed his daughters, likewise in response to an oracle from Delphi, in order to deliver the city from a plague or famine.

The naive and almost invariably senseless self-sacrifice of young men and women in war is a commonplace in Euripidean drama. In the *Iphigeneia at Aulis* Iphigeneia, the daughter of Agamemnon, lays down her life at her father's command in the mistaken belief that it will put an end to the rape of Greek women by barbarians. She even goes so far as to assert (l. 1394): 'One man's life is worth that of thousands of women.' Iphigeneia's death is all the more poignant and futile in view of the fact that, as the audience knows full well, it will serve merely to promote human suffering, for it is due to her sacrifice that the goddess Artemis consents to send a favourable breeze which enables the becalmed Greek fleet to sail to Troy. In the *Hekabê* it is high-minded preference for death over slavery that inspires the Trojan princess Polyxene to accept with equanimity her role as sacrificial victim to the shade of Achilles. In the *Children of Herakles* Makaria, Herakles' daughter, agrees to be sacrificed in order to save the lives of her brothers. Lastly in the *Phoenician Women* Kreon's son Menoikeus commits suicide in blind obedience to an oracle from Apollo which assures him that by so doing he will become the saviour of Thebes. In all these instances what Euripides is exploring is the fatal willingness of young people to lay down their lives for what they believe to be a noble and just cause, a quality which lays them tragically open to manipulation by their cynical elders.

Conclusions

It was Greek art above all which idealised the *kouros* and *kourê*, the young man and young woman at the height of physical perfection and attractiveness, and which made of this fleeting moment of life a veritable cult (see Figs. 22 and 23). All the more striking, therefore, is the absence of any clearcut division between adolescence and adulthood either in the Greek language or in the institutions of Greek life. For an Athenian male, both the sixteenth and eighteenth year marked significant stages in the passage to manhood. It has been suggested that 'One became an ephebe in the civic or military sense of the word at eighteen, but one became an ephebe in the phratry at sixteen' (Vidal-Naquet 1974, 177). But which milestone, if either, was judged to be more decisive? The twentieth year, when a young man completed his ephebic service, marked a further important transition. Attainment of the condition of *parthenos* was also pivotal, as is indicated by the custom of commemorating the deaths of those who died 'marriageable but unmarried' with a marble image of a *loutrophoros*, a vase used in the bridal bath connected with the marriage ceremony.

Fig. 26. Heroic delinquency. Attic red-figure *kylix* by Douris depicting a youthful Herakles cudgelling to death his lyre-teacher Linos with the leg of a broken chair, first quarter of the fifth century BC.

In our own society, dense with a mass of overlapping and intersecting areas of social interaction, the categories 'adult' and 'non-adult' can and commonly do shift their meaning according to context. Thus age of legal reponsibility, political majority and military call-up, not to mention the age at which one can drive a car, purchase alcohol, have intercourse or marry, form a cluster of essentially interrelated but partly discrete contexts which bestow the status of adulthood upon the individual according to their own technically circumscribed notions of social and personal responsibility. We expect the Greeks to be more dogmatic and simplistic in their categorisations than we are. But the testimony examined here demonstrates conclusively that they were not.

The literary evidence has suggested that there existed two complementary modes of dramatising the passage from childhood to adulthood in ancient Greece. According to the 'male' mode, the transition is in the form of a graduated enlargement of the social persona through a series of progressive identifications with an increasingly extended social group. Telemachos' maturation is thus presented in the *Odyssey* in terms of a series of social encounters which are designed to establish his reputation nationwide. In much the same way an Athenian youth was required to pass through a series of initiations which admitted him first to his *oikos*, then to his phratry, next to his deme, and finally to the state itself as a citizen with full political, civic and legal rights. According to the female mode, the transition takes the form of a violent rupture which severs for all time all links with the past. Instead of a graduated extension, there is an abrupt and violent irruption from the outside which shatters the world of innocence and play, as happens to Nausikaa during her encounter with Odysseus. We might say that the former mode views childhood and adulthood as organically related, the second as mutually exclusive.

Representations of coming in age in Greek literature are consistent with the fact that neither in Athens nor Sparta was there a graduated series of initiations for girls comparable to that which existed for boys, the reason being that girls did not undergo any extension of their social persona as they became adult. It may yet be argued that the one genuine rite of passage for girls was marriage itself. Even here, however, analogies with male initiation ceremonies are of dubious applicability, since – to anticipate what will be examined in the next chapter – marriage required the bride to pass from a condition of total legal and economic dependency upon her father or legal guardian to one of total legal and economic dependency upon her husband. From being some man's daughter she became some man's wife. In other words, whereas a youth came of age by moving outwards from *oikos* to *polis*, a girl came of age merely by being transferred from her natal *oikos* as *parthenos* to her marital *oikos* as *numphê*.

Finally, and to end on a somewhat frivolous note, though it would be extremely incautious to offer any comment upon the prevalence of juvenile delinquency either in Athens or elsewhere, there is enough to indicate that the phenomenon was not unknown. In addition to the painful drubbing which Strepsiades receives from his son in Aristophanes' *Clouds*, we may note that Alkibiades, when he was no longer a *pais*, is alleged to have struck his old schoolmaster with his fist simply because the wretched dunce did not possess a copy of Homer's works (Plu. *Alk*. 7). The hero Herakles was even more rebellious. He bludgeoned his music teacher Linos to death with his lyre (see Fig. 26).

5

Early Adulthood

> Ah, youth (*neotas*) is sweet!
>
> (Eur. *HF* 638)

The period of life covered by this chapter is approximately the age of nineteen to twenty-nine-plus in the case of a man and from marriageability to the birth of the first child in the case of a woman. In practice, however, it is often virtually impossible to differentiate the condition and status of a new bride from a wife of long standing, at least until menopause is reached. The reason for this divergence in the respective ages of the sexes is that we can no longer trace in parallel sequence the life patterns of Greek men and women.

The focus will essentially be upon the differing roles available to men and women within these age bands. Those available to men were military, civic, professional, social and domestic; those available to women were essentially marital and domestic. It has been stated that 'Marriage is for the girl what war is for the boy: for each of them these mark the fulfilment of their respective natures as they emerge from a state in which each still shared in the state of the other' (Vernant 1982, 23; cf. Loraux 1981, 40). What is striking is first how early that fulfilment was attained in the case of a woman; how late in the case of a man; and secondly how suddenly the transformation came about in the case of a woman; how lengthily in the case of a man. The attainment of manhood had its purest *raison d'être* in achievement on the field of battle; that of womanhood in service in the bridal bed.

Celibacy was not a valid option. Though Sparta imposed severe penalties on bachelors, no other state is known to have been so authoritarian and perhaps no other state needed to be. Even the fanatically misogynistic Hesiod concedes that the condition of those who remain single all their lives is no less unpleasant than that of those who marry, since bachelors have no one to look after them in old age and no one to succeed them as heirs (*Th.* 603-7). The condition of 'unmarried' as a classification therefore hardly exists in Greek thinking. In the case of a man, *êitheos*, which can signify 'unmarried', more precisely signifies 'a youth'. In the case of a woman, the assumption was that no eligible female would remain unmarried by choice: so 'unmarried' meant in effect 'unmarriageable' because of either ugliness or poverty. At least some freeborn and metic women would have chosen to become *hetairai* or prostitutes, rather than to go through life as old maids, since this would have afforded them independence, wealth and contact with the cultural life of their community, all of which would have been denied to them as spinsters.

A young adult male past ephebic age was perhaps most commonly classified as a *neos*, a term which covered the period from the twenties to the early thirties in Athens, but a somewhat longer span of years in other states (cf. Thuk. 5.43.2; below, p. 242). Other expressions include *neanias*, *neôteros* and *neaniskos*, though these could also apply to those of ephebic status. No term seems to have designated a young woman in her twenties, for the simple reason that the only noteworthy fact about a woman once she had passed puberty was whether she happened to be married. It is not surprising, therefore, that she is identified primarily in relation to her role as child-bearer: from being a marriageable *parthenos* at puberty she graduates to becoming a fully-fledged *gunê* upon the occasion of the birth of her first child, having passed through an intervening stage of social and biological development as a *numphê*, a term which was reserved for the brief interval from betrothal to motherhood.

The military and civic status of young adults

In Athens young men aged between nineteen and twenty-nine occupied an ambivalent position vis-à-vis the state. They were now eligible for hoplite service and probably liable to more frequent military call-up than any other age-group. At the beginning of the Peloponnesian War the Spartan king Archidamos cherishes the hope that the Athenians 'who flourish with numerous youth (*akmazontas … neotêti pollêï*)' will come out from behind their walls and challenge his army when they see their land being ravaged (Thuk. 2.20.2). The frequency of military call-up for those in this age-group accounts for the pathos that attends scenes of leave-taking in both literature and art from the time of Homer onwards. A prudent *neos* who was already head of his *oikos* would therefore make a will before going off on a military campaign (Isai. 6.3, 8; 11.8). Although permitted to attend the Ekklesia, *neoi* were not yet eligible for election to the Boule, probably due to the fact that whereas they were judged to have arrived at their physical *akmê*, intellectually speaking they were still underdeveloped.

Sparta seems to have held a similarly ambivalent attitude towards young men in their twenties. Known variously as *eirenes, hoi hêbôntes* and *ta deka aph' hêbês*, those of pure Spartan stock now became members of the regular army. In the fourth century it was this age-group which marched into battle at the head of the army (cf. Xen. *Hell*. 2.4.32 and 3.4.23). They could not yet be elected to the ephorate, however, and may well have been prohibited from attending meetings of the Spartan Apella or Assembly. For purposes of discipline, they were still under the jurisdiction of the *paidonomos* or supervisor of the *paides*, although this official could not himself punish miscreant *eirenes* but had to refer them to the ephors for judgment (cf. MacDowell 1986, 68). Although the law permitted them to wear their hair long 'as soon as they ceased to be ephebes (*euthus ek tês tôn ephêbôn hêkilias*)' as a sign of maturity (Plu. *Lyk*. 22.1; cf. Xen. *LP* 11.3), it judged them insufficiently adult to enter the agora and make their own purchases (Plu. *Lyk*. 25.1). Married *eirenes*, like their unmarried peers, were required to continue sleeping in a common dormitory, visiting their wives only stealthily at night (see below, p. 224). One important consequence of this bizarre regulation according to Plutarch was that 'some begat *paides* before they had seen their wives [naked] by daylight' (*Lyk*. 15.4-5). It is hard to resist the impression that this curtailment of their freedom was inspired in part by prudery. From the ranks of the *eirenes* the ephors appointed three *hippagretai* (cavalry-selectors) and these in turn each chose one hundred other *eirenes*, thus establishing a crack regiment of 300 *hippeis* or cavalry who acted as a bodyguard for the two kings (cf. Hdt. 8.124.3; Thuk. 5.72.4).

Spartan girls were strongly encouraged to take a leading role in the indoctrination of their male counterparts. As a mark of their identification with the aims and values of Spartan society, *parthenoi* were encouraged to mock goodnaturedly at

Fig. 27. Attic red-figure *skyphos* by the Pistoxenos Painter depicting Herakles and his old nurse Geropso, *c*. 470 BC.

neoi who had disgraced themselves and to sing the praises, quite literally speaking, of those who had achieved some distinction (Plu. *Lyk*. 14.3). In addition, since the security and continuance of the state depended upon the production of a new generation, *parthenoi* appeared at processions only scantily clad, so that the *neoi* who saw them should be aroused by what Plato circumspectly referred to as 'not the laws governing geometry [i.e. gravity?] but the laws governing eroticism' (15.1).

From the end of the fourth century BC onwards groups of *neoi* were organised into corporate associations which in a certain sense paralleled those to which *ephêboi* belonged. The principal function of such groups, which were regulated by an official known as a *gumnasiarchos*, seems to have been to stimulate athletic and gymnastic competitions. They flourished in the Hellenistic and Roman periods, particularly in Asia Minor. *Neoi* do not, however, appear to have been entrusted with executive authority. A rare exception is provided by a decree from Gortyn in Crete dating to the third century BC which legislated that disputes regarding the infringement of currency regulations are to be referred to a board comprising seven officials called the *neotas*, evidently a body constituted by *neoi*.

Generational conflict in Classical Athens

In the early decades of the fifth century BC the contrast between youth and old age became an extremely popular theme on Athenian red-figure vases. A well-known example is a drinking-cup by the Pistoxenos Painter (*c.* 480-470) which shows the youthful Herakles being accompanied to a music lesson by an old Thracian nurse who is white-haired, wizened and bowed with age, and with tattoos on her wrists and neck (Fig. 27). She is named Geropso, which we might perhaps render 'Senilia'. The contrast in ages between the two figures is accentuated by the vertical accent of the spear which Herakles carries upright, and the double crook in the staff which Geropso bears at an angle to the ground. The same distinction is exploited in sculpture, as in the so-called Ilissos grave-relief, which depicts a youth who gazes directly into the eyes of the spectator, while a grieving old man, probably his father, looks on sorrowfully (Fig. 28). Here the difference in age between the two figures serves to emphasise not only the pathos of early death but also the feebleness of unsupported senescence.

Artistic interest in the physical distinctiveness of youth and old age was almost certainly inspired in part by a developing awareness of the difference in outlook between the two age-groups. One of the best places to look for evidence of this difference is Aristophanes' *Clouds*, first produced in 423 and revised perhaps in 419 or 418, which contains a savage parody of the tensions and misunderstandings that exist between a father and his son. Though we do not know the exact age of the father, Strepsiades must be fairly elderly since he identifies himself as a *gerôn* (ll. 129, 746, 1457) and as a *presbutês* (ll. 263, 358). He is probably in his late fifties or early sixties. His son Pheidippides is about nineteen or twenty. The disagreement between the two begins, trivially enough, over their taste in music and poetry. When Strepsiades asks his son to sing a song by the sixth-century BC poet Simonides, he is told that it is old-fashioned to play the harp and sing while drinking 'like a woman humming while she is grinding corn' (ll. 1357-8). When he then asks him to recite a passage from Aeschylus, Pheidippides expresses utter contempt, praising instead the poet's younger contemporary Euripides. Struggling with difficulty to keep his temper, Strepsiades instructs his son to sing 'one of those ingenious songs that young men (*neôteroi*) know' (l. 1370). Scandalised by what he judges to be an

Fig. 28. Attic grave-relief from the Ilissos river depicting a naked youth and a grieving elder, probably his father, *c.* 330 BC. The emotional focus of the composition is emphatically on the youth.

outpouring of Euripidean depravity which issues from his son's lips, he can no longer contain himself and a fight ensues in which Strepsiades gets badly beaten up.

It may be argued that the generational conflict which Aristophanes explores in the *Clouds* is a perennial and universal one which has very little to tell us about the moral climate of late-fifth-century Athens, other than that the Athenians were remarkably like us. What is striking, however, is that the difference in artistic taste should be so marked that it contributed so strikingly to the generation gap. Mere comic exaggeration? Possibly. But the disagreement between father and son has implications that go far beyond mere aesthetic preference, and the point of that disagreement is very much the point of the play. Pheidippides, after thrashing his father for criticising Euripides, then goes on to prove by subtle logic that his behaviour is fully justified (ll. 1405ff.). The speech in which he defends his action is in part an Aristophanic showpiece designed to prove that the modern sophistry can justify the most morally abhorrent behaviour. At a deeper level, however, it articulates and justifies a studied contempt for old age that may well have been a hallmark of Athenian culture during the Peloponnesian war period. Pheidippides even goes so far as to assert that *gerontes* deserve to be punished when they misbehave because they are 'twice children (*dis paides*)' (l. 1417), an argument the force of whose logic Strepsiades actually concedes when he turns to address his peers (*andres hêlikes*) in the audience (l. 1437). The helpless condition of the elderly in the face of this irresistible rhetorical onslaught is pathetically illustrated by Strepsiades' description of his own humiliating descent into incontinence (ll. 1386-90). Second childhood indeed!

Aristophanes' *Clouds* lends strong support to the claim that in the final decades of the fifth century BC there existed in Athens a generation gap between those who were born under the Kleisthenic constitution established at the end of the sixth century on the one hand and those who had known nothing all their lives apart from the radical democracy instituted in the 460s on the other (cf. Forrest 1975). There is plenty of other evidence to support the claim. Thukydides' analysis of the voting pattern of the Athenian Assembly at the time of the despatch of the Sicilian Expedition in 415 suggests that sharp divisions along age lines surfaced in political debates. Nikias, who was about fifty-five at the time and bitterly opposed to the expedition, described the proposal as 'not the kind of thing that can be decided and acted upon by a young man in a hurry'. He sought his natural allies among *presbuteroi* and attempted to denigrate his opponent Alkibiades on the grounds that the latter, being a *neôteros*, was far too young to hold high military office (6.12-13). Alkibiades, who in 415 was in fact no mere stripling but a seasoned veteran of about thirty-five, responded by reproaching Nikias for attempting to create a division between young and old (6.18.6). He advocated instead a return to consensus politics which he rousingly described as 'the old system of our fathers who joined together in counsel, *neoi* and *geraiteroi* alike'.

The Sicilian debate in fact demonstrates two important tendencies of late-fifth-century Athenian politics: first that in 415 seasoned public speakers like Nikias expected to make political capital out of the fact that young and old constitute distinct and often opposed interest groups; and secondly that a belief was evidently cherished among the citizenry as a whole that in 'the good old days' consensus, and not the present factionalism, had been the order of the day. To what extent the intellectual climate of late-fifth-century Athens had brought about a genuine fracturing of the citizen body, to what extent it was erroneously perceived to have done so, and to what extent Nikias' appeal was merely a political rallying cry used by a self-interested politician seeking to gather the majority behind his banner is impossible to determine. In the event the decision to send the expedition to Sicily did produce a consensus of sorts, though not one which boded well for the success of the enterprise. Thukydides states (6.24.3):

> The *presbuteroi* thought that they would either conquer the places against which they were sailing or in any case with such a large force could come to no harm; the men in their prime (*hoi en têi hêlikiai*) had a longing for the sights and experiences of distant places, and were confident that they would return safely.

Athens as a youth-oriented culture

In view of the undoubted ascendancy enjoyed by the young in Athenian society it would hardly be surprising, if, as Theophrastos' portrait of the sixty-year-old Opsimath or Late-Learner (*Char.* 27) suggests, some senior citizens, reluctant to be perceived as dotards, cultivated an elaborate pretence of youthfulness. What in fact characterises the Late-Learner is not the desire to acquire learning for learning's sake, but a keenly felt psychological need to present himself to the world as one who is both abreast of the latest fashions and physically unimpaired by the ageing process. In his pitiful attempts to pit his strength against mere youngsters (*meirakia*) in competitions that require mental and physical stamina far beyond the command of his declining years, the Late-Learner is instantly recognisable and truly pathetic – surely the most pathetic among the thirty characters who populate Theophrastos' gallery of stock Athenians. To behave as if one were a *neanias* when one is in fact a *gerôn*, a form of aberrant behaviour identified in Greek by the verb *neanieuesthai*, is itself the product of a youth-oriented culture. Athens was not alone in producing such characters. Plutarch is likewise dismissive of the not unfamiliar present-day phenomenon of the man 'who, having lived blamelessly for many years under the same roof as his wife, kicks her out when he gets old and either lives alone or takes a mistress (*pallakidion*) instead of the woman he has wed (*gametê*)' (*Mor.* 789b = *Should Elders Take Part in Public Life?* 9).

Sexual activity of young males

The impression one receives of the young Greek male is of exuberant, guilt-free phallocentricity. The young Greek male seems to have required sexual novelty and evidently found it, with a variety of partners, both servile and freeborn, male and female. A graphic insight into the sexual mores of *neoi* is provided by remarks made by Ariston in his speech *Against Konon* (Dem. 54.14). His opponent, he says, in order to make light of his son's misconduct, will plead as follows:

> There are many people in Athens, the sons of gentlemen (*kaloi kagathoi*), who in the manner of *neoi* have playfully given themselves nicknames, and who call themselves Ithyphalloi (Erect-penises) and Autolekythoi (Self-stimulators), and that some of them have intercourse with *hetairai* (prostitutes), and that his son is actually one of them, and that he has often given and received blows on account of a *hetaira*, and that this is customary behaviour among *neoi*.

Although Ariston assumes that the jury will look with disfavour upon conduct of this kind, the opposition's claim that

Fig. 29. Tondo of an Attic red-figure *kylix* depicting a homosexual encounter between a boy and an older man, *c*. 470 BC.

it was common enough was probably true.

Whereas an adolescent Athenian male would have been the object of sexual attention from a man in his mid- to late twenties (see above, p. 187), the roles now became reversed and he was expected to play the part of an *erastês* himself. Homosexual activity took place in the *andrôn* or men's quarters as well as the gymnasium and was, or so it seems from depictions on Greek vases, a very public form of love-making. The *andrôn* was also the place where a young man would encounter *hetairai*. How a 'typical' young Athenian adult divided his attention between homosexual and heterosexual activity was perhaps a matter of individual preference and social conditioning, but it is probably safe to assume that healthily adjusted males would have been expected to have intercourse with partners of both sexes.

As we have seen already, homosexual attachments were believed to facilitate the transition from child to adult, though it must be stressed that this view seems to have been more prevalent among the aristocrats than among non-aristocrats. In Aristophanes' plays, and particularly in the *Clouds*, there is clear evidence of revulsion against homosexual practices on the part of the Athenian middle class. It is doubtful, moreover, whether homosexuality was much practised by men after they had married. For the most part wives would not, therefore, have had grounds for fearing that their husbands were romantically involved with another man, though they might well have had grounds for fearing that they were romantically involved with one or more *hetairai* (cf. Dover 1978, 171).

Given the inordinately high price set upon virginity in a bride, it is extremely unlikely that Greek girls were permitted to go out of the house unattended. As a result, too, of the absence of any stigma attaching to a young man who had intercourse with either a slave girl or a prostitute, few young people will have had their first experience of sex as something fast, furtive and forbidden. Whether the availability of sex for young males outside the constraints of marriage – outside, too, the constraints of what we would term today 'commitment' – encouraged the growth of sexual maturity, and whether that in turn disposed them to be tender and loving when they eventually married, is something upon which our sources shed no light.

But what of the *neos* who felt inhibited and repelled by the mere idea of sex? Euripides' *Hippolytos* is a classic case study of arrested emotional development in a young man who finds himself incapable of confronting his sexual identity. We do not know Hippolytos' exact age. Though he describes himself as an *anêr* (ll. 994, 1031), he is referred to as a *neanias* by Aphrodite and as a *neos* by his elderly servant (ll. 43, 114). My own impression is that he is probably in his early twenties – just at the age, in other words, when as a potential head of household he should be taking an active interest in members of the opposite sex. But Hippolytos shuns all contact with Aphrodite, physical sex personified so to speak, whom he contemptuously brands as 'a goddess adored at night-time' (l. 106), and devotes himself instead to the worship of her virgin rival Artemis. His exclusive attachment to Artemis and total rejection of Aphrodite constitute incontrovertible evidence of a serious, even fatal disequilibrium in his character.

The unnaturalness of the young man's behaviour becomes fully evident when it is set alongside the traditional Athenian picture of early manhood, aptly characterised as a compound of 'extravagance, pugnacity, thoughtlessness, drunkenness and sexual excess' (Dover 1974, 103). Hippolytos is the exact antithesis of this picture, as is demonstrated by his repeated description of himself as *sôphrôn*, a word which is usually translated as 'moderate' or 'self-controlled', but which in his mouth primarily connotes sexual continence. The presence of such exemplary continence in a *neos*, far from being interpreted as admirable, would surely have sent a warning signal to Euripides' audience who would have feared, and rightly so, for Hippolytos' emotional stability. The fact that Hippolytos is indeed unstable, and dangerously so, becomes fully apparent when he is confronted with the news that his stepmother Phaidra is in love with him. His reaction to this revelation is so violent, his vilification of the entire female sex so hysterical and so fanatical, that it almost seems as if he had been waiting for just such a pretext to abominate the sexual act in general (see above, p. 22). Euripides is far too subtle a dramatist merely to exhibit the destructive and negative side of Hippolytos' *sôphrosunê*, however. The opening scene of the play, in which Hippolytos and his companions are depicted returning from the hunt, illuminates the beauty of the ascetic life as personifed by the goddess Artemis (ll. 58-71), although the havoc which it wrecks in the course of the play leaves us in no doubt that such behaviour is pathological. To put it in psychoanalytical terms, it seems as if Hippolytos' *sôphrosunê* operates as a sublimation of his repressed sexual desire for the eternal *parthenos* that his patroness Artemis always remains.

Age at marriage

The earliest evidence for age at marriage in ancient Greece is provided by Hesiod (*Works and Days* 695-9) who advises his audience as follows:

> Bring a wife to your home when you are ripe (*hôraios*), not being much less than in your thirtieth year and not much more. This is the right age (*hôrios*) for marriage. Let your wife be four years past puberty (*tetor' hêbôöi*) and marry her in the fifth. Marry a *parthenikê* whom you can instruct in skilled accomplishments.

Hesiod's view is by no means eccentric. Later writers generally agree that a man should be at least in his thirtieth year when he marries. Solon (27.9 *IEG*) was of the opinion that the right time (*hôrion*) for a man to marry is between twenty-seven and thirty-four. Plato asserts in the *Republic* (5.460e) that he is 'at his peak (*akmê*) for marriage' in his thirtieth year, and in the *Laws* (4.721b and 6.785b; but cf. 6.772d) recommends passing legislation to the effect that a man should marry when he has reached his thirtieth year and before his thirty-fifth. Aristotle (*Pol.* 7.1335a29) proposed thirty-six as the ideal age.

Plentiful evidence suggests that well-to-do brides were often actually much younger than the age recommended by Hesiod. The law code from Gortyn in Crete, inscribed in the fifth century BC but much older in origin, states that an heiress (*patrôïôkos*) should marry 'in the twelfth year or older' (*IC* 4.72 xii 17-19), though this may not have been typical of lower-class brides. Athenian heiresses (*epiklêroi*) were expected to marry at thirteen (see above, p. 160) and the fictional Ischomachos married a girl who was not yet in her fifteenth year (Xen. *Oik.* 7.5). Philosophers by contrast tended to recommend that brides should be somewhat older. Plato (*Laws* 6.785b), for instance, gives fifteen to nineteen as the right age for a woman to get married, while Aristotle says she should be 'about seventeen' (*Pol.* 7.1335a29). It is likely that such pronouncements were intended as a corrective to contemporary practices in Athens and elsewhere, perhaps inspired in part by marriage patterns in Sparta where the age of bride and groom appears to have been more equal, eighteen to twenty in the case of the woman and the mid-twenties in the case of the man (cf. Cartledge 1981, 94-5).

Though the precise age-band covered by the concept of marriageability in Athens is impossible to fix, it seems to have extended from seventeen to thirty-five in the case of a man, and thirteen to twenty-five in the case of a woman. On the basis of sepulchral inscriptions it has been calculated that 'over 50 per cent of Roman girls of the *respectable classes* would have married by the age of fifteen' (Hopkins 1966, 260). The same is likely to have been true of Classical Athens, though we may question whether girls from the lower social strata married as early as those belonging to the middle and upper classes. It is further stated that in Rome 'husbands were typically nine years older than their wives' (op. cit., p. 262). The literary evidence from Athens suggests that the disparity in ages

Fig. 30. Attic grave-relief commemorating Ampharete and her grandchild, both deceased, *c*. 410 BC.

between husband and wife was even greater, perhaps as much as ten to fifteen years. It is sobering to reflect that, given the early age at marriage for women and the late age for men, the majority of women became grandmothers by the time they were thirty (Fig. 30); on the other hand, only a small percentage of the male population can have survived to become grandfathers, since a man would have needed to attain the age of sixty in order to see his first son wed (cf. Saller 1987, 30).

Why *did* the Athenians and other Greeks choose girls as marriage partners who were just out of puberty? The marked disparity in age between bride and groom is often, perhaps rightly, interpreted as a strategy for enforcing the subordination of women. Feminists in particular have suggested that the early age at which women were required to marry was dictated in part by the desire of Greek men to dominate their wives. There is after all 'nothing so effective as child-marriage for reducing a wife and mother to being a slave' (Toynbee 1969, 363). Certainly the fact that girls from well-to-do homes would have led completely sheltered lives before marriage meant that they were not only uneducated but also downright ignorant. Ischomachos states that his wife had 'up till then been closely supervised in order that she would see as little as possible, hear as little as possible and learn as little as possible' (Xen. *Oikon*. 7.5).

But though a philosopher might have regarded a woman whose mind was a complete blank as an exciting pedagogical challenge, it has to be conceded that the average Athenian may not have gone about his educative role with quite the same degree of *esprit*. Other considerations should, therefore, not be ruled out. First, as already noted, it is impossible to exaggerate the importance throughout antiquity which attached to the fact that one's bride should be a virgin (cf. Plu. *Comp. Lyk. and Num*. 4; *Mor*. 138e). Secondly, beliefs about human physiology may also have contributed to the discrepancy in ages. Aristotle, for instance, claimed that 'males who have intercourse while their bodies [or seed?] are still growing are harmed in respect of their growth' (*Pol*. 7.1335a27). He further alleged that the earliest seed which the male produces is infertile, owing to the fact that it is not sufficiently thick (*HA* 7.582a29-30 *T*; *GA* 2.747a2) and lacks sufficient vital heat because it has not been properly concocted (*GA* 2.739a10). Thus even if it proves fertile, the children whom it engenders will be somewhat small and weak (*HA* 5.544b16-17 *T*; cf. 7.582a18-20). Medical support for the belief that women should marry at or shortly after puberty is provided by Soranos (*Gyn*. 1.33) who argues that this is the safest age for child-rearing. Thirdly, as we have seen, there were fears for the emotional stability and physical well-being of *parthenoi* once they had begun to menstruate and a corresponding belief that their problems could best be solved by sexual intercourse (see above, p. 168). Finally, the large number of deaths in labour of women who were scarcely past puberty may paradoxically have served to keep women's age at marriage unnaturally low on the not wholly unreasonable grounds that if childbearing is hazardous even for a young woman, it must surely become more dangerous the older she becomes. In sum, the early age of marriage for Greek women is likely to have been determined by an unhappy mixture of sexual politics, male pride and medical ignorance.

Choosing a partner

To judge from literature, which is the only source of evidence available, the Greek aristocracy in the Archaic period produced an over-supply of eligible bachelors. It was to cope with this situation that there arose the custom of selecting a husband by competition, a recurrent story-tale motif in folklore and mythology. The procedure may have been intended not only to ensure that the bridegroom was virile and manly and thus capable of providing issue, but also to spare the bride's father the invidious task of having to discriminate between highborn youths on purely personal grounds, since his role was hereby limited to that of impartial judge in contests of skill. Herodotos' account (6.126-30) of how the tyrant Kleisthenes of Sikyon found a suitable husband for his daughter Agariste indicates that even men of his rank would seek to avoid giving offence to fellow aristocrats by behaving with exemplary deference towards the rejected suitors. Having made trial of the most eligible young men in all Greece by testing their skill in running, wrestling and table manners before bestowing the hand of his daughter on the Athenian Megakles, Kleisthenes presented each of the runners-up with a talent of silver as a consolation prize and expressed his regret at not having enough daughters to satisfy them all. To choose a son-in-law on purely personal grounds was undoubtedly the mark of an extremely powerful and independent ruler. In the *Odyssey* the Phaiakian king Alkinoös, though he knows nothing of Odysseus' background or personal circumstances, marks him out as an ideal son-in-law simply because Odysseus shares the same outlook on life (7.311-15).

In contrast to Archaic Greece, Classical Athens may have produced an over-supply of marriageable girls, as is indicated by the importance that attached to the dowry (see below). Among the well-to-do one of the principal criteria in choosing a suitable marital partner appears to have been wealth. As a result endogamy between an heiress or *epiklêros* and a close relative was common, to the extent that we hear of marriages between half-siblings born of a common father (though not of a common mother), marriages between first cousins, and even marriages between uncles and nieces. An *epiklêros thessa*, that is, an *epiklêros* belonging to the lowest (i.e. fourth) property group, had to be provided with a dowry by her nearest male relatives collectively.

Fig. 31. Detail of a Cretan *oinochoê* depicting a youth making a pass at a young woman who is with difficulty restraining (presumably) his wandering hands, *c*. 650 BC.

Restrictions in the choice of marital partner were imposed on members of certain Attic demes and perhaps as well on the members of particular kinship-groups (*genê*) or subdivisions thereof. Members of the deme of Pallene, for instance, were for some reason debarred from marrying those of Hagnous (Plu. *Thes*. 13.4). Other demes and *genê* probably operated a policy of positive discrimination by selecting their marital partners from a limited number of lineages. Some aristocratic families appear to have had a standing arrangement whereby their offspring regularly intermarried with noble families in other communities, like the Kypselids of Corinth who intermarried with the Philaidai of Athens, and the family of Gelon in Syracuse who intermarried with that of Theron in Agrigentum (cf. Gernet 1968, 350f.).

Whereas an Athenian male was free to contract a marriage from his eighteenth year onwards, an Athenian female could only do so at the instigation of her father or legal guardian whatever her age (cf. Xen. *Oikon*. 7.11). A passage of doubtful authenticity in Herodotos (6.122) reveals how unusual it was for a girl to exercise freewill in the choice of her husband. It tells us that the sixth-century BC aristocrat Kallias was remembered first for his hostility to the tyrant Peisistratos, secondly for his victories in the games, and thirdly for the fact that

> when his daughters reached marriageable age (*gamou hôraiai*) he gave them the most magnificent gift possible and one which delighted them: he gave to each the man whom she chose as husband from the entire population of Athens.

Helen's father Tyndareus is also said by Euripides to have 'allowed his daughter to choose as her husband the man to whom she had lost her heart in love' (*IA* 68-9), though in view of her notorious infidelity we may wonder whether the poet is perhaps casting doubts upon the wisdom of such accommodating behaviour. The ethnographic observation by Herodotos (1.93.4) that Lydian women 'give themselves away' further reinforces the normative nature of those Greek societies where the opposite procedure held good. Given the late age at marriage of Athenian men, it is a reasonable assumption that about a quarter or even as many as a third of all fathers failed to live to see their eldest daughter reach marriageable years, in which case the task of selecting a husband would normally have devolved upon her eldest brother. In some cases at least the latter would surely have been more amenable to suggestion than the father. Indications that in Athens young people did begin to exercise a measure of independence in the choice of their marriage partner are already to be found in Euripidean drama, notably in the two lost plays *Andromeda* and *Aiolos*, and the tendency becomes a common motif in New Comedy from the late fourth century onwards (cf. Fantham 1971; Humphreys 1983, 63).

The majority of marriages would have been arranged by the heads of the two *oikoi*, though some individuals employed the services of a professional matchmaker known as a *promnêstria*. In the popular imagination at least the capability of these women, some of whom probably doubled as midwives (cf. Pl. *Theait*. 149d), left something to be desired. Strepsiades in the *Clouds* (ll. 41-74) curses his own *promnêstria* for a truly inspired piece of mésalliance: whereas he is a thrifty countryman of humble origins, his wife is a spendthrift town aristocrat who is making him bankrupt. To make matters worse, she goes in for an *outré* style of French kissing, which conventional old Strepsiades finds offensive (l. 51).

In Classical Sparta, where in theory at least every potential Spartiate received an allotment of land at birth, it was the practice none the less that the rich married the rich. Though the dowry system as such did not exist, landed property was exchanged upon the occasion of a marriage. A particularly desirable catch was a *patrouchos*, the Spartan equivalent to the *epiklêros*, with the important difference that a *patrouchos* could inherit in her own right (cf. Cartledge 1981, 98). The consequence was that property tended to accumulate in the hands of the few, two-fifths of whom by the mid-fourth century, according to Aristotle (*Pol.* 2.1270a23-5), were women. Many girls from impoverished backgrounds must therefore have remained on the shelf. Hence the need for legislation penalising bachelorhood (see above, p. 199). Few Spartan women, when asked what marriage-settlement they brought to their husbands, would honestly have been able to answer, 'My family virtue' (Plu. *Mor.* 242b = *Sayings of Spartan Women* 24), as one haughty matron did. Good looks may none the less have given an attractive girl the edge over an otherwise well-endowed rival, particularly since *parthenoi* were obliged to wear minimal clothing at processions and public gatherings for the express object of catching the eye of a young man. Asked why his fellow-countrymen escorted their daughters out in public unveiled but their wives veiled, Charillos, an early king of Sparta, is said to have replied (Plu. *Mor.* 232c): 'Because our *korai* have to find husbands, whereas our *gunaikes* have to keep the ones by whom they are kept.'

The marriage ceremony

The formal requirements of an Athenian marriage ceremony were in two parts. The first was known as the *enguê*, a public agreement or pledge made in the presence of witnesses and resembling a bethrothal at which the size and composition of the dowry (*proïx*) were also stipulated. Herodotos (6.130) provides us with an example of the simple wording of the *enguê* in his account of the betrothal of Agariste:

> Kleisthenes called for silence and then said to the gathering: 'Suitors for the hand of my child (*pais*) ... I pledge (*enguô*) my *pais* Agariste to Megakles, son of Alkmaeon, according to the

> laws of the Athenians.' When Megakles replied that he accepted the pledge, the marriage (*gamos*) had been authorised (*ekekurôto*) for Kleisthenes.

The second part was the *ekdosis*, the formal handing over of the bride to the groom by her *kurios*, that is, her father or legal guardian, this action being accompanied by the transfer of the dowry to her new *oikos*. The *ekdosis* was a part of the *gamos* or wedding proper whose larger function was to integrate the new family member into her husband's *oikos*. Since Athenian girls were frequently betrothed well before they entered puberty, several years might elapse between the *enguê* and the *ekdosis*, and in the interval the groom was expected to pay for the support of his future wife since the *enguê* constituted 'not merely a betrothal but an act creative of the marital *kurieia*' by which she passed from the charge of one *kurios* to that of another (Wolff 1944, 51f.; cited by Sealey 1984, 120).

At the celebration of the *Apatouria* before the *ekdosis* the groom introduced his bride to his phratry in a ceremony which may have resembled that which he himself had undergone shortly after birth and then later at adolescence. Following his bride's formal acceptance by his *phratores*, the groom then performed a sacrifice known as the *Gamêlia*, which was also the name by which the entire ritual was known. The main purpose of the *Gamêlia* as a rite seems to have been to establish whether the groom was marrying the daughter of an Athenian citizen, for only if that condition was met would the male offspring of such a union be eligible for entry into the phratry. It is, however, entirely unclear what criteria the phratry would have used to determine whether the bride was the legitimate offspring of Athenian parents since, so far as we know, no public record of her birth actually existed. Perhaps the groom's phratry merely negotiated with that of the father of the bride in order to establish as far as possible her legitimacy. It is also uncertain whether the bride herself was required, or indeed permitted, to attend the ceremony, but the likelihood is that she was represented by her *kurios* who may have taken an oath to the effect that she was the legitimate offspring of Athenian parents. It must be emphasised that the *Gamêlia* did not function as a rite of passage for the bride since membership of the phratry was restricted to males. The ceremony merely conferred public approval upon the groom in the choice of his bride and public acceptance upon the bride as a potential bearer of Athenian children.

The winter month of Gamelion, as its name suggests, was the favourite time for Athenian couples to undergo the *gamos*, the ritual by which the bride was finally transferred from one *oikos* to another. This, too, was the month in which the sacred marriage of Zeus and Hera took place. The preference for Gamelion was not merely a matter of convenience or divine example; it may well reflect an underlying belief that marriageability occurred at a prescribed moment in a person's life, in the same way that the attainment of adulthood and citizenship occurred at an officially prescribed moment. On Crete, for instance, according to Ephoros (*FGrH* 70 F 149 ap. Str. 10.4.20): 'All those selected from the herd of *paides* are compelled to marry at the same time.' Lacking any narrative account of an Athenian wedding ceremony, we are forced to rely on evidence patched together from vase-paintings, drama and other sources. What follows is inevitably somewhat impressionistic.

The *gamos* negotiated the transfer of the bride from one *oikos* and status to another in accordance with the requirements of religion, just as the *ekdosis*, which constituted an element within the structure of the *gamos*, negotiated it in accordance with the requirements of the law. As in the case of pregnancy and childbirth, no one deity had exclusive or even overriding control. In Athens the deities most prominently associated with marriage include Aphrodite, Artemis, Demeter, Hera Teleia and Zeus Teleios, Hermes, the Moirai and Peitho (cf. Schmitt 1977, 1070 n. 29).

The ceremony began with a sacrifice known as the *proteleia* and/or *progameia*, literally 'preterminal' and 'premarital'. Pollux (*Onomast.* 3.38) writes with less than perfect clarity:

> The sacrifice (*thusia*) before the *gamos* is the *proteleia* and *progameia*. Not only brides (*numphai*) were said to perform the preterminal (*proteleisthai*) but also bridegrooms (*numphoi*). And the terminal (*telos*) is called the *gamos*, and those who have terminated are called wedded .... On this occasion at the *proteleia* they 'preterminate' [i.e. consecrate] girls (*korai*) to Artemis and the Moirai (Fates). And *korai* at this point cut off their hair to the goddesses.

The hair-cutting seems to have signified the symbolic death of a virgin's previous existence, and resembles that performed by Athenian youths at the *Koureôtis* (see above, p. 179). Possibly similar in meaning was the removal and consecration by the

Fig. 32. Detail of an Attic red-figure *pyxis* or cosmetic box depicting a bride being driven by chariot to the groom's house, late fifth century BC. The composition is framed by her natal *oikos* on the left and her marital one on the right. Torches indicate that the scene is taking place at night. The picture actually conflates the bride's departure with the *epaulia*, a ceremony which took place the following day, when the bride's property was conveyed to her new home. At the far left a woman, evidently the bride's mother, waves to the departing couple.

bride of the girdle she had worn since puberty, a rite alluded to by Pausanias (2.33.1) in the case of the *parthenoi* of Troizen who perform it in honour of Athena Apatouria. Either upon marriage or possibly upon reaching marriageable age girls formally dedicated items which may have included dolls, toys and musical instruments, a gesture which underscored the fact that their childhood had formally terminated (*AP* 6.280; cf. van Straten 1981, 90).

The bride (and possibly the groom, too) took a prenuptial ritual bath in holy water known as *loutra* drawn from a sacred spring (cf. Porph. *On the Cave of the Nymphs* 12; Eur. *Phoin.* 347 with schol.). Its function was primarily to mark the barrier between unwedded and wedded, but it will also have had the psychological effect of heightening awareness among the participants of the irreversible nature of the changes which they were about to undergo. The water was poured from a distinctively-shaped vase known as a *loutrophoros*. Miniature *loutrophoroi*, such as those which have been found at the Cave of Vari sacred to the Nymphs in east Attica, were probably offered to the deities who presided over the marriage, if they had not been dedicated previously at the time of betrothal (cf. King 1903, 303f.).

The ritual bath was followed by a wedding feast in the bride's house at which the bride herself, who remained veiled throughout, sat with other women apart from the men. It is probable that neither the groom nor any members of his family were present on this occasion. The bride underwent *makarismos*, that is to say, she was congratulated and pronounced *makêr* or 'blessed' by the assembled company. At nightfall the groom conveyed his bride, still veiled, from her original *oikos* to his own in a nuptial cart. She sat on one side of him and his best friend, known as the *paranumphos* or *parochos*, sat on the other. The party was accompanied by a torchlight procession which sung wedding hymns (*humenaioi*) in honour of Hymen, the god of marriage. Upon arrival at the groom's house, the bride was met by her mother-in-law (cf. Schol. Eur. *Phoin.* 344; Eur. *Tr.* 315). She was then conducted to the hearth, where she was formally placed under the protection of the household gods as a new member of the *oikos*. In the course of this ceremony bride and groom were showered with nuts and dried fruit (*katachusmata*), symbols of fertility and wealth, and then presented with a basket of bread by a *pais amphithalês* (see above, p. 145). At the climax to the whole proceedings the bride removed her veil with a ritual gesture known as *anakaluptêria*. Then the groom led her into the wedding-chamber and an *epithalamion* was sung, perhaps outside the closed door (cf. Sappho, frr. 104-17 *LP*). This, the first night which the bride passed in the house of the groom, was known as *epaulia* or 'camping out', evidently because she only had a few of her personal belongings with her (Hsch. and Sud. s.v.; cf. Redfield 1982, 193-4). *Epaulia* was also the name given to the day after the *gamos* when gifts were sent to the newlyweds by the bride's father and when members of the two families met for the first time during the course of the celebrations. In the case of a marriage involving an *epiklêros* and a close relative, it is possible that the groom was required to move to the *oikos* of his bride's legal guardian.

What conclusions can be drawn about the way Athenians viewed marriage on the basis of the imagery utilised by the *gamos*? Undeniably there is a heavy emphasis upon what appear to be negative elements, as evidenced by the fact that the bride is at first an alienated and veiled non-person within her own home, then a victim of abduction, and finally a prisoner in her new home. Viewed from a different perspective, however, these same features may be interpreted more sympathetically as a reflection of profound anxiety on the part of the new *oikos* lest the new union be interrupted or sabotaged. This ambivalence, which lies at the heart of the *gamos*, can be further demonstrated with reference to the *thurôros* or doorkeeper, who was appointed to prevent women from entering the bridal chamber while consummation took place (cf. Poll. *Onomast*. 3.42); it may also have been his role to prevent the bride from escaping. Judging by Sappho's description of him as having 'feet seven fathoms in length' (fr. 110 *LP*) it appears that he was perceived as a formidible figure.

On one level, therefore, the bride's alienation, abduction and imprisonment may be read as an expression not merely of male domination but also of male neurosis at the fear of losing what has recently been acquired. The fact that the bride is veiled and sits apart from the groom at the banquet, and the fact, too, that the wedding party departs for the new *oikos* at nightfall, should perhaps be regarded as metaphors for the profundity of the transition that she is undergoing – as if she were dying in her old *oikos* in order to be born again in the new. The relationship between the positive and negative aspects of Athenian marriage ritual are thus delicately poised: 'The negative tendency must not be denied, but it must of course be eventually overcome' (Seaford 1987, 106).

Absence of choice, abrupt severance from the natal *oikos*, and loss of virginity to a man who in many cases may have been a total stranger combined to make marriage a potentially traumatic experience for the bride, as the following fragment from Sophokles' lost play *Tereus* (fr. 524 *TGF*; *WLGR* no. 32) suggests:

> *Parthenoi*, in my own opinion, have the sweetest existence known to mortals in their fathers' homes, for their innocence always keeps *paides* safe and happy. But when we reach *hêbê* and can understand, we are thrust out and sold away from our ancestral gods and from our parents. Some go to strange men's homes, others to foreigners', some to joyless houses, some to hostile. And all this once the first night has yoked us to our husband, we are forced to praise and to say that all is well. (tr. M.R. Lefkowitz)

A remarkably similar representation of marriage occurs in the *Homeric Hymn to Demeter*, which tells how Persephone, the daughter of Demeter, while innocently plucking flowers in a meadow in the company of the daughters of Okeanos, is herself plucked from the face of the earth by the god of the underworld who has imperiously selected her to become his bride in Hades. The trauma which, though not described in the

Fig. 33. Attic *pelikê* attributed to the Marsyas Painter depicting Peleus' seizure of Thetis, *c*. 360–350 BC. Thetis is seeking to escape the clutches of her suitor by transforming herself into a serpent (see bottom left).

hymn, she surely experiences in consequence of her abduction is heightened by the advanced age of her suitor, his formidable identity as lord of the dead, and the subterranean location of their marital home. Viewed as archetype, the myth may be interpreted on many different levels, most notably perhaps as a symbolic enactment of the grief which mothers experience upon the occasion of their daughters' marriage and as an implicitly subversive commentary upon the violence caused to a *parthenos* by being abruptly torn from the sunlit world of childhood to the dark labyrinthine world of sexuality. But whereas the mythic solution is to contain and ease the mother's grief by effecting a compromise between the natal and marital *oikoi* in which the daughter will divide her time (two-thirds of eternity on Olympos with her mother, one-third in Hades with her husband), no such happy compromise existed in real life. What is perhaps most remarkable about the poem is that the perspective which it chooses, uncharacteristically for Greek literature in general, is that of the bride's own mother.

The Spartan marriage ceremony, at least in the form in which it has been preserved for us by Plutarch, appears at first glance to have been invested with an unhealthy undercurrent of savagery, transvestism and perversion. Here again, however, we must be wary of interpreting as an analogue of 'real life' what may at root be an enactment of the tensions which such a profoundly disruptive change of identity generated and of anxiety on the part of the marital *oikos* lest the new bride 'escape'. Plutarch (*Lyk.* 15.3) writes:

> Women get married by being abducted (*harpagê*), not when they are small and under-age (*aôroi*), but when they are in their prime (*akmazousai*) and ripe (*pepeiroi*). When the bride has been abducted, the bridesmaid (*numpheutria*) as she is called takes hold of her and shaves her hair off so that it is very short, dresses her in a man's cloak and sandals, and puts her to bed on a pallet alone and in the dark. Then the bridegroom (*numphios*) slips quietly into the room, not in a drunken stupor nor in a condition of exhaustion, but sober, as [he should be?] always, unloosens her girdle, and, raising her up, carries her over to the bed. After spending a short amount of time with her, he departs discreetly to wherever he was previously accustomed to spend the night in order to bed down with the rest of the *neoi*.

In Hellenistic times the *enguê* and the *ekdosis* fell out of use and marriage was effected merely by the signing of a written marriage contract, with or without the transfer of a *proïx*. From the point of view of changing social relationships in the Hellenistic world, it is instructive to note that a number of surviving contracts reveal that the bride was given away jointly by both her father and her mother. The following papyrus from Alexandria dated 92 BC, which sets out the terms of a marriage contract made between the bridegroom and the bride's brother, is typical in that it acknowledges the rights of the wife and lays down a code of behaviour to which the husband must adhere.

> Apollonia shall remain with Philiskos, obeying him as a wife should obey her husband, owning their property jointly with him. Philiskos, whether he is at home or away from home, shall furnish Apollonia with everything necessary and clothing and whatsoever is proper for a wedded wife, in proportion to their means. It shall not be lawful for Philiskos to bring home another wife in addition to Apollonia or to have a mistress or boy-lover, nor to beget children by another woman while Apollonia is alive nor to maintain another *oikos* of which Apollonia is not mistress, nor to eject or insult or ill-treat her nor to alienate any of their property with injustice to Apollonia. (tr. A.S. Hunt and C.C. Edgar in *Select Papyri* I no. 2 in *LCL*)

Husbands and wives

We cannot here undertake a full examination of the institution of marriage in Greek society. All I shall seek to do is to examine briefly the significance of two key concepts associated with the notion of a Greek marriage, namely *kratos* meaning 'authority, mastery, domination', and *homonoia* meaning 'likemindedness' or 'compatibility'.

To begin with, let us consider the infamous denunciation of wives written by the seventh-century BC poet Semonides of Amorgos. After listing nine types of awful women whom he likens to pigs, foxes, dogs, the earth, the sea, donkeys, ferrets, horses and monkeys, Semonides describes the bee woman who, uniquely among members of the female sex, is endowed with admirable qualities (fr. 7.83-93 *IEG*). The bee woman is industrious, causes her husband's property to increase, provides him with fine children, is beautiful, and does not gossip with other women about love. To cap it all, marriage to the bee woman is long-lasting and intimate, since 'she grows old with a husband whom she loves and who loves her'. How, we may inquire, does a man go about finding such a jewel? Unfortunately Semonides does not provide his audience with any tips. She is, he merely states, bestowed by Zeus. Consistent with the Greek inability to conceive of a constantly evolving personality or a constantly evolving relationship, the ideal woman is apparently ideal for all men, irrespective of individual temperament or preference. There is no comprehension here of the fact that a successful marriage is created by the fusion of both partners; on the contrary, the disposition of one's wife is premaritally predetermined.

The view that the number of bad wives in the world vastly outnumbers the number of good ones is a stock motif in Attic Comedy, as exemplifed by the following fragment ascribed to the fourth-century BC poet Euboulos (*CAF* II, p. 205f.116,117):

> I wish the second man who married would die an evil death. I don't wish evil upon the first man; he had no experience of that evil. The second man knew what kind of evil a wife was! [...] Oh honoured Zeus, shall I ever say something evil about women? By Zeus, may I perish if I do. They are the best possessions a man can have. If Medea was an evil woman, Penelope was a good thing; some might describe Klytaimnestra as evil, but I'd set Alkestis against her as good. Maybe someone will criticise Phaidra – but by Zeus there has to be another good wife! Who is it? Oh, poor me, I've got through the good women, and I still have so many dreadful ones to talk about.

The attitude towards marriage presented by Semonides and Euboulos should be treated with caution. These are jokes and not social statements, even if they were expected to strike a chord of recognition among Greek husbands. If we do treat them with some seriousness, however, what they suggest is that wives, despite their subordination, were perceived as possessing the power to make their husbands' lives thoroughly miserable. It is after all a fact of life that even if wives are opposed or thwarted by their husbands, they have ways of ensuring that their needs are not wholly ignored, by scolding, bullying or withdrawing their sexual favours (Ar. *Clouds* and *Lys.*; cf. Pomeroy 1988, 1340).

In a society like Classical Athens, where the husband was usually old enough to be his wife's father, a degree of paternalism and protectionism was perhaps inevitable. In Xenophon's *Oikonomikos* (7.10) Ischomachos indicates to his interlocutor Sokrates that he was not able to hold a rational conversation with his wife (her name, incidentally, is never given) until she had become 'manageable' and 'tamed'. The vocabulary which he uses to describe this condition, *cheiroêthês* and *etetithaseuto*, would be equally appropriate for the domestication of a wild beast. As soon as she attained 'rationality', Ischomachos saw it as his task first to point out to her that all the possessions in their house were held jointly, secondly to explain in minute detail her duties as mistress of the house, and thirdly to dissuade her from using any form of makeup. Instead she should make it her duty to acquire a healthy complexion by 'moistening and kneading the dough, and shaking out and folding away the cloaks and bedcovers' (10.11). Ischomachos claims that his wife docilely submitted to all this without a murmur of protest. The question is: how typical is Ischomachos and how typical is his wife? The fact that Ischomachos is intended to be representative of all that is finest and fairest in wife-rearing and that he is treated with unctuous reverence by Sokrates may suggest to the cynically-minded that Classical Athens witnessed some falling away from this noble 'ideal'. It is also possible that Xenophon intended his readers to treat this discussion with a measure of ironic detachment in view of the well-celebrated fact that the great philosopher was himself henpecked.

The most detailed treatise on the subject of marriage which survives from the ancient world is Plutarch's *Gamika parangelmata* or *Advice on Marriage* (*Mor.* 138b-146b). Though written in the Roman imperial period and from a philosophical perspective, it is founded on assumptions that were fairly standard among the educated upper class throughout Greek as well as Roman history. It provides a perfect illustration of antiquity's first law of conjugality, namely that the key to a happy marriage depends primarily upon a wife's readiness to submit unquestioningly to her husband's *kratos* whatever his qualities or defects (cf. Eur. *And.* 213-14). Yet it also provides the bride and groom with advice regarding the attainment of *homonoia* or *homophrosunê*, the quality which the Greeks consistently maintained to be the mark of an ideal marriage. Importantly from the point of view of the present investigation, the treatise demonstrates awareness of the fact that early married life is likely to impose an immense strain upon a young couple, even though the advice which it provides almost invariably shows greater sensitivity and deference to the needs and feelings of the husband.

Plutarch advises newly-weds to be on their guard against violent rows because their marriage has not yet had time to establish itself on secure foundations (138ef). The relationship between husband and wife is like that between horse and rider, and just as the rider must pay heed to the size of his horse in

Fig. 34. Attic grave-relief commemorating Hegeso, wife of Proxenos, *c*. 410 BC. She is gazing fondly at her wedding ring, perhaps in anticipation of reunion with her husband in Hades.

applying the reins, the husband must take care not to rein in his wife more tightly than is appropriate to her rank (139b). It is a wife's duty is to be visible when her husband is present, invisible when he is not (139c). While all the activities of a well-run household should be carried out by both parties in agreement (*hup' amphoterôn homonôöuntôn*), they should reflect the leadership (*hêgemonia*) and preference (*proairesis*) of the husband (139d). Reason rather than force is the best way to instil a sense of self-discipline in a woman (139e). A wife is to have no feelings of her own, but adapt herself to her husband's moods, whether cheerful or sombre (140a). If her husband is unfaithful with a *hetaira* or the maid, she is not to get upset or angry but appreciate that it is out of respect (*aidôs*) for her that he confines his outbursts of drunken lechery to outsiders (140b). It is not the woman's role to make sexual advances to her husband, though she should invariably submit to his (140c).*

*We may note in passing that what Plutarch has to say is in remarkably close *homonoia* with the advice which Mary Macaulay gives to wives in a

A wife is not to have any friends other than those whom she shares with her husband (140d). A good tip for preventing her from leaving the house is to hide her fancy shoes, expensive clothes and costly jewellery (142c). She must refrain from speaking in the presence of outsiders and gossip only with her husband (142d). A husband should govern (*archein*) his wife not as a master governs his slave but as the soul governs the body, that is, 'by sympathising with her and by being joined to her in goodwill' (142e). A wife must acknowledge that her mother-in-law will inevitably be hostile to her and try to cope with the situation by encouraging her husband to love her and not by seeking to alienate him from his mother (143ab). She should show more deference to her husband's parents than to her own and confide exclusively in them whenever she gets upset (143bc). If her husband becomes angry she should keep quiet, but when he falls silent seek to soothe him with comforting words (143c).

Once a woman's extravagance has been checked and she has made the necessary adjustments, the relationship between husband and wife should be based on mutual respect (*aidôs*), *homonoia* and goodwill (*eunoia*). Plutarch concludes by remarking that since a husband replaces and effectively anuls all the primary relationships (those of father, mother, brother, sister, etc.) which his wife acknowledged in her former, premarital condition, he must strive to become 'a guide, philosopher and teacher in all that is fairest and most holy' (145c).

This recipe for the attainment of perfect conjugal bliss should be balanced by a picture of the atmosphere inside a home where both partners know each other all too well and where, moreover, the wife has been unfaithful to her husband

---

manual entitled *The Art of Marriage* (1952; reprinted 1958): 'The wife who loves her husband should sometimes be prepared to welcome his advances even though at the time she herself does not feel any great desire' (p. 80). To women who fail to achieve 'satisfaction' (i.e. orgasm) when they are first married, Dr Macaulay counsels as follows: 'Until this is possible they can make it clear to their husbands that they are delighted to be the beloved and the desired, and that to be able to give so much pleasure brings them happiness. Most of those who give as generously as this will, with their husbands' help and patience, eventually be successful themselves.' In Athens male indiference to women's sexual needs left the latter with virtually no sexual outlet other than that provided by masturbation (cf. Pomeroy [1975, 87] with references to dildoes in Ar. *Lys*. 26-8 and Herod. *Mime* 6).

in the most public way imaginable. I am referring to the scene which takes place in *Odyssey* 4 at the palace of Menelaos and Helen in Sparta. Our first sight of Helen is when, led by unerring woman's instinct, she emerges from her perfumed boudoir 'like the goddess Artemis' just at the point when Telemachos is about to break down and weep at his host's incautious reference to the toils and tribulations of his father. She effortlessly restores the mood of the company by slipping a drug into the wine and then takes upon herself the delicate task of broaching the subject of her own infidelity by blaming Aphrodite for the moral blindness which caused her to elope with Paris (4.261-4). Menelaos, too, acquits his wife of all blame and appears to display nothing but the deepest reverence and affection for her. The quality of their *homonoia* is such, or so it would appear, that not even open discussion of Helen's notorious past can adulterate, so to speak, the tranquil harmony that pervades their home life.

That is one interpretation of the scene. But another is quite possible. How, we may inquire, can a husband live in *homonoia* with a wife who flaunted her immorality so openly and with such evil consequence for her entire race? Surely Homer intends us to probe beneath the veneer of this carefully staged play between the all-too-perfect hostess Helen and her all-too-compliant husband to the barely suppressed hostility that must characterise any marriage in which one partner has been flagrantly disloyal to another. The suggestion that all may not be quite as it seems is conveyed in the first instance by the comparison of Helen to the virginal and chaste Artemis. This outrageously inappropriate simile which heralds Helen's appearance should surely be interpreted as a piece of prescriptive irony, aimed at alerting the members of the audience to the fact that they are not to take everything that follows at face value. Secondly, the vision of Helen as the perfect hostess, ever attentive to men's needs and ever sensitive to their moods, must grate somewhat on her husband's nerves and evoke painful recollections in him of that former guest, the fornicator Paris, who found such over-gracious hospitality in that same room. The poet, I would suggest, is inviting his audience to share in the exquisite torture which Helen inflicts upon the most publicly proclaimed cuckold of all time, as she teases and tortures him with memories of his former humiliation.

Plutarch's *Advice on Marriage* and Homer's brief portrayal

of a tenuously balanced domesticity are not cited as complementary portaits of archetypal marital arrangements. They may or may not be characteristic of the different societies to which their authors belonged. Yet each is interesting because each represents a departure from what is often proclaimed to be the typical Greek marriage – whatever that may have been. Though Plutarch, like most Greek philosophers, undeniably regarded women as an inferior species, he none the less implies that under firm guidance they are capable of achieving a degree of spiritual and intellectual enlightenment that is comparable to that with which their husbands are more naturally endowed. The point of Homer's vignette, on the other hand, seems to be that a woman who combines a forceful personality with devastatingly good looks is more than a match for any man, irrespective of the latter's social rank.

In Sparta where it was the practice for women to marry at a much later age than in Athens and where bride and groom were therefore much closer in years, wives probably enjoyed considerable freedom and influence. Our sources certainly suggest as much, and their judgment upon Spartan women is negative in consequence. This is particularly true of Aristotle (*Pol.* 2.1269b-1270a) who composed a lengthy tirade on the subject, claiming that Spartan women were extremely forward and aggressive, that they devoted themselves to profligacy and extravagance, and that they completely dominated their husbands. We get a good insight into the kind of women we are dealing with from the following remark made by one such Spartan who, on being asked whether her husband had made love to her, chillingly replied: 'It wasn't that way round. I made love to him' (Plu. *Mor.* 242c = *Sayings of Spartan Women* 25). It is surely not fortuitous that the most formidable among the bunch of independent women whom we encounter in Aristophanes' *Lysistratê* is the Spartan Lampito, said to be capable of throttling a bull (ll. 80-4). The message that emerges from this is clear enough. But how accurate is it? Allowing for prejudice and comic exaggeration, it is, I believe, likely to be founded on truth. The facts are these: the age-difference between husband and wife was relatively narrow; there was a population shortfall which legislators ascribed to a shortage of wives; Spartan men did not establish themselves in their own homes until they were thirty, by which time their wives would have acquired considerable expertise in the handling of domestic affairs; and finally, there was an enormous concentration of wealth in female hands. All this made Sparta's women a powerful force in their society, unlike their counterparts anywhere else in the Greek world.

Finally, any consideration of the comparative status and importance of husband and wife in Greek society should take into account a conversation between the Persian king Dareios and his queen Atossa before the invasion of Greece, as reported by Herodotos (3.134). Dareios was allegedly prompted to take this huge step partly by his wife's desire to acquire Greek servant girls to wait upon her. If the Great King could be persuaded to undertake the largest expedition in human history while getting undressed to go to bed, *a fortiori* Greek husbands also occasionally took their wives' advice.

It is a striking fact that not a single surviving Archaic gravemarker from Attica commemorates a husband and wife jointly, whereas in the fourth century this type of commemoration becomes fairly standard, accounting for 88 out of approximately 600 funerary inscriptions (cf. Humphreys 1983, 111). While it cannot be assumed that this change necessarily reflects an accompanying enhancement of the values attaching to marriage over the same period, it does indicate that Athenian men now no longer presented themselves *exclusively* as athletes or soldiers as they had done in the preceding era.

Further evidence of increasing uxoriousness on the part of Athenian husbands is provided by the emergence of a comforting belief that the *oikos* would re-constitute itself in the afterlife, which became a feature of Athenian eschatology from the mid-fifth century onwards and was perhaps partly responsible for the spectacular rise in popularity of burial in family plots from *c.* 420 onwards (cf. Garland 1982, 125-76). The practice of joint burial of husband and wife within the same coffin or cinerary urn should also be considered in this context. When Admetos bids farewell to his dying wife he tells her to wait for him in Hades (Eur. *Alk*. 364-8):

> And make ready the room where you will live with me, for I shall have them bury me in the same chest as you, and lay me at your side, so that my heart shall be against your heart, and never, even in death, shall I go from you.

Evidently with the same image in mind Aristotle is said to have inserted in his will a request that his wife's bones be exhumed and buried with his (D.L. 5.16). Finally in Euripides'

Fig. 35. Fragment of an Attic black-figure *hydria* depicting elegantly attired women drawing water at a public fountain, *c*. 530 BC.

Suppliants (ll. 1020-1) Evadne throws herself onto her husband's funeral pyre in order that their flesh may actually roast together.

A wife's duties

The place of well-born married women, like their unmarried counterparts, was inside the home, secluded from the gaze of all but the immediate family. Except on family occasions, primarily birth, marriage and death, and at festivals such as the Thesmophoria from which men were excluded, they will have had little opportunity to associate with anyone outside the immediate family circle, as Medea (Eur. *Med*. 244-8) bitterly reflects:

> A man, when he's tired of the company of those in his home, goes out and cheers himself up ... whereas we women are forced to direct our attentions exclusively to one person.

Wives who belonged to poorer homes, by contrast, had far more opportunities to consort and gossip with other women, since they would have been required to perform outdoor tasks like fetching water from the communal well and washing clothes (Fig. 35).

Fig. 36. Detail of an Attic white-ground *oinochoê* attributed to the Brygos Painter depicting a woman holding a distaff in her left hand and spinning, *c*. 490 BC.

A wife's principal duties included child-rearing, supervising the slaves and running the household. She also had to provide education for her children for at least the first seven years of their life in the case of boys and until marriage in the case of girls. Although some women may have handed this task over to their household slaves, many would have taken their responsibilities very seriously. We can infer this from Herodotos' story of the Athenian women who, having been abducted by the Pelasgians and brought to Lemnos, taught their children to speak Attic Greek and indoctrinated them with Athenian values, greatly to the annoyance and discomforture of their masters (6.138.2; cf. also 4.78.1-3). Upon women, too, principally devolved the burden of looking after the sick, including both relatives and slaves, the latter obligation judged to be one of their least agreeable duties (Ps.-Dem. 59.56; Xen. *Oik*. 7.12 and 7.37).

In the economic sphere, married women were expected to contribute to the wealth of their *oikos*. What distinguishes the bee woman from the rest of the female race is, among other things, the fact that she causes her husband's property to grow and increase (Semon. fr. 7 *IEG*). It is not stated how she effects this miracle to take place, however, and it is quite possible that she does so merely by virtue of the dowry which she brings to her new home. The parting words uttered by Hektor to Andromache in the *Iliad* (6.490-3):

> Go inside the house and attend to your own affairs, to the loom and the distaff, and bid your servants to get on with their work; but as for war, that will be the concern of all men, especially for me, of those who are the sons of Troy.

are closely echoed by Telemachos in the *Odyssey* (1.356-9) with the modification 'but as for speech, that will be the concern of all men, especially for me, who holds the authority in this house'. Such sentiments classically delineate the bipolarity of male and female functions in Greek culture and indicate, too, the wife's obligation to contribute to the household's wealth. Spinning and weaving were in fact a 'high-status activity' (Sussman 1984, 90 n. 13). Kalypso (*Od.* 10.220-3), Kirke (*Od.* 5.61-2) and Helen (*Od.* 4.131-6) are all pictured at the loom, and when Agamemnon offers Achilles gifts of appeasement which include seven women from Lesbos, he is careful to mention that they are not only supremely beautiful but also highly skilled (*Il.* 9.128-30). A woman's skill in handicraft had such an important economic value in the Greek world that it was judged capable *in extremis* of preventing the disintegration of her *oikos*, for it is by pretending to weave a shroud for her father-in-law Laertes that Penelope kept the suitors at bay for nigh on twenty years. Aristophanes in the *Clouds* expected his audience to sympathise with the thrifty Strepsiades whose wife was a constant drain on his resources. Whether wives were expected to do heavy manual work would have depended upon the wealth of their *oikos* and the number of slaves which it owned, but many wives, not to mention daughters, would have been required to sew clothes, do the cooking, bake bread, milk the sheep and goats, make cheese, feed the hens, manufacture pots and pans, and work in the fields at harvest time.

Although it is often assumed that married women enjoyed greater freedom in the Hellenistic period than at any previous period of Greek history, it needs to be emphasised that most of our evidence for this epoch comes from Egypt, so it is question-

Fig. 37. A woman's world. Attic red-figure *epinêtron* or thigh-guard by the Eretria Painter depicting the interior of a *gunaikeion*, *c.* 425 BC. In the centre of the composition is a *loutrophoros*, a vase used for the bridal bath, indicating that preparations are being made for a wedding-ceremony.

able to what extent the alleged changes were 'due to native Egyptian influence ... and how far [they were] merely a continuation of the customs of Greek communities which had always been less repressive than Athens' (Humphreys 1983, 46; cf. Schaps 1979). We should at any rate be wary of assuming that there was any *radical* improvement in women's freedom. Admittedly in Theokritos' *Idyll* 15 two Alexandrian housewives are portrayed going out alone to witness the festival of Adonis, which would have been an uncommon occurrence anywhere in the Classical era. As their conversation reveals, however, it is still their husbands who do the shopping and who unilaterally take all the major decisions, like choosing where to live.

Divorcees and widows

An Athenian marriage was much less settled than the equivalent institution in modern western society. On the one hand, it could be dissolved simply by the husband expelling the wife from his *oikos*; on the other, a wife seeking a divorce could in theory simply remove herself from her marital home, though in practice she would have needed the approval and assistance of her former *kurios*. The latter's control over his daughter or ward did not entirely cease even when she married, for there are indications that he had the right to instigate divorce proceedings if he later determined that the alliance was unsuitable. A fragment of a New Comedy dated to the fourth or third century BC shows a daughter pleading with her father not to allow the fact that her husband has been bankrupted to constitute grounds for divorce (Anon. in Men. ed. Sandbach, p. 328 = *Select Papyri* III 34 in *LCL*). Though the passage does not make it entirely clear whether the father is compelling his daughter to divorce her husband or merely putting strong moral pressure on her to do so, the former interpretation would be entirely consistent with the fact that in the eyes of the law an Athenian woman remained a *pais* throughout her entire life. So we should probably think of a married woman not so much as alienated from her natal home as entrusted to her marital one (cf. Sealey 1984, 121).

Given the age-difference between men and women at marriage, most husbands probably predeceased their wives by several years. Many women would therefore have become widows in their late twenties or early thirties. Potentially at greatest risk were pregnant widows, whose interests and those of their offspring were safeguarded by the eponymous archon in the same way as those of orphans (Ps.-Arist. *AP* 56.7; above, p. 159). We gain some insight into the miserable plight of young widows from Euripides' *Alkêstis*, whose plot revolves around a wife's decision to lay down her life for her husband. She does so, however, not out of love – nowhere in the play is it suggested that Alkestis' motive in prefering death to widowhood is so high-minded – but simply because she cannot abide the prospect of having to raise fatherless children (ll. 287-9). Despite the economic discomforts to which widows were subjected, however, they would have enjoyed much greater personal freedom than married women.

Athenian law ensured that a married woman who came from a well-to-do background enjoyed a certain degree of economic security even if her marital status changed, since the dowry which she took with her to her new home remained in the possession of that home only so long as she herself was resident in it. If she was divorced, or if upon the death of her husband there was a move to eject her from his household – a not unusual occurrence, we may suspect, in the case of a woman who had produced no male offspring – then the dowry had to be returned to her natal *oikos*, so that it could be 're-used' in the not unlikely event of her re-marriage.

Extra-marital relationships

The notorious remark of Pseudo-Demosthenes (59.122):

> We have *hetairai* for physical excitement, mistresses (*pallakai*) to look after our daily comforts, and *gunaikes* to procreate legitimate children (*paidopoieisthai gnêsiôs*) and to act as trustworthy custodians for our households

illustrates the variety of sexual outlets available to a married Athenian male. A *pallakê*, whose condition resembled that of a concubine or modern common law wife, differed from an Athenian wife in that, although she cohabited (*sunoikein*) with her male partner, she occupied his *oikos* without having been handed over to it by her *kurios* and without the transfer of a *proïx*. The attention given by fifth-century BC tragedians to the *oikos* in which a husband's affections are divided between his wife and mistress may be evidence of a contemporary Athenian social phenomenon, since the *ménage à trois* is unlikely to be a traditional element in all the mythological outlines from which drama draws (Aes. *Agam*., S. *Trach*. and Eur. *And*.; cf. Humphreys 1983, 63). While a few liberated women (if any existed in Athens) may have preferred to be *pallakai* rather than wives, the great majority were forced to submit to this role for want of any better alternative, since a *pallakê* was extremely vulnerable and had no recourse to legal assistance from her *kurios* if she was abused or mistreated. Most *pallakai* would probably have been girls whose families, being unable to provide them with a dowry, were therefore glad to have them off their hands.

The status of the offspring of a *pallakê* is extremely difficult to determine, but we are not entitled to assume that they would all have been treated as illegitimate (cf. Sealey 1984, passim). Although Pseudo-Demosthenes (59.122) states that what distinguishes marriage from all other kinds of sexual union between men and women is the fact that the offspring of a *gamos* are legitimate and have legally defined rights not only as citizens, but also as members of an *oikos*, in the event of a manpower crisis, as in the period between 411 and 403/2 BC, the offspring of unions involving *pallakai* were definitely treated as legitimate (D.L. 2.26).

Women's fidelity was partly a function of the fact that they were confined almost wholly within the home. Public ceremonies, such as funerals, thus afforded a rare opportunity to attract the eye of a potential lover (cf. Lys. 1.8). In Egypt, where the conventional roles adopted by the sexes were reversed and women went outdoors while men stayed at home (cf. Hdt. 2.35.2), sexual mores, too, were turned upside down. Herodotos (2.111) tells a memorable anecdote about the blind Pharaoh Pheron, son of Sesostris, who was informed by an oracle that he would recover his sight only if he bathed his eyes in the urine of a woman who had never had intercourse with anyone except her husband. Pheron had to perform this unsavoury operation with the urine of almost every married woman in Egypt, including presumably that of his wife, until his sight was eventually restored. In gratitude and, no doubt, relief, he married the woman whose urine had proved to be efficacious and burned to death all those who had cheated on their husbands.

In Sparta, where wife-sharing for procreative purposes was countenanced by the law, outright infidelity appears to have been regarded as a very grave offence. Asked by an admirer whether she would be interested in having an extra-marital affair, a Spartan wife replied in words to this effect: 'I leave all decisions up to my husband. You'd better ask him' (Plu. *Mor.* 242b = *Sayings of Spartan Women* 23). The typicality of such unimpeachable propriety is impossible to determine, though we should note that Plutarch (*Lyk.* 15.10; *Mor.* 228bc = *Sayings of Spartans* 20) explicitly denied the existence of adultery in Sparta in early times. Perhaps the grim object-lesson supplied by Lakonian Helen served as an adequate deterrent.

Conclusions

Young men in the twenty to thirty age-group occupied the status of both adult and non-adult. They could fight and they could vote, but though they may have been eligible for election to senior military positions (see below, p. 280), there seems to have been no other executive office available to them. So what aspirations could *neoi* fulfil? In a democracy like Athens, exceptionally able and ambitious young men could begin to make a name for themselves as political speakers already in their early twenties. Alkibiades, for instance, was no more than twenty-three when he first rose to prominence as a public speaker. But this was an outlet which can only have satisfied a small minority. It is clear, too, that such precocity aroused loathing and that those who sought accelerated promotion as politicians were exposed to considerable abuse. Xenophon graphically describes (*Mem*. 3.6.1) how Ariston's son Glaukon 'when attempting to become a public speaker and to occupy a leading position in the state though not yet twenty years of age could not be restrained by any of his relatives or friends, even though he was dragged from the speaker's platform and made himself a laughing-stock'. Young men under thirty who adopted a high profile in the lawcourts likewise earned plenty of opprobrium (cf. Lys. 19.55). In the artistic field, Aeschylus, Sophokles and Euripides had all produced plays by the time they were thirty, though only Sophokles had been awarded a first prize. Aeschylus had to wait until he was forty to win a prize and Euripides until he was forty-four. Though Aristophanes may have been as young as eighteen when he produced his first comedy, the *Banqueters*, the fact that he did not put it on in his own name suggests that precocity in the arts may also have been viewed with some suspicion. By contrast, a woman's aspiration, as defined publicly, was to make a suitable match and provide her husband with sons.

As for social outlets, well-to-do *neoi* probably divided their time between the agora, palaistra and gymnasium in the daytime, and the *andrôn* at night. Theirs was a man's world. Their principal companions were their age-mates, those, in other words, with whom they had been initiated into the phratry and the deme and alongside whom they now fought in the army. Until marriage young girls also spent much time with their age-mates, though the opportunity for associating with members of their own sex would have been greatly reduced once they became married.

Though there is no certain evidence for bachelor apartments in the Greek world such as there were in Rome, some must have existed. Given the fact that the power of the Athenian *kurios* was severely curtailed when a young man reached legal and political majority, a considerable number of *neoi* must have been either affluent and independent or, like Pheidippides in Aristophanes' *Clouds* (ll. 12ff.), confident that their fathers would pay their bills.

Given the low life expectancy, many *neoi* must have come into their inheritance and assumed headships of families by the time they reached thirty. Considerable demands were placed upon people in this category, particularly in the case of those who inherited sizeable fortunes. First, they would have been under strong pressure to marry earlier than those whose fathers were still alive. Secondly, they became liable to the performing of liturgies immediately upon attaining majority at about eighteen. The defendant in a speech by Lysias (21.1) claims that he was required to produce a tragic drama at the Thargelia as soon as he passed his *dokimasia*, fund Pyrrhic dancers for the Greater Panathenaia and a male chorus for the Dionysia the next year, and subsidise a cyclic chorus for the Lesser Panatheneia the year after that – all this in addition to serving as a trierarch no fewer than seven times.

Neoi whose fathers were still alive were clearly expected to maintain a low profile in their own *oikos*. The defendant in another speech by Lysias (19.55) prides himself on the fact that although he is thirty years old, he has never once contradicted his father. Whether in reality young men, particularly young Athenians, were as deferential to their fathers as the speaker claims is another matter altogether. Many young couples must have begun married life in the household of the groom's parents, surrounded by unmarried siblings, other married brothers, their wives and children. Others presumably depended upon an allowance provided by the groom's father, supplemented by the interest accruing from the dowry.

There is evidence that after a wife had given birth to her first child her status in the household underwent a significant improvement. An epigram dating to the third century BC, which commemorates a woman who died in labour, refers to the deceased as 'neither what you would call a complete *gunê*, nor yet a *kourê*' (*Epigr. gr.* 505.4). Giving birth would have signalled a wife's further assimilation into the *oikos*. Whereas previously she had still been something of an outsider, by this action she became truly *oikeios*. The cuckolded husband in Lysias (1.6) ruefully reflects that after the arrival of his first child he became more trusting of his wife and bestowed upon her complete control over his property in the erroneous belief 'that the two of us had now achieved a condition of complete belonging-to-the-same-household (*oikeiotês*)'.

6

Elders and the Elderly

> Old age is a complete mutilation (*pêrôsis*). It possesses everything [i.e. all parts of the body] and yet they each lack something.
>
> (Demokritos *DK* 68 B 296)

When Sokrates asks a certain Charikles to suggest the age up to which Athenians are to be accounted *neoi*, the latter replies, 'Until they have reached the age when they are permitted to serve on the Council' (Xen. *Mem*. 1.2.35). That, as we know, was in the thirtieth year. By itself Charikles' answer should not of course be treated as authoritative. If there had been no room for argument Sokrates would not have put his question in the first place. Charikles' judgment gains support, however, from Thukydides' observation (5.43) that the politician Alkibiades, who was about thirty at the time of which he was writing, 'would have passed for a *neos* in any other city'. In Athens at least then, and probably elsewhere, the thirtieth year marked an important turning point in a man's life. At Sparta, for instance, it was almost certainly in his thirtieth year that a Spartiate was eligible to become an ephor (cf. MacDowell 1986, 167, citing Xen. *LP* 4.7).

Since adult Greek society was primarily organised on a two-generational principle, withdrawal from the ranks of the *neoi* was accompanied by immediate promotion to the *presbuteroi* or elders. It follows from this that the investigation of 'elders' in Greek society is essentially inseparable from that of its 'elderly'. The word *mesos*, which is the closest approximation in Greek to 'middle-aged', is used only rarely and never to my knowledge to describe a middle-aged woman. The essential bipolarity of adulthood is indicated by a cautionary tale told by Babrios (second century AD) about a middle-aged man which virtually seems to deny the actuality of middle age as an ontological reality (*Fable* 22):

> A man who was already middle-aged (*tên mesên echôn hôrên*) – he wasn't a *neos* any more, nor as yet a *presbutês*, but his white and black hairs were mixed up together – was still devoting his time to love affairs and carousing. He was sleeping with two women, one a *nea*, the other an old woman (*graia*). The *nea* wanted him to look like a young lover, the *graia* like someone her own age. The one who was in her prime plucked out the hairs which she found that were turning white, while the *graia* plucked out any black ones she came across. This state of affairs lasted until the two women bequeathed to one another a baldpate, having plucked out all his hairs.

Bipolarity is also exemplified in Greek mythology, as in the case of the brothers Hypnos (Sleep) and Thanatos (Death), who are depicted as charming and youthful on the one hand, and old and repellent on the other (cf. Mainoldi 1987, 30-8; see Fig. 38). Even the functioning of the bowels was governed by the principle of generational bipolarity, as the following Hippokratic aphorism indicates (*Aph*. 2.53):

> Those who, when they are *neoi*, have moist bowels fare better than those whose bowels are costive. In old age, however, they fare worse, since the bowels of geriatrics (*apogêraskontes*) are generally hard.

The term *presbutês* and its cognates were perhaps reserved for men between the ages of about twenty-nine to fifty-nine. A man was probably accounted a *gerôn* when he was no longer liable for military service at around fifty-nine. We may note that in Athens, upon attaining sixty and having served as arbitrators for one year (see below, p. 281), men apparently ceased in any formal sense to belong to an age-class and the name of their eponymous hero was bestowed upon the in-coming *ephêboi* of that year. Similarly in Sparta, a Spartiate was liable for military service until the sixtieth year, after which he was eligible to serve on the Gerousia or Council of Elders (see below, p. 282).

A woman was a *gunê* from the birth of her first child until her death. The word *graia*, which had a somewhat pejorative connotation, was probably applied to women past menopause. Menopause brought about a fundamental change in a woman's social identity by releasing her for the first time in her life from the confines of the *gunaikeion* and permitting her to appear in public unattended. As the fourth-century orator Hypereides (fr. 205 Blass) observed: 'A woman who leaves the home ought to be at a stage of life when those who come across her don't ask whose wife she is but whose mother she is.' Ironically the independence which women now achieved should probably be seen as a reflection not of their enhanced *status* but of their diminished *value*. Since women past menopause are no longer capable of supplying heirs, there was not the same need to ensure their protection as when they were of childbearing years. That may sound cynical but it fits the facts.

The status of the elderly and the care and attention which they receive from their relatives differs markedly from one human society to the next. How elders and the elderly are treated has, moreover, important implications not only for other age-groups in that society, but also for the rigidity or progressiveness of its political and social institutions. Since life expectancy for both men and women was well below fifty, we should naturally suppose that persons who attained old age would have been respected and influential. Certainly the Greek language suggests as much. Plutarch points out that the noun *geras* ('honour', 'privilege' or 'reward') and its cognate *gerairein* ('to venerate or honour') retain 'a sense of reverence (*onoma semnon*) which derives from the word *gerontes* ... because the latter hold kingly rank in city states by virtue of that wisdom (*phronêsis*) which nature ... only brings to perfect and complete fruition in old age' (*Mor*. 789f = *Should Old Men Engage in Public Life?* 10). What the evidence we shall be examining here seems to indicate, however, is that although conservative states such as Sparta do indeed appear to have retained a profound respect for the elderly, the same was far from true of Classical Athens. That is because the degree of respect accorded to seniority of years is closely related to the political system which that society espouses. Oligarchic regimes display a natural inclination towards gerontocracy, whereas democracies reveal the opposite tendency (cf. Glotz 1929, 97).

A word of caution at the outset. What passes for esteem, homage and sympathy for the elderly in one society may be interpreted as neglect, indifference or abuse in another (cf. Simmons 1945, 51). Nowhere is this better illustrated than in Herodotos' account (1.216.2) of compulsory euthanasia and endocannibalism among a nomadic people called the Massagetai who lived to the east of the Caspian Sea in the region known today as Turkman. Presumably because food was in short supply and because the elderly severely hampered the movement of the tribe, a maximum life-span or *ouros hêlikias* (literally, 'boundary marker of age) was instituted for all members of the community. Thus when one of their number reached very advanced years, all his relatives assembled and sacrificed him along with a number of cattle before boiling his flesh and eating it. Such a death, according to Herodotos, far from being interpreted as a mark of disfavour, was actually regarded as 'most felicitous'.

Life expectancy

There is little evidence with which to estimate the age structure of the population of ancient Greece. Greek funerary monuments, unlike Roman ones, rarely record age at death except in the case of extreme youth and extreme longevity. Only recently have archaeologists begun to collect data from skeletal remains which will, it is hoped, ultimately enable palaeodemographers to determine the deceased's age at death, though as yet no clear picture has emerged from their researches. Excavation reports rarely go further than categorising burials as either infant, child, youth or adult, and commonly they are far less precise than that (cf. Morris 1987, 58). In his study of sepulchral inscriptions, Hopkins (1966, 263) claims that in Rome the median age at death (i.e. the age by which 50 per cent of the population had died) was 34 years for wives and 46.5 for husbands. Similar results have emerged from Angel's (1972, table 28 on p. 94) study of skeletal remains from Classical Athens: 35 for women and 44 for men. Yet there are serious problems raised by these estimates. First, it is unlikely that those whose ages at death are recorded on gravestones are representative of the population as a whole, both because of the tendency of sepulchral inscriptions to over-represent the number of elderly decedents and because of the propensity of those who survive to old age to exaggerate their actual age (cf. Frier 1983, 336). Secondly, the technique for determining age and sex from skeletal material is still extremely rudimentary and the database is at present far too small to draw anything but the most tentative conclusions from it. It is probable for instance that Angel, whose figures are based on an analysis of the pelvis, has seriously underestimated the age of older women, perhaps by as much as ten years (cf. Golden 1981, 327). Hence the best that can be done at present is to calculate the proportion of adults to sub-adults within any given community (cf. Morris 1987, 58). What does seem clear is that women had a considerably lower life expectancy than men, as both the Hippokratic author of *Eighth-Month Foetus* (9) and Aristotle (see below) maintained. We may surmise that a woman's chances of surviving to old age were greatly reduced by the fact that she was expected to begin producing children soon after menarche.

Median age at death is not, of course, the same as 'when most people die'. The so-called mortality curve has peaks at birth, early childhood and the early twenties. Since there is no reason to suppose that Greece would have been an exception to this pattern, it is safe to conclude that if a person reached maturity, barring war and epidemics he or she probably had a reasonably good chance of surviving another 15-20 years. But the proportion of the total population which attained the age of sixty-five can only have been a small fraction of the 20 per cent that is forecast for Britain, for instance, by the end of this century (cf. Finley 1981, 157).

'No modern population has 3 per cent of its population as centenarians' (Hopkins 1966, 249). In antiquity probably less than 1 per cent attained the age of eighty, as is suggested by the fact that a short treatise falsely attributed to the satirist Lukian entitled *Makrobioi* or *The Long Lived* classifies anyone who lives to be eighty as *makrobios*. Since many Greeks can only have had an approximate notion of their exact age, however, the designation 'long lived' is likely to have been applied somewhat loosely. Diogenes Laertios (9.18.19) quotes an extract from a poem by the *makrobiôtatos* Xenophon of Kolophon in which the latter puts his own age at a hundred and nine, but revealingly adds: 'if indeed I know truly about these matters' (*DK* 21 B 8). In the absence of any universally accepted system of dating in the Greek world, a major event such as the Persian Wars might usefully serve as an objective criterion for determining a person's age. In another fragment of Xenophanes the speaker inquires (*DK* 21 B 22): 'Who are you and where do you come from? How old are you? What age were you when the Mede came?'

Total life span, as opposed to *mean longevity*, appears to have been no different in the ancient world than it is today. The fourth-century gravestone of the Athenian Euphranor of Rhamnous proudly records that the deceased was a hundred and five when he died, while another Athenian called Littias was a hundred. Though such claims must be treated with caution, there are several other reported instances of men surviving to this age. Life expectancy, contingent though it was upon wars, epidemics, place of residence and size of private income, probably remained approximately static throughout the Greek world, as is generally the case in agricultural societies that predate the 'demographic transition' (cf. Cipolla 1978, 87). That is in marked contrast to the situation which prevails in the modern world where, to give but one example, the brief interval between 1985 and 1988 has witnessed in Britain an increase in women's life expectancy of one year.

Notwithstanding the brevity of human life in ancient Greece, there was a strong conviction that three score years and ten constituted a person's full apportionment of years. Solon authoritatively declared (27.17f. *IEG*; cf. Hdt. 1.32.2) seventy to be the age when a man could receive 'the apportionment of death, not dying prematurely (*aôros*)'. Many writers claimed that the normal life span of a human being had originally been considerably longer. Josephus (*AJ* 1.107) credits Hesiod, Hekataios, Hellanikos, Akusilaos, Ephoros and Nikolaos with reporting that 'the ancients (*archaioi*) lived to be a thousand'. Certain races had a reputation for extreme longevity. The most celebrated were the long-lived Ethiopians whose life expectancy was put at a hundred and twenty (Hdt. 3.23). Their longevity was due to the fact that they ate boiled meat, drank milk, and bathed in fragrant spring water which was so lacking in density that even wood sank to its bottom. A people called the Seres, who are probably to be identified with the Chinese, were said to live to three hundred, thanks to an exclusive diet of water (*Makrob.* 5). Finally, the inhabitants of Mount Athos reputedly lived to a hundred and forty because of eating snakes' flesh which 'causes their heads and clothes to be free from creatures harmful to the body' (Isigonos ap. Pln. *NH* 7.2.27).

Explanations of longevity and ageing

Ancient explanations of longevity correspond remarkably closely to those which are currently in vogue. Ps.-Lukian in the *Makrobioi* cites climate, diet, occupation, physical fitness and mental alertness as factors in the promotion of long life, ascribing the longevity of philosophers and men of learning to the simple fact that they 'took good care of their bodies' (18). Of the so-called Seven Wise Men no fewer than three – Solon,

Thales and Pittakos – are said to have lived to a hundred, a circumstance, whatever its veracity, which implies that true wisdom was perceived to be a function of old age and conversely that old age can only be attained by living wisely. The secret of a long and healthy life was no doubt as eagerly sought in antiquity as it is today. Gorgias, a famous Sicilian rhetorician and sophist of the fifth century BC who lived to the grand old age of a hundred and eight, when asked to what he attributed his long life replied (*Makrob.* 23) that he had never accepted a dinner invitation from anyone, claiming in other words that he had refrained from over-indulging in food and drink.

Aristotle believed that ageing is due to the combined loss of bodily heat and moisture. People who reside in hot climates tend to live longer than those who inhabit cold regions because they 'cool down' more slowly (*Length and Shortness of Life* 465a9f.). Men live longer than women because they have more heat in their bodies to begin with and can retain it longer (466b10-17; 467a31-2; *GA* 4.775a13-14, 18-19). Those persons who over-indulge in sexual intercourse tend to age faster than those who exercise restraint because seed is a moist residue and cannot be replaced (*HA* 7.582a23f. *T*).* Aristotle's view of ageing is actually not dissimilar to the one we encounter in Greek myth, as exemplified by the myth of the sibyl who, having been granted eternal life from Apollo, was destined to shrivel until she became no larger than a cicada. Desiccated, bloodless and cold-bodied, yet endowed with a shrill and powerful voice, the cicada is the mythical symbol *par excellence* of extreme old age (cf. Brillante 1987, 49-89; King 1986, 24-6).

Medical interest in the elderly

Gerontology as a branch of medical inquiry had no ancient equivalent, though the Hippokratic corpus contains a

*The belief that sexual over-indugence is injurious to the health and shortens life expectancy was also upheld in the Victorian era. A phrenologist named Wells, the author of a work entitled *Vital Force, or Evils and Remedies of Perverted Sexuality, Showing How the Health, Strength, Energy, and Beauty of Human Beings are Wasted and How Preserved*, stated (p. 31) that someone had once informed him that he had experienced fifteen orgasms in twenty-four hours 'but that he had been subject to epileptic fits ever since'. Wells further claimed that if those who indulged nightly were instead to 'spend their powers usefully and naturally' their lives would be prolonged by many years.

scattering of observations concerning the physical condition of the elderly which evince an incipient interest in the process of ageing. *Aphorisms* (3.31), for instance, states that the elderly (*presbuteis*) are subject to:

> difficulty in breathing, catarrh accompanied by coughing, strangury [a disease of the urinary tract], difficult micturition, arthritis, nephritis, dizzy spells, apoplexy, cachexia, itching of the whole body, sleeplessness, watery discharge from bowels, eyes and nostrils, dullness of vision, glaucopia and hardness of hearing.

Like other phases of life, entry to old age was regarded as a physiological watershed, as the following passage from the *Koan Prognostications* (30.502) indicates:

> From this *hêlikiê* [i.e. forty-one] to sixty-two the body does not develop scrofulous swellings, nor stones in the bladder unless the stone is already present, nor rheum of the spine, nor nephritis, unless these illnesses continue from a previous *hêlikiê*, nor haemorrhoids, nor discharge of the blood, unless this is occurring already. These illnesses are absent until old age (*mechri gêrôs*).

In other words, the beginning of old age, or more precisely arrival at one's sixty-third year, which as we have seen previously (p. 4) was believed to be fraught with danger, heralded a period of life when the body became susceptible to a wide variety of ailments from which over the preceding twenty-one years it had been wholly immune.

The general lack of medical interest in the elderly may be explained as a reflection partly of the small number of geriatrics in the population and partly of professional helplessness in the face of the degenerative processes brought on by old age. It not only suggests that old people received little attention from doctors but hints as well at their emarginated social status. We need hardly doubt that the attainment of old age in Greek society was consequent upon the development of a robust and indomitable spirit of self-reliance.

Menopause

Medical writers agree that menopause generally occurs when a woman is in her forties. Aristotle (*HA* 7.585b2-5 *T*), for instance, states: 'In the majority of women menstruation (*ta katamênia*) ceases when they reach their fortieth year but in those who exceed this age it can last up to their fiftieth, and some women even give birth [around this age]' (cf. *Pol.* 7.1335a9; Pln. *NH.* 7.14.61; Sor. *Gyn.* 1.20.1). The author of *Koan Prognostications* (30.502) seems to suggest that the forty-second year is the modal age of menopause.

Like girls at menarche, women experiencing menopause were thought to be exposed to grave risks. Soranos (*Gyn.* 1.26.3-5) sought to alleviate these risks in the following way:

> In the case of women who are reaching menopause (*mêketi kathairesthai*) due to advancing years care must be taken that the cessation of menstrual flow (*tôn emmenôn hê apokopê*) does not occur abruptly .... The measures that are employed at the onset of menarche must now be brought into effect during the time when menstruation is about to cease .... In addition, use should be made of suppositories which are capable of softening and of injections which have the same effect, together with all the medicaments capable of making what is hardened become soft.

The violence and unpredictability of the physical and psychological changes that accompany menopause were no doubt a source of anxiety for men and women alike, even though the anxiety is unlikely to have been of quite the same intensity as that generated by menarche. Very probably the good offices of a female deity or deities were enlisted to guide the woman through this crisis, though our sources fail to shed any light upon the handling of menopause by ritual means. The fact that we have much less information about menopause than about menarche may be due to the fact that far fewer women encountered this experience (cf. Pomeroy 1975, 87). It would be useful to know whether menopause typically signalled the end of a woman's childbearing career or whether the fertility rate among older women had already sharply declined before this point was reached.

The threshold of old age

At the opening of Plato's *Republic* the reader is introduced to the elderly Kephalos, whom Sokrates describes as being 'on the threshold (*oudos*) of old age' (1.328e). The precise meaning of this expression is unclear, since the threshold in question may either be that which leads towards old age or that which leads from it to death. It is generally taken to mean the latter, despite the inherent improbability of describing an old man to his face as 'having one foot in the grave'. But the former interpretation cannot be ruled out, not least because it would lend support to the theory that the Greeks regarded old age as a separate phase of life, demarcated by an invisible boundary like other phases but unique in the fact that no rite of passage marked a person's entry to this final stage of his mortal journey. Further evidence that this is the correct interpretation is provided by the question which Odysseus puts to the swineherd Eumaios about his father Laertes whom he describes as having been on the threshold of old age when he departed for Troy yet who is still very much alive when he returns some twenty years later (*Od.* 15.347-50).

Just as it was Apollo who controlled the threshold that divides childhood from adulthood, so it was he who controlled one's entry to old age. In Kallimachos' *Hymn to Apollo* (ll. 12-15) *paides* are urged to be regular ministrants of the god 'if they intend to achieve marriage and to cut the grizzled locks of old age'.

The desirability of a long life

The ultimate rejection by Achilles of an old age devoid of fame in favour of an early death that brings eternal glory suggests, as it is clearly intended to do, the Homeric hero's studied contempt for longevity (cf. *Il.* 9.410-16). Insofar as it constitutes an essential component of the heroic military ethic upon which the whole foundation of the *Iliad* is laid, it cannot be taken as objective evidence of a widespread cultural rejection of old age, however. The more peaceful *Odyssey* upholds the notion that physical circumstances are all-important in determining whether old age is a burden or a joy. On the one hand, there is Odysseus' father Laertes who is depicted as leading the life of a destitute and broken-hearted recluse, living in squalour and pining for his lost son (*Od.* 11.195-6); on the other, there is Nestor 'growing old sleekly (*liparôs*) in his palace', in the comfort of material security and with his family around him, who exemplifies the very opposite condition. The fact that Odysseus prayed that he himself would reach 'sleek old age' demonstrates, moreover, that length of years, given comfortable circumstances, was indeed an estate to be desired (19.367-8). When Kroisos asked Solon

Fig. 38. Heroic contempt for longevity: the beauty of young death. Attic red-figure calyx-*kratêr* by Euphronios depicting Hypnos and Thanatos raising the corpse of Sarpedon, *c.* 515 BC.

who was the most blessed of men, the latter awarded first prize to an obscure and long-lived Athenian named Tellos, partly because he perished on the field of battle and had been awarded public burial with full military honours and partly because, being survived by both sons and grandsons, he died secure in the knowledge that his line would continue (Hdt. 1.30.4).

The lyric and elegiac poets commonly stigmatised old age as a condition which arouses distaste and loathing both in oneself and others. A poem by Mimnermos (1 *IEG*), who lived in Asia Minor in the second half of the sixth century BC, is a typical example of its kind:

> What kind of life, what kind of joy is there without golden Aphrodite? May I die when I no longer take any interest in secret love affairs, in sweet exchanges and in bed. These are the

> flowers of *hêbê*, pleasant alike for men and women. But when painful old age overtakes a man and makes him ugly outside and foul-minded within, then wretched cares eat away at his heart and no longer does he rejoice to gaze upon the sun, being hateful to *paides* and despicable to women. Such a grievous affliction has the god made old age.

It would, however, be extremely unwise to conclude from this kind of sentiment that Greeks of the Archaic period habitually regarded old age as a fate worse than death. Lyric poetry addressed itself first and foremost to the theme of love and love-making. The poet (or poetess), who typically adopted the persona of an experienced yet still vulnerable lover, was professionally bound by the conventions of the genre to rail insistently and repeatedly against the ravages of time.

Ageing is a particularly problematic issue in marriages between an immortal goddess and a mortal husband. Such ill-matched couples are merely asking for trouble in the long run, as in the case of Eos and Tithonos (*Hom. h. Aph.* 218ff.). Eos obtained the gift of immortality for her husband but not the gift of eternal *hêbê*, with the result that Tithonos eventually became so repulsive that his long-suffering wife was compelled to lock him away in a closet, where he babbles away endlessly to this day (ll. 233-8). A similarly ill-matched couple, Peleus and Thetis, whose marital problems were more straightforward, apparently elected to go their separate ways when Peleus began to age.

The mythological Geras, the personification of Old Age, is the offspring of Night and issued from the same womb as Doom, Fate, Death and other anti-social monstrosities (Hes. *Th.* 211-25). The image of old age as ugly, evil and a bane to mankind also occurs in a folktale known only from artistic representations on vases which depict Herakles subduing either a dwarf or, less commonly, a giant called Geras (Fig. 39). Yet mythology's essentially negative representation of old age and the elderly similarly manifests ambivalence upon close scrutiny. The folktale is actually a somewhat unpopular variant upon Herakles' much more familiar exploit against Thanatos, the personification of Death, which exemplifies the very opposite ideal by symbolising man's basic desire to postpone the hour of his death. The attempt to bargain with Death by supplying the gods of the underworld with a substitute-sacrifice is the basis of Euripides' *Alkêstis*, whose heroine agrees to lay down her life in order to extend her

Fig. 39. Detail of an Attic red-figure *pelikê* by the Geras (Old Age) Painter depicting Herakles in conversation with an emaciated and wizened Geras, the personification of old age, first quarter of the fifth century BC. Observe the swollen and repulsive genitals.

husband's life. As Admetos ruefully observes when castigating his elderly father Pheres for not offering to die in his place (ll. 669-72):

> It is fatuous the way that *gerontes* pray for death and complain of old age and long life. If death approaches them, not one of them wants to die and age is not a burden any more.

And Pheres, too, readily admits that life does not become less precious the closer one approaches its end. To state the obvious, dislike of old age hardly constitutes any eagerness for death. The chorus of Theban elders in Euripides' *Herakles' Madness* loathe old age precisely *because* it brings death in train (l. 649f.).

In the appropriate context the dislike of old age and its attendant horrors could be invoked as a reason for coming to terms with the loss of a loved one. Lysias in his *Epitaphios* which was written in *c*. 392 BC asserts (78-9) that the war dead are not to be mourned, on the grounds that they have escaped sickness and old age. One cannot help wondering how many of the bereaved were genuinely consoled by rhetorical claptrap of this kind. In Plato's dialogue *Hippias Major* (291de) it is claimed that the belief of the majority is that the highest condition attainable by a human being is 'to be rich, healthy, honoured throughout Greece, live to old age, and, after burying one's parents decently, to be decently laid out by one's own children and buried in magnificent style'. The same sentiment occurs in an inscription on an Athenian gravestone, where a deceased woman declares herself to have been 'blessed' in having set eyes upon her grandchildren before passing to the world below. It surely represents the majority view.

Physical plight of the elderly

Though old age is frequently denounced as 'hateful' or 'detestable' in Greek literature, most people did not, as they do today, have to look forward to a period of prolonged and increasing incapacitation while the body divested itself of its functions one by one. The majority of Greeks who reached advanced years were no doubt active and vigorous until their final illness which in the overwhelming majority of cases would have been mercifully brief, painless and uncomplicated. Even so, it is important to appreciate that the Greeks seem to have regarded dying (though not death itself) with as much trepidation as we do, evidently because the last stage of life's journey even in the ancient world had its portion of discomfort and misery. In fact a death that was not attended by lingering pain and sickness was so highly prized as to be regarded as the gift of the gods. An ideal world is therefore one where human beings experience neither hunger nor hateful sickness like the rest of wretched humanity, and where death comes in old age through the intercession of Apollo and Artemis whose painless arrows are the mythological explanation for the death that overtakes people in their sleep (Hom. *Od.* 15.409-11; cf. 11.171-3). The common desire for such an ideal death is surely, too, the reason for the prominence that is accorded to the brothers Thanatos and Hypnos (see Fig. 38), particularly on vases that are reserved for funerary use.

Notable, too, is the story of the Argive brothers Kleobis and Biton as narrated by Herodotos (1.31; see Fig. 23). After the two young men had performed an act of spectacular filial piety by dragging their mother in a cart to a festival in honour of Hera, their mother in gratitude prayed to the goddess to reward her sons with the greatest gift that could be bestowed upon any human being. That night Kleobis and Biton fell asleep in the sanctuary and never woke up, such a death being adjudged 'the fairest conclusion to life'. The anecdote not only reveals the extremely high value set upon death in sleep, here seen to be reserved exclusively for those of exceptional moral uprightness, but also underlines the *abnormality* of such a passage from this world to the next, since under normal circumstances death within a sanctuary was strictly forbidden (cf. Garland 1985, 45).

Economic plight of the elderly

Even in well-to-do circles there is unlikely to have been much inclination to pay excessive devotion to the elderly once they became infirm. Social values were such, moreover, that it would have been a matter of pride as well as economic necessity for an elderly person to demonstrate his or her usefulness in however humble a capacity until the very end of life. Thus Laertes, for instance, though he is of kingly stock, keeps himself occupied by tending his orchard in old age (*Od.* 24.226ff.).

While most Greek states afforded the elderly some degree of legal protection (see below), none took responsibility for their economic welfare or general well-being. Lexicographers refer cryptically to the existence of an institution known as a *gêroboskeion*, a word whose meaning approximately corresponds to 'old people's home', but it is possible that this is merely an invention of comic writers. In some states, Athens among them, senior citizens *qua* citizens would have been included in the periodic distributions of corn which were instituted in times of crisis, but no one seems to have been moved to suggest that the elderly were deserving of special support. The only category of citizens who received state support in old age were the parents of sons who died in war (cf. Pl. *Menex.* 248d). In all other cases the care of the elderly devolved entirely upon the family. The importance which the Athenians attached to the notion of filial piety in official contexts is indicated by the fact that one of the questions which an elected magistrate was required to answer before being allowed to assume public office was 'whether he treated his parents well' (Ps.-Arist. *AP* 55.3).

What proportion of the elderly lived alone and what proportion lived with their relatives is impossible to estimate, though the incidence of three and sometimes even four generations living under the same roof must have been considerably higher then than it is in modern western society.

In Athens men with property to bequeath but no heir to whom to bequeath it frequently had recourse to adoption, an expedient memorably described by Isaios (2.13) as 'the only refuge against isolation and the only possible consolation in life for childless persons'. Though lawcourt speeches dealing with cases of disputed adoption seek primarily to determine whether the claimant did or did not perform burial rites on behalf of his adoptive father, it is certain that the former was expected to discharge his filial duties during his adoptive father's lifetime as well (cf. Isai. 2.12). The fact that so little is said about the care of the elderly as a means of testing the validity of these claims presumably demonstrates that the burial of the dead constituted a more public demonstration of filial affection. In order to promote ties between adoptive father and adopted son, the law required that the latter should forego all kinship with his original father; only if he left a lawfully born son in his adoptive *oikos* was he permitted to return to his own family (cf. Ps.-Dem. 44.64). Unfortunately there is no evidence as to the age at which a childless man would typically adopt an heir.

What has been said so far about the economic plight of the elderly applies only to the well-to-do. The poor, both the men who had no fortune to bequeath and the women who had no dowries to reclaim, were immeasurably worse off. Athenian men could earn a modest income from jury service, though this occupation was available to any citizen over the age of twenty-nine and can hardly have provided a livelihood for all the old men who needed support. The impression which we receive from the plays of Aristophanes that the lawcourts were dominated by elderly jurymen or *gerontes hêliastai* may simply be a reflection of the exigencies of the Peloponnesian war which imposed so heavy demands upon Athenian manpower (e.g. *Knights* 255; *Wasps* 1060ff.; cf. Roussel 1951, 138).

If a widow had given birth to a son, then she was guaranteed support from the state throughout her life in the same way as the father of a soldier who had died in battle. If she had not borne a son by the time of her husband's death, however, she was dependent upon the goodwill of her late husband's *oikos*. Elderly spinsters, by contrast, were dependent upon their consanguineous relatives (cf. Schaps 1979, 83-4). It might in part have been to alleviate the economic privations of elderly women that Solon introduced a law permitting women above the age of fifty-nine to act as mourners at the funerals of those to whom they were not related, for which they presumably received at least a pittance (Ps.-Dem. 43.62). A more profitable source of income for women past the age of menopause was midwifery (see above, p. 62). Certain religious duties also devolved exclusively upon older women. Thus the Pythia at Delphi was, in earlier times at least, an old woman. Other examples include the priestess of the infant god Sosipolis at Elis and the priestess of Eileithyia (Paus. 6.20.2). It is possible that the *gerairai* or 'venerable ones', who assisted in rites connected with the cult of Dionysos Limnaios at Athens, were also, as their name suggests, chosen from the ranks of the elderly. Such duties were not particularly remunerative, however, even though they would have carried considerable prestige, and can have provided an income for only a very small minority of elderly women. I know of only one reference to women being granted a pension by the state outside the context of the conditions already described, though the instance may not be unique. Plutarch (*Arist.* 27.3) relates that the two daughters of Aristeides were awarded a pension of three obols per day (subsequently increased to one drachma) on the recommendation of Demetrios of Phaleron, evidently in recognition of their father's outstanding services to his country.

Spinsters

Of all categories of the elderly, it was the spinster who was regarded with most loathing. A common *hetaira* was at least performing a useful social function and may well have been viewed with greater favour than an old maid. Many of the most alarming and terrifying figures in Greek mythology, including Empousa, Medousa, Skylla, Lamia, the Graiai, the Fates and the Furies, are spinsters, a further indication of the vital importance that attached to childbearing, since spinsters are such either because they have rejected their biological role as childbearers or because their ugliness, deformity, poverty or unsociability makes them unacceptable bed-partners.

Though these outlandish products of the Greek imagination may be no infallible guide to the determination of cultural attitudes, they strongly suggest that the refusal or failure to co-habit with a man was viewed as a solitary and unnatural condition which bred nothing but rancour, frustration and emotional instability in a woman. If, as some scholars have argued, there existed a surplus of marriageable women in Athenian society (see above, p. 87), then spinsters would have formed a sizeable proportion among the citizen population (cf. Pomeroy 1973, 137). But the case is far from being proved.

Fig. 40. Archetypal Greek spinsters? Detail of a Protoattic *amphora* depicting two Gorgons in pursuit of Perseus, *c*. 670-650 BC.

Second marriages

Re-marriage was an option more available to men than to women except for those who were *epiklêroi*. When Alkestis agrees to die in Admetos' place, she does so on condition that he does not re-marry after her death. It is surely significant that the possibility that *she* might have re-married does not seem to enter into her calculations as an alternative way of safeguarding her children's interests (Eur. *Alk*. 287-9). Alkestis charges Admetos as follows (ll. 305-10):

> Do not marry again and provide our children with a stepmother who will not be so kind as I, who in jealousy will raise her hand to your children and mine .... For the newly arrived stepmother hates the children born to a former wife – she's deadlier than a snake.

The attitude towards stepmothers outlined here emphasises a very real source of tension in a society where the laws of inheritance more or less guaranteed that a second wife had to wage mortal combat for her economic rights. Her best recourse was to provide her husband with a son who would inherit at least a part of the estate when that husband died. In other words it was in her interests to undermine the affection which her husband felt towards the children of his first marriage as a way of consolidating her own position. To what extent this perception of the stepmother as fortune-hunter acted as a deterrent to entry into second marriages by ageing or elderly Athenians who had already raised one family is impossible to determine, but it seems probable that the new wife would have encountered antipathy if not outright opposition from the children of the first marriage.

In Greek literature second marriages are in fact almost invariably presented in a negative light, the common charge being that they lead to a loosening of the ties of affection binding parents to their children by a former marriage. In the *Odyssey*, for instance, Athena gives this stern warning to Telemachos concerning the likely consequences of his mother's marriage to one of the suitors (15.19-23):

> Take care that she doesn't remove property from your house against your wishes. For you know what kind of a spirit there is in the breast of a woman. She is eager to increase the house of the man who weds her but she gives no thought to her children or to her former husband once he is dead, nor does she ask about them.

Men are portrayed as acting equally callously. The plight of a divorced wife and her children consequent upon her upwardly mobile husband's second marriage constitutes the basis of the plot of Euripides' *Medea*, where the ex-wife's vulnerability is accentuated by the fact that she is a foreigner without kin in her husband's country and debarred from returning to her parental home. The Tutor to Medea's children sums up the situation in the opening scene of the play as he sadly comments

(76f.): 'Old ties give place to new ones. As for our master, he no longer has a feeling for this *oikos* of ours.'

Legal safeguards for the elderly

Athenian law was somewhat ambivalent in the safeguards that it afforded to the elderly. On the positive side, the *graphê goneôn kakôsis* or 'action concerning the mistreatment of parents' placed sons under a legal obligation not to beat their parents, but instead to provide them with food, accommodation and all due rites of burial. The requirement of the law extended to the care and protection of grandparents and great-grandparents as well, if these happened to be alive, as well as to adoptive parents. The only group not protected by the *graphê* were those who had farmed their sons out as prostitutes and those who had omitted to teach their sons a skill. The seriousness with which the neglect and ill-treatment of parents was judged in Athenian society is indicated first by the fact that the prosecutor, unusually in the case of a *graphê*, was exempt from penalty if he failed to secure one-fifth of the votes, and secondly by the very heavy sentence, namely total loss of civil and political rights, which was imposed upon offspring who were convicted as charged. But the fact that these legal safeguards were deemed necessary surely indicates that distressing cases of neglect and mistreatment were by no means unheard of in Athens.

Athens was by no means unique in using the law to enforce the care and protection of parents. A fragmentary inscription from Delphi states that anyone found guilty of failing to feed his parents was to be bound over and conveyed to gaol. Vitruvius (6, *Praef.* 3) goes so far as to state that regulations of this kind existed all over the Greek world and that what differentiated Athens from other communities was that she alone restricted protection to parents who had taught their sons a trade. Insecurity regarding the level of support which parents can expect from their children is already detectable in Hesiod, who reports that one of the characteristics of the present Age of Iron in its most degenerate phase will be the fact that 'men will not pay their parents the due reward for their rearing (*threptêria*)' (*Works and Days* 187-9; cf. Thgn. 821).

On the negative side, Athenian law limited the rights of the elderly by prescribing that testators were to be deprived of control over their estates if their heirs could prove that they had lapsed into senility, a condition referred to as *paranoia* (Isai. 4.16). Though we know little about the workings of this law, its wording may have been similar to Plato's recommendation in the *Laws* (11.929de) that if a man becomes insensate owing to illness, old age or peevish temper and wastes his property, his son shall be entitled to bring an action against him. If convicted the father 'shall henceforth no longer be master of his own estate but be debarred from handling the least part of it, and shall dwell in his own *oikos* as a *pais* for the rest of his life'. In other words a person convicted of senility was to be deprived of all legal and political rights and so revert to the condition of a minor. The *Life of Sophokles* (13; cf. Apul. *Apol.* 37.1-3) recounts that when Sophokles' son dragged his father into court in order to declare him incapable of managing his business affairs because of *paranoia*, the old poet, who was then ninety, replied to the charge by reading out to the jury some verses from *Oedipus at Kolonos*, the play he was currently working on, and then disingenuously inquiring: 'Does that play seem to be the work of an idiot?' It is pleasing to know that the jury found him innocent of the charge. No other instance of the law's application is recorded. The view that senility is a common accompaniment of old age was none the less widespread: Atossa, the wife of the Persian king Dareios, reminded her husband that as the body grows older, so the mind becomes blunter (Hdt. 3.134.3).

The evidence discussed here suggests that the structure of Athenian society was such that elderly parents were extremely dependent upon their offspring. Though fathers could charge their sons with criminal neglect, the latter could retaliate by accusing their fathers of senility. Moreover, since Athenian law required the testator to leave the bulk of his estate to his sons, fathers were not entitled to disinherit their heirs, unless they could secure a conviction against them on the charge of *goneôn kakôsis*.

Retirement

The headship of a family might in certain circumstances be voluntarily ceded to the son by his father. This is perhaps the reason why Odysseus holds both the headship of his household and the kingship of Ithaca, even though his father is still alive. The option of retirement is occasionally hinted at in Athenian literature: in Aristophanes' *Wasps*, for instance, it is Bdelykleon who handles the family affairs and takes charge of his father Philokleon, and in a private speech written by Isaios it is the adopted son and his wife who look after the elderly Menekles (2.10-12). Needless to say, for those at the lower end of the economic scale, whether self-employed or in the service of others, the option of retiring simply did not exist.

Elderly slaves

The role of a *paidagôgos* (see above, p. 122) is likely to have fallen mainly to elderly or infirm slaves. Zopyros became Alkibiades' *paidagôgos* simply because he was too old for any other kind of work (Plu. *Alk.* 1; cf. *Mor.* 4a = *On the Education of Children* 7); and Perikles, upon observing a slave break his leg, is said to have commented, 'There's another *paidagôgos*' (Hieronymos of Rhodes ap. Stob. *Flor.* 31.121). The Elder Cato (*De re rustica* 2.7) recommended the selling of slaves who were either old or sick 'along with everything else that is superfluous', but he omits to mention who would have been the likely buyer of such unattractive and seemingly unsaleable merchandise. Though elderly slaves figure frequently in Euripidean tragedy, occupying positions of trust and responsibility in royal households, it is unlikely that they would have been treated equally favourably in real life, particularly by those whose income was barely sufficient for their own needs. We are faced with the unpleasant conclusion that many of them, having outlived their usefulness, may simply have been left to die of neglect.

Representations of old age in literature

Both literary and artistic representations of old age tend either to caricature or to idealise the elderly, depending upon the outlook and intention of the author or artist. Comedy stresses the helplessness of age because helplessness is comic and pathetic. Platonic philosophy, by contrast, sees old age as offering an unrivalled opportunity for attaining the nearest approximation to human perfection, on the grounds that an elderly person is less likely than one who is young to be diverted from the call of philosophy by weak, bodily cravings and base, physical desires. Exactly the same polarities and prejudices can be detected among the researches of modern psychiatrists and psychoanalysts. As Post (in Sears and Feldman 1973, 123) reports:

> Some, under the impact of clinical experiences, stress decline and deterioration; others, basing themselves largely on the life histories and later productions of outstandingly gifted and creative persons, try to make us believe that personality developments can occur during old age which transcend levels reached during maturity.

Ambivalence towards old age and the elderly is embedded in the Greek language which, like English, possesses an assortment of complimentary and pejorative terms to describe the elderly. Those which correspond most closely to our modern notion of a senior citizen are *presbuteros*, *presbus* and *presbutês*, though these words can also describe a person in middle life. *Geraios*, *gerôn* and *gegêrakôn* tend to denote a 'geriatric'. Pejorative terms for the elderly include *Kronolêros* ('a babbler as old as Kronos'), *nôdogerôn* ('a toothless old man') and *tumbogerôn* ('an old man who is ready for his burial mound or *tumbos*'), all of which might be rendered idiomatically in English as 'old fart'. Kronos and Tithonos, who are both noted in myth for their advanced years, also serve as pet-names to describe a 'fuddy-duddy'.

The most memorable portrait of old age in Greek literature is that of Nestor who in Homer's *Iliad* holds the rank of senior adviser to the Greek overlord Agamemnon in the Trojan War. Since he claims to have seen two generations pass away and be 'now ruling over the third' (1.250-2), he must be in his late sixties or early seventies. Like many elderly people Nestor is garrulous, long-winded, self-opinionated, discursive, prone to lapsing into lengthy and somewhat irrelevant anecdotes about his past, by no means averse to singing his own praises, and highly critical of the younger generation which he views as vastly inferior to its predecessor. Despite these characteristics, he is none the less affectionately and respectfully drawn, and we need hardly doubt that he would have aroused affection and respect in a Greek audience.

At the beginning of the *Iliad* Nestor is characterised as 'a man from whose tongue flowed speech sweeter than honey' (1.249). It is due in large measure to his intervention in the military assembly that the war of words between Achilles and Agamemnon does not result in bloodshed. Later when Nestor offers advice to Agamemnon on how best to deploy his troops in battle, he chides the Greek chieftains for arguing 'like silly little boys (*paides nêpiachoi*) who have no practical experience of war' (2.337-8). His commander-in-chief, far from taking this as an insult to his own powers of leadership, pays the old man the extreme compliment of describing him as 'pre-eminent above the sons of the Achaians in public debate (*agora*)', and of declaring that if he had ten advisers of the calibre of Nestor Troy would soon be captured (2.370-4). Though Nestor's speeches are rambling and repetitive, he therefore performs an important and even vital function within the structure of the poem, not only as a touchstone of commonsense and prudence but also as a spokesman for justice and moderation. For all his infuriating circuitousness, he is not therefore to be perceived merely as a tedious old windbag.

In the world of the Homeric poems Nestor's authority and status are exceptional but by no means unique. The deference and respect due to the *gerontes* are exemplified in the phrase *geras gerontôn*, which alludes to all those privileges to which *gerontes* are entitled by virtue of seniority (cf. *Il.* 9.422). Of what did this *geras* consist? First, in the Achaian camp, on the citadel of Troy, and in the assemblies on Ithaca and Scheria, it is the *gerontes*, or at least a subdivision thereof, who occupy the foremost position as decision-makers. When the heralds are summoning the Achaians to assembly, Agamemnon invites the great-hearted *gerontes* to meet him beforehand in a secret counsel-session (*Il.* 2.53). Priam, too, is regularly assisted by seven elders of the people or *dêmogerontes* who hold their sessions on the wall at the Skaian Gate. No longer of an age to participate in war in an active capacity, they are described as 'good speakers, like cicadas which perch upon a tree in a forest and pour forth lily-like sounds' (*Il.* 3.150-2). Their influence is so great that it overrides even that of Hektor, as the latter ruefully observes when he recalls how the faintheartedness of the *gerontes* thwarted his planned offensive (*Il.* 15.721-3). Secondly, the oldest of the *gerontes* had the right to speak first, whether in the Council or in the Assembly. When Telemachos summons the assembly on Ithaca in order to air his grievances against the suitors, it is the *gerôn* Aigyptios who, by virtue of being *progenestatos* or oldest, is the first to speak in the debate and who demands to know on whose authority the meeting has been summoned (*Od.* 2.28-9). On Scheria Alkinoös invites a large number of *gerontes* to a banquet held in honour of Odysseus (*Od.* 7.189ff.): though they are not depicted as participating in any formal discussion, it is highly probable that they constituted a forum for consultation on matters of state business. Notably it is Echeneos, again the most elderly, who is the first to respond to Arete's suggestion that Odysseus should be furnished with gifts before his departure for Ithaca (*Od.* 11.343). Thirdly, *gerontes*, perhaps collectively, were instrumental in the ratification of important agreements, as is indicated by Hektor's musings upon whether to make a treaty with the Greeks and to ratify it with an oath taken by the elders, the so-called *gerousios horkos* (*Il.* 22.119). Finally, *gerontes* lead a much easier life than their juniors. They feast and deliberate on occasions when *kouroi* are guarding the fortifications around the Greek camp (*Il.* 9.65-75). We even hear of a special choice wine known as the *gerousios oinos* which was apparently reserved exclusively for *gerontes* (*Il.* 4.259).

The respect for the counsels of the elderly which we encounter in Homer seems to have been linked to the idea that wisdom is the property of persons of advanced years (see above, p. 248). When Nestor describes Diomedes as 'the best in council among all his peers', he is in effect damning him with faint praise by intimating that his understanding of the world is limited by the fact that he is merely a *neos* (*Il.* 9.53-9). It is appropriate, therefore, that it should be the luckless Elpenor, described as 'unsound in understanding (*phrenes*)', who is the one to fall from the roof of Kirke's palace upon waking from his drunken slumber, since he is in fact the youngest of Odysseus' companions (*Od.* 10.551-60; see above, p. 128).

In Greek tragedy old people usually appear in only a minor, supporting role, except where the dominant theme of the drama is the sufferings of innocent victims in war. The aged Hekabe, queen of Troy, was a particularly haunting symbol for Euripides of the unrelieved misery and utter degradation which is all too frequently the lot of the elderly. In both the *Hekabê* and the *Trojan Women*, where she occupies centre stage, Hekabe is forced to witness atrocities such as the sacrifice of her daughter Polyxene upon the tomb of Achilles and the slaughter of her infant grandson Astyanax who is hurled from the battlements of Troy. In tragedy power and influence in both the *oikos* and the *polis* tend to reside in those of middle years. Geriatrics are typically characterised either by their irascibility, as in the case of Teiresias in Sophokles' *Oedipus Turannos* and Oedipus and Kreon in Sophokles'

Oedipus at Kolonos, or by their feebleness, as in the case of the chorus of impotent old men in Aeschylus' *Agamemnon*.

In societies which, like our own, set high store by youthfulness, or at least by the appearance of youthfulness, the fabled capacity of elderly persons to undergo a seemingly miraculous rejuvenation is often an abiding preoccupation. This phenomenon unquestionably held a powerful grip over the Greek imagination. There were many reasons for this. First, it may have received some biological support from the example of snakes, cicadas and other creatures which annually shed their skin, also called *gêras* meaning 'old age' (cf. Arist. *HA* 5.549b25 *T*; Hsch. s.v. *gêras*). The sloughing off of old age is first referred to in Homer, but in a hypothetical context (*Il.* 9.445f.): Phoinix swears that he will not abandon Achilles even if a god vowed to strip away his old age (or outer skin) and render him 'a youth in the very prime of life'. Secondly, the cyclical view of life which the Greeks upheld (see above, p. 11) may have fuelled the belief in rejuvenation or rather age-reversal. Plato in the *Politikos* (271ab), for instance, claims that in a previous epoch it was the lot of the earthborn race, once having attained the status of *presbutai*, to become *paides* for the second time at the end of their life. When they died they returned to the earth, only to be resurrected later, thereby entering an endlessly repetitive cycle. A notable 'historical' instance of rejuvenation had to do with Hesiod, whose old age (*to Hêsiodeion gêras*) was proverbial for those of very advanced years, as the Suda informs us (s.v.). Aristotle in a lost work (fr. 565 *T*) quotes an unattributed epigram composed on behalf of the poet whose first line reads, 'Hail, you who were twice young (*dis hêbêsas*) and who twice experienced the grave', and he adds by way of explanation 'inasmuch as he outlived old age and was twice buried'. The explanation for the legend should probably be sought in the folk memory of a poet whose powers were undiminished in old age and whose place of burial was contested by rival claims of equal weight.

Returning to tragedy, an example of rejuvenation occurs in Euripides' *Children of Herakles* in the case of the elderly Iolaus, Herakles' nephew and companion-in-arms. When Eurystheus arrives at Marathon in order to kidnap the children of Herakles, the old man is resolutely bent on facing him in battle. The dramatist invests the scene of his arming for the coming struggle with considerable pathos and humour, as we see from the following exchange between Iolaus and an attendant who has reluctantly agreed to lead him into battle (ll. 732-40):

Iolaus	Hurry up, I couldn't stand to miss the battle.
Attendant	You're the one who's dawdling, not me.
Iolaus	Can't you see how fast I'm walking?
Attendant	I see that you think you are.
Iolaus	You'll say differently when you see me there.
Attendant	What are you going to do? (*Ironically*) I'd like to see you winning.
Iolaus	I'll smash my way through somebody's shield.
Attendant	If ever we get there, which I personally doubt.

Confounding our expectations Iolaus, in answer to his prayer to Zeus and Hebe, herself the divine personification of youthfulness, is transformed into an *ephêbos* (ll. 843-58) and achieves high military distinction by being personally responsible for the capture of the blackguard Eurystheus. What real significance lies behind Euripides' treatment of old age is hard to assess, other than that he seems to be intent, as so often, on turning our basic assumptions and expectations upside down, even to the extent, as here, of pursuing an inversion of reality to a ludicrous extreme. Iolaus' exploits are reported by a messenger in the usual manner of Greek tragedy and it is surely not accidental that the old man is not seen on stage again. A rejuvenated geriatric would have been too much of a handful even for Euripides – though not, as we shall see in a moment, for his contemporary Aristophanes.

By contrast, Laertes' divinely engineered rejuvenation in the *Odyssey* is a consequence of the revitalising effect which Odysseus' return has upon his father (24.367-74). Earlier the swineherd Eumaios reported to Odysseus that Laertes had been reduced to 'a raw old age' (15.357), a graphic way of saying that he had aged prematurely, because he has been mourning for his absent son and dead wife.

The elderly figure prominently in Attic Comedy, as they do in all comic theatre. Of the eleven surviving plays by Aristophanes, only the *Frogs* does not feature any geriatrics – evidence indeed that Aristophanes comprehended the rule, traditionally upheld in all drama, that satire and pathos go hand in hand. Typically the elderly are portrayed as either pitiable and helpless or bellicose and cantankerous, though occasionally both sets of characteristics are combined in the same person. A specially memorable and vivid portrait of a geriatric is that of Philokleon in Aristophanes' *Wasps*. The poet's fantasy is to depict the elderly Philokleon – just how elderly we are never told but he must at least be in his sixties – as a suitable case for Borstal, a superannuated delinquent who looks back wistfully upon his youth as a time when he was able to run riot and break the law with impunity. His sole remaining pleasure in life is to serve on the jury and pass waspish verdicts on those who break the law as a way of revenging himself on life for his physical decline. Though Aristophanes' caricature of Philokleon as a hyperactive teenager is on one level merely a comic inversion of real life, it none the less contains considerable psychological aptness as a stereotypical portrait of the frustrations of old age. The drama ends with Philokleon's rejuvenation (ll. 1341-87) accompanied by a complete change of role and shift in perspective whereby the words 'father' and 'son' virtually reverse their meanings (cf. MacDowell 1971, 307).

In the earlier *Acharnians*, produced in 425 BC when Aristophanes was perhaps only twenty, a chorus of elderly hoplites from the deme of Acharnai who had contributed to the defeat of the Persians at the battle of Marathon 65 years before serves as a personification of helpless but indomitable militancy. Although at the outset of the play they are implacably opposed to Dikaiopolis' private peace treaty with the Spartans, they swiftly change their minds when the hero points out that it is the elderly who are invariably sent off to the front line while the young are given sinecures like serving as ambassadors. After complaining that Athens maltreats her war veterans, the Acharnians evoke a memorable picture of themselves as the victims of persecution by sharp-witted youngsters in the lawcourts. Their description of their pitiable condition culminates in the image of 'Tithonos', an old man sucking on his toothless gums in a state of almost imbecilic bemusement, having been dazzled by the rhetorical fireworks of his younger legal adversary and now destined to be cheated of the very money which he had set aside to pay for his own coffin (ll. 687-91).

In his last surviving plays Aristophanes repeatedly extracts vicious humour from the ludicrous spectacle of over-sexed and frustrated old bags chasing after young men who are less than half their age. Arguably none of the poet's jokes is more unacceptable to modern taste, since what he seeks to arouse in his audience is pure loathing and contempt. In the communist and feminist state which the women of Athens establish in the *Ekkleziazousai* or *Women in Assembly*, a law is passed which states (ll. 1015-20):

> Motion passed by the women. If a *neos* desires a *nea*, he may not fuck her before screwing an old bag (*graus*) first. If the *neos* refuses, but still desires the *nea*, the female elders (*presbuterai*) are permitted to drag the *neos* along to court by his prick.

There then follows an indecent squabble between three old women who try to compel a young man to have sex with them before allowing him to gratify his desire with a young girl.

The variety of masks which were used, principally in Comedy, to classify varieties of old women provides further proof of the contempt with which this group was commonly regarded. Those mentioned by Pollux (4.150) include the *graïdion ischnon* (the little old shrivelled woman), the *graïdion lukainion* (she-wolf), the *graus pacheia* (obese old woman) and the *graïdion oxu* (sharp-tongued or sharp-witted old woman). The mockery to which old women were subjected on the stage may have something to do with the fact that wives who had passed the age of menopause were deemed to be no longer worthy of sexual attentions from their husbands. To what extent this was true in reality and to what extent it was merely a piece of comic invention is impossible to say. In view of the ease with which men could obtain extra-marital sexual gratification, however, it may well be that the less fortunate were treated as 'objects who had outlived their usefulness' (Bremmer 1985, 290).

Though the motif of the sex-starved old woman is not matched in Aristophanes by that of the sex-starved old man, this is more likely to be due to the fact that it was too near the bone and did not furnish the poet with useful material for comic invention, rather than that libidinal regression was unknown among elderly Athenian males. From around 470 BC onwards Athenian vase-painting manifests a vogue for depicting elderly satyrs with permanently erect penises which they direct with a vengeance towards maidenly maenads. Similarly in our two surviving examples of satyr plays, the *Kuklôps* of Euripides and the *Ichneutai* or *Trackers* of Sophokles, Pappasilenos, the hairy father of the chorus of young satyrs, is depicted as a hypocritical old reprobate much addicted to alcoholism and lechery. While this in itself may not tell us anything very culture-specific about the psychology of ageing Athenian males, it is of some interest that in the opinion of Theophrastos, a fourth-century BC writer, indecent exposure was a sufficiently widespread nuisance that the display of one's genitals to a freeborn woman was part of a stereotypical portrait of *Bdeluria*, for which 'Dirty Old Man' might serve as a not wholly inappropriate translation (*Char.* 11.2).

None of the material we have discussed so far makes any attempt to portray the realities of day-to-day living for the elderly. In fact there is no real discussion anywhere in Greek literature of what today are perceived to be *the* central issues facing millions of elderly people in modern society – loneliness, poverty, hunger, pain, cold, physical and mental decline, and the like. Arguably the opening scene of Sophokles' *Oedipus at Kolonos*, which dwells movingly on the frailty of old age as experienced by the elderly Oedipus, presents something of an exception. Oedipus' plight owes as much, however, to his self-inflicted blindness as to his length of years, and it is the combination of these two which gives the scene its unique emotional power.

Modern investigators of the cognitive changes associated with old age identify restriction of activities, difficulties in decision-making, rigidity, and decreasing communication with the outside world as common but not inevitable characteristics of the elderly (cf. Post in Sears and Feldman 1964, 125). The belief that these degenerative symptoms are not, however, the natural or necessary accompaniment to ageing became a fundamental tenet of the Platonic school of philosophy, though its origins, as we have seen, can be traced back to a much earlier period. It was partly with the intention of demonstrating that his master remained mentally alert and never lapsed into senility that Plato depicted Sokrates learning the harp in old age (*Euthyd.* 272d). Plutarch, too, is scathingly dismissive of old men who, having led full and active public lives, become increasingly introverted and slack as they grow older and who end up by confining themselves 'to the domesticity that befits women' (*Mor.* 784a = *Should Elders Take Part in Public Life?* 1). Elderly people, he argues, are uniquely well-equipped to govern and direct the affairs of state 'by virtue of their reason, their judgment, their outspokenness and their profound wisdom' (797ef).

What are commonly perceived as the drawbacks of old age actually constituted in Plato's eyes positive advantages on the grounds that they actively foster an increase in virtue and reason. When asked by Sokrates how he copes with old age, Kephalos tells an anecdote about the poet Sophokles who, when likewise asked by a friend whether his sexual drive had abated now that he had reached advanced years, replied: 'Don't even mention the subject – I'm delighted to have escaped the thing you talk of, as if I had escaped from a savage and raging beast that was my master!' (*Rep.* 1.329c). Though Kephalos in some ways comes closer to being identifiably human than any other elderly person in Greek literature, Plato's attitude towards him is none the less condescending, for the old fellow is paraded before the reader as an object of curiosity rather than as an individual with his own feelings and needs. Notably, he plays no further part in the *Republic* after the first scene and is dismissed by the author before the philosophical discussion gets seriously under way.

Plato's belief that impotency is more than adequately compensated for by increased rationality set the model for an ideal philosophical 'type' and greatly influenced later, Stoic thinking. The concept of cheerful resignation and philosophical detachment in the face of old age finds fullest expression in Cicero's dialogue *De senectute* or *Old Age*, the inspiration for which derives primarily from the portrait of Kephalos. Cicero, who puts his remarks into the mouth of the elderly Roman Cato, claims that old age's commonly perceived hallmarks, namely moroseness, querulousness and tetchiness, are in fact states of mind to which persons of any age are subject and not the exclusive property of the elderly. In other words, it is one's temperament and not one's age which determines whether one is happy in the twilight of one's days. Cato goes so far as to eulogise old age as the consummation of all life's travails, stating: 'The nearer I get to death, the more I feel like someone eventually sighting land who is about to anchor in harbour after a long voyage' – a thoroughly non-Greek way of looking at life.

Of all Greek writers it is Plato who manifests the greatest respect for the elderly, even going so far as to compare the reverence that is due to them with that which is paid to the gods. In the *Laws* (11.931a), an admittedly reactionary and repressive document written when Plato was in his seventies, he states:

> If anyone has a father or a mother of a grandparent alive, preserved inside the home and bedridden with age, let him remember that while there is such a figure to hallow his hearth

at home, no image can be more powerful, if the owner tends it properly and dutifully.

The 'image' to which Plato refers would seem to be a cult statue of a god, in whom, it was popularly believed, there resided some spark of the divine. Plato's view, though exaggeratedly phrased, was not wholly eccentric. The fourth-century orator Lykourgos (*Against Leok.* 94), for instance, states: 'The greatest impiety is not to spend our lives benefiting those from whom we have received the beginning of life and from whom we have ourselves obtained many good things.' Elsewhere in the *Laws* Plato describes education as 'the drawing and leading of children to the principle which has been pronounced right by the law and approved as truly right by the experience of the best and oldest men' (2.659d). He further comments that it is a universally observed custom that 'older men should rule and younger men submit' (3.690a; cf. *Rep.* 5.465a).

Confidence in the intellectual and moral superiority of the elderly was by no means confined to Plato, though it is in his writings that it is most prominently displayed. Demokritos, alert to the physical decline which accompanies old age, still regarded it as a time of life when the individual is finally capable of attaining self-fulfilment. Whereas strength and beauty constitute the good things of youth, he declared, 'The flower of old age is self-restraint (*sôphrosunê*)' (*DK* 68 B 294). Demokritos further characterised old age as 'the perfected good' on the grounds that an old man has been young, but a young man has not become old and so faces an uncertain future (*DK* B 295). He did not, however, accord unqualified respect to the elderly. An old man is agreeable, he states (*DK* 68 B 104), only if he is 'wily' and has 'a serious manner of delivery'.

Aristotle in the *Rhetoric* (2.1389b13-38) delivers what is surely one of the most devastating and depressing assaults upon the mental condition of the elderly ever written. Though it cannot be proved, his tirade seems almost to read as an intentional corrective to Plato's naive and sentimental fantasising upon the rewards of waning sexual desire:

> Older men or *presbuteroi* and those who have passed their prime or *parêkmakotes* have in most cases characters opposite to those of the young. For, owing to their having lived many years and having been more often deceived by others or made more mistakes themselves, and since most human things turn out badly, they are positive about nothing, and in everything they

Fig. 41. Detail of a statue of an elderly seer from the east pediment of the Temple of Zeus at Olympia, 465-457 BC.

show an excessive lack of energy. They always 'think', but 'know' nothing; and in their hesitation they always add 'perhaps', or 'maybe'; all their statements are of this kind, never unqualified. They are malicious; for malice consists in looking upon the worse side of everything. Further, they are always suspicious owing to mistrust, and mistrustful owing to experience. And neither their love nor their hatred is strong for the same reasons; but, according to the precept of Bias [one of the Seven Wise Men of Greece], they love as if they would one day hate, and hate as if they would one day love. And they are little-minded, because they have been humbled by life; for they desire nothing great or uncommon, but only the necessaries of life. They are not generous, for property is one of these necessaries, and at the same time, they know from experience how hard it is to get and how easy to lose. And they are cowardly and inclined to anticipate evil, for their state of mind is the opposite of that of the young; they are chilled, whereas the young are hot, so that old age paves the way for cowardice, for fear is a kind of chill. And they are fond of life, especially in their last days, because desire is directed towards that which is absent and men especially desire what they lack. And they are unduly selfish, for this also is littleness of mind. And they live not for the noble, but for the useful, more than they ought, because they are selfish; for the useful is a good for the individual, whereas the noble is good absolutely. (tr. J.H. Freese in *LCL*)

Representations of elders and the elderly in art

An interest in the elderly is detectable in vase-painting around the turn of the fifth century BC. A set-piece subject was the death of Priam, which is depicted on a famous hydria by the Kleophrades Painter: the aged king with bowed head awaits death at the hands of an almost preternaturally youthful Achilles, his grandson Astyanax strewn across his knees like a broken willow branch. One of the earliest attempts in sculpture to portray the infirmity and pathos of old age is that of the balding seer on the east pediment of the Temple of Zeus at Olympia dated *c.* 465-457 BC (Fig. 41). The old man is depicted reclining, resting his head on his hand, with a sagging belly and a deeply furrowed brow. There is a mixture of sad foreboding and terror in his pained expression. Empowered with prevision and therefore capable of foreseeing that the chariot race between Pelops and Oinomaos which is about to take place will have a fatal outcome, the seer stands as an epitome for the curse of old age, which is to have understanding in painful abundance but not the strength to act upon it. In its successful rendering of both the inner and outer predicament of old age the seer is practically unique in Greek art. The elderly marshals who direct the Panathenaic procession on the Parthenon frieze are by contrast merely embodiments of authority, for the artists have made no attempt to explore their inner state of consciousness.

The beginnings of an artistic interest in what might be described as the dignity of well-preserved middle-age coincides with the beginnings of an interest in old age, as indicated by the towering, athletic figure of Zeus in the centre of the east pediment at Olympia (Fig. 43; cf. Fig. 42).

It says much about the aims and ideals of Greek art as well as the bias of Greek society that there is no surviving study of an old woman which does more than portray her as the representation of an almost sub-human species of animal life which is at best abject and pitiable, at worst contemptible and repellent. A famous example from the Hellenistic period depicts an old drunk in a collapsed attitude on the ground. Still grasping her wineflask avidly in both hands, she gazes upwards with a stupefied expression on her face. Haunting though the study is, it lacks all compassion. Instead of inviting us to enter into the old woman's world as does the sculptor of the seer at Olympia, the artist of this work seeks to alienate

Fig. 42. Bronze statue of Zeus (or Poseidon), second quarter of the fifth century BC. Found in the sea off the coast of Artemisium.

the viewer from the physical and moral degeneration of old age.

Respect for the elderly: Athens versus Sparta

The rhetorician Thrasymachos of Chalkedon, who was active in the latter half of the fifth century BC, is said to have commented in an address to the Athenian Assembly (*DK* 85 B 1):

> I wish, men of Athens, that I were living in that period long ago when *neôteroi* were obliged to be silent, when matters did not

Fig. 43. Fragmentary statue of Zeus from the east pediment of the temple of Zeus at Olympia, 465-457 BC.

compel them to speak out, and when *presbuteroi* guided the polis surely.

By the early fourth century contempt for the elderly had widely come to be perceived as a distinctive feature of the Athenian national character, and one which sharply distinguished it from its Spartan counterpart. The earliest explicit comparison between the two communities' attitudes towards the elderly is contained in Xenophon's *Memorabilia* (3.5.15) where Perikles despairingly demands: 'When will the Athenians respect their

Fig. 44. Pentelic marble statue of an exhausted old woman bearing a basket of vegetables, second century BC.

presbuteroi the way the Spartans respect theirs, instead of despising everyone older than themselves, beginning with their own fathers?' Deference towards old age as a characteristically Spartan virtue is already alluded to by Herodotos (2.80.1), who claims that the Egyptians along with the Spartans alone of all Greeks observe the custom whereby *neôteroi* stand aside for *presbuteroi* when they pass them in the street and rise when they enter the room. Among the complaints which Sokrates levels against extreme democracy in Plato's *Republic* (8.563a) is the fact that the old tend to be overawed by the young whom they imitate 'for fear they be thought disagreeable and authoritarian'. Though Sokrates does not refer specifically to Athens, there can be little doubt that his home town was uppermost in Plato's mind when he made this observation. Plutarch (*Mor.* 235d. = *Sayings of Spartans* 55) tells the anecdote that when an elderly Athenian was looking for a place to sit in the theatre of Dionysos, the only members of the audience who stood up and offered him theirs were some Spartan ambassadors sitting in the front row who happened to be official guests of the Athenian state. On witnessing this act of courtesy, the audience broke out into spontaneous applause, whereupon one of the Spartans turned and quipped to his companions: 'These Athenians certainly know how to recognise good manners, but not how to put them into practice.'

Spartan respect for the elderly was as much a function of social structure as of social conditioning. It was the duty of *presbuteroi* and magistrates to supervise the punishment meted out by *eirenes* to *paides* (Plu. *Lyk.* 18.3). *Presbuteroi* were also the only group permitted to use a light when walking in the dark (Xen. *Lak. Pol.* 5.7; cf. MacDowell 1986, 69). Their privileges entailed responsibilities, however. It was regarded as disreputable for members of this age-group to be seen constantly loafing about in the agora; instead they were expected to spend the greater part of the day exercising in the gymnasia and conversing in the Leschai, not talking about money-matters, but setting a good example by praising noble deeds and censoring base ones (Plu. *Lyk.* 25.1-2). There is no evidence as to whether elderly women enjoyed comparable prestige in Spartan society.

The establishment of close personal ties between a young Spartiate and an older mess companion may well have helped to bridge the gap between the two generations, just as the absence of any such bonding mechanism served to widen it in Athens (cf. Reinhold in Bertram 1976, 27). Given the whole tenor of Periklean democracy no less than the structure of its primary institutions, namely the Assembly and the lawcourts, it was perhaps inevitable that father and son should confront one another daily across the generational divide as *neos* and *presbuteros* in debating theatres which tended to polarise their differences and foster discord. Yet it is at least conceivable that the youth revolution eventually produced a backlash. This would explain why in the fourth century *neoi* commonly found it necessary, or at least judicious, to justify their appearance as prosecutors in civil lawsuits (e.g. Dem. 29.1; 44.1). Likewise in his address to the Council on the occasion of his public scrutiny a young man called Mantitheus alludes to the irritation and hostility that were felt towards *neôteroi* who attempted to speak in the Assembly (Lys. 16.20).

We should be wary, however, of any excessive simplification in the antithesis between Athens and Sparta, not least because belief in a supposedly Golden Age when youth was innately deferential towards its elders appears to have formed part of a collective Greek perception of modern decadence that was by no means confined to Athens, even if, inevitably, that is where most of our evidence for it originates (cf. Roussel 1951, 170). A hint is already detectable in the *Iliad* when Nestor remarks at the beginning of his long speech in Book 1: 'In former times I associated with better warriors than you and they never made light of me' (l. 260f.). A part of the problem in weighing the evidence we have been considering lies in the fact that the Athenians were more self-critical than the Spartans.

Lower and upper age limits for public office

In many Greek communities the acquisition of full political, legal and civil rights postdated by as much as a decade the attainment of adulthood. In Athens, for instance, citizens were not eligible to be members of the 'Solonic' Council of Four Hundred nor the later Kleisthenic Council of Five Hundred until they had entered their thirtieth year. This was also the lower age-requirement for serving as a dikast, i.e. as a member of an Athenian jury (Dem. 24.150; Ps.-Arist. *AP* 63.3). On the other hand, men under twenty-nine seem to have been eligible for senior military posts, including the generalship (*stratêgia*). Likewise the fortieth year was also a milestone in terms of official trust and responsibility. Both the board of *sôphronistai* and probably as well the *kosmêtês*, officials responsible for disciplining the *ephêboi*, had to be at least in their fortieth year, as did the *chorêgoi* or leaders of boys' choruses. As already noted, military service for an Athenian lasted until the the fifty-ninth year, upon the attainment of which the only position available to an elder by virtue of seniority was the relatively humdrum one of being judicial arbitrators or *diaitêtai* in cases where both prosecution and defence preferred to settle out of court. The period of incumbency only lasted one year and could not be extended (Ps.-Arist. *AP* 53.4).

Although Plato in the *Laws* (6.759d) went so far as to make the sixtieth year the minimum age requirement for holding a priesthood and Aristotle in the *Politics* (7.1329a31-4) recommended that priests should be appointed only from those who were too old to serve the state in a more active capacity, there is no evidence to indicate that in Athens either suggestion was actually adhered to in practice, though some priesthoods were reserved exclusively for the elderly.

To what extent Greek communities imposed an upper age limit for public office is very difficult to determine, but such evidence as we have suggests it was the exception rather than the rule. Aristotle in the *Politics* (3.1275a15-19) describes *gerontes* who have been 'released from duty (*apheimenoi*)' as 'citizens in a sense' and observes (4.1297b14-16) that at Malea on Crete the magistrates (*archontes*) were chosen from men on active military service. He would surely have cited more important communities if they, too, had adopted this practice. Aristotle's further claim that 'in some communities the citizen body (*politeia*) consists not only of those who are currently serving as hoplites, but also of those who have served' clearly indicates that these same communities divested persons who were no longer capable of military service of either some or all of their political rights. To judge from the career of the Athenian politician Phokion, who was elected to the post of general (*stratêgos*) no fewer than 45 times and who last held it about the age of eighty, there did not exist any upper age limit for senior military officers at Athens. It also seems most improbable that there was any upper age limit for councillors or magistrates. In the ideal state envisaged by Plato in the *Laws*, however, no senior magistrate is to be above the age of sixty-nine or in some cases seventy-four. The custodians of the law or *nomophulakes* are to be permitted to hold office until the age of sixty-nine (6.755ab), whereas the auditors (*euthunoi*) are to be eligible until seventy-four (12.946c).

Political authority of the elderly

Sparta

The question whether any Greek community deserves to be labelled a gerontocracy depends ultimately not on how much deference was accorded to men of advanced years but on how much political power was invested in them constitutionally. In Sparta the chief decision-making body was the Gerousia, a council of *gerontes* in the strict sense of the word which comprised the two kings plus 28 over-fifty-nine-year-olds 'who were judged to be outstanding in virtue' (Plu. *Lyk*. 26.1). It is by no means certain, however, whether there was a comparable lower age limit for eligibility to the supervisory board consisting of five ephors who monitored the conduct of the kings.

Once elected to office, members of the Gerousia were in power for life and accountable to no one (cf. Arist. *Pol*. 2.1271a5-6). On what basis their election took place is not known, but it is possible that it may have had something to do with proximity of kinship to the royal houses since, as Herodotos (6.57.5) tells us, when one of the kings was absent the member of the Gerousia who was most closely related to him took over his vote. The Gerousia had two main functions. First, it had the right of *probouleusis*, i.e. the right to determine whether a proposed law should be put before the whole assembly of citizens for ratification (Plu. *Agis* 11.1). Secondly, it was the supreme court of law in the land, being empowered to hear cases for which the penalty was either death, exile or loss of civil rights (Xen. *LP* 10.2; Plu. *Lyk*. 26.1; cf. Arist. *Pol*. 4.1294b31-4). Xenophon actually states that it was due to the fact that the Gerousia had control over the death penalty that old age was held in greater honour in Sparta than 'the vigour of those who were in their prime or *akmazontes*'. It is also possible that at moments of crisis the Gerousia had the right to issue instructions to the kings in concert with the ephors. Herodotos (5.40) describes an occasion when the ephors and *gerontes* ordered King Anaxandridas to take a second wife because he had failed to produce an heir from his first wife. Other boards of elders also wielded considerable power in Sparta, such as the *presbutatoi phuletôn* or elders of the tribes who were charged with the inspection of newborn infants (see above, p. 88). Very possibly this same body may have been called upon to supervise the entry of children and youths into their various age-classes.

Sparta was not alone among Greek communities in weighting its constitution in favour of the elderly. A charter granted to Cyrene in Libya by Ptolemy I of Egypt at some date between 322/1 and 308/7 BC laid down that the 500 members of the Council, the 100 members of the Gerousia, the five generals, the five ephors and almost certainly as well the nine custodians of the law must all be at least forty-nine years old.

Athens

The only occasion in Athenian history when the elderly are known to have been assigned powers by virtue of their advanced years was in the winter of 413/2 BC, immediately after the calamitous defeat of the expedition which had been sent out to Sicily two years previously. On this occasion the democratic constitution was suspended and 'a board of older men (*archê tis presbuterôn andrôn*)' appointed 'to give their advice on the situation, whenever the occasion arose' (Thuk. 8.1.3; cf. Ps.-Arist. *AP* 29.2). This board consisted of ten *probouloi* or councillors, later increased in number to thirty, who were appointed on a temporary basis to tide Athens through a particularly critical period. The minimum age requirement of the *probouloi* is not known, but at least one member of it, the poet Sophocles, was over eighty at the time, while another, Hagnon, the father of the politician Theramenes, was almost certainly over sixty. The prominence of ten or thirty Athenian elders at a time of almost unprecedented national emergency only serves to underline, however, how little their counsels counted for under normal conditions. Their appointment may well have had something to do with the fact that the debate in the Assembly which originally approved the expedition to Sicily had, as already noted, divided along age lines.

The fact that Nikias' appeal to the elderly on that occasion failed to carry the vote has implications not only for the decision-making processes and political tendency of Athenian democracy in general, but also for the age structure of the Assembly, which, in view of the ravages inflicted by the

Peloponnesian war and the plague, probably contained a preponderance of men under thirty. The failure of his appeal may even contain part of the reason why a community like Athens became a democracy in the first place. Had the average citizen been more innately respectful towards his elders, I doubt it would have been necessary to pass laws requiring children to look after their parents. It was precisely because Athenian culture encouraged the individual to set himself on a level of political equality with the entire citizen body that he was able to rise to the challenge of full, participatory democracy. Political systems largely reflect, and are to some measure the product of the social infrastructure out of which they have grown. As in the modern world, so in antiquity, gerontocracies are not noted for radical solutions, while societies which undergo rapid changes tend to manifest little respect for the elderly.

Euthanasia and suicide

Although ancient physicians lacked the capability to prolong human life, it is evident that the means by which to shorten life were readily available. To be sure, beliefs about the afterlife militated strongly against both practices, since both *biothanatoi* and *aôroi*, that is, those who took their own lives and those who died prematurely, constituted abnormal and unhappy categories of the dead to which no god-fearing pagan would have sought entry. The Hippokratic oath, which required those who took it 'not to administer a poison to anybody when asked to do so and not to propose such a course', expressly ruled out both mercy killing and assisted suicide. As was true in the case of the earlier discussion about the injunction against abortifacients, however, the existence of this clause in the oath indicates that such practices were not unknown. Moreover, it is highly improbable that a Greek physician would have considered the prolongation of the life of a helpless invalid as necessarily consistent with medical ethics. In the *Suppliants* Euripides makes a plea for what today would technically be called patho-euthanasia, the withdrawal of life support systems and drugs from the terminally ill, when he puts into the mouth of one of his characters the following statement (ll. 1109-11):

> I can't stand people who drag out their life with food and drink and magic spells, trying to keep death out of the way.

Plato, too, though strongly opposed to suicide, praises the legendary physician Asklepios for refusing to prolong the lives of those who were incurably sick (*Rep*. 3.407d-408b).

Philosophers were somewhat divided on the subject of euthanasia. A fragment of Demokritos (*DK* B 160) pragmatically states: 'To live badly is not to live senselessly, immoderately, or impiously, but to spend a long time dying.' The conclusion seems to be that suicide is an acceptable alternative. Plato, on the other hand, as we have seen, idealised old age as a period of liberation from the tyranny of sexual passion and one which is most naturally akin to the philosophical ideal: he omitted to mention that the decline of one's sexual drive is inevitably accompanied by a painful deterioration in one's physical and often mental health as well. His assertion that the death which comes to a man in old age is 'the easiest of deaths, one that is accompanied by pleasure rather than by pain' (*Tim*. 81e) seems to imply that he regarded the suicide of the elderly for whatever reasons as morally unacceptable. Among the Stoics, by contrast, it was a point of honour for the very aged to terminate their existence before entering their dotage. When Zeno, the founder of the school, at the age of ninety-eight stumbled and fell upon entering the Assembly in Athens, he barked back at Pluto, the god of the underworld, 'I'm on my way. Why are you shouting?' The philosopher subsequently went home to starve himself to death, evidently seeing in this trivial incident evidence of an irreversible and unacceptable physical decline (D.L. 7.28; cf. Luk. *Makrob*. 19).

The compulsory slaughter of the elderly by peoples who lived outside the Graeco-Roman world is widely reported by ancient writers. Whether there is any veracity in such claims is impossible to tell, but their significance for the present study lies chiefly in the fact that the Greeks and Romans found such practices alien and barbaric.

Signs of impending death

The Hippokratic author of *Aphorisms* (7.87) lists the following as signs of impending death. Clinically detached though the passage is, its conclusion, which is obviously inspired by Homer, possesses a haunting beauty that verges on the lyrical:

> The right testicle chilly and withdrawn is a sign of death. Blackening nails and toes that are cold, black, hard and

> clenched reveal that death is near. So do livid fingernails and dark lips which hang down and are turned outwards. A patient who feels dizzy and turns away, who relishes peace and who is gripped by sleep and heavy lassitude, has no hope of recovery. If he raves somewhat, does not recognise people, does not hear or understand, that is a sign of death. So, too, is vomiting through his nose when he drinks. These clearer signs occur at the very point of death. Immediately the bowels enlarge and become puffy. The boundary of death (*horos thanatou*) is reached when the heat of the soul (*psuchê*) has gone past the navel to the part above the diaphragm, and all the moisture [in the body] has been burnt up .... And the *psuchê*, leaving the edifice of the body, hands over the cold, mortal image (*eidôlon*) to bile, blood, phlegm and flesh.

The rest is silence. As a prosaic Greek proverb puts it, the corpse can't bite (*CPG* II, p. 542.4a).

Conclusions

The modern emphasis upon middle age has no ancient equivalent. The brevity of human life ensured that the evils commonly attributed to this phase of life were assimilated to those attributed to old age. Or, to phrase it differently, while perhaps no Greek ever complained of feeling middle-aged, many middle-aged Greeks as we would identify them today may have complained of feeling old.

Broadly speaking Greek society does not appear to have been any more age-oriented than it was child-oriented. For a privileged minority old age may have been relatively pleasant, but for the majority, both physically and psychologically speaking, it must have been burdensome in the extreme.

A priori the influence and prestige of the elderly is likely to have been more pronounced in a largely illiterate society such as Sparta where there were few written records and where the aged served as repositories of knowledge and folkloristic wisdom. Progressive and highly literate societies such as Athens do not manifest the same tendency. In fact the conspicuous failure of Athenian democracy to address the problems facing the elderly is, arguably, a reflection of its pragmatic and unsentimental judgment upon the marginality and essential worthlessness of this age-group for society as a whole, as compared with the economic and political value of other age-groups. Yet it is also due to the fact that the elderly constituted only a very small fraction of the population as a whole and that their welfare was the exclusive concern of the family.

It is probably safe to assume that in every Greek community a certain number of elderly people of both sexes featured prominently in formalised and ceremonial contexts as priests, advisers, officiants and the like. In particular, it would be useful to know whether elderly persons had a leading role as controllers of ceremonies connected with critical periods in the life-cycle, as frequently attested by anthropologists, since this would have granted them an important manipulative facility. All that we know is that in Sparta it was *presbutatoi* who determined which offspring should be reared.

There were two functions in Greek society which, if not exclusively reserved for the elderly, were most appropriate to persons of advanced or advancing years, namely that of the seer and the midwife. Both acted as mediators between the human and divine worlds and both functioned virtually autonomously in their respective spheres of expertise.

The status of the elderly within the Greek family is extremely difficult to assess. Nominally at least headship of a family devolved upon the most senior male, who in many cases might not, of course, have been particularly elderly. We should naturally expect there to exist some correlation within a single community between the political prominence of the elderly on the one hand and their standing and prestige in the family on the other. However, there is no way of testing, say, whether elders as a group enjoyed less prestige and privileges in the Athenian home than they did in its Spartan equivalent.

A final observation. Given the fact that able-bodied men were frequently absent from the home, it is probable that inter-generational ties developed between the very young and the very old, such as seem to have been deliberately fostered in Sparta. In view of the age-difference between men and women at time of marriage, however, grandfathers must have been in much shorter supply than grandmothers.

Conclusion

Human life in the ancient world was confronted with lethal danger and opposition both at the biological and social levels. The physical world was deemed to be resistant to the production, growth and socialisation of the individual to a marked degree. Conception, gestation, birth, growth, entry to adulthood and survival to old age could be successfully accomplished only if they were assisted at every juncture by divine intervention. Whereas in our society the attainment of a full term of years is now regarded with an almost confident inevitability, in ancient Greece the view was held that only if one performed the proper rituals, only if one mobilised the support and goodwill of the gods, only if the natural resistance of the physical world could be negated and overcome, would human life flourish and prosper.

All societies are obliged to deploy their human resources as effectively as they can. In ancient Greece one's working life as defined by eligibility for military service in the case of a man and fertility in the case of a woman extended approximately from the years seventeen to fifty-nine and fourteen to forty-plus respectively. Yet very few men and an even smaller proportion of women ever reached 'retirement age' in their role as soldiers and childbearers – proof, if proof were needed, of the central and equivalent importance of warfare and childbearing.

How others see us and how in turn we see ourselves is in part a function of physiological changes that occur in the human body. But it is also a consequence of the judgment which society has passed upon the usefulness of the *hêlikia* or age-group to which we belong. It is the function of any system of age-categorisation to provide a common stock of references and a mode of self-recognition by which the members of a particular community can achieve a sense of corporate identity. The study of age-categorisation thus constitutes an important aspect of axiology. It cannot be undertaken without an awareness of the needs and ideals of the society that produced it and which it in turn serves. In undertaking this inquiry I have sought to demonstrate that the Greek way of life, as that form of words has been interpreted throughout this investigation, reflects a particular, perhaps even unique social reality. Like other ways of life (our own included) it taught the Greeks their place in the community, and in so doing it served both to liberate and to inhibit their energies.*

Homêlikia or peer-group bonding was an inconstant factor in Greek history, as it is in modern societies. Consider the close and enduring ties that are maintained throughout life by American high school and college graduates of the class of a particular year, for which there is no Bristish equivalent. Judging from the dearth of evidence relating to age-classes from the Hellenistic period, the ability to define oneself as the member of a particular age-group within a particular community may have been one of the many casualties of the greatly expanded and far more open-ended world created by the conquests of Alexander the Great. Not entirely lost, *homêlikia* survived in archaising institutions such as the *ephêbeia*, though these had now been stripped of their original functions.

The Greeks tended to regard man's personality as something fixed and unchanging, not, as we do, as a constantly evolving continuum (cf. Pelling 1989). Words like *nêpios*, *pais, ephêbos, neos*, and *gerôn* identified periods of life that were perceived as self-contained units with their own highly specific age-related character traits. Psycho-social and biological change was largely confined to the divisions between age-categories. Hence the anxiety which Greek culture focussed upon the junctures which marked the transition from one age-class to the next. As a consequence, Greek age-terminology tended to carry with it a far heavier 'cultural load' than does its English equivalent. *Neos*, to take an example, conveyed much more than is ever imparted by the term 'young man'. It is of course an undeniable fact that age contributes to the conditioning of

*The inhibiting effect of age-stereotyping is pointed out in the following letter to the *Independent* (20/7/88) from John Allrey, Director of Research into Ageing (London EC4): 'Our failure to harness the wisdom and skills of those who have retired will continue as long as we fail to recognise that, with some exceptions, people need not even be described as "physically old" at seventy-five .... A national change in attitude to the elderly will encourage people to face the last third (or more) of their lives with greater optimism to the benefit of themselves, their families, their friends and the nation.'

human behaviour, but so do family background, childhood experiences, relationship with one's parents, and so on. Of these we hear virtually nothing. It is the almost exclusive concentration upon personality traits which are essentially age-linked and basic human drives such as lust, greed, fear and pride that makes the delineation of character in Greek literature often appear so irredeemably naive.

There is one final point to grasp which modifies almost all the foregoing. Written into the text of this book is an unavoidable class bias. We have already noted that coming of age functions as an extended process only in communities and social groups which have privileges to confer upon those seeking entry to their ranks. But the same point holds true for other transitional points as well. The economically depressed and the socially downtrodden have neither the motivation, leisure nor means to dramatise life's divisions as do those who enjoy high economic and social status. There are two obvious consequences that stem from this. First, the poor enjoy greater social freedom than the rich; and secondly, their lives are far more drab and undistinguished on the temporal plane. At the extreme end of the spectrum is the slave who, with perfect aptness, is designated a *pais* all his life. On one level much of what we have been examining is the artificial insertion of high drama, with all its many exits and entrances, into the palpable obscure passage of time.

Fig. 45. Terracotta figurine depicting a child being taught to write by an elderly man, possibly his grandfather or *paidagôgos*.

Glossary

ageneios – literally 'beardless'; age-categorisation used in athletics to denote those in the middle group between *paides* and *andres*
agôgê – the Spartan educational system
akmazôn (pl. *akmazontes*) – young man who has reached his *akmê*
akmê – the peak of one's physical condition
akoitis – wife or legal bed-partner (from *koitê*, bed)
alochos – wife or legal bed-partner (from *lechos*, bed)
amblôsis – abortion or miscarriage
apogêraskôn (pl. *apogêraskontes*) – geriatric
apothesis (verb *apotithêmi*) – exposure
anêbôs – prepubertal person of either sex
anêr (pl. *andres*) – husband or adult male
aôros – one who is under age; one whose life is cut off in its prime
bouagos – ox-leader or leader of Spartan year-class
brephos (pl. *brephê*) – embryo, foetus or neonate
damar – wife (Archaic, from *damazô*, subdue)
diaphthora – abortion or miscarriage
eirên (pl. *eirenes*) – Spartan youth from his twentieth to his thirtieth year
êitheos – unmarried youth
ekthesis (verb *ektithêmi*) – exposure
ektrôsis, ektrôsmos – abortion or miscarriage
embruon – embryo, foetus or neonate
ephêbos – ephebe; in Athens the period of military training from about seventeen to nineteen; in Sparta that from about thirteen to nineteen
epi dietes hêban – to be two years past puberty (in Athens the period from the cutting of the *koureion* to admission to the *ephêbeia*)
epikuêsis – superfetation
erastês – the senior partner of a homosexual relationship
erômenos – the junior partner of a homosexual relationship
geraiteros – a person who is over-age (e.g. for military service)
gerôn (pl. *gerontes*) – old man or senior citizen; approximately, a man aged about sixty or over
gerousia – council of old men; in Hellenistic and Roman times, an association of old men
gonê – seminal emission; embryo
graïdion (dim. of *graus*) – little old woman

graus – old woman; more specifically perhaps, a woman past menopause
gunê (pl. *gunaikes*) – mature woman or wife; woman who has given birth to her first child
hebdomas (pl. *hebdomades*) – period of seven years
hêbê – puberty; in Athens the age at which an adolescent youth is presented to his phratry
hêlikia (Ionic *hêlikiê*) – period of life; in Athens one of forty-two year-groups approximately covering the ages eighteen to fifty-nine
hetaira – prostitute; literally, a female companion
homêlikia (Ionic *homêlikiê*) – sameness-of-age; those belonging to the same year-group or *hêlikia*
hôrê – the moment of one's physical peak
klimaktêrikos – climacteric; a year of one's life (especially one's sixty-third) when the body is particularly susceptible to illness
koros (Ionic *kouros*) – young man; in Homer a man of military age
korê (Ionic *kourê*) – young woman
krupteia – the Spartan secret police; the period of military service for Spartan youths aged about seventeen to nineteen
kurios – legal guardian (father, eldest brother, etc.)
lechô – parturient woman or one who has recently delivered
maia – midwife
meirakion – lad or youth
meirakullion (dim. of *meirakion*) – lad or youth
mesos – middle-aged person
mothax (pl. *môthakes*), *mothôn* (pl. *mothônes*) – boy of impure Spartan descent who has been admitted into the *agôgê*
nea – young woman
neanias – young man
neaniskos (Ionic *neêniskos*) – young man (dim.)
neos – young man; one who belongs to a youth organisation for those in their twenties
neôteros – young man; person of military age
neotês – youth; those of military age (collective); in Crete *neotâs* denotes a board of officials representing the *neoi*
nêpios – infant or young child; intellectually immature adult (pejorative)
numphê – bride, young wife or wife who has just given birth; woman who is at the interval between the status of *parthenos* and *gunê* (i.e. between marriage and the delivery of her first child)
numpheutria – bridesmaid
numphios – bridegroom
omphalêtomos – midwife; literally 'navel cutter'
ouros hêlikias – maximum lifespan; literally 'boundary marker of age'
paidagôgos – person, usually a slave, responsible for the welfare of a freeborn boy
paidarion (dim. of *pais*) – little child or slave

paidika (dim. of *pais*; pl. used as sing.) – the junior partner of a homosexual relationship
paidion – embryo, foetus or neonate; little child; young slave
paidoktoneô – commit infanticide (used only very rarely of exposure)
pais – child or young person of either sex; slave; in Sparta a youth in a year group approximately aged eighteen
parthenos – marriageable but unmarried woman (less commonly, man)
patrôïôkos – heiress (Crete)
phthora – abortion or miscarriage
presbuteros, presbutês – senior citizen, elder or elderly person
promnêstria – matchmaker
teknon – offspring or child of either sex
titthê, titthênê – wet-nurse
threptos – foundling child
tropheus – dry-nurse
trôsmos – abortion or miscarriage
tumbogerôn – old fart

Notes

Introduction

3 **The hebdomadal system.** See especially Hipp. *Peri hebdomadôn* or *Weeks* (5), as edited by West (1971, 365-88), where the seven ages are referred to as *paidion, pais, meirakion, neêniskos, anêr, presbutês* and *gerôn*. (Note that in Poll. *Onomast.* 2.4 where the same list is given *presbutês* and *gerôn* are transposed). The text is variously dated. For a full discussion of the properties inherent in the number seven, see Roscher (1906). For references to the hebdomadal system in later literature, see Eyben (1972, 685 n. 4). For climacterics, see Eyben (1973, 229).

4 **Threefold division of life.** For exhortations to the three generations in funeral orations, see Thuk. 2.44-5; Pl. *Menex.* 246d-248e (parents of the dead, the dead and their peers, and sons of the dead); and Hyper. *Epitaph.* 31 (*hoi p*[*resbuteroi*], *hoi hêlikôt*[*ai, hoi*] *neôtero*[*i kai paides*]). For threefold age-classes in competitive athletics, see Golden (1981, 18-20). Recent excavations carried at Eretria have brought to light a cemetery (late eighth/early seventh century BC) where newborn babies, adolescents and adults were accorded separate burial treatment (Bérard 1970, 51).

6 **Fourfold division of life.** See also the reference to 'birth, *choës, ephêbia* and marriage' in *IG* II^2 1368.130 (Athens, before AD 178). Strictly speaking, however, these terms do not denote periods of life but rather the intervals between one period and another (cf. Burkert 1985, 237). For later controversy among the supporters of the fourfold system (e.g. as to whether youth is warmer than childhood and whether old age is moist or dry), see Eyben (1972, 679). There is extensive discussion of the various systems of identifying the ages of man in Censorinus *DN* 14.

Analogies between the human life-cycle and the seasons, etc. For Perikles' comparison between the spring removed from the year and the *neotês*, see Loraux (1975, 12). For the traditional attribution of this observation to the *epitaphios* of Samos, see Wilamowitz (*Hermes* 12 [1877] p. 365 n. 51) with the discussion in Girard (1919, 227-8) and Loraux (1975, 9 n. 34). Cf. also Hdt. 7.162 where Greece, being deprived of the assistance of Syracusan troops, is likened by Gelon to a year from which the spring has been removed. Seasonal changes could also be used to denote the transience of human life, as in Hom. *Il.* 6.146-9 where Glaukos famously remarks: 'As are the generations of leaves, so are the generations of men .... One generation of men comes to flower while another is passing away.' Cf. also Lucr. 5.330f. (the world is in its first youth); and 5.826f. (Nature is worn out, like an exhausted woman past childbearing years). Ov. *Met.* 15.199f. reverses the analogy by inquiring: 'Do you not see the year taking on the four seasons in imitation of life?' *Karpos* as 'embryo': Hipp. *Seventh-Month Foetus* 1 and Demokritos (*DK* 68 B 148); *hersê* as 'young and tender animal': Hom. *Od.* 9.222 and cf. *LSJ*[9]; *anthos hêbês* as 'bloom of youth': Hom. *Il.* 13.484, Pi. *P.* 4.158 and Aes. *Supp.* 663; *hôra* or *hôrê* as 'springtime of life': Mimn. 3.1 *IEG* and Aes. *Supp.* 997; *thallos* as 'offspring': Hom. *Il.* 22.87, *Od.* 6.157, *Hom. h. Dem.* 66 and 187, Pi. *O.* 6.68 and Eur. *El.* 15. See p. 145 for *pais amphithalês*. Seasonal analogies in Galen include 16.102, 16.345, 16.424 and 19.374 *K*. The most thorough investigation of the association between ages of life and the cycle of the seasons, times of day, etc., is by Boll (1950, 156-224). In general cf. also E. le Roy Ladurie (*Histoire de la France rurale* II [Paris 1975] p. 542) who observes that shepherds' calendars conventionally divide human life into twelve units each of which is six years in length, by analogy with the agricultural year. For the earliest attested instance of the view that man is a microcosm of the cosmos, see Demokritos (*DK* 68 B 34: as quoted by David, a sixth-century AD Neoplatonist). See Furley (1987, 157f.) and Lloyd (1966, 250ff.).

9 **Influence of age on character**. See Eyben (1973, 235-8) for further references.

2 ***Embruon* used in a post partum sense**. E.g. Hom. *Od.* 9.245; Arist. *PA* 3.676a17; Sor. *Gyn.* 2.67.2.

3 ***Numphê***. See further Chantraine (1946-7, 228-9; 1974-80, 758), M. Detienne (*Les jardins d'Adonis* [Paris 1972] p. 157f.), King (1983, 112) and Schmitt (1977, 1068). For the opposition between *parthenos* and *numphê*, cf. Sappho's epithalamion, fr. 114 *LP*.

4 **Reckoning a person's age in years**. In the case of Classical Athens there are essentially three possibilities, as Booth (1988) has recently pointed out: (1) the period between birth and the first day of the new civil year after its birth was regarded as an infant's first year and it became 'two years old' on new year's day; or (2) it became 'one year old' at the turn of the first civil year after its birth; or (3) it became 'one year old' at the turn of the second civil year after its birth. Although Booth argues convincingly for (3), we still have to reckon with the fact that Athenians themselves were at times somewhat confused as to their exact age. For the claim that the Greeks and Romans employed ordinals where we would understand a cardinal, see Halkin (1948, 354-70) and Waltz (1949, 41-53). On this whole subject see further pp. 180 and 327.

6 **Biography**. The only Greeks whose life-histories we can reconstruct with some accuracy are Plato, Aristotle and Alexander the Great. Among the Romans the list includes Pompey, Cicero, Caesar and the

Julio-Claudian emperors. The earliest biography of a woman to survive from the ancient world is St Gregory of Nyssa's *Life of Saint Macrina*, for which see Momigliano (in Arrigoni 1985).

1. Conception and Pregnancy

17 **Women's biological need for sexual intercourse**. Cf. Hipp. *Diseases of Women* 1.1 where it is maintained that 'Women who have not had children suffer more severely during menstruation.' For further references see Lloyd (1983, 84 n. 102). Much less frequently a woman is advised to refrain from intercourse (loc. cit., n. 103). The belief that intercourse was essential for women's health was also shared by Plato (*Tim.* 91c). So, too, Pln. *NH* 28.10.44 reports: 'Many kinds of illnesses are cured by the first act of intercourse or by a woman's first menstruation.' (I cite regularly from Pliny in this and the following chapter because he was undoubtedly familiar with Greek embryological treatises, notably Book 7 of Arist.'s *HA*.) For the contrary opinion, that the emission of seed is harmful and that permanent virginity in both men and women is healthful, see Sor. *Gyn.* 1.30-2. For discussion of gynaecological problems together with their underlying social implications, see Lefkowitz (1981, 13ff.).

Female authorities. See Lloyd (1983, 60 n. 6 and 63 n. 11). The women mentioned by Pliny include Salpe, Lais, Elephantis, Olympias, Sotira and Antiochis. Nothing is known of any of them, though Salpe and Sotira are identified as midwives (*obstetrices*). As Lloyd notes, Pliny appears to be citing written material and, if this is the case, we can take it that by the first century AD at the latest some medical writers were women.

Sources. For discussion of the importance of embryological analogies for Presocratic cosmogony, particularly in the writings of Anaximander (*DK* 12 A 10.33-7) and the Pythagoreans, see Baldry (1932, 27-34) and Vernant (1962, 104-7). Cf. also the Orphic idea that the cosmos began as a world-egg (*DK* 1 A 12 and B 12, 13), which Aristophanes parodies in *Birds* 693-97. A useful but not invariably accurate summary of the embryological concerns of the Presocratics is to be found in Censorinus (*DN* 4.2-13.6). For further discussion, see Burkert (1972, 37). Embryological and gynaecological works in the Hippokratic corpus include the following: *Peri aphorôn* (*Sterile Women*), *Peri epikuêsios* (*Superfetation*), *Peri gonês* (*Seed*), *Gunaikeia* (*Treatise on Women*), *Peri gunaikeiês phusios* (*Nature of Women*), *Peri heptamênou* (*Seventh-Month Foetus*) [two existing treatises under this name], *Peri nousôn* (*Diseases*) IV, *Peri oktamênou* (*Eighth-Month Foetus*) and *Peri partheniôn* (*Illnesses of Virgins*). All are attributed to the so-called Knidian school of Hippokratic medicine, for which see I.M. Lonie ('The Cnidian treatises of the Corpus Hippocraticum', pp. 1-13 in *CQ* n.s. 15 [1965]). For the transmission of the gynaecological treatises, see the bibliography cited by Preus (1975, 257 n. 4). The question which (if any) of the works in the Hippokratic corpus are genuine writings of Hippokrates cannot be discussed here. My own use of the term 'Hippokratic' merely signifies 'belonging to the school said to have been founded by Hippokrates'.

19 **Allusions to reproduction in Plato**. The following description of a male orgasm as provided by Diotima in *Symp.* 206d, which 'treats ejaculation of semen by the male ... as a *tokos* of that with which the male is pregnant' (Dover 1980, 147), will serve as an example of Plato's oblique style of reference:

> When *to kuoun* (that which causes pregnancy or conceives) draws near to the beautiful, it becomes genial and exhilarated, and engenders (*tiktei*) and begets (*gennai*). But when it draws near to the ugly, it becomes sullen and gloomy, contracts (*suspeiratai*), turns away, coils up (*aneilletai*) and does not beget (*gennai*), but bears *to kuêma* [the part which conceives?], being held in check, only with discomfort. Therefore <*ptoiêsis*, arousal> becomes big with that which causes pregnancy and with that which swells (*spargônti*) through being stirred by the beautiful, as a result of the satisfaction which results from possessing [the beautiful] and being released from great birth-pangs.

Herophilos of Chalkedon. Herophilos' lost work *Anatomy* is quoted by Galen (4.596-97 *K*) in *Peri spermatos* or *Seed* 2.1. For his influence on later medical writers, see Lloyd (1983, 108 with n. 189).

The human womb. Greek words for 'womb' include *hustera* (or pl. *husterai*), literally 'the part which follows or comes after'; and *mêtra*, (or pl. *mêtrai*), literally 'the mothering area'. As Lefkowitz (1981, 13) points out, these expressions are 'politely vague'. They seem to include what today are called the oviducts (cf. Peck, p. 17 in Arist. *GA* [*LCL*]). There is no description of the female organs of reproduction in any work in the Hippokratic corpus. The term used by Herophilos for ovaries is *orcheis* (cf. Galen 4.596.6 *K*), which also describes the testicles. See Littré (1853, VIII p. 2), Lloyd (1983, 108f.) and Phillips (1987, 142). For a detailed discussion of the uterus and vagina, see Sor. *Gyn.* 1.6 who illustrated his work with pictures (preserved in some manuscripts) showing positions of the foetus *in utero*. Hanson (1987, 598) graphically describes the ancients' image of a woman's uterus as that of a 'jug, worn by her upside down'.

Dissection of the human body. The theory, based on *HA* 7.583b15ff. *T*, that Aristotle himself performed dissection on human embryos cannot be substantiated, as Lloyd (1983, 27) notes. There is also compelling evidence to indicate that Aristotle was averse to dissecting adult human cadavers (cf. *HA* 1.494b21ff. *T*). His knowledge of human anatomy seems to have derived from his dissection of animals and from observing persons who had been wounded. See van Staden (1975, 184). It is not known for certain when dissection was first practised in the ancient world, but Herophilos has a strong claim to being the first to establish it on a regular basis (cf.

Celsus, Proem to *De Medicina* 23-6). In addition, Diokles of Karystos, a pupil of Aristotle, wrote a lost book entitled *Anatomy*. For the controversy about the pre-Alexandrian use of dissection in general, see L. Edelstein ('The history of anatomy in antiquity', pp. 247-302 in *Ancient Medicine* [Baltimore 1967]) and Phillips (1987, 140). Soranos' attitude towards dissection was somewhat ambiguous. In the preface to his discussion of female anatomy in *Gyn*. 1.5 he dismisses the practice as 'useless', but goes on to acknowledge the need to be acquainted with its findings 'for the sake of profound study'. Even in the second century AD the opportunities for examining a cadaver were rare and when they did present themselves were not invariably put at the service of research. See Lloyd (1975) and van Staden (1975, 185-6).

20 **The origins of sexual dimorphism**. The description of the creation of woman in Hes. *Th*. may be compared with the marginally more hostile version in *Works and Days* 57-95. Though Hes. comes across in both as a rabid misogynist, in *Th*. he comments at ll. 602-12 with some feeling upon the evils of growing old without a wife. For women as a separate *genos*, see also Semonides fr. 7 *IEG* ('The god made women's minds separately in the beginning'). In Pl. *Tim*. 90e women are depicted as a secondary race created out of a combination of cowards and malefactors. See further Lloyd (1983, 95). Like Hesiod, Plato also imagines a golden era when 'political constitutions did not exist nor did men possess wives or children because all were born anew out of the earth, remembering nothing of their former lives' (*Plt*. 271e-272a). For autochthonous generation, see Arist. *Pol*. 2.1269a5 and Pi. *N*. 6.1. Cf. also Hes. *Works and Days* 143-5: men of the bronze race were sprung from ash trees.

23 **Conception**. Soranos (*Gyn*. 1.43.5) alleges that it is possible for the seed to be retained for some length of time in the seminal ducts without conception taking place. The expulsion of semen could be induced, he claims (1.46.2), by alarm, grief, unexpected joy, mental upset, violent physical exercise, the forcible holding of one's breath, coughing, sneezing, undergoing a beating, falling down, lifting heavy objects, leaping, sitting on hard chairs, etc. Cf. also Ps.-Arist. *Sterility* (636b39-637a5) which warns that if more seed is produced than the womb can retain, thereby resulting in its expulsion, a woman may erroneously suppose that conception has not taken place.

Whether there is any truth in the belief that the retention of semen after intercourse influences the chances of a conception occurring remains even today somewhat uncertain. Guttmacher (in Ellinger 1952, 112) writes: 'It is now presumed that most pregnancies are due to direct intracervical insemination, and that the strictly vaginal portion of the semen has very short lasting fertilising ability.' Yet modern physicians continue to recommend that women who have difficulty in conceiving should lie on their back for half-an-hour or more after intercourse with their hips raised above the level of their shoulders.

For the image of woman as soil, see S. *Trach*. 31-3 (with P.E.

Easterling's commentary [1982] ad loc.), Men. (*CAF* III, p. 205.720) and Aes. *Septem* 752-6 (I am grateful to Helen King for these references). See further Vernant (1985, 171-2).

As for the perennially absorbing but admittedly peripheral question as to whether men or women derive more satisfaction from sexual intercourse, the Hesiodic *Melampodia* (fr. 275 *OCT*) records that the seer Teiresias, who had been both a man and a woman and was thus uniquely qualified to pronounce upon the issue, asserted that if intercourse is divided into nineteen parts, the man experiences nine parts of the satisfaction, and the woman ten parts. (For a slightly different version of the same story, see Eustath. [ad Hom. *Od.* 1665.42-7]). Contrariwise the writers of the Hippokratic school argued that although a man's orgasm is briefer, it is actually more intense than that of a woman since the secretion of his sperm takes place 'suddenly ... as the result of a more violent disturbance (*tarachê*) of his system' (*Seed* 4).

6 **Recommended ages for procreation**. See Phil. *Gym.* 28 for the alleged physical characteristics of children born to parents who are advanced in years, namely soft skin, collarbones shaped like ladles, prominent veins and a weak muscular system. Modern medicine has actually detected no correlation between the health of the offspring and the age of its father, though the best age for a mother to procreate, both for her own safety's sake and for that of her baby, is between the ages of about seventeen and thirty-five, or, according to a more narrow reckoning, twenty and twenty-nine.

The newspaper *Le Monde* (17 February 1988) in an article entitled 'Sex after 60' assured anxious French readers that men can actually father children until they are eighty or over.

7 **Intercourse as a possible source of pollution**. For the general dearth of evidence to indicate that menstruation was regarded by the Greeks as a source of pollution, see Parker (1983, 100-3). In the Classical period menstruating women do not generally seem to have been debarred even from entering sanctuaries. For the Christian era (third century AD), however, there exists a very fragmentary purity regulation from Therasia (*LSCG* 99, as emended by Immerwahr [1971, 235-8]) which contains an allusion to *ta katamênia* (menstruation). All this is in striking contrast to the horrific chemical properties ascribed to the menses throughout antiquity, for which see e.g. Arist. *Dreams* 459b-460a and Pln. *NH* 7.15.64-5 (contact with it turns new wine sour, renders crops barren, causes seeds to wither, clouds the surface of mirrors, blunts iron, dulls the gleam of ivory, kills colonies of bees, rusts bronze and iron, fills the air with a terrible stench and infects dogs with rabies).

A possible indication that the Greeks regarded sex as ritually dirtying resides in the fact that *ekmiainomai*, which means literally 'pollute thoroughly', can be used both of a voluntary and involuntary ejaculation (cf. Ar. *Frogs* 753 with schol.), though it is uncertain whether the verb should be taken in its literal sense. See Dover (1973, 60f.) for the suggestion that the Greeks became more inhibited in their use of sexually explicit language in the course of the Classical period.

For an extensive list of legislation banning sexual intercourse within a sanctuary, see Parker (1983, 74f. with n. 4) who notes that later laws sought to introduce a moral dimension by distinguishing between licit and illicit intercourse (i.e. with a prostitute or another man's wife). For washing before entering a sanctuary after having had intercourse, cf. a sacral law of the second century AD found at Sounion relating to the Asiatic Moon goddess Men which instructs 'persons who have eaten garlic or pork or been with a woman (*apo skordôn kai choireôn kai gunaikos*)' to purify themselves before entering the sanctuary (*LSCG* 55.3f.). Cf. also the dialogue between Kinesias and Myrrhine in Ar. *Lys*. 911-13: on the insistence of her husband, Myrrhine agrees to have intercourse in the cave of Pan and then to wash in the spring called Klepsydra before returning to the Acropolis. See J. Henderson's commentary (1987, ad loc.). For divine retribution consequent upon the violation of the ban, see the story of Araüktes as told in Hdt. 9.116-20 and Xen. *Ages*. 5.7.

28 **Predominance of sperm**. Onians (1951, 111 and 178-82) plausibly connects the birth of Athena from Zeus' head with the belief that seed, being stored in the head, issued by way of marrow to the spine. For discussion of the myth of the double birth of Dionysos, see Dodds' commentary (1960, 78f.) on Eur. *Ba*. 88-98. Dodds suggests that the myth owes its origin to the fact that the marrow contained in the thigh-bones was believed to constitute the 'stuff of life'. At *Ba*. 94f. it is stated that 'Zeus straightaway received Dionysos in the secret recesses of birth (*lochiois* ... *thalamois*), hiding him in his thigh-bone (*kata mêrôi* ... *kalupsas*)'. The myth is occasionally represented in art (see Dodds, loc. cit. for references).

Keuls (1985, 41) interprets this and other such miraculous birth myths as evidence of what she calls 'uterus envy' on the part of the Greek male. It is just as likely, however, that they were intended to explain the widely attested phenomenon of men experiencing the symptoms of pregnancy. They may even contain an allusion to the practice recorded by anthropologists known as couvade, by which the father is put to bed and treated as if he were undergoing the trauma of birth. We learn, for instance, that at a festival held in honour of Ariadne on Cyprus a young man (*neaniskos*) 'lies down and imitates the sounds and actions of a woman in labour' (Plu. *Thes*. 20.4).

It is noteworthy that both in Hesiod's *Theogony* and in the approximately contemporary *Catalogue of Women* genealogical trees are for the most part matrilinear, with the mother as the grammatical subject of the sentence. There is thus some evidence of a system of belief by which the procreating role of the female, far from being overshadowed by that of the male, was actually regarded as determinative. For matrilinear descent, cf. also Hdt.'s account (1.173.4-5) of the Lykians who, uniquely to his knowledge, take the mother's name instead of the father's.

9 **Reproductive theories**. 'Pangenesis' is not an original Greek word, being adopted from Charles Darwin's theory that each cell reproduces itself exactly by contributing materially to its future offspring. As Lloyd (1979, 217) notes, the forcefulness of Aristotle's onslaught against the doctrine lies not in the presentation of new empirical data but in his close examination of the coherence and cogency of his opponents' doctrine. Eyben (1972, 679) usefully defines *perittôma* in its Aristotelian usage as 'that which is left over when the living organism, by acting upon the nutriment which it has taken, has provided itself with a sufficient supply for its upkeep'. Some of the excess is mere waste material (i.e. excrement), whereas other is useful, producing marrow and hair as well as semen. See also Peck (1945, 32-4).

It is only comparatively recently that the different roles of the male and female reproductive organs have been properly understood. The seventeenth-century British physician William Harvey, who discovered the circulation of blood, advanced the theory that an embryo was formed entirely out of menstrual blood and that semen made no physical contribution but merely served to 'activate' the female (s.v. Genetics in *OCM*).

Sex differentiation. My summary of the leading Presocratic views on the subject is mainly taken from Censorinus *DN* 6.4-6.8 (but note that Censorinus' testimony of Anaxagoras' views is at variance with that of Arist. and therefore likely to be in error). In ancient China, where the left side was regarded as more honourable than the right, the reverse theory was upheld, namely that a male embryo was carried on the left side of the body (cf. Lloyd 1962, 61). For a critique of the theories advanced in *Seed* and *Regimen*, see Lloyd (1983, 91-3). One of the most striking facts about both works is that the contribution of both partners is judged to be exactly equal, either one being capable of determining the sex of the embryo.

Genetic transmission. For Soranos' discussion of whether the embryo is affected by the mother's psychological state, see Lloyd (1983, 174f.). While not commenting on the veracity of anecdotes of women producing babies that resemble monkeys, Soranos endorses the general point that the state of mind of the mother may have an important influence on the child produced, by observing (*Gyn*. 1.39.2): 'It is good that the offspring (*ta gennômena*) be made to resemble the soul when it is stable and not deranged by drunkenness.'

On the subject of eugenics, see the interesting article by Fortenbaugh (1975) on its treatment in Plato. In *Rep*. Plato recommends the introduction of a deceptive lottery in order to ensure that the best men and women mate most frequently. In *Laws*, however, the best and worst are to be encouraged to intermarry in order that they can produce 'moderate' offspring (772e-773a). Finally, in *Phil.* the Stranger claims that when individuals marry their like over several generations the results of their union are deplorable (310c-e). Fortenbaugh sees the explanation for this reversal in attitude in what he terms Plato's doctrine of psychic dichotomy, i.e. the doctrine that a combination of temperamental opposites constitutes the ideal reproductive blend.

35 **Superfetation**. Superfetation is first mentioned by Herodotos (3.108) who claims that the hare 'alone of all creatures can conceive during pregnancy'. A case history of an alleged superfetation occurs in Hipp. *Epid.* 5.11 involving a woman from Larissa who delivered a superfetation, which is described simply as 'flesh (*sarx*)', forty days after giving birth to a girl 'with a wound on her hip'. In mythology Herakles and his brother Iphikles are examples of offspring produced by superfetation (cf. Pln. *NH* 7.11.49). Aristotle reports the memorable instance of an adulterous woman who by superfetation produced one child resembling her husband and the other resembling her lover (*HA* 7.585a16f. *T*). The Hippokratic treatise *Superfetation* is inappropriately named; only the first chapter actually deals with this topic. For modern evidence regarding the phenomenon, see Guttmacher in Ellinger (1952, 127f. n. 23).

36 **Fertility and sterility**. Regarding a woman's incapacity to conceive as constituting grounds for divorce, see the story told in Hdt. 5.40 of the Spartan king Anaxandrides whose wife was childless and who was consequently urged by the ephors to divorce her. When he refused to do so, the ephors proposed instead that he should take a second wife. Anaxandrides agreed and henceforth maintained two separate *oikoi*, thus establishing a Spartan precedent. That the king here found himself in conflict with offialdom should alert us to the possibility that a happily married yet childless couple may have come under intense parental pressure to divorce. Examples of contempt for childlessness include Eur. *And.* 201f., where Andromache, a *pallakê* (see p. 238) who has provided Neoptolemos with a son, taunts her rival Hermione, Neoptolemos' wife, for being childless. The fifty Pallantidai are said to have despised Aegeus for his childlessness (Plu. *Thes.* 3.5): their contempt reflected the fact that without an heir to the throne his rule was extremely vulnerable to external threat (13.1). For a prayer for the blessing of children (*euteknia*), see Eur. *Ion* 452-91. It is addressed primarily to Athena and Artemis but with the intention that they should beseech Apollo to give the childless Xouthos a favourable response to his request for a child. Athena is invoked to ensure that the ancient line of Erechtheus which she first propagated should not die out (ll. 469-71). Cf. also *AP* 6.276 where Artemis is invoked in order to provide Hippe with both a husband and children. Prayers for children constituted a regular feature of epithalamia, cf. Theok. 18.50-1; Aes. fr. 43 *TGF*. See Borthwick (1963, 228). Very likely there was a highly profitable trade in magic cures for childlessness, such as the *pharmaka* which Medea administered to Aegeus (Plu. *Thes*. 12.2).

For Ithmonike's and Kleo's pregnancies, see *IG* IV^2 121.3-22 = Edelstein (1945, II p. 221ff. T423). Credulity in such matters was not the exclusive property of the Greeks. Cf. the alleged precocity of Zoroaster who 'laughed on the same day that he was born' (Pln. *NH* 7.16.72). The American newspaper *The Sun* carried a leading article on 5 April 1988 whose headline read: 'Woman gives birth to two-years old baby. Child walks and talks after three days.'

For the proverbial fertility of Egyptian women, see Arist. *HA* 7.584b7-8 *T*. The Aphrodite worshipped on Mount Hymettos is most likely to have been Aphrodite Ourania, the Athenian goddess most closely associated with sexual love and fertility.

Among the more fanciful cures for sterility was 'a pessary made out of the excrement of babies which has been discharged in the womb', which according to Pliny (*NH* 28.13.52) is recommended by 'very celebrated authorities'. For allusions to fertility and sterility in the medical writers, see Preus (1975, 243-5). For instances where Hippokratic writers insist that women should not be unduly anxious if they are unable to conceive or miscarry, see Lloyd (1983, 85 n. 106). The test for sterility recommended in *Aph*. 5.59 is also described in Sor. *Gyn*. 1.35.2, though the latter does not make it clear whether it was still being administered in the second century AD. Regarding remedies for male sterility or impotency, cf. the comic playwright Epicharmos of Syracuse (*fl*. 485-467 BC) who recommended that afflictions of the testes and genitalia could be cured by the application of a cabbage leaf (*DK* 23 B 61). The joke is presumably at the expense of equally bizarre remedies current in the fifth century BC. For magical cures for impotency, see Hopfner (1938, 267-73). Pliny (*NH* 7.16.73) claimed that the fertility of seed (*ubertas seminum*) is becoming exhausted by what he calls 'the conflagration towards which our age is now heading'.

Pregnancy. For the use of analogy in embryological writings, see King (1988). Other examples of the oven analogy include Hdt. 5.92 (necrophilia is a case of putting one's loaves into a cold oven); Ar. *Peace* 891-3 (members of the Athenian Boule keep their 'saucepans' in Theoria's 'oven'), and Artem. *Onirok*. 2.10 *T* (dreaming of a hearth or oven means that you are going to have a child).

For a summary of ancient views on embryonic and foetal development, see Cens. *DN* 5.5-6.2. Among the authorities cited are Alkmaion (*DK* 24 A 13) who denied that anything could be known about the subject; Empedokles (*DK* 31 A 84) who, like Aristotle, maintained that it is the heart 'which chiefly contains the life of man'; and Diogenes of Apollonia (*DK* 64 A 27) who stated 'from liquid comes flesh, from flesh bone, nerves and other parts'. For the ancient controversy as to whether the embryo/foetus breathes before birth, see the evidence cited by Baldry (1932, 26-7 with n. 9). Galen, who provides an extensive critique of the work of preceding writers on the subject in *Peri kuoumenôn diaplaseôs* or *Formation of the Foetus* (4.652-702 *K*), maintained that the liver is the first organ to be formed and that the heart begins to develop only after the veins have subdivided. For the importance and influence of Galen's study of foetal blood-flow, see Siegel (1968, 59-63).

Like modern medical writers, Soranos (*Gyn.* 1.46.1) also regards pregnancy as 'divisible into three phases (*trichronos*)', though perhaps less in accordance with a fully worked out system of foetal development than with concern for the proper treatment of the pregnant woman. For the terms *ekrusis* and *ektrôsmos*, see also Cens. *DN* 11.10 who states that an *ekrusis* is discharged after six or seven days and is watery, an *ektrôsmos* after a longer period and is bloody (cf. Hipp. *Eighth-Month Foetus* 9.2). As Egerton (1975, 309) notes, Aristotle usually discusses reproduction alongside life chronology (average and maximum longevity, recommended ages for procreating, etc.) because he was interested to establish whether there existed a correlation between length of gestation and length of life.

For length of gestation, see Cens. *DN* 7.2-11.12 with Diepgen (1937, 160ff.). For the question 'When is the baby due?' as preserved on Egyptian papyri, see Montevecchi (1979, 113-17) on *P. Oxy.* 46.3312. For criticisms in the Hippokratic corpus of women's calculations about how advanced their pregnancy is, see Lloyd (1983, 68 and 76-8) and Hanson (1987, 596). Guttmacher (in Ellinger 1952, 125) quotes an English obstetrician called Thomas Eden who reported a pregnancy which lasted '336 days after the beginning of the last menses and 315 days from the last coitus'. For *Nutriment* 42, see Hanson (1987, 589-602). See further p. 43, for the 'impossibility' of a successful eight-month pregnancy.

46 **The pregnant woman**. With regard to prenatal gymnastics Sprague (1984, 277) points out that the recommendation in *Laws* 7.789b-d ties in neatly with Plato's theory that each human being is a microcosm in which are reflected the cosmic motions of the whole universe (cf. *Tim.* 44b, 88de, 90c). For cults which were established with the express object of averting miscarriages and perinatal deaths of infants, see Paus. 2.3.6-7 and 8.23.7. For pregnancy and pollution, see Parker (1983, 48f.). The sacral law (third century BC) relating to the mysteries of Demeter at Lykosoura (*LSCG* 68.12-13) provides an exception to the general rule that pregnant women, like women who were nursing, were not ordinarily regarded as polluting. For acts of violence committed against pregnant women, see Montevecchi (1979, 115).

48 **Contraception**. The fragment by Archilochos is preserved on a papyrus in Cologne which was first published by Merkelbach and West (pp. 97-113 in *ZPE* 14 [1974]). On *Nature of the Child* (13), see Lonie (1981, 160-2) and Hanson (1987, 596). Littré (1839, VII p. 463) supposed that the 'blighted ovum' was merely uterine mucus. See Preus (1975, 254). Guttmacher (in Ellinger 1952, 116) comments on

Nature of the Child (13) as follows: 'Such activities would never cause the expulsion of a sound, well-embedded pregnancy, but might readily cause the expulsion of an unhealthy, already semi-detached ovum, which would have been aborted within the next few hours or days even if the woman had remained quietly in bed.' Whatever the nature of the object discharged it was certainly not an embryo, which at six days is virtually invisible to the naked eye.

On contraception in general, see Eyben (1980-1, 7-10), Krenkel (1978, 197-303), Salmon (1955, 61ff.), Pomeroy (1975, 68ff. and 164ff.) and Vatin (1970, 232ff.). Eyben (1980-1, 8) argues, tendentiously in my view, that the absence of evidence on contraception is probably to be explained 'by the fact that the practice was generally accepted and gave little offence'. For a critique of the efficacy of Greek methods of contraception, see Preus (1975, especially pp. 250-1). *Seed* (2) alleges that men who have had incisions made in the vessels behind the ears can emit 'only a trickle of enfeebled and infertile sperm'. The frequency with which this operation was performed as a method of birth control is not indicated. As Preus (1975, 241-3) notes, however, enemy populations were occasionally castrated in order to render them more tractable and docile. Cf. Hdt. 6.9 and 32; Hom. *Od*. 22.474; Pl. *Laws* 3.695b; Xen. *Kyr*. 7.5.60-5. Detailed information about contraception in the ancient world dates only from the period of the Roman Empire, for which see Hopkins (1965a, 124-51). Hopkins claims (p. 124) that 'aspects of ancient contraceptive theory were as advanced as any modern theory before the middle of the nineteenth century'. This was certainly not true of ancient Greece. I do not comprehend his further contention that 'The intensity of the desire not to beget or not to conceive (is) an important factor in increasing the efficiency of most contraceptive methods' (op. cit., p. 126).

Abortion. The fullest account of abortion in antiquity is that of Nardi (1971) who covers the period from the sixth century BC to the sixth century AD and claims to be able to detect an increasingly negative attitude towards abortion over the course of time, determined by a growing conviction in the rights of the unborn child. This theory was previously advanced by Dölger (1933, 1-51) and effectively countered by Crahay (1941). See also den Boer (1979, 272-88), Hähnel (1937, 224ff.) and Thalheim, s.v. *Amblôsis* in *RE* 1.2 (1894) cols. 1804-5.

For the *pesson phthorion*, see Nardi (1971, 60ff. and 66). For the pollution caused by abortion and miscarriage, see Parker (1983, 354-5). As Eyben (1980-1, pp. 43-4 with n. 139) points out, the Hippokratic oath merely mentions the most common and most dangerous abortifacient; it does not condone the use of other devices. Edelstein (1967, 15) goes so far as to assert that a Greek doctor who adhered to the rules laid down in the oath may actually have been in the minority. For the dangers of abortion in advanced pregnancy, see Hipp. *Illnesses of Women* 1.25. On Lys. fr. 8 *T*, see Eyben (1980-1, 21 with n. 62) and Nardi (1971, 82ff.). For the laws ascribed to Lykourgos and Solon banning abortion, see Pseudo-Galen (19.179 *K*). Their authenticity is defended by Dölger (1933, 10-12), but generally rejected (e.g. Nardi 1971, 33-41). On Arist. *Pol.* 7.1335b24-6, see Oppenheimer (1975) who suggests that the moment 'when sensory perception and life begin' should, on the basis of *HA* 7.583b2-27 *T*, be estimated around the fortieth day. See also Golding and Golding (1975, 356) and Eyben (1980-1, 37f.). For the Orphic attitude, see Eyben (1980-1, 56). For the Stoic attitude, see Dölger (1933, 21-2, 29) and Eyben (1980-1, 38 with n. 123). For the Pythagorean attitude, see Ps.-Gal. *Pros Gauron peri tou pôs empsuchoutai ta embrua* (*Against Gauros: Concerning the Question whether Embryos are Ensouled*) with Edelstein (1967, 19 n. 46). See also Carrick (1985, 110-50). Cathartic law of Cyrene: *SEG* IX 72 = *LSCGS* 115B, ll. 24-7 with Nardi (1971, 132-4). For other inscriptions involving abortion, see Eyben (1980-1, 56f.). The first ancient author, Greek or Roman, unequivocally to condemn abortion is Ovid (cf. *Am.* 2.13 and 14). His rejection of the practice is based primarily on the senselessness of hazarding one's life in order to preserve one's beauty but also on the need to maintain Roman manpower at full strength. See Eyben (1980-1, 51-2 with n. 157).

57 **Sexual abstinence**. For the 'anti-sexual ethos' of the Thesmophoria, which was reflected in other ways besides sexual abstinence, see Parker (1983, 81-3).

2. Childbirth

59 **Sources**. Vase-paintings and sculpture reveal little of value for our study. Apart from Attic grave-reliefs commemorating women who died in childbirth, depictions of birth are almost wholly confined to the realm of mythology. Since a divine birth is by definition an abnormal event and since as well it is its abnormal features that the Greek artist tends to portray, little evidence can be gleaned from it.

61 **Birth setting**. For the *gunaikeion*, see Walker (1983). Many such quarters may have been situated in the upper part of the house (e.g. Lys. 1.9). Cf. also Xen. *Oikon.* 9.2-5 and *Mem.* 3.8. If privacy could be guaranteed it is just possible that some women may have preferred to give birth out of doors, as is suggested by several divine birth myths. For the 'primeval childbed (*ôgugion lechôion*)' where Rheia gave birth to Zeus, see Kall. *h. Zeus* 10-14. For the palm tree (*phoinix*) which Leto suppported herself against when she gave birth to Apollo, see *Hom. h. Del. Ap.* 117 and *h. Del.* 209-11. As Mary Lefkowitz points out to me, however, myths are of dubious value in determining 'real life' birth settings since a human dwelling might have been considered an inappropriate location for the birth of a deity. Giving birth within a sanctuary was judged to be an extreme form of defilement liable to imperil the entire community, as in the case of Auge who, by giving birth to Telephos in the temple of Athena at Tegea, caused a blight to descend upon the whole land. Iphigeneia's pointed criticism in Eur. *IT* 380-4 of Artemis' hypersubtle logic in prohibiting persons who have been in contact with spilled blood, childbirth or a corpse from entering her sanctuary while herself delighting in 'homicidal sacrifices' is, as Parker (1983, 34) points out, an indication of fifth-century unease about such 'amoral rules of purity'.

Exclusion of men from the birth. The presence of a male figure on funerary reliefs commemorating women who died in childbirth (see Fig. 3) cannot be used to furnish evidence that men regularly participated at a birth, since they are merely an iconographic device for evaluating the impact of the event in terms of its effect on the deceased's family circle.

Midwives and assistants. The most detailed account of the duties of the midwife is provided by the early chapters of Sor. *Gyn.* (discussed at length in Lloyd [1983, 168-78]), which is in effect a textbook of instruction in the techniques of the profession. Herophilos of Chalkedon also wrote a lost treatise entitled *Midwifery*, from which Soranos quotes. Soranos' stipulation that the midwife should be 'literate in order to comprehend her art through theory' may be interestingly compared with an advertisement placed in the *Gazette de Montréal* in 1787 by a certain Alexandre Serres, Master of Surgery, who gave notice that he proposed to give a course in midwifery for 'the surgeons of Montreal as well as for the midwives, who are for the most part unlearned in this delicate art which demands as much theory as practice'. For the pride which midwives take in their skill in cutting the navel, see Pl. *Theait*. 149d. The same passage states that their sphere of expertise included the ability to forecast 'what kind of woman should unite with what kind of man in order to produce the finest children'.

On the division of labour between men and women in childbirth, see Lloyd (1983, 70 and 73f.). For the purposes to which incantations and spells were generally put, see Rohde (1925, 320 n. 82). In Hom. *Od.* 19.457f. the sons of Autolykos staunch the flow of blood from Odysseus' wounded knee by singing *epôidai*. Incantantion during labour may similarly have been intended to prevent excessive bleeding. For the swapping of a stillborn for a live infant (though without the assistance of a midwife), see Hdt. 1.112-13. For midwifery in the ancient world, see also the fascinating account of the duties of the *hasnupallas* (literally 'the woman who knows the internal organs') in Hittite birth ritual, as described by Pringle (1983, 128-41).

Deaths of women in labour. On the deaths of women in labour with particular reference to the Spartan law on tomb-monuments, see Loraux (1981, 37-67). The emendation to Plu. *Lyk.* 27.2 by K. Latte is defended on the grounds of epigraphical evidence (principally by *IG* V.1 713-14, 1128 and 1277 where *lechô* is appended to the name of the deceased). It is accepted by Cartledge (1981, 95 with n. 72), D.H. Kelly

(*GRBS* 22 [1981] 33-4 n. 9), Loraux (1981, 37) and Pomeroy (1975, 36 with n. 8), even though it has no ms. support. For case histories of illnesses among pregnant and postpartum women, see Hipp. *Epid.* 1 *Fourteen Cases* 4, 5, 11, 13; *Three Cases* 10-12; 3 *Sixteen Cases* 2,3,14. It is noteworthy that in none of these instances is there any reference to the condition of the newborn.

66 **Deities of childbirth**. The extreme antiquity of the worship of birthing goddesses in the ancient world has been dramatically confirmed by recent excavations conducted under the direction of Dr Edgar Peltenburg of Edinburgh University at Paphos on Cyprus (as reported in *The Times* of 22 January 1988). These have brought to light pottery and stone figurines dated *c.* 3000 BC which include a 10-inch model of a woman apparently seated on a birthing stool with the head and arms of her infant shown emerging from the womb. It is one of the earliest portrayals of childbirth to be found anywhere in the world.

Eileithyia. Excavations carried out in a cave at Amnisos on Crete have revealed a continuous series of pottery finds extending from Neolithic to Roman times. At least partial continuity of worship here from the Late Minoan to Roman period is suggested by a clay tablet found at nearby Knossos which records the following dedication: 'Amnisos, for Eleuthia [*sic*], one amphora of honey.' The cave, which it is tempting to identify with the one mentioned by Homer as being sacred to Eileithyia (*Od.* 19.188), seems to have owed its sanctity partly to the anthropomorphic suggestiveness of its rock formations. Close to its entrance is an 'oval elevation like a belly with a naval', while in its centre rises 'a stalagmite resembling a female figure' (Burkert 1985, 25). For the tablet from Knossos, see Chadwick (1958, 125).

The goddess's importance is indicated by the frequent references to her in hymns which allude to divine births (e.g. Kall. *h. Zeus* 12; *h. Del.* 132). Athena, who sprang fully-formed from the head of Zeus (see p. 28), was appropriately termed *aneileithuia* or 'she who was born without the aid of Eileithyia' in Eur. *Ion* 453. See Pingiatoglou (1981, pls. 2-6) for representations in vase-paintings. Eileithyia is characterised by the epithets *mogostokos* ('she of the difficult birth') and *lusizônos* ('she who loosens the cord or girdle'). Once in Homer the plural Eileithyiai (*Il.* 11.270f.) occurs but elsewhere (e.g. *Il.* 16.187, 19.103; cf. Hes. *Th.* 922) the goddess is singular.

A Spartan temple of Eileithyia is recorded by Pausanias (3.14.6) and Archaic figurines of the goddess have been found in the local sanctuary of Artemis Orthia (cf. R.M. Dawkins, *The Sanctuary of Artemis at Orthia* [London 1929] p. 51). In Athens the cult was sufficiently prominent for Plato to regulate that in the ideal state envisaged in the *Laws* (6.784a) 'mothers should assemble daily for at least twenty minutes at the temple of Eileithyia'.

There is a useful discussion of the cult in Pingiatoglou (1971) who cites literary and epigraphical evidence for fifty-one sanctuaries of Eileithyia on the Greek mainland and islands of the Aegean. See ibid. pp. 120-43 for representations of the Eileithyia(i) in art. Further discussion of these and other childbirth deities is to be found in Price (1978).

Artemis. It is entirely appropriate that Artemis, a deity associated with childbirth, should have caused her mother Leto no pain 'either when she was carrying her or when she delivered her' (Kall. *h. Art*. 24). Artemis is also alleged to have assisted at the birth of her brother Apollo when she was only one day old. Though Calame (1977, I, p. 293) may be technically correct in identifying Eileithyia as the goddess of delivery from travail, and Artemis as the protectress of the newly born (cf. D.S. 5.73.4-6), it is unlikely that the Greek mind insisted upon a rigid demarcation of their spheres of influence. Cf. Brelich (1969, 191 n. 222) for the 'political tendency' of linking together related cults. The fourth-century cathartic law of Cyrene makes it plain that Artemis was a prenatal as well as postnatal goddess, since it stipulates that a pregnant woman should make an offering of the feet, head and skin of a young animal before giving birth, or of a full-grown animal after delivery, should she omit to sacrifice beforehand (*SEG* IX 72; *LSCGS* 115B, ll. 15-23). See Parker (1983, 345f.). For the cult of Artemis Lochia ('of childbirth'), see Eur. *IT* 1097ff., *Supp*. 958ff. and *SIG*³ 1219.34 (Gambreion, third century BC). Calame (1977, 292) believes that the Spartan cult of Artemis Orthia had associations with infancy as well as adolescence.

Iphigeneia. For the name Iphigeneia, see Calame (1977, I, p. 292 n. 234), who denies that it is a contracted form of *iphi gennasthai poiousa* (she who makes [the child] to be born possessed of strength)', as is often alleged, on the grounds that the morpheme *-genês* (fem. *-geneia*) is always intransitive. Calame argues instead that her designation indicates that Iphigeneia favoured and promoted 'vigorous births', i.e. by giving the mother the strength to endure a painful delivery.

Hekate. For Hekate as childbirth deity, see the testimonia cited in Rohde (1925, 322 n. 91). She was probably invoked both as a goddess of transitions and crossings and in her capacity as go-between for humans and gods.

Moirai. For the association between the Moirai and birth, cf. Eur. *IT* 206f. (*lochiai Moirai*); Pi. *O*. 6.42, *N*. 7.1; Pl. *Symp*. 206d; and Paus. 8.21.3. See Borthwick (1963, 228 n. 12) and Dodds (1960, 79).

Genetyllides. Cf. Ar. *Clouds* 52; *Lys*. 2; *Thesm*. 130 (*potniai Genetullides*), all with schol. ad loc.; Ps.-Luk. *Am*. 42. Hsch. and Sud. s.v. *genetullis* write: 'Her name comes from 'births (*geneseis*)' and she resembles Artemis.' See further Borthwick (1963, 237 with n. 49). The Genetyllides (or Genetyllis in the singular) presided over the hour of birth (*genetê*) which was the moment when an infant was believed to receive its due apportionment of 'glorious gifts' from the gods' (e.g. Hom. *Il*. 24.534f.).

Kalligeneia. Cf. Ar. *Thesm.* 298 with schol.; Hsch. s.v. *Kalligeneian*; Alkiphr. 2.37.2 (where *ta Kalligeneia* is referred to as a *hêortê* performed by Athenian women); Nonnos *Dion.* 6.140 (where Kalligeneia is the name of the *eupais tithênê* or 'nurse blessed with fine children' of Persephone).

Labour and delivery. For the *ôkutokion*, see Hipp. *Nature of Woman* 1.77; *Sterile Women* 3.224; Arist. *Thesm.* 504; Thphr. *HP* 9.9.3. See Sor. *Gyn.* 2.3 for a detailed description of the appearance and construction of the *diphron maiôtikon*. As the name suggests, such chairs were evidently the personal property of the midwife. Cf. Diepgen (1937, 179).

Arist. *Pol.* 7.1336a15-21 notes that some barbarians bathe newborn babies (*ta gignomena*) in a cold river so as to accustom them to the cold. Michell (1964, 166) improbably suggests that the bathing of newborn Spartan babies in wine may have been prompted by 'primitive hygienic motives' on the grounds that wine acts as a mild antiseptic. On the importance of an infant's first bath, see Parker (1983, 50f. with n. 69).

76 **Caesarean section**. Pliny (*NH* 7.9.47) alleges that the elder Scipio Africanus and Julius Caesar among other notable Romans were born as a result of the mother dying in labour, and that Caesar 'was so called from the fact that the uterus of his mother was cut open (*caeso matris utero*)'. In fact 'Caesarean' may either derive from *caedere*, 'to cut', or from the Lex Caesarea which prohibited the burial of a woman who died in pregnancy until the foetus had been cut from her uterus. The earliest recorded instance of a Caesarean operation dates to 1500. As late as the seventeenth century it was almost always fatal for the mother, however, and only with the discovery of antibiotics in the 1940s did the procedure finally become relatively safe. See D. Trolle, *The History of Caesarean Section* (Copenhagen 1982).

Embryotomy. See Sor. *Gyn.* 4.9-13 for further details. Soranos also refers dismissively to a complicated system of pulleys which were attached to the birthing stool for the purpose of extracting the foetus (2.3.3). For the surgical instruments used in these operations, see Milne (1907, 152-8). The only evidence to suggest that there existed any instruments for delivering a foetus alive is provided by a reference to *mêchanai iêtrou* in *Superfetation* (15), but, as Milne (p. 155f.) points out, *mêchanai* here 'may mean any mechanical aid such as a fillet, or even assistance with the fingers of the accoucheur'. For a Christian denunciation of embryotomy, see Tertullian (*De anima* 25) who castigates Hippokrates, Asklepiades, Erasistratos, Herophilos and Soranos for using an instrument called an *embruosphaktês*, a bronze rod for killing live infants.

77 **Premature births**. See Burkert (1972, 263) and K. Deichgräber (*Hippokrates über Entstehung und Aufbau des menschlichen Körpers* [Leipzig 1935] p. 20) for further evidence in Hippokratic writings of the belief that even numbers are weak and more likely to incur misfortune. See also Thesleff (1965, 59).

79 **Monstrous births**. The horror and fascination aroused by abnormal births are a universal fact of human experience. In Empedokles' physical system a period of monsters and deformities represent the second stage in his fourfold evolutionary cycle (*DK* 31 B 61). See Kirk, Raven and Schofield (1983, 302-5). It is alleged by Ailian (fr. 47 *T*) that when the Lokrians ceased to remit the maiden tribute, their wives were afflicted with a disease which caused them to bear crippled and monstrous children (*empêra kai terata*). See Fontenrose (1978, 132 and Q 232 [280 BC]: not genuine) and below p. 192. For monstrosity as a consequence of oath-breaking, cf. also Hes. *Works and Days* 235; Aischin. 3.111 (oath of the Delphic Amphiktyony). See Roussel (1943, 13). For Arist.'s discussion of monstrosity in *GA* 4, *HA* 6 and *Phys*. 2, see Louis (1975, 277-84). Arist. confines his investigation to higher vertebrates and a few species of birds, and is particularly interested in malformations consisting of either an excess or lack of parts. There is no discussion of monstrous births in the Hippokratic corpus.

0 **Day-superstition**. On the whole the Greeks do not appear to have attached much importance to later birthdays in life, with the result that Herodotos (1.133.1) makes it a matter for ethnographic comment that the Persians were 'accustomed to celebrate the day each was born most of all'. On day-superstition generally, see West (1978, 348).

1 **Swaddling the newborn**. For examples of *sparganiôtai* in Greek art, see Klein (1932, 1 with pls. 1 and 2). It was almost certainly due to a belief in the superiority of right over left that Soranos (*Gyn*. 2.42.2), who himself endorsed swaddling, recommended that the right hand should be unswaddled before the left (cf. Lloyd 1983, 176). Cf., however, his rejection (2.14) of Thessalian methods of swaddling on the grounds that they are too harsh.

3 **Thank-offering for delivery**. For the Nymphs, see A.J.B. Wace and M.S. Thompson (*ABSA* 15 [1908-9] pp. 243-7) and Borthwick (1963, 236f.). Usually in epigrams it is the mother who makes the offering, whereas in *AP* 6.271 a joint offering is made by both husband and wife. See further Gow and Page (1965, II p. 453f.). Similar dedications are referred to in *AP* 6.202 and 272 (to Artemis); 6.200 and 274 (to Eileithyia). Mommsen's theory (*Philologus* 58 [1899] pp. 343ff.) that *rakos* (literally 'a ragged or tattered garment'), an article frequently referred to in the inventories, should be interpreted as a sanitary napkin soiled with a young girl's first menstruation is rejected by Linders (1972, 58), who sees it instead as a comment upon the defective quality of the dedication.

4 **Exposure**. Roussel (1943, 12) convincingly suggests that the prominence of myths relating to the exposure of infants derives ultimately from the anxiety which the group to which the infant will belong experience 'at the arrival of an infant charged with ambiguous possibilities'. In Egypt newborn children may have been abandoned on public rubbish dumps or *koprônes*, as is indicated by the frequent occurrence of names such as Kopreus, Kopriairetos, etc., which were commonly bestowed on slaves. Cf. Perdrizet (1921, 85-94), rejected by

Pomeroy (1983, 1341). Perdrizet (p. 92) suggests that the exposure of a newborn infant in such circumstances may have constituted 'an almost juridical process indicating absolute renunciation to the right of inquiry or entitlement concerning the child on the part of the parent', but a no-questions asked policy surely operated whenever an infant was exposed. The practice of exposure seems to have been introduced into Egypt by the Greeks (D.S. 1.80 and Str. 17.2.5).

For the Milesian evidence regarding the probable exposure of girls, see G. Kawerau and A. Rehm (*Das Delphinion im Milet* [Berlin 1914] nos. 34-93). Similar to *P. Oxy*. 4.744 is Apul. *Met*. 10.23.3: a husband who is about to go on a voyage instructs his pregnant wife that if she delivers a female infant she should kill it. See Patterson (1985, 107-11) for a valuable critique of Engels, Golden and Pomeroy.

For the Spartan practice, see MacDowell (1986, 52-4; 71) and Roussel (1943, 5-17). It is uncertain whether Spartan girls as well as boys had to be inspected because Plutarch refers to the infant by sexually neutral words such as *genêthlon* and *paidarion*. Roussel (p. 16), who is of the opinion that the examination was connected with the apportionment of property, maintains that it was exclusive to male children, since they were 'presumptive heirs of the estate and liable to military obligations'. This seems to me improbable, given the importance that attached to the fitness of Spartan mothers-to-be (p. 25). See also Cartledge (1981, 90). MacDowell (p. 53) suggests that meetings of the *presbutai* for the purpose of inspection were possibly held once a month, but it would surely have been both practical and humane to hold them more frequently. For Aristotle's requirement of abortion in the case of deformity, see Golding and Golding (1975, 355f.).

For *sunektithemena*, see G. Glotz s.v. *Expositio* in *DS* II (1892) cols. 933-4. Note that baby Kyros was dressed in grave clothes when he was handed over to Harpagos for exposure (Hdt. 1.109.1). For the legal status of an exposed child who has been rescued, see Dem. 58.19 and 59.40; Lys. 23.12; Isok. 17.14; Men. *Arbitr*. passim. See further Harrison (1968, 71 with n. 3). For the rights of a Roman father over his exposed child, see Rawson (1986a, 172).

As Wiedemann (1987, 29 n. 3) observes, there is no comprehensive study of exposition and infanticide in the ancient world. Older studies include G. Glotz (op. cit., cols. 930-39); A. Mau s.v. 'Aussetzung' in *RE* II.2 (1896) cols. 2588-9. The most thorough recent account is that of Eyben (1980-1, pp. 5-82; p. 12 n. 28 for bibliography). For the Hellenistic evidence, see Pomeroy (1983). For the Roman evidence, see Hopkins (1983, 225f.) who believes it to have been 'common enough among the rich and powerful'. Infanticide as a practice adopted in most places and most periods of history as a means of conserving the resources of the family and community has only recently began to attract the ethnographical attention it deserves. For a succinct account, see W.L. Langer, 'Infanticide: a historical survey', pp. 353-65 in *History of Childhood Quarterly* 2 (1974-5). Langer (p. 361) notes that as late as the 1860s the British press was reporting the frequent discovery of dead infants who had been abandoned in parks, under bridges, in ditches and even in cesspools, to the extent that the *Morning Star* in 1863 was moved to declare that the practice was becoming 'a national institution'. Yet even today the American press reports with sickening regularity the discovery of so-called 'trashcan' babies.

93 **Amphidromia**. Conflicting lexicographical testimonia furnish most of the evidence for the Amphidromia, viz. Harp., Hsch. and Sud. s.v.; Apostol. 2.56. Cf. also Pl. *Theait*. 160e with schol. Hsch. s.v. *dromiamphion êmar* states: 'They run naked with the child in their arms'. The same entry claims that the Amphidromia is held 'on the seventh day after birth'. With the exception of the schol. to Pl. *Theait*., the runners are invariably described as male. On the 'contamination' of the sources and for an attempt to resolve it by proposing that girls were named on the seventh day after birth, boys on the tenth, see Deubner (1952, 374-7). The Amphidromia has been interpreted both as a purification of the child by fire and as an ordeal by fire. Cf. Rohde (1925, ch. 9 n. 72) and Stengel s.v. *Amphidromia* in *RE* I.2 (1894) cols. 1901-2. Samter (1901, 62) was the first to note that Pl. *Theait*. (160e-161a) clearly indicates that it was 'not only a ceremony of purification but also one of adoption'. For further discussion, see Furley (1981, 65-70) and Parker (1983, 51 with n. 71 for bibliography). For the role of the hearth in domestic worship, see Burkert (1985, 255). It is possible that Demophoön's baptism by fire in *Hom. h. Dem*. 239ff. is intended to be an aetiological explanation of the Amphidromia (*pace* Richardson 1974, 232).

94 ***Optêria***. Cf. Eur. *Ion* 1127; Kall. *h. Art*. 74; Nonn. *Dion*. 5.139; schol. on Aes. *Eum*. 7.

Magic charms. For artistic representations of infants wearing amulets, see Klein (1932, 7f.). The string to which the amulet was attached seems to have been hung from one shoulder and passed under the other arm, cf. Fig. 8 and Klein (pl. VIId and g).

95 **Tenth-day ceremony**. Cf. Ar. *Birds* 494 and 922f. with schol.; Dem. 39.22 and Ps.-Dem. 40.28; Eur. *El*. 1126 and fr. 2 *TGF*; Isai. 3.30 and 70; Hsch. s.v. *dekatên thuomen*; Sud. s.v. *dekatên hestiasai* and *dekateuein*. Hsch. s.v. *amphidromia* alleges that it is at the Amphidromia that the child is assigned its name, as does the schol. on Ar. *Lys*. 757. For the seventh-day festival, see Arist. *HA* 7.588a8-10 *T*; Harp. s.v. *hebdomeuomenou* and Hsch. s.v. *hebdomai*. See further Deubner (1909, 648f.) and Golden (1981, 4).

Circumcision. See Dover (1978, 129f.) and Keuls (1985, 68). There is an attempt to exploit the distinction between circumcised and uncircumcised penises for comic effect on a famous Caeretan hydria which depicts Herakles attacking the attendants of the Egyptian king Busiris (Dover, R 699 = Athens *NM* 9683 = *ARV* 554.82). As Dover notes, however, the painter has actually depicted the Egyptians not circumcised but merely with foreskins pulled back, evidently because he has never seen a circumcised penis.

96 **Pollution**. Law of Cyrene: *SEG* IX 72; *LSCGS* 115B, ll. 15-23 with Parker (1983, 336). For the pollution of childbirth with comprehensive testimonia on the subject, see Parker (pp. 49-52, with n. 67; 352-3) who proposes that impurity as a result of contact with a parturient generally lasted three days. For 40-day periods (*tessarakontades*) in other medical contexts, see Hipp. *Seventh-Month Foetus*, esp. 7 and 9, and Arist. *HA* 7.587b4 and 6 *T*.

Vis-à-vis a general understanding of how childbirth was regarded in Greece it may be instructive to note that whereas *lechô* emphasises the confinement of birth, its root being derived from bed (*lechos*), the equivalent term in Hittite-Luwian (*wiwiskitallas*) emphasises the pain of birth, its literal meaning being 'the one who keeps on wailing'.

97 **Lochial discharge**. For references see Hipp. *Epid.*: 1 *Fourteen Cases* 4; 3 *Sixteen Cases* 2,14. As Guttmacher (in Ellinger 1952, 118) notes, until the introduction of the clinical thermometer and the realisation of the significance in variations of the pulse as an indicator of health, the lochial discharge figured prominently as a subject of discussion in modern medical handbooks.

98 **Numbers of offspring per family**. See Eyben (1980-1, 5-7 with bibliography cited in n. 1), Gomme (1933, 75ff.), Lacey (1968, 164ff.), Wilkinson (1979, 21, 32-3) and Engels (1980, 117 n. 21). Golden (1981a, 318 n. 7) has suggested that in Classical Athens, where women were on average producing children over a 25-year period from the age of fifteen to forty, the birth-rate may have been as high as over six children each. It is likewise estimated that the average number of children born to a 'married' woman in agricultural societies is 'at least five' (Cipolla 1978, 87). From the evidence of pelvic scars Angel (1984, table 3.1b, p. 55) has calculated that in the period from 650-300 BC the average adult female gave birth '5.0' times, whereas in the period 300 BC – AD 120 the figure was '3.4?'

On Pol. 36.17.5-10 and the Hellenistic period generally, see Eyben (1980-1, 24 with n. 68), van Hook (1920, 143f.), Brunt (1971, 141), Landry (1936, 1ff.), Bérard (1947, 303-12), Rostovtzeff (1967, I, p. 96, II, pp. 623-6; III, pp. 1464-5 and 1547), Tarn and Griffith (1974, 100-2) and Vatin (1970, 228ff.).

Fertility is in fact a function of many factors including tradition, prosperity and accessibility. See also R.R. Kuczynski (*Measurement of Population Growth* [1935] p. 104f.) who notes that modern statistics indicate that the birth-rate falls in time of war by between one fifth and one third. Variations can be extremely marked, even over a short period of time. In England and Wales 1951 saw the final end to the disturbance in the fertility rate caused by the Second World War and its aftermath, 1964 the attainment of a peak level of fertility, and 1977 of a minimal level (cf. *Population Trends* 52 [*HMSO* 1988] p.

15f.). A similar decline may have occurred in Classical Greece at the time of the Peloponnesian War.

For the motives for procreating as advanced by Athenian authors of the Classical era, see Raepsaet (1971, 80-110). They include: guaranteeing one's prosperity, providing for one's support in old age, handing down one's wealth, ensuring that funerary and post-funerary rites will be properly conducted on one's behalf, preserving one's *oikos*, and preserving the state from extinction.

0 **Population policy**. For the Spartan custom of wife-sharing, see Michell (1964, 55-61) and MacDowell (1986, 85-6). For the status of children produced in this way, see Michell (pp. 56-7) who is of the opinion that they were not entitled to claim a part of the paternal inheritance but only an endowment without a *klêros*. The Spartan laws relating to fertility are all ascribed to Lykourgos, but some at least are likely to have been introduced in response to the fifth- and fourth-century crisis.

For the population policies of Plato and Aristotle, see Golding and Golding (1975) and Eyben (1980-1, 32-7). At Pl. *Rep*. 5.461bc there is another possible reference to abortion. Even if this is the case, however, we cannot be certain whether Plato is recommending the practice indiscriminately or merely advocating that defective children should not be raised as guardians. For the ideal number of 5040 households, see Moreau (1949, 603ff.). For bibliography on the various interpretations of Pl. *Laws* 5.740b-e, see Eyben (p. 32 n. 102).

Population policies were also implemented in Rome. Dionysios of Halikarnassos (2.15; cf. 9.22.2) ascribes to Romulus a law requiring every citizen, on pain of forfeiting half his property, to raise all male children and his firstborn girl unless the child was either monstrous or deformed, in which case it could be exposed on condition that five of his neighbours agreed. Several Greek myths, including that of Kadmos and Niobe, appear to reflect the desire to implement a primitive kind of population policy. See Daube (1977, 13).

For Athens' exclusion of childless men from high office, cf. *ML* 23.18 (Decree of Themistocles: trierarchs required to have children; Ps.-Arist. *AP* 4.2 (Drakonian constitution: generals and hipparchs); and Dein. 1.71 (unspecified laws: rhetors and generals). See further Rhodes (1981, 114 and 510-11).

3. The Growing Child

Pais. Nouns cognate with *pais* include *paidion, paidarion* and *paidiskos*. See Poll. *Onomast*. 2.9. *Paidion* could even be used of a foetus or unborn child (see p. 42). As Golden (1985, 93) notes, only if modified by an adjective or participle could *pais* signify a baby. Cf. *paides nearoi* in Hom. *Il*. 2.289 and *paida neon gegaôta* in *Od*. 19.400. The claim made by *LSJ*[9] and Chantraine (1974-80, 848) that *pais* refers specifically to the father and *teknon* to the mother should be discounted (Golden, p. 91). In Sparta *pais* denoted children from about the age of seven to twelve but also those specifically aged eighteen (Plu. *Lyk*. 16.4-6; Xen. *Lak. Pol*. 2.2-11), whereas in Athens it was the official designation for a young man from earliest infancy until the attainment of ephebic status (cf. Ps.-Arist. *AP* 42.1). For *pais* denoting a pathic, cf. Xen. *Anab*. 7.4.7. The so-called *kalos*-inscriptions on Greek vases which celebrate a young man's beauty frequently state simply '*pais* is *kalos*'. *Pais* meaning 'slave' is not confined to Athenian usage; it occurs also, for instance, in Hipp. *Epidem*. passim. For girls treated as slaves, cf. Hdt. 6.137.3 (quoted p. 136). A mark of the inferior status shared by both women and children is the fact that they both were required to be seated at a symposium, in distinction to men who customarily reclined (Xen. *Symp*. 1.8). For women, children and slaves as morally inferior beings, see Pl. *Rep*. 4.431c. For the comparable social status of children, slaves and women, see references in Golden (1981, 56-84).

Proportion of children to whole population. For modern Britain see *Population Trends* 48: '1837-1987: 150 years of the General Register Office' (HMSO 1987) p. 27, which states that the under-fifteen and over-sixty age groups are currently 'about equal'.

108 **Infant mortality**. For infant diseases and disorders, see also Sor. *Gyn*. 2.50-7 where reference is made to inflamed tonsils, rashes, itches, catarrh, coughing, touches of sun, fever and diarrhoea. Quite aside from the perennial hazards which the newborn face, this group is particularly vulnerable at times of famine, a frequent occurrence throughout Greek history and one that is often associated with war. See Angel (1945, 330) for the remains of 175 infants, the majority of them newborn, discovered in a Hellenistic well; their deaths are possibly connected with the Sullan siege of 84 BC.

Hopkins (1966, 263) states that his estimate of 28 per cent infant mortality 'correlates with the predominance of agriculture, low average income, and scarcity of doctors and of useful medical knowledge, which together distinguish the Roman Empire and other pre-industrial societies from modern industrial societies'. In modern industrial societies an even higher incidence of infant mortality has been recorded, however. In 1901 in Montreal, which had the distinction of being the most dangerous city in the western world for a newborn child, one out of three babies died before the age of one.

Regarding the problems of health and hygiene connected with swaddling, we may note the following injunction in *The Byrthe of Mankynde*, which was published in the sixteenth century: 'Shift the child's clouts often, for the piss and dung. When the child is seven months old you may (if you please) wash the body of it twice a week with warm water till it be weaned.' A further disincentive to the regular changing of the bands which operated until the nineteenth century in Europe was the belief that if they were removed over-frequently the newborn would be deprived of its nurturing bodily juices.

1 **Divine protection of the growing child.** For discussion of *kourotrophoi*, see Price (1978, passim) who includes a list of all the chief deities, *daimones* and heroes, together with testimonia. As she rightly points out (p. 200), it is impossible to make any strict division between protectors of childbirth and childhood. In Athens and Attica the chief deity was known simply as *kourotrophos*, whom Price (pp. 105-12) identifies with Ge or Earth. Divine nurses in myth include Athena, nurse of Erechtheus (Hom. *Il.* 2.547f.); Diktymna, nurse of Zeus (Crete); Eirene, nurse of Ploutos (Athens); Hera, nurse of Herakles; Iris, nurse of Hermes; and Themis, nurse of Apollo (*Hom. h. Del. Ap.* 123-5). In Kall. *h. Del.* 2 and 276 the island of Delos is said to be *kourotrophos* of the infant Apollo. In *AP* 6.271 a thank-offering to Artemis for a successful delivery apparently concludes with a prayer for the child's protection and growth. Cf. also *AP* 6.281: prayer to the Mother of the Gods to bring Aristodike to 'the bounds of girlhood (*peirata kourosunas*)', i.e. marriage. On theories of physical growth, see Eyben (1972, 685f.). Cf. also Pln. *NH* 11.87.216: particularly at puberty human beings are observed to get rid of a certain *nodum* (impediment to their growth?); and 7.16.73: a child has attained half his future stature by the age of three.

Nurses. Letter to Phyllis about hiring a wet-nurse: Thesleff (1965, 123f.; Lefkowitz and Fant 1982, no. 110). For the regimen recommended for wet-nurses, see Sor. *Gyn.* 2.24. See also the rules of conduct for a wet-nurse called Didyma set out in a contract from Egypt dated 13 BC (Berlin papyrus 1107; *WLGR*, no. 179). The contract lays down that the nursing period is to last for sixteen months. Cf. *Hom. h. Dem.* 221 where Metaneira engages Demeter to rear her child 'until he reaches the full measure (*metron*) of *hêbê*'. For other *titthai* and *trophoi* in literature, see Bremmer (1985, 287) and Golden (1981, 89-90). In support of his hypothesis that wet-nursing was intended to minimise the impact of a child's death on its parents 'by driving a wedge between parent and child', Bradley (1986, 220) cites Stone (1979, 83). But Stone is referring to a situation where a child actually boarded out with its wet-nurse. That, so far as we know, was not the case in either Greece or Rome. It might be argued that in tragedy mothers and children are often separated by a nurse (e.g. Klytaimnestra-Nurse-Orestes; Phaidra-Nurse-Hippolytos), but such instances are anything but typical: Klytaimnestra has no maternal instinct whatsoever for Orestes, and Phaidra is only a stepmother to Hippolytos. See Golden (1981, 113 n. 12) for a list of sepulchral inscriptions commemorating nurses. As Lefkowitz (1987, 154) points out, wet-nursing was 'perhaps the only occupation that in antiquity was practised exclusively by females'.

In *Hom. h. Dem.* 226-30 *hupotamnon* is apparently either 'a plant cut off at the bottom' evidently to be used in witchcraft or, more probably, a 'borer' or 'worm', perhaps that which was thought to cause pain during teething. If *hulotamnon* is read then it should mean some kind of charm 'cut into the wood', whereas *oulotamnon* may again be 'the worm of teething'. See *LSJ*[9] s.v. and T.W. Allen and E.E. Sikes (*The Homeric Hymns* [London 1904] p. 35). For the duties of nurses in addition to breast-feeding, such as pre-chewing food and, later, instruction, see Golden (1984, 310).

118 **Weaning and teething**. Plato (*Phdr*. 251c) uses the image of teething to identify the period when the soul is just beginning to grow wings. Cf. also the Homeric expression 'nursed on gall' (e.g. *Il*. 16.203) which describes a person with a stubborn will.

121 **Registration of an Athenian infant in a phratry**. See Deubner (1932, 232-4) for testimonia and discussion. Harp. s.v. *meion* writes: 'a sacrifice (*thuma*) which those introducing the children (*hoi tous paidas eisagontes*) provide for the *phratores*'. According to the so-called Demotionid Decrees, the names of those who had been certified were recorded in a *grammateion* or register which was evidently stored in the phratry archives (*IG* II^2 1237.20f.; *SIG*^{3} 921). For the variant oath cited in this document, see Sealey (1984, 122). For registration in *genê*, cf. Andok. 1.127; Dem. 59.59-61, with Golden (1981, 6f.). Among members of the Labyad phratry at Delphi the approval of the *patria* (Doric equivalent of the *genos*) was a necessary prerequisite for admission into their own ranks at the festival of the Apellai (cf. Buck 1955, no. 52 A 23ff.). For late registration, cf. Ar. *Frogs* 418; Dem. 43.11, 14 and 82; Isai. 6.21-2; Lys. 30.2. For the possibility that girls were also registered, see Isai. 3.73, 75-6, 79 with Cole (1984, 236 and n. 19). For birth-notices on Egyptian papyri, see Wallace (1938, 400 n. 58).

122 ***Choës***. See Garland (1985, 82f., 161f.) and Golden (1981, 12-15). As further evidence that the age of four was thought to mark an important stage in a child's development, cf. Kall. *h. Ap*. 58f. where it is stated that it was at this age that Apollo first established a settlement on Delos. It is somewhat bizarre, and perhaps to be seen as a mark of barbarian stupidity, that the nomadic Libyans delayed inoculating their children against catarrh until they were four years old (Hdt. 4.187.2).

124 **Toys**. See Beck (1975, ch. 7) for illustrations. There is an apparent reference to *neurospasta* in Plato (*Laws* 644de) where the Athenian compares all living creatures to puppets which have been manufactured by the gods and which are capable of being manipulated by their own emotions.

125 **Games**. See Beck (1975, ch. 9) for illustrations. For the bronze fly, see also Hsch. s.v., Eust. ad *Il*. 1243.29 and Herond. 12.1. For *drapedinda*, see *Et. Mag*. 286.48-53. For the cooking-pot, see Poll. *Onomast*. 9.110, 113 and 114 (from which the extract is taken) and 125; and Hsch. and Sud. s.v. *chutrinda*. See H. Blümner (in A. Baumeister, *Denkmäler des klassischen Altertums* [Munich and Leipzig 1885-8] s.v. Kinderspiele, pp. 778-81) and Lambin (1975). For representations of games in art, see Klein (1932, 9-22 with pls. 7-22).

127 **Innate deficiency in intelligence as a mark of childhood**. For a possible example of a child displaying a greater depth of understanding than its parent, see Hdt. 5.51.2 where Kleomenes' eight- or nine-year-old daughter Gorgo makes a timely intervention to prevent her father from being bribed. As Dover (1974, 104) notes, however, Hdt. does not indicate whether Gorgo was 'genuinely perceptive' or merely hit upon the truth by chance. Dover (1974, 102) has rightly described the passage from infancy to late middle age as seen through Athenian eyes as 'a continuous development of rationality'. Cf. Hyp. 6.28 and Aischin. 1.39. As Hes. *Works and Days* 441-7 (see above, p. 9) indicates, however, this view was not confined to Athens. Cf. also Plu. *Mor.* 909cd where the Herakleitan and Stoic view is cited that an individual's mental faculties are enlarged with the onset of puberty at around fourteen. See also Edmund's discussion (1977, 300) of Homer's derogatory use of *nêpios* to describe adults who are in a state of what he calls 'mental dislocation'. The term is applied to Patroklos, Odysseus' men and the suitors, all of whom are victims of self-inflicted doom.

Fiendish monsters. See Ar. *Frogs* 293, *Ekkles.* 1056 and *Wasps* 1177; Dem. 18.130; and Plu. *Mor.* 2.1040b. In Kall. *h. Art.* 66-71 the disobedient *kourai* of Okeanos are terrorised by a Hermes who appears to them with his face whitened with ash and 'pretends to play the Mormo (*mormussetai*)'. Note as well the striking use of this verb in Kall. *h. Del.* 297 where it describes the childish terror experienced by *kourai* at the prospect of marriage.

The teachability of virtue. The philosophical principles raised by this question cannot be treated here. See Kerford (1981, 131-8) for a detailed discussion of *Prot.* and other relevant texts that bear upon the issue.

Athenian education. See Beck (1975, chs. 2-4) for illustrations. For the absence of infant schools throughout Greece, see Marrou (1948, 142-3). The only evidence known to me regarding the public provision of education for Athenian children is provided by a decree of uncertain date found at Eleusis honouring a certain Derkylos 'especially with regard to the education of the *paides* in the deme' (*IG* II^2 1187; *SIG*^{3} 956). The exceptional nature of the reference does not, however, warrant the conclusion that 'the word *paides* stands for boys of ephebic age' (F. Mitchel, *Hesperia* 33 [1964] p. 45 n. 35).

On women's lack of education in Athens, cf. Cantarella (1987, 73-6) who points out that of all the female poets belonging to the sixth to fourth centuries BC (some nine in all) who are known to us not one is an Athenian. The iconographic evidence for the education of girls is discussed by Beck (1975, ch. 10).

Spartan education. For the *mothakes*, see MacDowell (1986, 46-51). The earliest reference to the institution is in Xen. *Hell.* 5.3.9. Sons of helots may also have been eligible, cf. Hsch. μ 1538. For the punishment of Spartan boys, see Plu. *Lyk.* 17.2 and Xen. *Lak. Pol.* 2.2. Cf. also Xen. *Lak. Pol.* 6.1-2, where it is stated that every Spartan man rules (*archein*) other men's sons as well as his own. For Spartan pederasty, see Bremmer (1980, 279), Cartledge (1981, 22) and Golden

(1981, 163-74) who are of the opinion that it was 'institutionalised', and MacDowell (1986, 61-5) who rejects the view that homosexual relations were regulated by law. Michell (1964, 195) refuses to discuss the subject altogether, for fear that it will upset what he calls his and our 'equanimity'. For education at public expense in the Hellenistic period, see Hands (1968, D 49-51, etc.). Herodotos (1.136.2) speaks approvingly of a Persian boy's education which lasted from five to twenty and taught him only three things – to ride, shoot and speak the truth.

141 **Representations of childhood in biography**. For this section I am greatly indebted to Christopher Pelling, who kindly provided me with a copy of an article entitled 'Childhood in biography', which he gave as a talk at Manchester University on 13 March 1987. The insights which his paper contains led me to modify my overall interpretation of the perception of childhood in the ancient world.

144 **Representations of children in Greek art**. See Humphreys (1983, 108). Funerary *lêkythoi* depicting children: *ARV* 743, 1239. Funerary monuments commemorating Mnesagora and Nikochares: Clairmont (1970, no. 22 and pl. 11); Garland (1985, fig. 19).

The role of children in religion. For temple service, see also the discussion of the *Arkteia*, on p. 187. Judging from Eur. *Ion* ll. 82-183, duties may have included sweeping the precinct each morning, performing simple lustrations, and scaring away the birds so that their droppings did not befoul the sanctified ground. For dithyrambic choruses, see Golden (1981, 16 and 38 nn. 50-2). Athenian boy-choruses also competed at the Hephaisteia and Prometheia (*IG* II^2 1138.11). For priesthoods reserved for children, see Burkert (1985, 98). Cf. also the case of Lysimache, pristess of Athena Polias, who held this post for 64 years and can hardly have been more than a child when first appointed: Paus. 1.27.4; Pln. *NH* 34.19; cf. Davies (*APF* no. 4549) and Garland (*ABSA* 79 [1984] p. 94). For the *pais aph' hestias*, see Harp. s.v. *aph' hestias mueisthai*, with Golden (1981, 15f. and 38 n. 49). For *amphithaleis*, see Nilsson (*GGR* I, p. 118), Oepke (1934, 42-56) and Redfield (1982, 193). For the somewhat tenuous link between children and purity, see Parker (1983, 79 with n. 21), who, citing *TLL* s.v. *impubes* col. 706 bottom, draws attention to the post-Classical belief in the efficacy of the urine of an 'intact boy (*pais aphthonos*)'. For child heroes, see Eitrem in *RE* VIII.1 (1912) s.v. *Heros*, col. 1118. For the deposit of children's bones at Knossos, see P. Warren (in R. Hägg and N. Marinatos, *Sanctuaries and Cults in the Aegean Bronze Age* [Stockholm 1981] pp. 155-66); and Burkert (1985, 37). For a Cretan offering of first-born children (*anthropôn aparchai*) sent to Delphi in fulfilment of a vow, see Plu. *Thes*. 16.2. Discussion of sacred functions involving *parthenoi* is generally reserved for the next chapter.

147 **Mothers and fathers**. For the various meanings of *têlugetos*, see Richardson (1974, 200 with bibliography). S. *Ant*. 905-12 is often compared with Hdt. 3.119 where Intaphrenes' wife elects to save the life of her brother in preference to those of her husand and children. It is sometimes suggested that the degree of affect between brother and sister was unusually close in Greek society – even closer than that which generally existed between parent and child. Humphreys (1983, 71), for instance, writes: 'It is hard not to feel that the society which produced and appreciated the joy of the recognition scene between Elektra and Orestes in Sophokles' *Elektra*, and the total absorption in plotting together of the same pair in the *Elektra* of Euripides, was one in which the brother-sister relation was often close and affectionate.' It must not be overlooked, however, that the situation in which Elektra and Orestes find themselves is highly atypical since they have been separated for many years and are united in a common cause; they are thus less subject to sibling rivalry than might otherwise be the case. For a review of Slater, granting limited importance to unconscious conflicts in Greek culture while demanding (rightly) that much closer attention be paid to the literary texts and contexts in which the myths appear, see Foley (1975, 31-6).

Mythology abounds in instances of father-son conflict which often involve the father's deposition by the son, but it is surely somewhat tendentious to assume that these tales tell us anything about the father-son relationship that is exclusive to Greek society. For the suggestion that the prototype for the mother of the timocratic man was Plato's own mother Periktione, see U. von Wilamowitz (*Platon* 1: *Leben und Werke* [Berlin 1919] p. 429). For the theory that there is an inverse correlation between 'structural naming' (e.g. naming a son after his paternal grandfather) and parental involvement with children as individuals, see Stone (1979, 409) with Humphreys (1983, 77 n. 13). W.B. Stanford (*The Ulysses Theme* [Oxford 1954] p. 60), detects, spuriously in my view, 'a latent father-son antagonism' between Odysseus and Telemachos in the *Odyssey*. For a father's intimate involvement with his infant son, cf. Ar. *Clouds* (1380-5) where Strepsiades claims that he had to look after his son's babyish needs. However, the joke may simply be intended as a comic inversion of real life and symptomatic of the dominance of Strepsiades' wife. Herodotos suggests that abuse of the father-daughter relationship is a classic hallmark of an authoritarian personality. Thus the Pharaoh Cheops prostituted his daughter in order to finance the building of his own pyramid (2.126), while his successor Myrkerinos raped his, in consequence of which she hanged herself (2.131).

For grave monuments set up by parents commemorating the deaths of children, see Humphreys (1983, 108). For child burial, see further Bremmer (1983, 96-8) and Garland (1985, 78-86). Plu. *Mor*. 612ab states that 'by ancestral and ancient customs and laws ... people do not bring libations to the infant dead (*nêpioi*) nor do they perform for them any of the rites which it is natural to perform for the dead, for they have no share in the earth nor in earthly matters, nor do they stay beside the burial spot or at the monument or at the laying out of the body and sit beside the corpse'. Bremmer (p. 97) wrongly takes *neos* in Arist. fr. 611.28 *T* as a reference to a dead child. Roman children who died before they were 40 days old were buried in the wall of the house (Fulgentius, *Expositio sermonum antiquarum* 560.7, quoted by Bremmer).

According to Pln. *NH* 7.36.121 the most spectacular example of filial devotion in the entire world was recorded in the case of a plebeian woman of lowly circumstances who nourished her mother with her own breasts while the latter was in prison. The daughter's piety was rewarded by the mother's release from prison and by the fact that both were awarded maintenance at public expense for life. In addition, a temple of Piety was consecrated at the spot where the incident occurred. Cf. also the cautionary tale of the fate that befell those who abandoned their parents when Etna erupted (Lykourg. *c. Leok.* 95-6). For two divergent views of the father-son relationship in Men. *Sam.*, see Grant (1986, 172-84) and Lloyd-Jones (1972, 119-44).

157 **Parental authority and the legal rights of children**. See Harrison (1968, I, pp. 70-81). Harrison (p. 74) observes that the Athenian father 'never in historical times enjoyed a power remotely resembling the Roman father's *ius vitae ac necis*', that is, the right as a father to execute one's own children. He is also of the opinion (p. 70) that 'in its origins parental authority in Greece belonged to a wholly different pattern of family life from the Roman'. Solon's enactment depriving fathers of the right to maintenance from their sons in old age if they failed to teach them a trade (Plu. *Sol.* 22) should not be interpreted as an acknowledgment of the fact that a male child does have certain inalienable rights but rather of the reciprocity of obligation in antiquity. For references to the mistreatment of children, see Golden (1985, 101). For the possibility that a son who had been recognised as his father's legitimate offspring had the right to prosecute his father for failing to enlist him in his phratry or, later, in his deme, see Harrison (p. 78 with n. 1). For the criminal responsibility of children, see Golden (1981, 12) who notes that in Antiphon's *Second Tetralogy* it is suggested that a boy could be convicted and banished for murder. A further example of the difficulty of retrieving one's estate if it was squandered by one's guardian is described in Dem. 38: even though Nausimachos and Xenopeithes brought a successful action for 80 talents against their ex-guardian Aristaichmos, the case was still being contested fourteen years later.

158 **Orphans**. For *orphanos* in the sense of 'fatherless' see Chantraine (1974-80, 829) and Boisacq (1950, 719). The primary meaning of the word is 'deprived of' or 'bereft of'. For orphaned girls, see Hes. *Th.* 448 who comments that although Hekate was an only child (*mounogenês*) she none the less received honour from all the immortal gods because Zeus himself watched over her interests. For Athenian orphans, see the decree of Theozotides (403/2 BC) which was introduced to protect the children of those who gave their lives opposing the Thirty Tyrants (Stroud 1971, 280-301; translated in Harding, *TDGR* 2 no. 8). As we learn from Lysias' speech *Against Theozotides* the decree was exceptional in that it excluded illegitimate and adopted children (Papyrus Hibeh [third century AD] in Grenfell and Hunt, *The Hibeh Papyri* I [London 1906] pp. 49-55, no. 14). The assurance of state support for orphans 'until puberty (*mechri hêbês*)' is given briefly at the close of Perikles' Funeral Speech (Thuk. 2.46.1). Cf. also *IG* I^2 6 + 9 = *LSCG* 3C.38-42 which refers to privileges accorded to orphans at the Eleusinian Mysteries (mid-fifth century). In the imitation *epitaphios* delivered by Aspasia in Pl. *Menex.* orphans of the war dead are said to be protected by 'the highest authority in the state' (i.e. the eponymous archon) and when they come 'to man's estate (*eis andros telos*)' they will be provided with full military equipment (249a). In addition to the fact that the state took care of their offspring, the war dead received burial at state expense. The two privileges are obviously complementary, being designed to provide the Athenian citizen-soldier with a kind of life insurance policy. For orphans and *orphanistai* in other Greek states, see Bolkestein (1939, 276-9). For commentary on Ps.-Arist. *AP* 56.7, see Rhodes (1981, 635f.).

4. Coming of Age

4 ***Parthenos***. For *parthenos* used to denote women who are not virgins, see Pi. *P.* 3.34 (Koronis); S. *Trach.* 1219 (Iole); Eur. *Ion* 502 (Kreousa); Ar. *Clouds* 530-2 (the playwright describes himself as a mere *parthenos* when he 'exposed' his first play). The 'beautiful evil' fabricated by Zeus in Hes. *Th.* 572 and *Works and Days* 63 is said to be a *parthenos* or *parthenikê*. L. Deroy ('Le culte du foyer dans la Grèce mycénienne', pp. 26-43 in *RHR* 1950) has proposed that *parthenos* originally designated 'one who attends to the hearth'. The etymology of the word remains uncertain, however.

Kouros. For *kouros* used of a foetus, see Hom. *Il.* 6.59 and Kall. *h. Ap.* 212, 214; and of a newborn child, see Konon 33.3. For its application in Homer, see Jeanmaire (1939, 26-43). Jeanmaire (p. 33) is of the opinion that the description of Thoas in *Il.* 15.281-4 as one who is 'expert at throwing the javelin, a fast runner, almost without rival among the Achaians as a speaker in the agora where *kouroi* compete in debate' constitutes 'the model for a perfect *kouros*'.

6 ***Hêbê, ephêbos*, etc.** For the archaic formulation *epi dietes hêban*, meaning 'to be two years past *hêbê*', see Harp. s.v., Hyp. fr. 223 Sauppe, *Et. Mag.* 359.17 and Bekker *Anecd.* I, 255.15. In Athens the son of an *epiklêros* or heiress was entitled to take possession of his estate when he was 'two years past puberty (*hama hêbêsêi epi dietes*)', i.e. in his eighteenth year, cf. Dem. 46.20, Isai. 8.31, 10.12, etc. The period seems to be the interval between the cutting of the *koureion* and entry to the *ephêbeia* (cf. Booth 1988). See also Tazelaar (1967, 145) and Rhodes (1981, 503). For the use of *hêbê* in epigrams commemorating the war dead irrespective of age, see Loraux (1975, 19-24). Likewise the

expression *hêbês metron*, which occurs commonly in Hom. and Hes., seems to denote the entire period of liability to military service, i.e. 'the full measure of adult prime' (Tazelaar 1967, 143f.). The earliest attested use of the word *ephêbos* in an Athenian source belongs to the year 343 (Aischin. 2.167; Dem. 19.303).

167 **Age of puberty**. As Eyben (1972, 689) notes, the reason why Aristotle associates the production of sperm with the breaking of the voice is because he believed that the sexual organs and the voice box are both connected by channels to veins that issue from a similar place in the heart (cf. *GA* 7.787b20ff.; 4.776b15-17).

For age of puberty in both Greece and Rome, see Amundsen and Diers (1969, 125-32). The testimonia, which apart from Arist. are all late, include Caelius Aurelianus *Gyn.* 1.24 (ed. M.F. and I.E. Drabkin in *Bull. Hist. Med.* Supp. 13 [Baltimore 1951] p. 7); Gal. 17.ii.792 *K*; Rufus in Orib. *Coll. Med. lib. inc.* 18 (ed. J. Raeder [Leipzig 1933] 6.2.2, pp. 107f.); Sor. *Gyn.* 1.20.1; and Vindicianus, *Gyn.* pp. 450f. in ed. V. Rose (Leipzig 1894). All these authorities are in general agreement that puberty occurs in both males and females in the fourteenth year. The extent to which average age of puberty can vary over the course of time is indicated by the fact that in western Europe over the period 1830-1960 it fell 'by some four months per decade' (Hopkins 1965, 311). The Roman jurists fixed puberty at fourteen for a boy and twelve for a girl (Macr. *Comment. in S. Scip.* 1.6.71 *T*). So, too, in England the legal age of puberty is fourteen in boys and twelve in girls. Arrival at puberty could be used to calculate a person's age. In *Works and Days* 695-9 Hes. recommends that a man should marry a girl who is 'in the fifth year past puberty'.

168 **Vulnerability at puberty**. For the *Peri partheniôn*, see King (1983, 113-18). I take it that the switch between *parthenos* and *gunê* in the treatise is deliberate and indicative of the fact that the author regards menarche as a highly significant turning point in the life of a young woman. See also Hipp. *Aph.* 3.28 where it is stated: 'Diseases which persist among *paidia* and do not cease around *hêbê* or, in the case of girls, around menarche, are likely to become chronic (*chronizein*)'. Galen (17.i.825 *K*) maintained that the onset of puberty actually reduced susceptibility to illnesses such as epilepsy, quintan fever, kidney complaints, etc., on the grounds that the body now became warmer and drier. For other references to menarche, see Gourevitch (1984, 81-8). Belief in the need to curb pubescent girls is also implicit in Herodotos' observation (5.6.1) that the Thracians do not restrain *parthenoi* but 'allow them to have intercourse with anyone they like'. On the healing powers ascribed to the first seminal discharge and menstruation, see Eyben (1972, 684). Cf. also Pln. *NH* 28.10.43: a virgin who touches with her right thumb an epileptic who has fainted revives him immediately.

Telemachos. See Clarke (1963, passim) for the significance of the *Têlemacheia* for the *Odyssey* as a whole and for further discussion of the transformation which Telemachos undergoes in the course of it. Telemachos is more commonly described as a *neos pais* (e.g. *Od.* 4.665, 18.217), but occasionally as a *neos anêr* (3.24). Of the situation on Ithaca at the outset of the poem, Clarke (p. 129) aptly writes: 'Ithaca is trapped in the weakness of its leaders, the weakness of old age' – Odysseus' aged and superannuated father Laertes – 'and the weakness of youth, senility and adolescence'. A preoccupation with ages and ageing is detectable throughout the *Odyssey*, Odysseus himself being a quintessentially middle-aged figure. Clarke (p. 133) appropriately describes Books 3 and 4 as 'a baptism into the heroic life'. Telemachos' isolation at the beginning of the poem is heightened by the fact that he has no brothers or sisters living close by and no friend of either sex in whom to confide. Although he is accompanied to the mainland by a group of companions who are bound to him by 'friendship' none is ever identified by name and we are left with the impression that their association with him is of a purely formal nature (cf. *Od.* 2.291f., 408). For the absence of character development in Telemachos in the second half of the poem, see U. von Wilamowitz (*Die Heimkehr des Odysseus* [Berlin 1927] p. 106). For *kratos* used of authority in the home, see Hdt. 4.26.2 who observes that Skythian wives are unique in being *isokrateës* with their husbands.

74 **Violent rupture**. The violence of the rupture from the world of childhood becomes almost a topos in Greek literature. Notable examples include a fragment of S. *Tereus* (fr. 583 Radt), where Prokne speaks feelingly of being thrust from her ancestral gods and her parents upon the occasion of her marriage; and an autobiographical poem by Erinna (*Greek Literary Papyri* no. 120 in *LCL*), where in a manner clearly calculated to shock her audience the poetess juxtaposes her loss of childhood beside her loss of virginity.

Rites of passage. Burkert (1985, 260) claims: 'The formation of the rising generation appears almost the principal function of religion, where ritual concentrates on the introduction of adolescents into the world of adults.' See Jeanmaire (1939), Brelich (1969) and Vidal-Naquet (1974, 163-85). See also Sourvinou-Inwood's (1971a, 172-7) masterly critique of Brelich. For the Cretan initiatory ritual, see E. Bethe ('Die dorische Knabenliebe', pp. 438-75 in *RhM* [62] 1907), Bremmer (1980, 285f.), Burkert (1985, 261), Jeanmaire (1939, 421-60) and Willetts (1965, 115f.). Dover (1978, 189-90) describes it as 'a special local variant irrelevant to the problems of the origins of the homosexual ethos' and regards it as of only marginal value to a general understanding of Greek homosexuality. There is no allusion to the rite in the law-code of Gortyn. For the typical age-difference between an *erômenos* and an *erastês*, see Dover (1978, 87) and Golden (1984, 321-2).

8 **The Spartan *ephêbeia***. See Forrest (1980, 52f.), Jones (1967, 36f.), Michell (1964, 171-3) and Vidal-Naquet (1975, 182f.). For conflicting interpretations of the terminology in the Strabo gloss, see Diller (1941, 501), Billheimer (1947, 99-104), MacDowell (1986, Appendix), Marrou

(1946, 229) and Michell (1964, 169-70). See also the bibliography cited in Calame (1977, I, p. 280 n. 209). Other sources for Spartan age-classes include Xen. *LP*, Plu. *Lyk*. (especially 16.7, 16.12 and 17.4), a gloss in Hdt., entries in Hsch. and Phot., and a few inscriptions. The disagreement in our sources regarding the ages at which Spartan males graduated from one category to another is explained by Tazelaar (1967, 152) by the theory that boys could be classified *either* according to the requirements of the law *or* according to their physical development. On the possibility that *mikizomenos* is a false form of *mikichizomenos*, see MacDowell (p. 163f.). For the *krupteia*, see Jeanmaire (1913, 121-50) and Vidal-Naquet (1968, 153-4). Jeanmaire (p. 147) draws attention to the importance which the shedding of blood plays in military societies as a way of symbolising the end of childhood; this, he argues, explains the significance of the assault upon the helots. Very little else is known about the institution. See Plu. *Lyk*. 28 and Pl. *Laws* 1.633b (with scholia). Calame (1977, I, pp. 350-7) has attempted to reconstruct a cycle of initiations for Spartan girls which was designed to confer adult status upon them, but his theory has failed to persuade. See Cartledge (1981, 91 n. 42).

179 ***Koureôtis***. See Hdt. 1.147; and Isai. 6.22. Votes for each candidate could either be cast secretly or openly (Dem. 43.82). Candidates were required to sing and to recite poetry (Pl. *Tim*. 21b). Of special interest is the Demotionid Decree (*IG* II² 1237 = *SIG*³ 921) dated 396/5 BC, for which see U. von Wilamowitz (*Aristoteles und Athen* [Berlin 1893] II, pp. 260ff.), Wade-Gery (1958, 118-34) and Parke (1977, 89). The age of youths at the time of the *koureion* cannot be fixed with certainty, cf. J. Labarbe (*BAB* 39 [1953] p. 372f.), Golden (1981, 9f.) and Cole (1984, 234f.). The equivalent festival among Dorian and West Greek communities was called the Apellai.

It must be emphasised that the lexicographers (cf. Poll. *Onomast*. 8.107; Hsch. s.v. *koureôtis*; and Sud. s.v. *koureôtês*) fail to clarify whether Athenian boys underwent two successive registrations, at birth and at adolescence, or merely one.

Hair-cutting. In antiquity *kouros* and *korê* were plausibly derived from the same etymological root as *koureion* (cf. Str. *Geog*. 10.3.8). If that view is correct, then the primary meaning of *kouros* may be 'one who has recently dedicated his *koureion* and who is therefore distinguishable from the mass of longhaired warriors', as Jeanmaire (1939, 37f.) suggests.

The many examples of sacrificial hair-cutting in Greek literature include Achilles cutting off a lock of hair which had been pledged to his native river Spercheios and placing it on the bier of Patroklos (Hom. *Il*. 23.141-53); Orestes dedicating a *threptêrios plokamos* or 'nurturing lock of hair' to his native river Inachos as a thank-offering for his upbringing (Aes. *Ch*. 6); Delian *paides* and *korai* cutting their hair in mourning for the two Hyperborean girls who died on Delos (Hdt. 4.34 with Paus. 1.43.4); Delian girls making an offering of their hair to *parthenikai*, and boys of their first growth of beard to *êitheoi* (Kall. *h. Del*. 296-9); unmarried Troizenian *korai* dedicating a lock of their hair in honour of Hippolytos in a prenuptial ceremony (Eur. *Hipp*. 1425f.; Paus. 2.32.1); and Megarian *korai* offering first-clippings before marriage at the tomb of the *parthenos* Iphinoë (Paus. 1.43.4). In Theseus' day it was customary for 'those leaving the ranks of the *paides* (*hoi metabainontes ek paidôn*)' to go to Delphi and offer the first clippings of their hair to Apollo (*aparchesthai tôi theôi tês komês*), a practice still performed in the fourth century BC by the personification of Mikrophilotimia or Petty Pride (Plu. *Thes*. 5; cf. Thphr. *Char*. 21.3). A votive statue stood in Athens of a *pais* dedicating a lock of his hair to his river Kephisos (Paus. 1.37.3). For further testimonia, see Bremer s.v. 'Haartracht' und 'Haarschmuck' in *RE* VII.2 (1912) col. 2118, Frazer (*Pausanias* vol. 3, pp. 279-81) and Burkert (1985, 373f. n. 29). The custom of hair-cutting may already have existed in Minoan times, cf. A. Evans (*The Palace of Minos* [London 1921-36] IV, p. 480). There is evidence to suggest that in some parts of Greece a child's hair was cut for the first time upon entering puberty (*AP* 6.279, *IG* I2.5.173.4 [Paros, fourth century BC]). In other parts, however, it was cut extremely early (*AP* 6.155 and 7.482). See Gow and Page (1965, II, p. 285).

Oinistêria. G.H. Chase and C.C. Vermeule (*Greek, Etruscan and Roman Art* [Museum of Fine Arts, Boston 1963] p. 139) have suggested that an Attic relief in Boston dated to the early fourth century BC showing Herakles and Hermes approaching a shrine dedicated to Herakles Alexikakos ('Warder off of evil') was dedicated by a youth who had just participated in the *oinistêria*. Cf. Garland (1987, Appendix III no. 68). For Herakles' connections with youth, see Woodford (1971, 214). Hebe, the personification of youth, became his wife after his apotheosis, and his shrines frequently had gymnasia attached to them.

Enrolment on the deme register. See the discussion of Ps.-Arist. *AP* 42.1-2 in Rhodes (1981, 495-502, esp. 497f.). There has been considerable discussion as to whether *oktôkaideka etê gegonotes* should be rendered 'having attained eighteen years of age' or 'having entered upon one's eighteenth year', for which see Rhodes (loc. cit.), Sealey (1957, 195-7) and Carter (1967, 51-7). Support for the latter view derives largely from Dem. 27. But even if the former interpretation is correct, we still do not know whether the period between one's last birthday as a *pais* and one's enrolment in the deme register was counted for official purposes as a year in itself (cf. Davies *APF*, p. 125). For the *lêxiarchikon grammateion*, see *IG* I^2 79.5-7; Isai. 7.27; and Lyk. *c. Leok*. 76. It is likely that all Athenian youths, including the *thêtes*, were so registered (cf. Rhodes 1972, 173 n. 3). The ceremony took place around the turn of the Attic year (Dem. 30.15, with Sealey 1957, 195). It is an interesting fact, as noted by Goldhill (1987, 64), that the ritual associated with war-orphans disappears just at the time when the evidence for the Athenian ephebate begins. For an Athenian male's right at seventeen to marry without the consent of his father, see Dem.

40.4 and Lys. fr. 24 Thalheim, with Harrison (1968, I, p. 18 with n. 5). For the procedure of *apokêruxis*, see Dem. 39.39. Harrison (1968, I, pp. 75-7) believes that the religious sanctions implicit in *apokêruxis* (exclusion from domestic worship) account for the fact that it was so rarely invoked, on the grounds that 'public sentiment would have condemned its use except in extreme cases'.

183 **The Athenian *ephêbia*.** For the change from black to white *chlamus*, see *IG* II^2 2090.10f. (AD 165/6) and 3606 (*c.* AD 175) with Roussel (1941, 163-5). According to Philostratos (*VS* 2.1.5, p. 59 ed. Kayser), the black *chlamus* had been worn as a token of remorse at the killing of the Argive herald Kopreus whom the Athenians slaughtered when he was clinging in supplication to the altar of the Herakleidai.

For the ephebic oath (not mentioned by Aristotle) cf. also Lykourg. *Against Leok.* 76, Poll. *Onomast.* 8.105-6 and Stob. *Flor.* 43.48. All versions are given in translation in Harding (*TDGR* 2.109). For the stele from Acharnai, see G. Daux (*Charistêrion eis A.K. Orlandon* [Athens 1965] I, pp. 78-84). As both Tod and Daux note, the association of deities summoned to witness the oath epitomise Athenian military prowess, fertility, prosperity, territory and social stability. For alleged echoes of the oath in Aeschylus, Sophokles and Thukydides, see Siewart (1977, 102-11). For the conflicting testimonia regarding the precise moment in an ephebe's cursus when the oath was administered, see Vidal-Naquet (1982, 162, n. 5). For the archaeological evidence regarding the border forts, see Ober (1985); none of it is earlier than the fourth century BC. For the participation of ephebes at the Great Dionysia, see Pickard-Cambridge (1968, 59-61). As Goldhill (1987, 59) points out, there is no evidence for the role of ephebes in the procession earlier than the late second century BC (cf. *SEG* XV 104). For the antiquity and history of the ephebate, see Rhodes (1981, 494f.) and briefly Roussel (1921, 459-60). The earliest ephebic inscriptions date to 334/3 (see O.W. Reinmuth, *Mnemosyne* Supp. 14 [1971] for the fourth-century series). For the importance of Epikrates' reform, see F.W. Mitchel (*G&R* 12 [1965] pp. 189-204). See also Pélékidis (1962), Marrou (1948, 105-12), and N. Robertson (*Historical Reflections* 3 [1976] pp. 3-24). For the myth, see Vidal-Naquet (1968, esp. 150-3), who provides (n. 9) an extensive list of its sources. On the ambivalent status of the Athenian *ephêbos* (too young for hoplite combat but inscribed on the deme register), see also Loraux (1975, 7). Registration documents relating to the admission of boys to the ephebate have survived on Egyptian papyri. See Carter (1967, 54) with e.g. *P. Oxy.* 1202 (*Loeb Select Papyri* 2.300 in *LCL*).

The civic significance of the Athenian ephebate in connection with the Great Dionysia is discussed in a provocative article by Winkler (1985) who regards it as 'a social event focused precisely on the ephebes'. The evidence for his theory is based primarily on the fact that tragic plots are rich in ephebic themes, and secondly on the twin suppositions that ephebes (1) sat *en bloc* in the central wedge of the auditorium, and (2) constituted the members of tragic-satyric choruses.

For S. *Phil.* as a dramatisation of the passage from childhood to adulthood conducted via the conversation between the ageing hero Philoktetes and the ephebe Neoptolemos which occupies virtually the entirety of the play, see Vidal-Naquet (1982, 161-84).

87 **Dedication to the gods upon coming of age**. Cf. also *AP* 6.309 where a ball, rattle, set of knucklebones and spinning-top, all described as 'the playthings of youth (*kourosunês paignia*)', are dedicated. Gifts were also offered to parents, nurses, etc. Cf. *Hom. h. Dem.* 168 and 223 (awarded to nurse); Hes. *Works and Days* 188 (to parents); Theokr. *Epigr.* 20 (to nurse). and Aes. *Ch.* 6 (to river).

Arkteia. Other interpretations of Ar. *Lys.* 641-47 include Sourvinou-Inwood (1971, 339-42) who has suggested that Aristophanes is alluding to only two age-categories, namely the *arrhêphoria* and *arkteia*, and that the terms *aletrides* and *kanêphoroi* merely denote the functions corresponding to these categories; and Brelich (1969, 230ff. and 265ff.) who argues from analogies with age-categorisation found elsewhere in the Greek world that the divisions correspond to what he terms 'an institutional reality'.

Testimonia for the *Arkteia* are collected by Brelich (1969, 248 n. 44). See in particular Hsch. s.v. *arkteia*; Sud. s.v. *arktoi*; and schol. Ar. *Lys.* 645. The Brauronia was probably penteteric, cf. Ar. *Peace* 876, Ps.-Arist. *AP* 54.7 and Poll. *Onomast.* 7.107. For *kratêriskoi*, see L. Kahil ('Autour de l'Artémis attique', pp. 20-33 in *AK* 8 [1965]; 'Rites et mystère', pp. 86-98 in *AK* 20 [1977]; and 'Le cratérisque d'Artémis et le Brauronion de l'Acropole', pp. 252-63 in *Hesperia* 50 [1981]). There has been lengthy discussion about the meaning and significance of the ritual. See Robertson (1983, 278-80), who rejects the view that the *Arkteia* performed any initiation function whatsoever; Lloyd-Jones (1983, 87-102); and Cole (1984, 238-43).

1 ***Arrhêphoroi***. In addition to Paus. 1.27.3, cf. Harp. and Hsch. s.v. *arrhêphorein*; Sud. s.v. *Chalkeia*; and schol. on Ar. *Lys.* 642. The etymology of *arrhêphoros* is uncertain. *LSJ*[9] derive it from *hersephoros* meaning 'dew carrier'. For the number of *arrhêphoroi* and their length of residence on the Acropolis, see Robertson (1983, 276f.). For further discussion of the office, see Burkert (1985, 228f.) and Garland (1984, 93f.).

2 ***Parthenoi* as priestesses**. For the Lokrian *parthenoi*, see Fontenrose (1978, 131-7, with 131 n. 10 for ancient testimonia and modern bibliography) who argues that the ritual may have been first instituted as late as the third century BC; and Graf (1978, 61-79) and Bremmer (1983, 98-9) who detect – wrongly in my view – initiatory symbolism in the conditions of office. A fragmentary treaty (*IG* IX.1^2 706) dated *c.* 280 BC provides details of compensation to be provided by the state for the girls' clothing, upbringing and other expenses. For the very rare instances in Greek religion of virgin priestesses serving for life, see

Parker (1983, 92-3). They include Paus. 9.27.6 (Herakles' priestess at Thespiai); and the fictional Theonoe in Eur. *Helen*.

193 **Choirs of *parthenoi***. See Calame (1977, passim). Classical epitaphs which allude to a woman's *hêlikia* include *Epigr. gr*. 73 and 78. For Sappho's circle, see Burnett (1983, 209-28) and Dover (1978, 173-9). We never hear of *thiasoi* of Athenian girls comparable to those which existed elsewhere in Greece.

194 **Sacrifice of *parthenoi***. For virgin sacrifice in war, see Burkert (1983, 65-6). For its occurrence in tragedy, see the discussion in Loraux (1985, 62-5) who sees it as a 'catharsis of the imagination' whereby the audience is permitted to 'think the unthinkable'. For the Leokorion, see Thuk. 6.57.3 and Ps.-Arist. *AP* 18.3. It is possibly to be identified with a sanctuary situated at a crossroads in the north-west corner of the Athenian Agora (cf. Camp 1986, 47f.).

196 **Coming of age as an indeterminate categorisation**. Vidal-Naquet (1974, 182f.) seems to regard Sparta as unique among Greek *poleis* in failing to establish a precise age at which its youth became full citizens, whereas in actuality the same flexibility seems to lie embedded in the structures of all age-systems we have been considering. His observation (loc. cit.) that 'it is hard to tell whether adulthood at Sparta was an extension of childhood; or whether childhood was rather an anticipatory preparation for the life of an adult and a soldier' serves in my view as an excellent characterisation of all Greek societies.

198 **Delinquency**. For ephebic delinquency, aided and abetted by the father, see the charges made against Konon and his sons in Dem. 54.3-9.

5. Early Adulthood

199 **Roles available to women**. On the limited life-patterns available to women in myth, see Lefkowitz (1981, 42). Sepulchral inscriptions conventionally eulogise women as faithful wives and loving mothers. See Schaps (1977, 23-30).

Penalties imposed on bachelors. Ariston (ap. Stob. *Flor*. 67.16) states that in Sparta there existed a *nomos agamiou* (law against non-marrriage), *opsigamiou* (late marriage) and *kakogamiou* (marriage with a social inferior?). Cf. also Plu. *Lys*. 30.7. Poll. *Onomast*. 3.48 alleges that *agamiou dikai* or legal proceedings regarding non-marriage exist 'everywhere' throughout Greece. This is undoubtedly an exaggeration. They certainly did not exist in Athens. See Harrison (1968, I, p. 19 with n. 1).

200 ***Neos*, etc.** For the age-span covered by such terms, see Forbes (1933, 5 with nn. 17-20) and Hopfner (1938, 233-6) who cite examples of its use in connection with all the stages from infant to young man inclusive.

Military and civic status of young adults. For the alleged non-professionalism of the Athenian military as compared with the arduous training programme of the Spartans, see Loraux (1986, 150-1).

For the Spartan *eirenes*, see MacDowell (1986, 66-8 and 166). The exact span of years covered by the term *eirên* cannot be established with certainty. My use of it here to denote Spartiates in the twenties age-group owes more to convention than to conviction. Tazelaar (1967, 142), adopting the suggestion of Ollier (*Xénophon: la République des Lacédémoniens* [Paris 1934] p. 34), believes that what prevented the *eirenes* from doing any shopping was merely the fact that they lived in military barracks and were on full-time active service. I see it rather as a mark of their sub-adult status.

Forbes (1933) lists some seventy associations of *neoi* in the Graeco-Roman world. The earliest evidence for their existence comes from Troizen, if the restoration to *IG* IV 749.6 as proposed by M. Fraenkel is correct. See also Poland, s.v. *Neoi* in *RE* XVI.2 (1935) cols. 2401-9. Gortyn Decree: *IC* IV 162.7-10, cf. 163.6 (fragmentary). For discussion of the *neotas*, see Willetts (1965, 131f. and 187-91). In *IC* IV 164 the participle *neotateuonta* occurs.

03 **Generational conflict in Classical Athens**. An early piece of evidence for the conflict between youth and age is provided by Aes. *Agam*. where emphasis is laid on the fact that: 'The one generation has created the situation; the toil and suffering remain for the next' (Freyman in Bertram 1976, 68). In this drama generational conflict embroils the divine world as well as the human, notably in the oppositon between the Erinyes and the younger Olympians. See A.J. Podlecki (*The Political Background of Aeschylean Tragedy* [Ann Arbor 1976] p. 79). It seems likely that the seeds of generational conflict had already been laid by the time of the Persian Wars at the latest. Hdt. 7.142.1 states that in 480 BC the *presbuteroi* were outmanoeuvred in the interpretation of the oracle concerning the wooden walls which Athens received before the battle of Salamis.

9 **Hippolytos**. Carter (1986, 52-6) sees in Euripides' characterisation of Hippolytos evidence that some Athenian noble youths in the 420s 'were rejecting their traditional place in society and choosing a private life instead' (p. 52). In support of this interesting theory, he draws attention to Hippolytos' words at ll. 986ff. where the latter declares that he is unskilled at addressing a crowd, but 'rather proficient' before a small number of men of his own age. North (1947, 5) claims that Hippolytos 'shows himself to be one-sided in a way peculiarly repugnant to the Greeks', but my point is rather that he is not yet of an age when *sôphrosunê* is an entirely appropriate or even healthy characteristic. Cf. also F. Zeitlin (P. Burian, *Directions in Euripidean Criticism: a Collection of Essays* [Durham 1985] p. 56) who describes Hippolytos' rejection of love as 'the self's radical refusal of the Other' which is 'needed ... for constructing an adequate model of that self and for defining it socially in a network of proper relations'.

210 **Age at marriage**. See in general West (1978, 327) and Golden (1981, 158-9 n. 41; 1981a, 322 with n. 21). The Athenian Mantitheos (Ps.-Dem. 40.4), who married in his eighteenth year at the insistence of his father, was evidently a youthful exception. The bridegrooms of New Comedy also behave as if they are immature in years, though there is no evidence to indicate that they actually were. For the Gortyn Code, see Willetts (1965, 19 and 78; 1967, 27 and 79). For the age of marriage partners in Sparta, see Xen. *Lak. Pol.* 1.6 who states that Lykourgos ordained that 'marriages should take place when partners are at the peak of their physical condition (*en akmais tôn somatôn*)'. Cf. also Plu. *Lyk*. 15.3 and Plu. *Kleom*. 1.1.

Brunt (1971, 138) argues, fancifully in my view, that the early age at marriage of Roman girls (and hence, it might be argued, of Greek girls) was due in part to the prevalence of infanticide which required prospective husbands to 'pre-empt' their brides by marrying them as soon as possible. In Rome from the time of Augustus until the sixth century AD the legal minimal age for a girl to get married was twelve and for a boy fourteen (D.C. 54.16.7). Women were obligated to marry by the time they were twenty, men by the time they were twenty-five.

For the husband as educator, see Plutarch's advice to a recently married young man that he should strive to become for his wife 'a guide, philosopher and teacher in all that is fairest and most holy' (Mor. 145c).

214 **Choosing a partner**. For the *epiklêros*, see Schaps (1979, ch. 3). The miserable lot of the henpecked husband of an *epiklêros* became a stock joke in fourth-century Comedy, cf. Alexis (*CAF* II, p. 350.146 = *WLGR* 35) and Men. (fr. 333 Körte = *WLGR* 37). For marriage among the poor, see Schaps (1979, 78-81). For Sparta, see Toynbee (1969, 356-64), Redfield (1977-8, 158-61) and Cartledge (1981, 94-102). The fact that the Spartans were aggressively competitive in this as in all other areas of life is suggested by the existence of the previously-cited law against bad marriage, as Cartledge (1981, 96) points out. According to Plu. *Lys*. 30.5 it was expressly intended to prevent marriages being contracted by persons wishing merely to improve their financial situation.

217 **The marriage ceremony**. States which under certain conditions are known to have provided brides with dowries include Thasos, Rhodes and Iasos (cf. *Thasos* 1.141.5; D.S. 20.84.3; *ASAA* n.s. 29-30 [1967-8] pp. 445-53). The evidence for Athens is inconclusive. Cf. Plu. *Arist*. 27 for the claim that the state provided dowries for the daughters and grand-daughters of Aristeides. There is a full discussion of the subject in Pomeroy (1982, 115-35).

For fifth-century Attic vases depicting the marriage ceremony, see Jenkins (1983, 137-45). These occasionally depict the bride being lifted into the nuptial cart by the groom. A closely-related motif is that of the groom laying his hand upon the bride's wrist at the moment of entry into her new home. Though such images are clearly suggestive of mock abduction (cf. Sourvinou-Inwood 1973, 17), Jenkins has wisely pointed out that they should not necessarily be interpreted literally since they may be intended merely to symbolise the bride's social and metaphorical death and rebirth as she passes from one *oikos* to another. For marriage as abduction in art, see further Sourvinou-Inwood's investigation (1987, 131-53) of the theme of erotic pursuit in Athenian red-figure vase-paintings. Identifying the principal pursuer as Theseus, 'the Athenian ephebe par excellence', she interprets the capture of the girl as 'a test in the context of the ephebic experience, comparable to the capture of an animal' (p. 137).

References to the *Gamêlia* include Dem. 57.43, 69; Isai. 3.76, 79; 6.64; 8.18; Poll. *Onomast.* 8.107; and schol. on Ar. *Ach.* 146. For discussion, see Cole (1984, 236-8).

For the *proteleia* and hair-sacrifice, see Eur. *IA* 718, Pl. Com. 174.5, Pl. *Laws* 774e with Burkert (1983, 62.f). Cf. also Plu. *Arist.* 20: couples who are about to marry sacrifice to Eukleia (possibly Artemis). For the removal of the girdle, see Schmitt (1977, 1063) who notes: 'The subtle game of putting on and removing the girdle punctuates the sexual life of a Greek woman.' In addition to removing it before marriage, she also takes it off before sexual intercourse and before giving birth. In Hes. *Th.* 570ff. and *Works and Days* 72ff. it is Athena who ties the girdle around Pandora. For *katachusmata*, see Samter (1901, 1-14). For *anakaluptêria*, see Pherekydes (*DK* 7 B 2) with Brückner (1907, 79-122). Extended descriptions of the ceremony can be found in Deubner (1925, 210-23), Nilsson (1960, 243-50) and Pomeroy (1988, 1333-42). For literary references to the marriage ceremony, see Seaford (1987, 106). For the dynamics of the relationship between the *enguê* (administered by men) and the *gamos* (administered by women) see Redfield (1982, 186-98). In what may be taken as a general statement upon the function of ritual, Burkert (1983, 63) states with particular reference to the wedding ceremony: 'The rituals do not mitigate the transition; rather, they stress it by creating inhibitions and guilt.'

Keuls (1985, 112) aptly defines Persephone's fate in *Hom. h. Dem.* as 'premature marriage to an unknown husband at the command of a callous and remote father'. All the three factors cited here are likely to have obtained in many 'real life' marriages. The notion that marriage is a conspiracy on the part of the male relatives of the bride is also implicit in the hymn, for not only does Zeus fail to answer Persephone's appeal for help at the moment of her abduction (20f.) but he also connives with Aïdoneus, who happens to be his brother, in keeping his niece's whereabouts secret. The myth of Persephone is compared by Schmitt (1977, 1065-8) with the charter myth of the Apatouria, in that both involve ruses and both are associated with transitional moments in young people's lives. For the distinction between the carefree life of the *parthenos* and the careworn life of the *gunê*, see S. *Trach.* 141-52.

4 **Hellenistic marriage contracts**. The earliest surviving Greek marriage contract dates to 311/10 (*Elephantine Papyrus* 1; cf. Pomeroy 1988, 1341).

5 **Husbands and wives**. For the atypicality of the hostile attitude to

women expressed by Semonides fr. 7 *IEG*, see Lloyd-Jones (1975). The necessary subordination of the wife to the husband is, according to Aristotle (*Pol.* 1.1254b10-12), merely one among a number of hierarchical relationships ordained by nature for the good of both parties, other examples being that of the body to the soul, the emotions to the intellect, domesticated animals to man, and slaves to their masters. As Aristotle further notes, the Greeks did not have any word which specifically describes the union or *suzeuxis* between a man and a woman. (For the absence, too, of any Indo-European word for marriage, see Benveniste 1969, 239-44.)

Inscriptions on gravestones testify to close emotional ties between married couples (cf. Lefkowitz 1983, 36 and 40). A perfect demonstration of *homonoia* occurs in the *Odyssey* where Penelope by cheating at the loom exhibits the same wiliness to preserve her *oikos* as Odysseus does in his travels to preserve his own life. Cf. also the recognition scene towards the end of the poem in which Homer pointedly compares the joy experienced by Penelope at the sight of her long-lost husband to that of a shipwrecked sailor who has finally escaped to dry land (23.233-40). For what is surely Homer's own personal view of marriage, see Odysseus' remarks to Nausikaa in *Od.* 6.182-5. For Helen's adultery, cf. also *Il.* 3.351-4 where Menelaos sees the issue exclusively in terms of a personal feud between himself and Paris (Arthur 1973, 17). For adultery with particular reference to Comedy, see Fantham (1975, 71).

Because intercourse between husband and wife is conventionally depicted in Greek art by the loosening of the belt or girdle which holds up the overfold of a woman's chiton whereas *hetairai* are often shown naked, Keuls (1985, 114-16 with figs. 99 and 100) has argued that wives were partially robed when they made love with their husbands. But the convention is surely more likely to reflect a desire on the part of the artist not to offend good taste, rather than to constitute an objective statement upon the limits of carnal knowledge. Even the Spartans eventually saw their wives naked – or so Plutarch (see p. 201) implies.

233 **A wife's duties**. On women's seclusion, see Pomeroy (1975, 79-84). Schaps (1977, 323-30) puts forward the interesting theory that the orators avoided using women's names as a form of etiquette except in the case of 'women of shady reputation, women connected with the speaker's opponent and dead women' (p. 328). On the remarks made by Hektor and Telemachos, see Arthur (1973, 14) who rightly observes that they occur 'at those points where the women involved … threaten to overstep the limits of their prerogatives as females, and in a context which makes it clear that they are being deliberately excluded from participating in decisions which affect them directly'. Redfield (1982, 195) goes somewhat too far in describing weaving as 'the transforming power of women [which] symbolises their power to bring peace out of war'. Philosophers sought to justify the theory that a woman's place is in the home by appealing to the biological and emotional differences between the two sexes which rendered women unfit for undoor work (cf. Xen. *Oik*. 7.22-6). The association between women and the home is discussed in detail by Vernant (1985, 152-215; especially p. 163).

36 **Divorcees and widows**. For an Athenian father's rights in regard to his daughter after her marriage, see Harrison (1968, I, p. 19, 30ff. and 74). We hear very little about the plight of widows in Greek society. Widows of the Athenian war dead were expected to keep a very low social profile, to the extent of almost total invisibility (Thuk. 2.45.2). *A fortiori* other widows must have been even more emarginated. See Golden (1981, 328f.). For influential widows in fourth-century Athens, see Humphreys (1983, 47).

1 **Increased status of the wife upon the birth of the first child**. The comment by the husband in Lys. 1.6 accords remarkably closely with a phenomenon observed in modern rural Greece, of which Doumanis (1983, 35) writes: 'After the birth of her first child the status of the traditional woman changed considerably .... The attitude of the whole extended family would shift from tolerance to acceptance and affection for her as the mother of their tiny kinsman .... At this time the husband's behaviour towards his wife would also undergo fundamental changes. He would begin to talk to her more freely before other members of the family.' See further Loraux (1981, 40f.). For the opposition between *alochos*, wife as established member of the *oikos*, and *akoitis*, wife as lover, see Chantraine (1946-47, 223-5).

6. Elders and the Elderly

2 **Greek society as two-generational**. Already in the Homeric poems distinctions between *neoi* (or *kouroi*) on the one hand and *gerontes* on the other are prevalent, with the expression *neoi êde gerontes* signifying all adult male members of a community. For example, when Aigyptios opens the debate called by Telemachos on Ithaca, he asks: 'What compelling need has overtaken one of the *neoi* or one of the *progenesteroi?*' (*Od*. 2.28f.; cf. *Il*. 9.35f.).

3 **Liability for military service**. In Athens and probably elsewhere the heaviest military burden undoubtedly fell on those aged twenty to fifty. Only in the event of an emergency would ephebes and the fifty-plus age-group have been called up (cf. Thuk. 1.105.4-5; Lykourg. *c. Leok*. 39-40). Most probably the entire *hêlikia* was called up when its turn fell due, with the exception of those who were sick or otherwise disabled (cf. Ps.-Arist. *AP* 53.7). In Athens before 335 BC a register comprising the names of all members of the 42 year-classes was displayed on whitewashed boards. After 335, however, the names were enrolled on bronze tablets or *stêlai* set up in front of the Council House beside the statues of the eponymous heroes of the ten Athenian tribes. For a Spartiate's liability for military service for '40 years from coming of age (*tettarakonta aph' hêbês*)', see Xen. *Hell*. 5.4.13. Even Sparta's kings

were not exempt, cf. Plu. *Ages*. 24.2. The requirement of military service for those within the twenty to sixty age-group appears to have been standard throughout Greece. See F. Jacoby (*Apollodors Chronik* [Berlin 1902] p. 45). For sixty or thereabouts as the age at which a man was judged to be a *gerôn*, see Byl (1974, 114) who cites instances of this usage in Plato (*Parm*. 127b; *Rep*. 5.460de) and Aristotle (*Pol*. 7.1335b29-37).

Elderly women. See Bremmer (1985) who convincingly argues (p. 275) that 'the onset of menopause and old age ... brought about a fundamental change in the relationship between men and women', primarily evident in the increased freedom and independence enjoyed by women in this age-group. Cf. the 'freedom' of Demeter in *Hom. h. Dem*. (ll. 101-4) who is likened by the poet to 'an ancient woman who is debarred from child-bearing and the gifts of garland-loving Aphrodite'. Later evidence relating to the freedom of older women includes Lys. 1.15; Eur. *Hel*. 435ff. and *Tro*. 194ff.; and Thphr. *Char*. 28.3. See also Henderson (1987, 113) for the emphasis on female solidarity among older women in Aristophanic Comedy, due in part to their freedom of movement. It must be emphasised, however, that the same degree of independence is unlikely to have been enjoyed by all social categories. Aristocratic Greek women were unquestionably restricted in their freedom of movement, whatever their age.

It is widely reported among anthropologists that women above childbearing years enjoy extensive freedom. Simmons (1945, 64), for instance, writes that among the Omaha Indians young women and girls had to sit in a dignified manner, whereas old women could sit with their feet stretched out in front 'for this was the privilege of age'.

245 **Life expectancy**. On the life expectancy of those who survive the ailments of early childhood, cf. the claim of the sixteenth-century physician Jerome Cardano of Pavia to be able to cure any patient not younger than seven and not older than seventy (cited by Cipolla 1978, 90).

For the period from 650 BC to the end of the Classical era, Angel (1984, table 3.1b [p. 55]) puts the life expectancy of males and females who survive to the age of fifteen and over at 44.1 and 36.8 years respectively. For the period from 300 BC to the end of the Hellenistic era, his figures are 41.9 and 38.0 respectively. There is brief discussion of longevity in the Greek world in Grmek (1983, 162-5). In modern non-industrial societies, median age at death is put at around thirty-five years. In modern Britain life expectancy is currently seventy-one years for men and seventy-seven for women, and the ranks of the elderly (especially those who are over eighty-five) are growing faster than any other age group. For the problems in using Roman sepulchral inscriptions for calculating the average age at death of men and women, see Hopkins (1966, passim). Hopkins concludes that the evidence is 'irremediably obfuscated by the patterns of commemoration' (p. 263). He puts the expectation of life at birth among the Roman population at above twenty and probably under thirty. For the usefulness of epigraphic material for calculating life-expectancy, see the bibliography cited by Frier (1983, 343 n. 20). For Littias, Euphranor and other long-lived Athenians, see Humphreys (1983, 107). For the comparative life expectancy of men and women in Athens, see Golden (1981, 326f.). For an estimated pattern of mortality in Athens, cf. A.H.M. Jones (*The Athenian Democracy* [Oxford 1957] p. 82).

The term '*horos* (Ionic *ouros*) *tês zôês* or *hêlikias*', which means 'the boundary of life', conveys the idea of an upper limit of years which cannot be exceeded. Cf. Hdt. 1.32.2, 74.2, 216.2; Bacch. 5.144; D.L. 1.55; and Pln. *NH* 7.49.160-1. Hence *gamou horos* in Pl. *Laws* 6.785b is to be understood as the upper age limit at which one should marry. As expressed in mythological terms, one's personal allotment of years was determined by the *moira thanatou* or 'fate of death'. Mimnermos' couplet (fr. 6 *IEG*) 'O that the *moira thanatou* would come upon me when I reach sixty, troubled neither by sickness nor by sorrow' is said to have been altered by Solon to read 'when I reach eighty' (fr. 20 *IEG*).

For a list of 128 so-called 'famous Greeks' who attained the age of sixty or more, see Richardson (1933, ch. xiii). They include Sophokles (ninety), Euripides (about eighty), Plato (eighty-one) and Isokrates (ninety-eight). But it is highly questionable whether much reliance should be placed on biographical 'evidence' relating to year of birth. For doubts about the proclaimed longevity of philosophers, see L. Jerphagon ('Les mille et une morts des philosophes antiques', pp. 17-28 in *Revue Belge Phil. Hist.* 59 [1981]). Even in a highly bureaucratic society such as Graeco-Roman Egypt the ages recorded on papyri are merely approximations, neatly rounded off to the nearest five years (cf. Carter 1967, 53). As Hopkins (1966, 249) points out: 'The number of claimed centenarians in a population can often be considered a function of illiteracy rather than of longevity.' Thus in a Roman census taken in AD 74 several persons domiciled in the backward region between the Apennines and the Po declared themselves to be between a hundred and twenty and a hundred and forty years old (Pln. *HN* 7.49.162-4).

7 **Explanations of longevity and ageing**. On Aristotle's theory of ageing, see Egerton (1975, 309f.) and Eyben (1972, 680-2). It continued to find advocates in the second century AD (cf. Gal. 1.522, 1.582 19.344, 19.374 *K*). On Arist.'s comments on the comparative longevity of the sexes, see Lloyd (1983, 103). Finley (1981, 161) characterises Greek geriatrics as 'a highly selected assemblage, men who possessed both great luck and great toughness, physiological and psychological'. It is noteworthy that there are very few recorded instances of women living to great ages, either because of the (even greater) difficulty in establishing their exact number of years, because their longevity was not considered significant enough to record for posterity, or because the phenomenon was practically unknown.

For the belief that longevity is – or at least ought to be – a just reward for good behaviour, see the anecdote told in Hdt. 2.133 of the ill-fated

Pharaoh Myrkerinos whose life was cut short because he sought to alleviate the sufferings of his people, an action deemed contrary to the will of the gods. The belief that old age and goodness are functionally related is widely reported by anthropologists, as Simmons (1945, 221) notes. Cf. also the promise made by the Lord to the Israelites in Exodus 20:12: 'Honour thy father and thy mother that thy days may be long ....'

Confirming the testimony of the sophist Gorgias, *The Times* of 30 December 1987 reported that Anna Williams, believed to be the oldest woman in the world, who died in a Swansea nursing home at the age of a hundred and fourteen, attributed her longevity to a 'no-pills policy' and a 'meat and two veg diet'. The Olympian equivalent, namely a diet of nectar and ambrosia, is presumably the biological justification for the fact that the gods are eternally deathless and ageless. Explanations of longevity based on diet continue to dominate our thinking. Finley (1981, 158) engagingly suggests that 'in the retsina regions of the ancient world there was a somewhat higher life expectancy (and therefore a somewhat higher percentage of the elderly) than in the sapa regions', on the grounds that sapa, a kind of syrup used to sweeten wine, was prepared over a slow fire in leaden vessels, thereby causing increased mortality and decreased fertility among drinkers.

248 **Medical interest in the elderly**. Although the elderly are unlikely to have received much in the way of medical attention, Lloyd (1983, 64) rightly points out that the Hippokratic treatises pay considerable attention to the differences between young and old with regard to both diagnosis and treatment.

249 **Menopause**. See Gourevitch (1984, 89-91) and Amundsen and Diers (1969a) for references to menopause in Greek and Roman literature. In modern Italy most women experience menopause betwen forty-five and forty-nine, the modal age being forty-six.

250 **The 'threshold of old age'**. Other references include Hom. *Il.* 22.60; Hes. *Works and Days* 331; and Hdt. 3.14.10.

252 **Old age in lyric and elegiac poetry**. See the discussion of the treatment of old age in lyric and epic poetry by Byl (1976, 238-44). Anakreon was especially 'remembered' for possessing exceptional sexual vitality in old age. Cf. Sud. s.v. *Anakreôn*, *AP* 7.23, 9.239, etc., with G. Giangrande ('Sympotic literature and epigram', pp. 93-177 in *Entr. H.* 14 [1968] 109-11 with n. 2).

The most provocative poem on the subject of old age is Anakr. 358 *PMG*, in which the elderly poet complains that a girl from Lesbos despises him because of his white hair and instead 'gapes towards another (feminine gender)'. On the grounds that Lesbian girls were uncommonly addicted to fellatio Giangrande (1973, 129-33) has ingeniously proposed that what the girl is gaping after is not another girl as is usually assumed, but at Anakreon's pubic hair which has not yet turned white.

253 **Old age in mythology**. For Herakles' contest with Geras, cf. Dover (1978, R 422) = Paris G234 = *ARV* 286.1642 (Geras Painter no. 16).

Other examples include *ABV* 491.60, *ARV* 284.1, 653.1 and 889.160. The motif is discussed by Robinson (1933, ch. vi). In Gades (Cadiz) there was an altar dedicated to Geras (Philostr. *Ap. Ty.* 5.4.190). For the representation of old age on vases, in sculpture and the minor arts, see Robinson (1933, chs. vii-x). Among the divine and mythological figures commonly depicted as elderly are Hades, Charon, Nereus, Anchises, Priam and Nestor. According to the Hesiodic Myth of the Five Ages (ll.113-16) 'miserable old age' did not afflict the Golden Age, and appears to be unique to the present Age of Iron, which will be destroyed 'when men are born with hoary locks' (l. 181). For other legends as to how old age originated, see Simmons (1945, 218f.).

55 **Physical plight of the elderly**. For other examples of death in sleep being the reward for virtue, see Mainoldi (1987, 17). For Hypnos as an agent of death, see ibid. pp. 39-45. On the wisdom of not preserving the lives of those who are useless both to themselves and to the community, see Pl. *Rep*. 3.407d-408b.

It may help to put the public Greek neglect of the elderly into some sort of financial perspective by pointing out that health-care expenditure on the elderly in the USA is expected to reach $200 billion by the year 2000. See D. Callahan, *Medical Goals in an Ageing Society* ([New York] 1987).

57 **Adoption**. There was no upper age limit for adoption in Athens, though the adopters themselves had to be adult (cf. Harrison 1968, I, p. 84). See Aischin. 3.21 for a law forbidding magistrates from being adopted until they had rendered their accounts.

58 **Spinsters**. On mythical spinsters, see the references in Henderson (1987, 126f.). Hdt. (4.117) reports that among the military-minded Sauromatai there was a law that no *parthenos* was permitted to get married until she had killed a man in battle, and that many, unable to fulfil this condition, grew old and died in spinsterhood. The only unrepellent middle-aged spinster in Greek myth is Hestia, who received a special dispensation from Zeus to be a perpetual virgin (*Hom. h. Aph*. 26-8).

59 **Second marriages**. Investigation has revealed that some 53 instances of re-marriage recorded in the orators and other literary sources, 30 of which involve women and 23 men. At least 34 of these re-marriages resulted in the birth of offspring.

61 **Legal safeguards for the elderly**. Cf. Thalheim in *RE* X.2 (1919) s.v. *kakôsis* cols. 1526-28, and the bibliography cited by Reinhold (in Bertram 1976, 20). For the Athenian law see Aischin. 1.28; And. 1.74; Isai. 8.32; Lys. 13.91; Ps.-Arist. *AP* 56.6; and D.L. 1.55 (stating it was instituted by Solon). See further Harrison (1968, I pp. 77f.). For the Delphic law, see Lerat (1943, 68-86) who emphasises the extreme severity of the punishment which 'assimilates the wrongdoer to a *kakourgos*, almost to a slave' (p. 84f.). The Delphic manumissions indicate that slaves were commonly enfranchised on condition that they look after their masters in old age, an obligation known as

gêrotrophia (cf. *GDI* 1723.10-12). Herodotos informs us that Persian sons, too, were expected to look after their parents (7.38-9), though in Egypt, where gender roles were inverted, this task fell to the daughters (2.35.4).

262 **Retirement**. E.g. *AP* 6.1; 5; 18f.; 25-30; 46; 63. Cf. also Kimon's dedication of his horse's bridle in Plu. *Kim*. 5.2. For discussion see Finley (1981, 168).

263 **Elderly slaves**. Examples of elderly slaves in Eur. include the servant of Elektra in *El*. 487ff.; the servant of Agamemnon in *IA* 115ff.; the servant of Kreousa in *Ion* 725ff.; the portress of Theoklymenos and the servant of Menelaos in *Hel*. 437ff., 700ff.; the nurse of Phaidra in *Hipp*. 176ff.; the tutor of Medea's children and her nurse in *Med*. 1ff.; and the servant of Antigone in *Phoin*. 88ff.

Representations of old age in literature. In Stob. *Antholog*. (fifth century AD) citations on old age ranging over a period of some 700 years are arranged under the two headings 'Praise of Old Age' and 'Blame of Old Age'. For what the comparison is worth, Stob.'s compendium lists twenty-six passages under 'Praise' and fifty under 'Blame' (4.25). Cf. also his nine citations under 'Old Age is not burdensome'. Studies of the depiction of old age in a variety of literary genres have been conducted by Byl (1974, 1975, 1976, etc.). His somewhat limited approach is to categorise authors according to whether they essentially valorise or denounce old age.

264 **Terminology for the elderly**. See Poll. *Onomast*. 2.13-16. Pejorative terms for the elderly inevitably occur mainly in Comedy but there is no reason to assume that they were invented by the Comic poets. For uncomplimentary epithets describing old age, such as *dusônumos* (ill-omened), *oulomenos* (deadly), *ponêros* (grievous), etc., see the citations in Richardson (1933, 7f.).

Nestor. For an analysis of the rhetorical techniques employed by Nestor in his speech in Book 1, see Dio *Or*. 57. There is a detailed discussion of Nestor's speech in Book 1 in Schofield (1986, 28f., with bibliography). Valuable though Schofield's comments are, it is incorrect to state that 'Tact is the hallmark of Nestor's *euboulia*' (p. 29). In the Council in Book 2 the old man is nothing if not outspoken. See also Finley (1981, 164). On Nestor's garrulousness, cf. also *Od*. 15.195-201 where Telemachos, eager to return home, appeals to Peisistratos to help him avoid being trapped by his father as he had been previously – for fear, presumably, of being subjected to another interminable narrative.

265 ***Gerontes* in Homer**. The theory proposed by Kahrstedt (1922, 246 and 375) that the *gerontes* are not necessarily 'elders' in the strict sense of the word, but merely heads of the senior branch of the family, and further that *gerôn* has as its primary meaning not 'elder', but one who is in receipt of *geras* or privilege, ignores, as Jeanmaire (1939, 19f.) points out, 'one of the most striking characteristics of ancient societies, which is to attach precisely the idea of honour to that of old age'. My brief

survey of the treatment of old age in Homer is greatly indebted to Jeanmaire's discussion of the subject (op. cit., pp. 11-26). There is also a useful treatment in Glotz (1929, 46-9).

66 **Old age in Tragedy**. Though the elderly Teiresias and Oedipus admittedly possess, in addition to irascibility, an eerie, supernatural understanding of the ways of the world, that is surely due in no small measure to the fact that the former is a seer and the latter a hero-elect.

The elderly, like other weak and defenceless members of society (e.g. war captives, suppliants, etc.), constitute a popular collective persona for tragic choruses since the conventions of Greek drama normally required that a chorus should not actively intervene in the outcome of events. In Aes. *Agam*. the chorus, who, since they were too old to be conscripted for war, must now all be in their seventies, are of course capable of displaying outrage at Klytaimnestra's murder of her husband but are conveniently (for the playwright) disqualified from either preventing it or avenging it. Cf. the chorus in Eur. *HF* who lament the passing of youth (ll. 637-54) and wait around helplessly while Herakles slaughters his wife and children (875ff.). Of the tragedians it is Euripides who most insistently exploits the pathos of old age (cf. Byl 1975, 135-9). For an analysis of the imagery that is regularly used in Tragedy to describe the elderly (e.g. *eidôlon* or image, *ptanon oneiron* or fleeting dream, etc.), see Brillante (1987, 49-54).

It has been claimed that Kadmos and Teiresias in *Ba*. 170ff. represent a 'miracle of Dionysiac rejuvenation' (Murray and Nihard [*Problème des Bacchantes*] pp. 44f.). As Dodds (1960, 90) points out, however, neither figure is exactly an ideal witness to the new faith. Dodds concedes, however, that lines 187-90, where Kadmos invites his partner to forget that he is old and the latter replies 'I feel in my prime (*hêbô*)', do describe 'a traditional Dionysiac effect'. For Dionysos as rejuvenator, see the Iacchos hymn sung by the Chorus in Ar. *Frogs*, especially ll. 345-9. Cf. also Pl. *Laws*. 2.666b where it is said that 'Dionysos gave wine as a helpful medicine against the crabbedness (*austêrotês*) of old age, so that we might grow young again (*anhêban*).' On this topic generally, see further Bond (1981, 91) and Richardson (1933, 3-5).

8 **Old Age in Comedy**. Dover (1972, 129f.) rightly detects in Philokleon's juridical ferocity the hint of 'a nasty kind of compensation for the inferior status which necessarily follows physical enfeeblement'. Rejuvenation was a stock motif in Old, Middle and New Comedy. In the surviving plays of Ar. it occurs in *Birds* (Peisthetairos), *Knights* (Demos), *Peace* (Trygaios) and *Wealth* (Ploutos). See Byl (1977a). Ar. also wrote a play called *Geras* or *Old Age*, whose chorus of old men undergo rejuvenation (*CAF* I, pp. 422-7, frr. 125-48 esp. 141). A similar transformation seems to have taken place in Pherekrates' *Graes* or *Old Bags* (*CAF* I, pp. 153-5, esp. fr. 35) in which old women take control of the city – the ultimate Greek fantasy, we might suppose. Finally, the New Comedy poet Philemon wrote a play called *Ananeoumenê* or *The*

Rejuvenated Woman (*CAF* II, p. 480.8). On the subject of sloughing off old skin, see McCartney (1929, 176) who quotes the following comment made by a Mohave squaw: 'Indians don't die. They shed their skins like snakes and we burn up the old skins so that they can be used again.' Cf. also Kallimachos' wish to become a cicada 'in order that I may divest myself of *gêras*' (*Ait.* fr. 1.33-5 Pfeiffer).

The image of the older woman seeking amatory attachment and unable to control her sexual desires seems to have been proverbial to judge from allusions to old women who 'get hot', 'go boar-hunting' or 'play the bacchant'. Cf. Bekker, *Anecd.* 33.20 (*graus anathuai*) and *CPG* I, pp. 57, 228 and 234. Of the scene in *Ekkles.* Finley (1981, 164) writes, 'I know of no more unrelieved cruelty in Greek or Roman literature ...'. The motif of the sex-starved old bag also receives prominent attention in Ar. *Pl.* 959-1095. As Henderson (1987, 108 and 128) points out, the portrayal of old women in Attic Comedy is not invariably negative. In Ar. *Lys.* and *Thes.*, for instance, the chorus of older women are represented in a sympathetic and even heroic light.

270 **Old age in satyr plays**. Consistent with his general thesis that tragedy was essentially preoccupied with ephebes (above, p. 328), Winkler (1985, 52f.) ingeniously interprets the satyr play as 'a military graduation play in which high-spirited cadets take their taskmasters to task'.

271 **Old age in Platonic philosophy**. It is worth noting that Plato is not invariably deferential towards the elderly. In *Laws* 1.645e-646a, for instance, he unflatteringly describes an old man as a 'twice child (*dis pais*)' – evidently a Greek cliché (see p. 205). As Byl (1974) rightly notes, familiarity with the portrait of Kephalos has unduly influenced the modern perception of Plato's evaluation of old age. The view that it is outlook on life which determines whether one is happy or unhappy in old age is not confined to Plato. Cf. Anaxandrides, *FAC* IIb, p. 74 no. 53.

273 **Old age in Aristotle**. There is discussion of Arist. *Rhet.* in Byl (1974, 122-6) and Boll (1913, 89-145). Byl argues with some justification that the similarities between Pl. and Arist. in respect to old age outweigh their differences; and that Arist.'s criticisms mainly reflect his preoccupation, as a biologist, with the physical ravages of time, much less his opinion as to whether or not the elderly should be held in high honour.

280 **30th- and 40th-year age-requirements**. For 30th-year age-requirements, see 'Drakon' in Ps.-Arist. *AP* 4.3; Dem. 22.1.1; Xen. *Mem.* 1.2.35 (404/3); and Ps.-Arist. *AP* 30.2 and 31.1 (Council elected under the Five Thousand in 411 BC). The heliastic and possibly also the bouleutic oath required incumbents to swear that they were at least in their thirtieth year (Dem. 24.150; see Rhodes 1972, 194f.; 1981, 116 and 389f.). For the age of *stratêgoi*, about which we have no evidence at all, see W.K. Pritchett (*The Greek State at War* [California 1974] II, p. 63 n. 17) who argues that the lower age-requirement should not be fixed at the thirtieth year on the analogy of the Athenian Boule and the lawcourts, since the *stratêgia* was 'an exception to the general rules as regards, first, election by the populace, and second, re-election'. Admittedly an Athenian was eligible for the trierarchy at twenty (see above, p. 241), though the *stratêgia* was harldy analogous to that office either. The 30th-year requirement for the generalship is accepted uncritically by Davies (*APF*, 18).

For 40th-year age-requirements, see Ps.-Arist. *AP* 42.2 and 56.3. For the age of the *sôphronistai* and *kosmêtês*, see Rhodes (1981, 504). The twenty *probouloi* appointed to supplement the original ten in 413 had to fulfil the requirement, as did the ten *katalogeis* who had to draw up a register of the Five Thousand (cf. Ps.-Arist. *AP* 29.2 and 5; see below, p. 344). Rhodes (1981, 625f.) believes that the 40th-year rule for regular appointments was an innovation of the fourth century.

1 ***Diaitêtai***. Cf. also Poll. (*Onomast.* 8.126) and other lexicographers who claim that these officers were elected 'from those who are above fifty-nine years old (*ek tôn huper hexêkonta etê gegonotôn*)'. *Diaitêtai* were first appointed in 399/8. See Rhodes (1972, 172; 1981, 591). For inscriptions recording *diaitêtai*, see *IG* II^2 1294 + 2409 with D.M. Lewis (*ABSA* 50 [1955] pp. 27-36). The fact that those who failed to comply with the requirement to serve as *diaitêtai* suffered loss of civic rights or *atimia* (Ps.-Arist. *AP* 53.5) provides conclusive proof that in Athens those above military age did normally retain all their rights.

Minimum age requirements for priesthoods. It is not known whether an Athenian had even to be over thirty in order to hold a priesthood, but the evidence on the whole suggests not. Certainly there does not appear to have been any minimum age requirement for the high-ranking priesthood of Athena Polias (see above). For the contrary practice elsewhere, cf. the edict of Ptolemy I, dated 322/1-308/7 which required that priests of Apollo be chosen from the *gerontes*, who are defined as being those who were at least fifty years of age (*SEG* IX 1.24-6). On this topic see also Parker (1983, 87) and Simmons (1945, 164f.).

Upper age limit for public office. See Rhodes (1972, 1 with n. 8). Regarding the probable absence of any upper age limit for *bouleutai*, Rhodes notes that Sokrates was well over sixty when he served on the Council in 406/5 (Apollod. and Dem. Phal. ap. D.L. 2.44 with Xen. *Hell.* 1.7.15, etc.).

2 **Political authority of the elderly: Sparta**. See MacDowell (1986, 7 and 127). For the exercise of *probouleusis*, which Plu. *Agis* 11.1 describes as a manifestation of the *kratos* or power of the *Gerousia*, see also Forrest (1967, 11-19). Homicide is the only offence which is known certainly to have come before the *Gerousia*. Possibly it was up to the ephors to decide at a pre-trial hearing whether a case was sufficiently serious to fall within the jurisdiction of that body. A fragment found in a Vatican palimpsest apparently refers to an investigation conducted by the ephors before a trial by the *Gerousia*. See further Keaney (1974, 179-94) and MacDowell (1986, 138).

The Spartan *Gerousia* had nothing in common with the numerous

Gerousiai which are referred to in inscriptions from the first century AD onwards, particularly those found in Asia Minor and the Aegean islands. These *Gerousiai* were associations, numbering on average about a hundred people, whose funds were used largely for the provision and maintenance of burial grounds and for the perpetual commemoration of the dead. See further Hogarth (1891).

For the charter to Cyrene, see *SEG* IX.1 ll. 16-34 which contains the provision that if the full complement of councillors from the fifty-plus age group cannot be found, then the shortfall should be made up from those who are forty-plus.

283 **Political authority of the elderly: Athens**. Since '*presbuteros*' like '*neôteros*' did not denote a specific number of years, all that is known about the age of the *probouloi* is that the twenty elected subsequently to the first ten had to be over forty (Ps.-Arist. *AP* 29.2). Regarding their individual ages, Sophokles was born in *c*. 496 (Kirchner *PA* 12834) and Hagnon before 470 (Davies, *APF* 227-8; Kirchner *PA* 171). For bibliography on the *probouloi*, see Rhodes (1981, 373).

284 **Euthanasia and suicide**. Scholarly opinion is divided as to whether euthanasia was widely practised in the ancient world. Deichgräber (1932, 36) denies that it was, whereas Edelstein (1967, 11f.) asserts the opposite. There is simply not enough data to decide the issue either way, though the lack of evidence may itself in part be due to an understandable reluctance on the part of ancient writers to speak openly on the subject. Other references to the killing of the elderly by barbarians include D.S. 3.33.5; Plu. *Mor*. 328c; Str. 11.8.6 and 11.11.8; Porph. *Abst*. 4.21; and Procop. *Gothic Wars* 2.14. See further Finley (1981, 169) and Bremmer (1983, 103f.). For attitudes towards euthanasia among the Pythagoreans, Plato and Aristotle, see Carrick (1985, 134-44).

286 **Marginality of the elderly**. Bremmer (1983, 103f.) has attractively suggested that since *gerontes*, along with *numphai, êitheoi* and tender *parthenikai*', are among the first dead to be encountered by Odysseus during his visit to Hades (*Od*. 11.38-41), they may have constituted 'a special category of the dead with infranormal status'.

287 **The elderly as controllers of rites of passage**. For the anthropological evidence, see Simmons (1945, 124) who writes: 'The aged, especially men, have frequently been associated with secret societies, and have thereby been able to increase their authority through the instrumentality of well-guarded secrets and elaborate, sometimes very severe initiatory rites .... The manipulative facility of these rituals and the opportunities which they have afforded aged persons to control the conduct of others can hardly be appreciated without firsthand experience with some of the cases.'

Bibliography

Periodical titles are abbreviated according to the form in *L'Année Philologique*.

ABV = Beazley, J.D. (1962) *Attic Black-Figure Vase-Painters*. Oxford, Clarendon.

Amundsen, D.W. and Diers, C.J. (1969) 'The age of menarche in classical Greece and Rome', pp. 125-32 in *Human Biology* 41.

——— (1969a) 'The age of menopause in classical Greece and Rome', pp. 79-86 in *Human Biology* 42.

Angel, J.L. (1945) 'Skeletal material from Attica', pp. 279-363 in *Hesperia* 14.

——— (1946) 'Social biology of Greek culture growth', pp. 493-533 in *American Anthropologist* n.s. 48.

——— (1969) 'The bases of palaeodemography', pp. 427-37 in *Amer. J. of Phys. Anthrop*. 30.

——— (1972) 'Ecology and population in the eastern Mediterranean', pp. 88-105 in *World Archaeology* 4.

——— (1975) 'Paleoecology, paleodemography and health', pp. 167-90 in S. Polgar (ed.), *Population, Ecology and Social Evolution*. The Hague and Paris.

——— (1984) 'Health as a crucial factor in the changes from hunting to developed farming in the eastern Mediterranean', pp. 51-73 in M.N. Cohen and G.L. Armelogos (eds.), *Paleopathology at the Origins of Agriculture*. Orlando, etc.

Ariès, P. (1960) *Centuries of Childhood*. Harmondsworth.

Arrigoni, G. (ed.) (1985) *Le donne in Grecia*. Roma-Bari.

Arthur, M. (1973) 'Early Greece. The origins of the western attitude towards women', pp. 7-58 in *Arethusa* 6.

——— (1982) 'Women and family in ancient Greece', pp. 532-47 in *Yale Review* 71.4 (July).

——— (1983) 'Origins of the Western attitude toward women', pp. 7-58 in *Arethusa* 6.1.

ARV = Beazley, J.D. (1963) *Attic Red-Figure Vase-Painters*, 2nd ed. Oxford, Clarendon.

Ashmead, A. (1978) 'Greek cats: exotic pets kept by rich youths in fifth-century Athens as portrayed on Greek vases', pp. 38-47 in *Expedition* 20.3.

Baldry, H.C. (1932) 'Embryological analogies in Presocratic cosmogony', pp. 27-34 in *CQ* 26.

Balme, D.M. (1962) 'Development of biology in Aristotle and Theophrastus: theory of spontaneous generation', pp. 91-104 in *Phronesis* 7.

Barton, S.C. and Horsley, G.H.R. (1981) 'A Hellenistic cult group and the New Testament churches', pp. 7-41 in *JbAC* 24.

Beck, F.A.G. (1964) *Greek Education 450-350 B.C.* London.

——— (1975) *Album of Greek Education: the Greeks at School and at Play*. Sydney.

Benveniste, E. (1969) *Le vocabulaire des institutions indo-européennes*, vol. 1. Paris.

Bérard, J. (1947) 'Problèmes démographiques dans l'histoire de la Grèce antique', pp. 311ff. in *Population* 2.

Bérard, C. (1970) *Eretria: Fouilles et recherches*, vol. 3 (= *L'héroön à la porte de l'Ouest*. Bern.

Bertram, S. (ed.) (1976) *The Conflict of Generations in Ancient Greece and Rome*. Amsterdam.

Billheimer, A. (1946) *'Ta deka aph' hêbês'*, pp. 214-20 in *TAPhA* 77.

——— (1947) 'Age-classes in Spartan education', pp. 99-104 in *TAPhA* 78.

Biscardi A. (1984-85) 'Mariage d'amour et mariage sans amour en Grèce, à Rome et dans les évangiles', pp. 205-13 in *Annali della Fac. di giur. di Genova* 20.

Blayney, J. (1986) 'Theories of conception in the ancient Roman world', pp. 230-6 in Rawson 1986.

Boardman, J. (1974) *Athenian Black Figure Vases*. Thames and Hudson, London.

den Boer, W. (1979) *Private Morality in Greece and Rome: Some Historical Aspects* (= *Mnemosyne Supplement* 57). Leiden.

Boisacq, W. (1950) *Dictionnaire étymologique de la langue grecque*, 4th ed. Heidelberg.

Bolkestein, H. (1939) *Wohltätigkeit und Armenpflege im Vorchristlichen Altertum*. Utrecht.

Boll, F. (1913) 'Die Lebensalter. Ein Beitrag zur antiken Ethologie und zur Geschichte der Zahlen' in *Neue Jahrbücher für das klassische Altertum*, reproduced in *Kleine Schriften zur Sternkunde des Altertums*, 1950. Leipzig.

Bond, G.W. (1981) *Euripides' Heracles with Introduction and Commentary*. Oxford, Clarendon.

Bonner, C. (1950) *Studies in Magical Amulets, chiefly Graeco-Egyptian*. Ann Arbor, Michigan.

Booth A. (1988) 'The age for reclining', talk given at the McMaster Symposium on Symposia (Sept. 1988). To be published by the Univ. of Michigan Press in 1990.

Bork, A. (1961) *Der junge Grieche*. Zurich.

Borthwick, E.K. (1963) 'The Oxyrhynchus musical monody', pp. 225-43 in *AJPh* 84.

Bradley, K.R. (1986) 'Wet-nursing at Rome: a study in social

relations', pp. 201-29 in Rawson 1986.
Brelich, A. (1969) *Paides e Parthenoi* (= *Incunabula graeca* 36). Rome.
Bremmer, J.N. (1980) 'An enigmatic Indo-European rite: paederasty', pp. 279-95 in *Arethusa* 13.2.
——— (1983) *The Early Greek Concept of the Soul*. Princeton.
——— (1985) 'La donna anziana: libertà e indipendenza', pp. 275-98 in Arrigoni 1985.
Brillante, C. (1987) 'Il vecchio e la cicala', pp. 49-89 in Raffaelli 1987.
Brückner, A. (1907) 'Athenische Hochzeitsgeschenke', pp. 79-122 in *AM* 32.
Brunt, P.A. (1971) *Italian Manpower 225 B.C.–A.D. 14*. Oxford.
Bryant, A.A. (1907) 'Boyhood and youth in the days of Aristophanes', pp. 73-122 in *HSCP* 18.
Buck, C.D. (1955) *The Greek Dialects*. Chicago.
Burkert, W. (1966) 'Kekropidensage und Arrhephoria', pp. 1-25 in *Hermes* 94.
——— (1972) *Lore and Science in Ancient Pythagoreanism*, tr. E.L. Minar Jr. Cambridge, Mass.
——— (1983) *Homo necans: the anthropology of ancient Greek sacrificial ritual and myth*. Berkeley.
——— (1985) *Greek Religion: Archaic and Classical*, tr. J. Raffan. Oxford.
Burnett, A.P. (1983) *Three Archaic Poets: Archilochus, Alcaeus, Sappho*. London.
Byl, S. (1974) 'Platon et Aristote ont-ils profesé des vues contradictoires sur la vieillesse?', pp. 113-26 in *LEC* 42.
——— (1975) 'Lamentations sur la vieillesse dans la tragédie grecque', pp. 130-9 in *Le monde grec: Hommages à Claire Préaux*. Brussels.
——— (1976) 'Lamentations sur la vieillesse chez Homère et les poètes lyriques des VIIème et VIème siècles', pp. 234-44 in *LEC* 44.
——— (1977) 'Plutarque et la vieillesse', pp. 107-23 in *LEC* 45.
——— (1977a) 'Le vieillard dans les comédies d'Aristophane', pp. 52-75 in *AC* 46.
——— (1978) 'Lucien et la vieillesse', pp. 317-25 in *LEC* 46.
——— (1983) 'La vieillesse dans le corpus Hippocratique', pp. 85-95 in *Actes du IVème colloque international Hippocratique*. (Lausanne 21-26 September 1981).
CAF = Kock, T. (ed.) *Comicorum Atticorum Fragmenta*, 3 vols. Leipzig 1880-88.
Calame, C. (1977) *Les choeurs de jeunes filles en Grèce archaïque*, 2 vols. Urbino.
——— (1984) *Amore in Grecia*, 3rd ed. Roma-Bari.
Calderini, A. (1970) 'L'indicazione dell' età individuale nei documenti dell' Egitto greco-romano', pp. 317-25 in *Rass. Ital. Lett. Class.* 2.
Cameron, A. (1932) 'The exposure of children and Greek ethics', pp. 105-14 in *CR* 46.
Cameron, A. and Kuhrt, A. (1983) *Images of Women in Antiquity*.

London and Canberra.
Camp, J. (1986) *The Athenian Agora: Excavations in the Heart of Classical Athens*. London, Thames and Hudson.
Cantarella, E. (1987) *Pandora's Daughters: the Role and Status of Women in Greek and Roman Antiquity*, tr. M.B. Fant. Baltimore.
Carrick, P. (1985) *Medical Ethics in Antiquity: Philosophical Perspectives on Abortion and Euthanasia*. Holland.
Carter, J.M. (1967) 'Eighteen years old?', pp. 51-7 in *BICS* 14.
Carter, L.B. (1986) *The Quiet Athenian*. Oxford, Clarendon.
Cartledge, P. (1981) 'The politics of Spartan pederasty', pp. 17-36 in *PCPhS* n.s. 27.
——— (1981a) 'Spartan wives: liberation or licence', pp. 84-105 in *CQ* n.s. 31.
——— (1987) *Agesilaos*. London 1987.
Chantraine, P. (1946-47) 'Les noms du mari et de la femme, du père et de la mère en Grèce', pp. 219-50 in *REG* 59-60.
——— (1974-80) *Dictionnaire étymologique de la langue grecque*. Paris.
Cipolla, C.M. (1978) *The Economic History of World Population*, 7th ed. Harmondsworth.
Clairmont, C. (1970) *Gravestone and Epigram*. Mainz.
Clarke, H.W. (1963) 'Telemachus and the Telemacheia', pp. 129-45 in *AJPh* 84 (reprinted in C. Nelson (ed.) *Homer's Odyssey*, [California 1969]).
CMG = *Corpus Medicorum Graecorum*. Leipzig 1908-.
Cohen, Y.A. (1964) *The Transition from Childhood to Adolescence*. Chicago.
Cole, S.G. (1984) 'The social function of rituals of maturation: the Koureion and the Arkteia', pp. 233-44 in *ZPE* 55.
CPG = Leutsch, E.L. and Schneidewin, F.G. (eds.). (1958) *Corpus Paroemiographorum Graecorum*, 2 vols. Hildesheim.
Crahay, R. (1941) 'Les moralistes anciens et l'avortement', pp. 9-23 in AC *10*.
Daube, D. (1977) 'The duty of procreation', pp. 10-25 in *PCA* 74.
Davies, *APF* = Davies, J.K. (1971) *Athenian Propertied Families: 600-300 B.C.* Oxford, Clarendon.
Deichgräber, K. (1932) 'Die arztliche Standesethik des hippokratischen Eides', in *Quellen und Studien zur Geschichte des Naturwissenschaften u. d. Medizin* 3.
Deubner, L. (1909) 'Birth', pp. 648f. in vol. 2 of J. Hastings (ed.), *The Encyclopaedia of Religion and Ethics*. Edinburgh and New York.
——— (1925) 'Hochzeit und Opferkorb', pp. 210-23 in *JdI* 40.
——— (1932) *Attische Feste*. 2nd ed. rev. by B. Doer in 1966. Hildesheim.
——— (1952) 'Die Gebräuche der Griechen nach der Geburt', pp. 374-7 in *RhM* 95.
Dewald, C. (1981) 'Women and culture in Herodotus' *Histories*', pp.

91-125 in Foley 1981.

Dickison, S.K. (1973) 'Abortion in antiquity', pp. 159-66 in *Arethusa* 6.

Diepgen, P. (1937) *Die Frauenheilkunde der alten Welt* (= *Handbuch der Gynäkologie*, ed. W. Stöckel, 12 Bd, 1 Teil). Munich.

Diller, A. (1941) 'A new source of the Spartan ephebia', pp. 499-501 in *AJPh* 62.

DK = Diels, H. (1935) *Die Fragmente der Vorsokratiker*, 5th ed. revised by W. Krantz, 2 vols. Berlin.

Dodds, E.R. (1960) *Euripides' Bacchae with commentary*. 2nd ed. Oxford, Clarendon.

Dölger, F.J. (1933) 'Das Lebensrecht des ungeborenen Kindes und die Fruchtabtreibung in der Bewertung der heidnischen und christlichen Antike', pp. 1-51 in *Antike und Christentum* 4.

Doumanis, M. (1983) *Mothering in Ancient Greece: from Collectivism to Individualism*. London.

Dover, K.J. (ed.) (1968) *Aristophanes' Clouds*. Oxford, Clarendon.

——— (1972) *Aristophanic Comedy*. London.

——— (1973) 'Classical Greek attitudes to sexual behaviour', in *Arethusa* 6.1.

——— (1974) *Greek Popular Morality in the Time of Plato and Aristotle*. Oxford.

——— (1978) *Greek Homosexuality*. London.

——— (1980) *Plato: Symposium*. Cambridge.

DS = Daremberg, Ch. and Saglio, E. (1877-1919) *Dictionnaire des antiquités grecques et romaines d'après les textes et les monuments*. Paris.

Dufays, J.M. (1985) 'Réflexions sur un vieux fantasme: l'homme enceint', pp. 71-9 in *STHist* 1.

Easterling, P.E. (1977) 'The infanticide in Euripides' *Medea*', pp. 177-91 in *YCS* 25.

Edelstein, E.J. and Edelstein, L. (1945) *Asclepius: a collection and interpretation of the testimonies*. 2 vols. Baltimore 1945.

Edelstein, L. (1937) 'Greek medicine in its relation to religion and magic', pp. 238ff. in *Bulletin of the History of Medicine* 5.

——— (1967) *Ancient Medicine*, ed. O. and C.L. Temkin. Johns Hopkins, Baltimore.

Edmunds, S.T. (1977) 'Homeric *nepios*', pp. 299-300 in *HSCP* 81.

Egerton, F.N. (1975) 'Aristotle's population biology', pp. 307-30 in *Arethusa* 8.2.

Ellinger, T.H. (1952) *Hippocrates on Intercourse and Pregnancy*. New York.

Engels, D. (1980) 'The problem of female infanticide in the Greco-Roman world', pp. 112-20 in *CP* 75.

Epigr. gr. = Kaibel, G. (ed.). (1878) *Epigrammata graeca ex lapidibus conlecta*. Berlin.

Erdmann, W. (1934) 'Die Ehe im alten Griechenland', in *Münchener Beiträge zur Papyrusforschung der antiken Rechtsgeschichte* 20.

Etienne, R. (1977) 'Ancient medical conscience and the life of children', pp. 131-63 in *Journal of Psychohistory* 4.

Eyben, E. (1972) 'Antiquity's view of puberty', pp. 677-97 in *Latomus* 31.

——— (1973) 'Roman notes on the course of life', pp. 213-38 in *Ancient Society* 4.

——— (1973a) 'Die Einteilung des menschliches Lebens im römischen Altertum', pp. 150-90 in *RM* 116.

——— (1980-81) 'Family planning in Graeco-Roman antiquity', pp. 5-82 in *Ancient Society* 11-12.

FAC = Edmonds, J.M. (ed.). *The Fragments of Attic Comedy*, 3 vols. Leiden.

Falkner, T.M. (1989) '*Epi gêraos oudôi*: Homeric heroism, old age and the end of the Odyssey', forthcoming in Falkner and de Luce.

Falkner, T.M. and de Luce, J. (1989) *Old Age in Greek and Latin Literature*, forthcoming.

Fantham, E. (1971) '*Heautontimoroumenos* and *Adelphoi*: a study of fatherhood in Terence and Menander', pp. 970-8 in *Latomus* 30.

——— (1975) 'Women in New Comedy', pp. 44-74 in *Phoenix* 29.

FGrH = Jacoby, F. (ed.) (1923-58) *Die Fragmente der griechischen Historiker*. Leiden.

Finley, M.I. (1981) 'The elderly in classical antiquity', pp. 156-71 in *G&R* 28 (published also in *Ageing and Society* 4 [1984]).

Foley, H.P. (1975) 'Sex and state in ancient Greece': review of P.E. Slater, *The Glory of Hera*, pp. 31-6 in *Diacritics* 5.4.

——— (1981) *Reflections of Women in Antiquity*. New York, London and Paris.

Fontenrose, J. (1978) *The Delphic Oracle*. Berkeley.

Forbes, C.A. (1933) *'Neoi': a Contribution to the Study of Greek Associations* (= *Philological Monographs* [published by the American Philological Association] no. 2). Connecticut.

Ford, C.S. (1964) *A Comparative Study of Human Reproduction* (reprinted from the 1945 ed.). New Haven.

Forrest, W.G. (1967) 'Legislation in Sparta', pp. 11-19 in *Phoenix* 21.

——— (1968) *A History of Sparta*. London.

——— (1975) 'An Athenian generation gap', pp. 37-52 in *YCS* 24.

Fortenbaugh, W.W. (1975) 'Plato: temperament and eugenic policy', pp. 283-305 in *Arethusa* 8.2.

Fraser, P.M. (1953) 'An inscription from Cos', pp. 35-62 in *Bulletin de la Société Archaeologique d'Alexandrie* 40.

Freedman, L.Z. and Ferguson, V.M. (1950) 'The question of "painless childbirth" in primitive cultures', pp. 363-72 in *American Journal of Orthopsychiatry* 20.2.

French, V. (1988) 'Birth control, childbirth and early childhood', pp. 1355-62 in Grant and Kitzinger 1988.

Frier, B. (1983) 'Roman life expectancy: the Pannonian evidence', pp.

328-44 in *Phoenix* 37.

Furley, W.D. (1981) *Studies in the Use of Fire in Ancient Greek Religion*. New York.

Furley, D. (1987) *The Greek Cosmologists*, vol. I: 'The formation of the atomic theory and its earliest critics'. Cambridge.

Garland, R.S.J. (1982) 'A first catalogue of Attic peribolos-tombs', pp. 125-76 in *ABSA* 77.

——— (1982a) 'Greek drinking parties', pp. 18-21 in *HT* vol. 32 (June).

——— (1983) 'Death without dishonour: suicide in the ancient world', pp. 33-7 in *HT* vol. 33.

——— (1984) 'Religious authority in archaic and classical Athens', pp. 75-123 in *ABSA* 79.

——— (1985) *The Greek Way of Death*. London and Ithaca N.Y.

——— (1986) 'Mother and child in the Greek world', pp. 40-6 in *HT* vol. 36.

——— (1987) *The Piraeus*. London and Ithaca N.Y.

——— (1987a) 'Greek geriatrics', pp. 12-18 in *HT* vol. 37 (Sept.).

GDI = H. Collitz et al. (eds.) (1884-1915) *Sammlung der griechischen Dialekt-Inschriften*. Göttingen.

George, S. (1982) *Human Conception and Fetal Growth: a Study in the Development of Greek Thought from the Presocratics through Aristotle*. Diss. Pennsylvania.

Germain, L.R.F. (1969) 'Aspects du droit d'exposition en Grèce', pp. 177-97 in *Rev. hist. de droit fr. et étr.* 47.

——— (1975) 'L'exposition des enfants nouveau-nés dans la Grèce ancienne. Aspects sociologiques', pp. 211-46 in *Recueils Jean Bodin* 35.

Gernet, L. (1968) *Anthropologie de la Grèce antique*. Preface by J.-P. Vernant. Paris.

GHI = Tod, M.N. (1946 and 1948) *Greek Historical Inscriptions*, 2 vols. Oxford, Clarendon.

Giangrande, G. (1973) 'Anacreon and the Lesbian girl', pp. 129-33 in *QUCC* 16.

Ginouvès, R. (1962) *Balaneutiké: recherches sur le bain dans l'antiquité grecque* (= *BEFAR* 200). Paris.

Girard, P. (1919) 'L'année a perdu son printemps', pp. 227-39 in *REG* 32.

Glotz, G. (1929) *The Greek City and its Institutions*, tr. N. Mallinson. London.

Golden, M. (1981) *Aspects of Childhood in Classical Athens*. Diss. Toronto.

——— (1981a) 'Demography and the exposure of girls at Athens', pp. 316-33 in *Phoenix* 35.

——— (1984) 'Slavery and homosexuality at Athens', pp. 308-24 in *Phoenix* 38.

——— (1985) ' "*Pais*", "child" and "slave" ', pp. 91-104 in *AC* 54.

——— (1988) Review of B. Rawson (ed.), *The Family in Ancient Rome*, pp. 78-83 in *EMC* n.s. 32.

——— (1988a) 'Did the ancients care when their children died?', pp. 152-63 in *G&R* 35.2.

Goldhill, S. (1987) 'The Great Dionysia and civic ideology', pp. 58-76 in *JHS* 107.

Golding, M.P. and Golding, N.H. (1975) 'Population policy in Plato and Aristotle: some value issues', pp. 345-58 in *Arethusa* 8.2.

Gomme, A.W. (1933) *The Population of Athens in the Fifth and Fourth Centuries B.C.* Oxford.

Gordon, R.L. (ed.) (1981) *Myth, Religion and Society*. Cambridge and Paris.

Gourevitch, D. (1984) *Le mal d'être femme: la femme et la médicine dans la Rome antique*. Paris.

Gow, A.S.F. and Page, D.L. (1965) *The Greek Anthology: the Hellensitic Epigrams*, 2 vols. Cambridge.

Graf, F. (1978) 'Die lokrischen Mädchen', pp. 61-79 in *Studi Storico-Religiosi* 2.

Grant, J.N. (1986) 'The father-son relationship and the ending of Menander's *Samia*', pp. 172-84 in *Phoenix* 40.2.

Grant, M. and Kitzinger, R. (eds.) (1988) *Civilization of the Ancient Mediterranean: Greece and Rome*, 3 vols. New York.

Grmek, M.D. (1958) *On Ageing and Old Age* (= *Monogr. bibliog*. 5.2). La Haye, Junk.

——— (1983) *Les maladies à l'aube de la civilisation occidentale*. Paris.

Hähnel, R. (1937) *Der kunstliche Abortus im Altertum*, pp. 224ff. in *Archiv f. Geschichte d. Medizin* 29.

Halkin, L. (1948) 'Le problème des "decem menses" de la IVe Éclogue de Virgile', pp. 354-70 in *LEC* 16.

Hands, A.R. (1968) *Charities and Social Aid in Greece and Rome*. London.

Hanson, A. (1987) 'The eight-months' child and the etiquette of birth: *obsit omen*!', pp. 589-602 in *Bull. Hist. Med.* 61.

Harris, W.V. (1982) 'The theoretical possibility of extensive infanticide in the Graeco-Roman world', pp. 114-16 in *CQ* n.s. 32.

Harrison, A.R.W. (1968) *The Law of Athens*, 2 vols. Clarendon, Oxford.

Harrison, G.A. and Boyce, A.J. (1972) *The Structure of Human Populations*. Oxford, Clarendon.

Haynes, M.S. (1962) 'The supposedly Golden Age for the aged in Ancient Greece: a study of literary concepts of old age', pp. 93-8 in *Gerontologist* 2.

——— (1963) 'The supposedly Golden Age for the aged in Ancient Rome', pp. 26-35 in *Gerontologist* 3.

Henderson, J. (1987) 'Older women in Attic Old Comedy', pp. 105-29 in *TAPhA* 117.

Hogarth, D.G. (1891) 'The Gerousia of Hierapolis', pp. 69-101 in *JPh* 19.

Hollinshead, M.B.B. (1979) *Legend, Cult and Architecture at Three*

Sanctuaries of Artemis. Diss. Bryn Mawr 1979. Ann Arbor, Michigan.

van Hooff, A.J.L. (1983) 'Old age in ancient Greece (= Oud-zijn in het oude Hellas'), pp. 141-8 in *Tijdschrift voor Gerontologie en Geriatrie* 14.4.

van Hook, La Rue (1920) 'The exposure of infants at Athens', pp. 134-45 in *TAPhA* 51.

Hopfner, T. (1938) *Das Sexualleben der Griechen und Römer*, vol. 1, part 1. Prague.

——— (1938a) 'L'impotenza e i suoi rimedi', pp. 267-73 in Calame (1984), first published in Hopfner 1938.

Hopkins, K. (1965) 'The age of Roman girls at menarche', pp. 309-27 in *Population Studies* 18.

——— (1965a) 'Contraception in the Roman Empire', pp. 124-51 in *Comparative Studies in Society and History* 8.

——— (1966) 'On the probable age structure of the Roman population', pp. 246-64 in *Population Studies* 20.

——— (1983) *Death and Renewal* (= *Sociological Studies in Roman History*, vol. 2). Cambridge.

Hubbard, J.K. (1989) 'Old men in the youthful plays of Aristophanes', forthcoming in Falkner and de Luce.

Humphreys, S.C. (1974) 'The *nothoi* of Kynosarges', pp. 88-95 in *JHS* 94.

——— (1978) *Anthropology and the Greeks*. London.

——— (1980) 'Family tombs and tomb cult in Classical Athens: tradition or traditionalism', pp. 96-126 in *JHS* 100.

——— (1983) *The Family, Women and Death*. London.

Humphreys, S.C. and King, H. (eds) (1982) *Mortality and Immortality: the Anthropology and Archaeology of Death*.

Hussey, E. (1972) *The Presocratics*. London and New York.

IC = Guarducci, M. (ed.) (1935) *Inscriptiones Creticae*. Rome.

IEG = West M.L. (ed.) (1971) *Iambi et Elegi Graeci ante Alexandrium cantati*, 2 vols. Oxford, Clarendon.

IG = *Inscriptiones Graecae*.

Immerwahr, H.R. (1971) 'A purity regulation from Therasia purified', pp. 235-8 in *Hesperia* 40.

Jeanmaire, H. (1913) 'La cryptie lacédémonienne', pp. 121-50 in *REG* 26.

——— (1939) *Couroi et Courètes. Essai sur l'education spartiate et sur les rites d'adolescence dans l'antiquité hellénique*. New York 1975.

Jenkins, I. (1983) 'Is there life after marriage? A study of the abduction motif in vase paintings of the Athenian wedding ceremony', pp. 137-45 in *BICS* 30.

——— (1986) *Greek and Roman Life*. London.

Joly, R. (1966) *Le niveau de la science hippocratique: contribution à la psychologie de l'histoire des sciences*. Paris.

Jones, A.H.M. (1967) *Sparta*. Cambridge, Mass. 1967.

Jordan, B. (1983) *Birth in Four Cultures: a Crosscultural Investigation of Childbirth in Yucatan, Holland, Sweden and the United States*, 3rd ed. Quebec and London.

K = Kühn, C.G. (ed.) (1821) *Claudii Galeni Opera Omnia*, 20 vols. Leipzig (reprinted Hildesheim 1964).

Kahrstedt, U. (1922) *Griechische Staatsrecht*, vol. 1. Sparta.

Karras, M. and Wiesehöfer, J. (1981) *Kindheit und Jugend in der Antike: eine Bibliographie*. Bonn.

Keaney, J.J. (1974) 'Theophrastus on Greek judicial procedure', pp. 179-94 in *TAPhA* 104.

Kember, O. (1973) 'Anaxagoras' theory of sex differentiation and heredity', pp. 1-14 in *Phronesis* 18.

Kerford, G.B. (1981) *The Sophistic Movement*. Cambridge.

Keuls, E.C. (1985) *The Reign of the Phallus*. New York and Toronto.

King, L.S. (1903) 'The cave at Vari: vases', pp. 320-7 in *AJA* 7.

King, H. (1983) 'Bound to bleed', pp. 109-27 in Cameron and Kuhrt 1983.

——— (1986) 'Tithonus and the tettix,' pp. 15-35 in *Arethusa* 19.1.

——— (1988) 'Making a man: becoming human in early Greek medicine'. Paper presented at the Constantinus Africanus Colloquium at Exeter.

Kirchner, *PA* = Kirchner, J. (1901-3) *Prosopographia Attica*, 2 vols. Berlin.

Kirk, G.S., Raven, J.E., revised by Schofield, M. (1983) *The Presocratic Philosophers*. Cambridge.

Klein, A. (1932) *Child's Life in Ancient Greece*. Columbia.

Krenkel, W.A. (1975) 'Hyperthermia in ancient Rome', pp. 381-6 in *Arethusa* 8.

——— (1978) 'Familienplanung und Familienpolitik in der Antike', pp. 197-203 in *Würzburger Jahrbücher für die Altertumswissenschaft* 4.

Labarbe, J. (1953) 'L'âge correspondant au sacrifice du *koureion* et les données historiques du 6è discours d'Isée', pp. 358-94 in *BAB* 39.

——— (1957) *La loi navale de Thémistocle. (= Bibliothèque de la faculté de philosophie et lettres de l'Université de Liège*: fascicule 143). Paris.

Lacey, W.K. (1968) *The Family in Classical Greece*. London, Thames and Hudson.

Lambin, G. (1975) 'Les formules de jeux d'enfants dans la Grèce antique', pp. 168-77 in *REG* 88.

Landels, J.G. (1979) 'An ancient account of reproduction', pp. 94-113 in *Biology and Human Affairs* 44.

Landry, A. (1936) 'La dépopulation dans l'antiquité gréco-romaine', pp. 1-33 in *RH* 177.

Lang, M. (1977) *Cure and Cult in Ancient Corinth: a Guide to the Asklepieion*. American School of Classical Studies at Athens, Princeton.

LCL = *Loeb Classical Library*.

Lefkowitz, M.R. (1981) *Heroines and Hysterics*. London.

——— (1983) 'Wives and husbands', pp. 31-47 in *G&R* 30.1.

——— (1986) *Women in Greek Myth*. London.

——— (1987) 'Women in Greece', pp. 146-55 in *Storia della Storiografia* 12.

——— (1988) 'Feminist myths and Greek mythology', pp. 804, 808 in *TLS*, 22-28 July.

Linders, T. (1972) *Studies in the Treasure Records of Artemis Brauronia found in Athens*. Stockholm.

Littré, E. (1839) *Oeuvres complètes d'Hippocrate*. Paris (reprinted Amsterdam 1961).

Lloyd, G.E.R. (1962) 'Right and left in Greek philosophy', pp. 56-66 in *JHS* 82.

——— (1966) *Polarity and Analogy: Two Types of Argumentation in Early Greek Thought*. Cambridge.

——— (1975) 'Alcmaeon and the early history of dissection', pp. 113-47 in *Sudhoffs Archiv* 59.

——— (ed.) (1978) *Hippokratic Writings*. Harmondsworth.

——— (1979) *Magic, Reason and Experience. Studies in the Origin and Development of Greek Science*. Cambridge.

——— (1983) *Science, Folklore and Ideology*. Cambridge.

Lloyd-Jones, H. (1972) 'Menander's Samia in the light of the new evidence', pp. 119-44 in *YCS* 22.

——— (ed.) (1975) *Females of the Species: Semonides on Women*. London.

——— (1983) 'Artemis and Iphigeneia', pp. 87-102 in *JHS* 103.

Lonie, I.M. (1981) *The Hippocratic Treatises 'On Generation', 'On the Nature of the Child' and 'Diseases IV'*. Berlin.

Loraux, N. (1975) '*Hebe et andreia*: deux versions de la mort du combattant athénien', pp. 1-31 in *Ancient Society* 6.

——— (1977) 'La belle mort spartiate', pp. 105-20 in *Ktema* 2.

——— (1978) 'Sur la race des femmes et quelques-unes de ses tribus', pp. 43-87 in *Arethusa* 11.

——— (1981) 'Le lit, la guerre', pp. 37-67 in *L'Homme* 21.

——— (1985) *Façons tragiques de tuer une femme*. Paris.

——— (1986) *The Invention of Athens: the Funeral Oration in the Classical City*, tr. R. Forster. Cambridge, Mass. and London.

Louis, P. (1975) 'Monstres et monstruosités dans la biologie d'Aristote', pp. 277-84 in *Le monde grec: hommages à Claire Préaux*. Bruxelles.

LP = Lobel, E. and Page, D. (eds.) (1955) *Poetarum Lesbiorum Fragmenta*. Oxford, Clarendon.

LSAM = Sokolowski, F. (ed.) (1955) *Lois sacrées de l'Asie mineure*. Paris.

LSCG = Sokolowski, F. (ed.) (1969) *Lois sacrées des cités grecques*. Paris.

LSCGS = Sokolowski, F. (ed.) (1962) *Lois sacrées des cités grecques. Supplement*. Paris.
LSJ[9] = Liddell, H.G., Scott, R., Jones, H.S. (1940) *Greek-English Lexicon*, 9th ed. Oxford.
Lucas, D.W. (1946) 'Hippolytus', pp. 65-9 in *CQ* 39.
MacDowell, D.M. (ed.) (1971) *Aristophanes' Wasps*. Oxford, Clarendon.
——— (1986) *Spartan Law* (= *Scottish Classical Studies* 1). Edinburgh.
McCartney, E. (1929) 'On the shedding of skin by human beings', p. 176 in *Classical Weekly* 22.
Macaulay, M. (1952) *The Art of Marriage*. Harmondsworth.
Mainoldi, C. (1987) 'Sonno e morte in Grecia antica', pp. 9-46 in Raffaelli 1987.
Mansfeld, J. (1971) *The Pseudo-Hippocratic Text: 'Peri Hebdomadon' ch. 1-11 and Early Greek Philosophy*. Assen.
Marrou, H.I. (1946) 'Les classes d'âge de la jeunesse spartiate', pp. 216-30 in *REA* 48.
——— (1948) *A History of Education in Antiquity*, tr. G. Lamb. Wisconsin 1982 (first published as *Histoire de l'education dans l'antiquité* [Paris 1948]).
Mead, M. (1928) *Coming of Age in Samoa: a Psychological Study of Primitive Youth for Western Civilization*. New York.
Mead, M. and Newton, N. (1967) 'Cultural patterning of perinatal behavior', in S.A. Richardson and A.F. Guttmacher (eds.), *Childbearing: its Social and Psychological Aspects*. Baltimore.
Michell, H. (1964) *Sparta*. Cambridge.
Mikalson, J.D. (1983) *Athenian Popular Religion*. Chapel Hill and London.
——— (1986) 'Zeus the father and Heracles the son in tragedy', pp. 89-98 in *TAPhA* 116.
Milne, J.S. (1907) *Surgical Instruments in Greek and Roman Times*. Oxford.
ML = Meiggs, R. and Lewis, D. (1969) *Greek Historical Inscriptions to the end of the Fifth Century BC*. Oxford.
Montevecchi, O. (1979) *'Posôn mênôn estin'*, pp. 113-17 in *ZPE* 34.
Moreau, J. (1949) 'Les théories démographiques dans l'antiquité grecque', pp. 603ff. in *Population* 4.
Morris, I. (1987) *Burial and Ancient Society: the Rise of the Greek City State*. Cambridge.
Moulinier, L. (1952) *Le pur et l'impur dans la pensée des Grecs d'Homère à Aristote* (= *Études et commentaires* 12). Paris.
Mulhern, J.J. (1975) 'Population and Plato's Republic', pp. 265-81 in *Arethusa* 8.2.
Nag, M. (1962) *Factors affecting Human Fertility in Non-industrial Societies: a Cross-cultural Study* (= *Yale Univ. Publications in Anthropology*). Yale.

Nardi, E. (1971) *Procurato Aborto nel Mondo Greco-Romano*. Milan.

Néraudau, J.-P. (1984) *Être enfant à Rome*. Paris.

Nettleship, R.L. (1901) *Lectures on the Republic of Plato*, 2nd ed. London.

Nilsson, *GGR* I = Nilsson, M.P. (1967) *Geschichte der griechischen Religion*, vol. 1, 3rd ed. Munich.

Nilsson, M.P. (1908) 'Die Grundlagen des Spartanischen Lebens', pp. 308-40 in *Klio* 12.

——— (1960) 'Wedding rites in ancient Greece', pp. 243-50 in *Opuscula* 3.

Noonan, J.T. (1970) 'An almost absolute value in history', pp. 1-59 in J.T. Noonan (ed.), *The Morality of Abortion: Legal and Historical Perspectives*. Cambridge.

North, H.F. (1947) 'A period of opposition to *sôphrosynê* in Greek thought', pp. 1-17 in *TAPha* 78.

——— (1966) *Sophrosyne and Self-knowledge in Greek Literature*. Ithaca.

van Nortwick, T. (1989) 'Do not go gently ...: *Oedipus at Colonus* and the psychology of aging', forthcoming in Falkner and de Luce 1989.

Ober, J. (1985) 'Fortress Attica: defence of the Athenian land frontier 404-322 B.C.', *Mnemosyne* 38.

OCM = Gregory, R.L. (ed.) (1987) *The Oxford Companion to the Mind*. Oxford and New York.

Oepke, A. (1934) '*Amphithaleis* im griechischen und hellenistischen Kult', pp. 42-56 in *Archiv f. Religionswissenschaft* 31.

Onians, R.B. (1951) *The Origins of European Thought about the Body, the Mind, the World, Time and Fate*. Cambridge.

Opie, I and Opie P. (1959) *The Lore and Language of School Children*. Oxford.

——— (1969) *Children's Games in Street and Playground*. Oxford.

Oppenheimer, J.M. (1975) 'When sense and life begin: background for a remark in Aristotle's *Politics* (1335b24), pp. 331-43 in *Arethusa* 8.2.

Osborne, R. (1987) 'The viewing and obscuring of the Parthenon frieze,' pp. 98-105 in *JHS* 107.

PA = Kirchner, J. (1901-3) *Prosopographia Attica*. Berlin.

Parke, H.W. (1977) *Festivals of the Athenians*. London, Thames and Hudson.

Parker, R. (1983) *Miasma*. Oxford, Clarendon.

Patterson, C. (1985) ' "Not worth rearing": the causes of infant exposure in ancient Greece', pp. 103-23 in *TAPhA* 115.

Peck, A.L. (1945) *Aristotle: Parts of Animals*. (*Loeb Classical Library*), 2nd ed. London.

Pélékidis, Ch. (1962) *Histoire de l'éphébie attique des origines à 31 avant J.-C.* (*Éc. Fr. Ath., Travaux et Memoires*, 13) Paris.

Pelling, C. (ed.) (1989) *Characterization and Individuality in Greek Literature*, forthcoming.

Peradotto, J. and Sullivan, J.P. (1984) *Women in the Ancient World: the 'Arethusa' Papers*. New York.
Perdrizet, P. (1921) 'Copria', pp. 85-94 in *REA* 23.
Phillips, E.D. (1987) *Aspects of Greek Medicine* (first published as *Greek Medicine* [1973]). Philadelphia and Kent.
Piaget, J. (1969) *Science of Education and the Psychology of the Child* (first published as *Psychologie et Pédagogie* [Paris 1969]). Harmondsworth 1977.
Pickard-Cambridge, A. (1968) *Dramatic Festivals of Athens*, 2nd. ed. revised by J. Gould and D.M. Lewis. Oxford, Clarendon.
Pingiatoglou, S. (1981) *Eileithyia*. Diss. Würzburg.
PMG = Page, D.L. (ed.) (1962) *Poetae Melici Graeci*. Oxford, Clarendon.
Pomeroy, S.B. (1973) 'Selected bibliography on women in antiquity', pp. 125-52 in *Arethusa* 6.
——— (1975) *Goddesses, Whores, Wives and Slaves: Women in Classical Antiquity*. New York and London.
——— (1982) 'Charities for Greek women', pp. 115-35 in *Mnemosyne* 35.
——— (1983) 'Infanticide in Hellenistic Greece', pp. 207-22 in Cameron and Kuhrt 1983.
——— (1984) 'Copronyms and the exposure of infants in Egypt', p. 1341 in *Atti del XVII Congresso di Papirologia*. Naples.
——— (1988) 'Greek marriage', pp. 1333-42 in Grant and Kitzinger 1988.
Preus, A. (1975) 'Biomedical techniques for influencing human reproduction in the fourth century BC', pp. 237-63 in *Arethusa* 8.2.
——— (1977) 'Galen's criticism of Aristotle's conception theory', pp. 65-85 in *Journal of the History of Biology* 10.
Price, T. (1978) *Kourotrophos. Cults and representations of the Greek nursing deities*. Leiden.
Pringle, J. (1983) 'Hittite birth rituals', pp. 128-41 in Cameron and Kuhrt 1983.
Pundel, J.P. (1969). *Histoire de l'opération césarienne dans la médicine, l'art et la litérature, les religions et la législation. La prodigieuse évolution de la césarienne depuis l'antiquité jusqu'aux temps moderns*. Brussels.
Raepsaet, G. (1971) 'Les motivations de la natalité à Athènes aux Vème et IVème siècles avant notre ère', pp. 80-110 in *AC* 40.
Rawson, B. (ed.) (1986) *The Family in Ancient Rome*. Kent.
——— (1986a) 'Children in the Roman Familia', pp. 170-200 in Rawson 1986.
RE = Wissowa, G. (ed.) (1893-) *Paulys Real-Encyclopädie*. Stuttgart.
Redfield, J. (1977-78) 'The women of Sparta', pp. 146-61 in *CJ* 73.2.
——— (1982) 'Notes on the Greek wedding', pp. 181-201 in *Arethusa* 15.1 and 2.
Rhodes, P.J. (1972) *The Athenian Boule*. Oxford, Clarendon.
——— (1981) *A Commentary on the Aristotelian Athenaion Politeia*.

Oxford, Clarendon.

Richardson, B.E. (1933) *Old Age among the Ancient Greeks* (= *The Johns Hopkins Studies in Archaeology* no. 16). Baltimore.

Richardson, N.J. (1974) *The Homeric Hymn to Demeter*. Oxford, Clarendon.

Robert, L. (1968) 'De Delphes à l'Oxus. Inscriptions grecques nouvelles de la Bactriane', pp. 416-57 in *CRAI*.

Robertson, N. (1983) 'The riddle of the arrhephoria at Athens', pp. 241-88 in *HSCP* 87.

Rohde, E. (1925) *Psyche: the Cult of Souls and Belief in Immortality among the Ancient Greeks*, tr. W.B. Hillis. London and New York.

Roscher, W.H. (1906) *Die Hebdomadenlehren der griechischen Philosophen und Artze*. Leipzig.

Rose-Neil, W. (1984) *The Complete Handbook of Pregnancy*. London and Sydney.

Rostovtzeff, M. (1941) *Social and Economic History of the Hellenistic World*, 1st ed. Oxford, Clarendon.

——— (1967) *Social and Economic History of the Hellenistic World*, 2nd ed. Oxford, Clarendon.

Roussel, P. (1921) Review of Alice Brenot, *Recherches sur l'éphébie attique et en particulier sur la date de l'institution* (Paris 1920), pp. 459-60 in *REG* 34.

——— (1941) 'Les chlamydes noires des éphèbes athéniens', pp. 163-5 in *REA* 43.

——— (1943) 'L'exposition des enfants à Sparte', pp. 5-17 in *REA* 45.

——— (1951) 'Étude sur le principe d'ancienneté dans le monde héllenique du 5è siècle avant J.-C. à l'époque romaine', pp. 123-227 in *Mémoires de l'Institut National de France, Académie des Inscriptions et Belles-Lettres* 43.

Saller, R.P. (1987) 'Men's age at marriage and its consequences in the Roman family', pp. 21-34 in *CP* 82.1.

Salmon, P. (1955) 'La population de la Grèce antique', pp. 34-61 in *Bull. Soc. Roy. belge Géogr.* 79.

Samter, E. (1901) *Familienfeste der Griechen und Römer*. Berlin.

Saunders, J.B. de C.M. (1963) *The Transitions from Ancient Egyptian to Greek Medicine*. Kansas.

Schadewaldt, W. (1933) 'Lebenzeit und Greisenalter in frühen Griechentum', pp. 285-92 in *Die Antike* 9.

Schaps, D.M. (1977) 'The woman least mentioned', pp. 323-30 in *CQ* 27.

——— (1979) *Economic Rights of Women in Ancient Greece*. Edinburgh.

Schmitt, P. (1977) 'Athene Apatouria et la ceinture', pp. 1059-77 in *Annales ESC* 32.

Schofield, M. (1986) 'Euboulia in the *Iliad*', pp. 6-31 in *CQ* n.s. 36.1.

Seaford, R.A.S. (1987) 'The tragic wedding', pp. 106-30 in *JHS* 107.

Sealey, R. (1957) 'On coming of age in Athens', pp. 195-7 in *CR* n.s. 7.

——— (1984) 'On lawful concubinage in Athens', pp. 111-33 in *CA* 3.
Sears, R.R. and Feldman, S.S. (eds.) (1973) *The Seven Ages of Man: a Survey of Human Development – Body, Personality, Ability – through Life*. California.
Segal, C. (1974) 'The Homeric Hymn to Aphrodite: a structuralist approach', pp. 205-12 in *CW* 67.
——— (1986) 'Tithonus and the Homeric *Hymn to Aphrodite*: a comment', pp. 37-47 in *Arethusa* 19.1.
Shaw, B.D. (1987) 'The age of Roman girls at marriage', pp. 30-46 in *JRS* 77.
Siegel, R.E. (1968) *Galen's System of Physiology and Medicine*. Basel and New York.
Siewert, P. (1977) 'The ephebic oath in fifth-century Athens', pp. 102-11 in *JHS* 97.
Sifakis, G.M. (1979) 'Children in Greek Tragedy', pp. 67-80 in *BICS* 26.
*SIG*³ = Dittenberger, W. (ed.) (1915-24) *Sylloge Inscriptionum Graecarum*, 4 vols, 3rd ed. Leipzig.
Simmons, L.W. (1945) *The Role of the Aged in Primitive Society*. Yale.
Sissa, G. (1984) 'Une virginité sans hymen. Le corps féminin en Grèce ancienne', pp. 119-39 in *Annales ESC* 39.
Slater, P.E. (1971) *The Glory of Hera: Greek Mythology and the Greek Family*. Boston, Mass.
Sourvinou-Inwood, C. (1971) 'Aristophanes' *Lysistrata* 641-7', pp. 339-42 in *CQ* 65.
——— (1971a) Review of A. Brelich, *Paides e parthenoi*, pp. 172-7 in *JHS* 91.
——— (1973) 'The young abductor of the Locrian pinakes', pp. 12-21 in *BICS* 20.
——— (1981) 'To die and enter the house of Hades: Homer, before and after', pp. 15-39 in J. Whaley (ed.), *Mirrors of Mortality: Studies in the Social History of Death*. London.
——— (1987) 'A series of erotic pursuits: images and meanings', pp. 131-53 in *JHS* 107.
Sprague, R.K. (1984) 'Plato and children's games', pp. 275-84 in D.E. Gerber (ed.) *Greek Poetry and Philosophy: Studies in Honour of Leonard Woodbury*. California.
van Staden, H. (1975) 'Experiment and experience in Hellenistic medicine', pp. 178-99 in *BICS* 22.
van Straten, F.T. (1981) 'Gifts from the gods', pp. 65-151 in Versnel 1981.
Stone, L. (1979) *The Family, Sex and Marriage in England 1500-1800*. Harmondsworth.
Strömberg, R. (1954) *Greek Proverbs: a Collection of Proverbs and Proverbial Phrases which are not listed by the Ancient and Byzantine Paroemiographers*. Göteberg.
Stroud, R.S. (1971) 'Greek inscriptions: Theozotides and the Athenian

orphans', pp. 280-301 in *Hesperia* 40.

Sussman, L.S. (1984) 'Workers and drones: labor, idleness and gender definition in Hesiod's beehives', pp. 79-93 in Peradotto and Sullivan 1984.

T = Teubner edition.

Tarn, W.W. and Griffith, G.T. (1974) *Hellenistic Civilization*, 3rd ed. London.

Tazelaar, C.M. (1967) '*Paides kai ephêboi*. Some notes on the Spartan stages of youth', pp. 127-53 in *Mnemosyne* 20.

TDGR = Badian, E and Sherk, R.K. (eds.) *Translated Documents of Greece and Rome*. Cambridge.

Temkin, O. (1953) 'Greek medicine as science and craft', pp. 213-25 in *Isis* 44.

TGF = Nauck (ed.) (1964) Suppl. B. Snell. *Tragicorum Graecorum Fragmenta*, 2 vols. Hildesheim.

Thesleff, H. (ed.) (1965) *The Pythagorean Texts of the Hellenistic Period*. Abo.

Thompson, W.E. (1972) 'Athenian marriage patterns: re-marriage', pp. 211-25 in *CSCA* 5.

Tolles, R. (1941) *Untersuchungen zur Kinderaussetzung bei den Griechen*. Diss. Breslau.

Toynbee, A. (1969) *Some Problems in Greek History*. Oxford.

Turner, V.W. (1969) *The Ritual Process*. London.

Valentine, C.W. (1956) *The Normal Child and Some of his Abnormalities*. Harmondsworth.

Vatin, C. (1970) *Recherches sur le mariage et la condition de la femme mariée à l'époque hellénistique*. Paris.

Vermeule, E. (1987) 'Baby Aigisthos and the Bronze Age', pp. 122-52 in *PCPS* n.s. 33.

Vernant, J.-P. (1962) *The Origins of Greek Thought*. Ithaca 1982.

——— (1982) *Myth and Society in Ancient Greece*, tr. J. Lloyd. London.

——— (1983) *Mythe et pensée chez les Grecs*. Paris.

Vernant, J.-P. and Vidal-Naquet, P. (1982) *Mythe et tragédie en Grèce ancienne*. Paris.

Versnel, H.S. (1981) *Faith, Hope and Worship: Aspects of Religious Mentality in the Ancient World*. Leiden.

Vidal-Naquet, P. (1968) 'The Black Hunter and the origin of the Athenian ephebeia', pp. 147-62 in Gordon 1981. First published simultaneously in 1968 in *Annales ESC* 23, pp. 947-64, and in *PCPhS* n.s. 14, pp. 49-64. Page references are from Gordon 1981.

——— (1974) 'Recipes for Greek adolescence', pp. 163-85 in Gordon 1981. First published in J. Le Goff and P. Nora (eds.) *Faire de l'histoire*, vol. 3. Paris 1974. Page references are from Gordon 1981.

——— (1982) 'Le Philoktète de Sophocle et l'ephébie', pp. 159-84 in Vernant and Vidal-Naquet 1982.

——— (1986) *The Black Hunter*. Baltimore and London.

Wade-Gery, H.T. (1958) *Essays in Greek History*. Oxford.

Walcot, P. (1987) 'Plato's mother and other terrible women', pp. 12-31 in *G&R* 34.1.

Walker, S. (1983) 'Women and housing in classical Greece: the archaeological evidence', pp. 81-91 in Cameron and Kuhrt.

Wallace, S. (1938) *Taxation in Egypt*. Princeton.

Walz, R. (1949) 'Ordinal et cardinal: une "règle" caduque', pp. 41-53 in *REA* 51.

Weiss, K.M. (1972) 'A general measure of human population growth control', pp. 337-43 in *Amer. J. Phys. Anthrop*. 37.

Weissman, P. (1965) 'Sophocles' *Antigone*, the psychology of the Old Maid' in *Creativity in the Theater: a Psychoanalytic Study*. New York.

West, M.L. (1966) *Hesiod: Theogony, edited with Prolegomena and Commentary*. Oxford, Clarendon.

——— (1971) 'The cosmology of "Hippocrates", De Hebdomadibus', pp. 365-88 in *CQ* n.s. 21.

——— (1978) *Hesiod: Works and Days, edited with Prolegomena and Commentary*. Oxford, Clarendon.

Wilkinson, L.P. (1979) *Classical Attitudes to Modern Issues*. London.

Willetts, R.F. (1965) *Ancient Crete: a Social History*. Toronto and London.

Winkler, J.J. (1985) 'The ephebes' song: *tragôidia and polis*', pp. 26-62 in *Representations* 11.

WLGR 1982 = Lefkowitz, M.R. and Fant, M.B. (1982) *Women's Life in Greece and Rome*. London and Baltimore.

Wolff, H.J. (1944) 'Marriage law and family organisation in ancient Athens: a study in the interrelation of public and private law in the Greek city', pp. 43-95 in *Traditio* 2.

Woodford, S. (1971) 'Cults of Heracles in Attica', pp. 211-25 in D.G. Mitten, J.G. Pedley and J.A. Scott (eds.) *Studies Presented to George M.A. Hanfmann* (= *Harvard University Monographs in Art and Archaeology* no. 2). Mainz.

Zahn, R. (1970) 'Das Kind in der Antiken Kunst', pp. 21-31 in *Forschungen und Berichte* (from the Berlin Museum) 12.

Zapperi, R. (1983) *L'homme enceint*. Paris.

Index Locorum

References to the pages of this book are given in bold type.

General Index